WE THE PEOPLE

a publication of
THE AMERICAN HISTORY RESEARCH CENTER
MADISON · WISCONSIN

WE THE PEOPLE

The Economic Origins of the Constitution

By FORREST McDONALD

THE UNIVERSITY OF CHICAGO PRESS

CHICAGO & LONDON

LIBRARY OF CONGRESS CATALOG CARD NUMBER: 58-14905
THE UNIVERSITY OF CHICAGO PRESS, LTD., LONDON W.C.1

To PROFESSOR FULMER MOOD
of the University of Texas,
*in appreciation of his
inspiration and guidance*

Preface

THE study of history in the United States before the advent of Frederick Jackson Turner and Charles A. Beard was largely confined to what Beard called "barren political history." Both men had that rarest of gifts, the ability to burst free from convention and to look at things in a new way. Each, by a bold formulation and coherent expression of ideas that had been "in the air" for some time, opened new vistas that promised to liberate historians from the fruitless wastes they had been traveling. Turner did so with his essay on the significance of the frontier in American history. Beard did so with his book *An Economic Interpretation of the Constitution of the United States.* Such was the powerful persuasiveness of the two works that each of them altered the course of American historiography, and such was the personal force of the two men as teachers that each breathed new vitality into the study of American history.

And so they served. But as they served, so also did they solidify. Brilliant lights cast dark shadows, and Beard's lights and shadows proved to be as restrictive as had been the conventions which Beard himself had overturned. Hence a newly blazed trail degenerated into a well-worn rut, and no historian who followed in studying the making of the Constitution has been free from Beard's view of it. And as with Beard and the Constitution, so with Turner and the West.

Beard's book can be and has been viewed in three principal lights: as propaganda, as historical methodology, and as history. The first view, to which Beard himself added considerable support, consciously or unconsciously, in his presidential address before the American Historical Association,[1] is that the book was written as a contribution to the cause of the progressive movement, of which Beard was an ardent supporter. At the time Beard's book was first published, in 1913, many progressives were convinced that the Constitution was a barrier to social and economic progress, and they sought to break down what they considered slavish adulation of the document. According to this view Beard served the cause by charging (or demonstrating) that "that group of demigods," the Founding Fathers, had merely been rich men designing a scheme for the more effective exploitation of the poor.[2] Beard himself repeatedly denied that he had written his book for any political purpose, and he denied that he had charged the Founding Fathers with any impropriety. On the other hand, there is no room for doubt that many reformers have used the conclusions of the book as a justification for demands that little or no attention be paid to the Constitution.

The work was also extremely significant in its contribution to historical methodology. As the first thoroughgoing economic interpretation of any major aspect of American history to gain wide acceptance, its influence on the methods and theoretical basis of the study of history in the United States was tremendous. On this ground, as on the grounds of its political implications, the book has been as widely discussed and as much attacked [3] as it has been influential. It is probably also true that the acceptance of the book in this aspect, as in its political

[1] Charles A. Beard, "Written History as an Act of Faith," presidential address before the American Historical Association, Urbana, Illinois, December 28, 1933, printed in the *American Historical Review*, 39:219–229 (January, 1934).

[2] A clear statement of this view, together with numerous footnote references to other such statements, is contained in Richard Hofstadter's "Beard and the Constitution: The History of an Idea," in the *American Quarterly*, 2:195–213 (Fall, 1950).

[3] The most recent and from all accounts the most thorough critical analysis of Beard's methodology is Robert E. Brown's *Charles Beard and the Constitution: A Critical Analysis of "An Economic Interpretation of the Constitution"* (Princeton, 1956). I am familiar with Professor Brown's thinking on the subject, and have read several reviews of the book, but have thought it best to refrain from reading the book itself until the present work is published.

aspect, has hinged largely on the emotional and philosophical predispositions of its readers.

It is as history that the book has been least quibbled about, for however one may challenge Beard's logic or his methods or question whether his data prove his case, and however stinging the epithets one may hurl at him, his array of documented data itself has, for the most part, gone unchallenged and, except in terms of Beard's thesis, unexplained. Accordingly, despite the great to-do over the political and methodological implications of the book, its account as history gradually came into almost universal acceptance.

The purpose of the present work is to examine Beard's thesis as history. To do so, I have followed a rather unorthodox method. For purposes of this book I have accepted, without qualification, Beard's system of interpretation and his system of testing it. His pages, he wrote, were "frankly fragmentary"; he sketched in broad outlines and left it for others to fill in the details. In so far as possible, I have filled in the details.

Having written the book before writing this preface, I know how it comes out: economic interpretation of the Constitution does not work. This being the case, one may ask, why bother to write the book? I offer two reasons. The first, quite frankly, is to clear the decks. I propose to follow this volume with two more, in which I shall attempt to write something meaningful about the making of the Constitution. In doing so I should like to be able to avoid not only the shadow of Mr. Beard but also those of others, to write without pausing at every point along the way to answer questions that I do not consider valid. I hope that the present work will, if nothing else, at least make it clear that many of the questions that have been asked are out-of-context questions. And out-of-context questions are no more valid than out-of-context quotations. Which leads to the second reason for writing this book. I believe that by examining Beard's system of interpretation as history something of a fundamental nature can be learned about the process of attempting to understand history.

The list of persons to whom I am indebted is virtually endless. Dozens of librarians and archivists from Maine to Texas and from Wisconsin to Georgia showed great kindness in digging up manuscripts for me and even more in letting me browse unattended through their rich collections. The Social Science Research Council and Mr. Lem Scarborough provided generous financial assistance. The Chrysler Corporation and the UAW-CIO built a marvelous Plymouth automobile which, though old when I got it, uncomplainingly carried me the equivalent of thrice around the globe in my search for data.

Dean Roy F. Nichols of the University of Pennsylvania, Professor Richard P. McCormick of Rutgers University, Professor C. Perry Patterson of the University of Texas, and Dr. Clifford L. Lord of the State Historical Society of Wisconsin read the entire manuscript and took the time to give me the benefit of their critiques. The following persons generously read parts pertaining to individual states of which they have specialized knowledge, and thus helped me weed the manuscript of many errors of detail: Mrs. Mary Bryan of the Georgia Historical Society (Georgia), Dr. J. Harold Easterby of the South Carolina Archives (South Carolina), Professor William C. Pool of Southwest Texas State College (North Carolina), Dr. Robert Thomas of the Hooker Electrochemical Company (Virginia), Mr. Paul S. Clarkson of Baltimore (Maryland), Professor John A. Munroe of the University of Delaware (Delaware), Professors Richard P. McCormick (New Jersey) and Broaddus Mitchell (New York) of Rutgers University, Miss Mary T. Quinn of the Rhode Island Archives (Rhode Island), and Professor Robert Brown of Michigan State University and Mrs. B. Katherine Brown (Massachusetts).

Two persons, Professor Fulmer Mood and Miss Livia Appel, have contributed so much—he as teacher, she as editor, and both as friends—that I cannot begin to express my gratitude. I only hope that in this and in future work I may, in some measure, justify their investment in me.

FORREST McDONALD

Madison, Wisconsin

Contents

PART FOUR: SIGNIFICANCE OF THE DATA

PART ONE: INTRODUCTION

I

Charles A. Beard's Pioneer Interpretation
of the Making of the Constitution

THE day was Monday, September 17, 1787, the place Philadelphia. The long and, as tradition has it, steaming hot
summer was finally ending.[1] Throughout the city, serenely unaware that historians were one day to know this as the Critical
Period of American history, Philadelphians were busy prepar-
ing a record wheat crop for export. Inside a crowded room in
the State House (later to be rechristened Independence Hall)
thirty-odd men penned their signatures to a document they had
styled a "Constitution for the United States of America."

There was no exuberance, no display of enthusiasm, and very
little reverential solemnity. Fourteen members of the body had
previously walked out for one reason or another, most of them
because they had personal business they considered more de-
serving of attention or because the hot clash of personalities had
been too much for them. Even now, at the very end, a half
dozen men were wrangling about minor details, and three
others flatly refused to sign the instrument. Another group was
already worrying about and planning for the strenuous campaign for ratification which lay ahead. Mostly, however, the
atmosphere pervading the room was one of exhaustion and a
sense of relief that the four-month ordeal was over.

[1] The New York *Daily Advertiser* reported on July 23, 1787, that "the heat
of the weather, on Tuesday the 3d instant, in Philadelphia, was 91 degrees of
Fahrenheit's thermometer in the shade." In his diary, which is printed in Max
Farrand's *The Records of the Federal Convention of 1787* (3 vols., New
Haven, 1911), 3:552–554, William Samuel Johnson made brief daily notations
about the weather in Philadelphia during the Convention. More days were
described as "hot" or "very hot" than as "cool." September 17 was described
as "cold."

The importance of the event insured that the making of the Constitution of the United States would become the subject of debate, study, and writing for many years to come. In addition the actors in the drama helped to fan the flames of debate and to provoke perhaps even more writing than the subject itself warranted. Almost as if to vex future scholars, the members of the Philadelphia Convention kept their proceedings secret and passed down to historians only the most fragmentary of notes; the Constitution was deliberately couched in ambiguous language; the disputants in the contest over ratification clouded both the contest and the conditions that shaped it by publishing reams of misleading, often fantastic propaganda. Partly because of the nature of the event, partly because of the chaotic record left by the participants, the mountains of historical writings on the subject have often been colored by emotionalism and shrouded in confusion. The men in the Convention have been depicted as a group of demigods, a band of ruthless conspirators, and virtually every intermediate brand of humanity. The document has been characterized at one extreme as scarcely less sacred than the Holy Bible, at the other as the greatest single barrier to the progress of social justice. Interpretation of the ratification has run the gamut from the noblest act of a free people under divine guidance to an unprincipled *coup d'état*.

Early in 1913 there emerged from this historiographical maze a work that was destined to become a classic. In that year Charles A. Beard, then a young professor of politics at Columbia University, published his *An Economic Interpretation of the Constitution of the United States*, a brilliant, challenging, and provocative study that has towered over everything else written on the subject, before or since. No other work on the making or the nature of the Constitution has been so much debated, so widely known, and ultimately so widely accepted.[2]

The central points in the thesis advanced by Professor Beard were these: "Large and important groups of economic interests

[2] The work was published by the Macmillan Company in April, 1913, and was reprinted seven times before August, 1935, when it was reissued with a new Introduction. The text proper is the same in the two editions and the pagination is identical.

were adversely affected by the system of government under the Articles of Confederation, namely, those of public securities, shipping and manufacturing, money at interest; in short, capital as opposed to land." After failing to safeguard their rights, "particularly those of the public creditors," through the regular legal channels, these groups called a convention in the hope of obtaining "the adoption of a revolutionary programme." (p. 63) In other words, the movement for the Constitution originated with and was pushed through by "a small and active group of men immediately interested through their personal possessions in the outcome of their labors. . . . The propertyless masses were . . . excluded at the outset from participation (through representatives) in the work of framing the Constitution. The members of the Philadelphia Convention which drafted the Constitution were, with a few exceptions, immediately, directly, and personally interested in, and derived economic advantage from, the establishment of the new system." (p. 324)

In essence, then, the Constitution was "an economic document drawn with superb skill by men whose property interests were immediately at stake; and as such it appealed directly and unerringly to identical interests in the country at large." (p. 188) It was based "upon the concept that the fundamental private rights of property are anterior to government and morally beyond the reach of popular majorities." (p. 324)

The system "consisted of two fundamental parts—one positive, the other negative." The positive part comprised four great powers conferred on the new government: "taxation, war, commercial control, and disposition of western lands." This meant for the manufacturers a protective tariff; for trade and shipping groups, tariffs and other legislation against foreign shipping; for money interests the prevention of "renewed attempts of 'desperate debtors' like Shays"; and for public creditors, ample revenues for the payment of their claims. The negative portion placed restrictions on the states: "Two small clauses embody the chief demands of personalty against agrarianism: the emission of paper money is prohibited and the states are forbidden to impair the obligation of contract." (pp. 154–179 *passim*)

In the contest over ratification, Beard concluded, only about a fourth of the adult males were eligible—or interested enough—to vote on the question, and the Constitution was ratified by no more than a sixth of the adult males. In five states it was "questionable whether a majority of the voters participating . . . actually approved the ratification." "The leaders who supported the Constitution in the ratifying conventions represented the same economic groups as the members of the Philadelphia Convention; and in a large number of instances they were also directly and personally interested in the outcome of their efforts." (p. 325) Of the voters on ratification, those favoring the Constitution were "centred particularly in the regions in which mercantile, manufacturing, security, and personalty interests generally had their greatest strength." The holders of public securities "formed a very considerable dynamic element, if not the preponderating element, in bringing about the adoption of the new system." The opposition, on the other hand, came almost exclusively from the agricultural regions and from the areas in which debtors had been formulating paper-money and other depreciatory schemes. (pp. 290, 291) In short, "the line of cleavage for and against the Constitution was between substantial personalty interests on the one hand and the small farming and debtor interests on the other." (p. 325)

If from this tightly and skillfully woven system of ideas are extracted those parts which are essentially nonconjectural—which are susceptible, in other words, of a reasonable degree of validation or invalidation as historical facts, and upon which the interpretative superstructure is erected—three propositions come into clear focus, namely that:

1. The Constitution was essentially "an economic document drawn with superb skill" by a consolidated economic group "whose interests knew no state boundaries and were truly national in their scope." [3] (pp. 188, 325)

---

[3] Beard carefully and explicitly denied that he was charging the members of the Convention with writing the Constitution for their personal benefit. The question, he said, was whether they can be considered, because of their own personal experience with certain forms of property which were adversely affected under existing conditions, as representatives of holders of such property in general. Beard, *Economic Interpretation*, 73. This is a subtle but valid and important distinction, often overlooked by Beard's critics.

2. "In the ratification, it became manifest that the line of cleavage for and against the Constitution was between substantial personalty interests [approximately identical to those which had been represented in the Philadelphia Convention] on the one hand and the small farming and debtor interests on the other." (p. 325)

3. "Inasmuch as so many leaders in the movement for ratification were large [public] security holders [as were most members of the Philadelphia Convention], and inasmuch as securities constituted such a large proportion of personalty, this economic interest must have formed a very considerable dynamic element, if not the preponderating element, in bringing about the adoption of the new system. . . . Some holders of public securities are found among the opponents of the Constitution, but they are not numerous." (pp. 290, 291n)

It was perhaps inevitable, in view of the immaturity of American historiography at the time Beard wrote, and the fact that his work was a piece of pioneering, that he should have based his case on an ingenious polarization of facts, assumptions, and inductive and deductive reasoning. Furthermore, while a substantial body of *theory* of economic interpretation of history had been developed long before Beard's time, no systematic methodology had yet been formulated by American historians for applying such theory to the analysis of specific historical phenomena. Thus to implement and substantiate his pioneering thesis Beard had to pioneer also in the matter of methodology. If his book is to be fruitfully examined, it is therefore necessary at the outset to analyze it in terms of these components: the facts presented, the assumptions made, the logic employed, and the methodology applied.

The work consists of eleven chapters. The first is a general introduction to the subject by way of an essay on historical interpretation in the United States. At the end of the chapter Beard summarizes the theory of economic determinism and states, as a methodological ideal, the "requirements for an economic interpretation of the formation and adoption of the Constitution." First it would be necessary to compile economic biographies of all persons connected with the framing and adop-

tion of the document. These data would lay the ground for a
consideration of the following proposition:

Suppose it could be shown from the classification of the men who
supported and opposed the Constitution that there was no line of
property division at all; that is, that men owning substantially the
same amounts of the same kinds of property were equally divided
on the matter of adoption or rejection—it would then become apparent that the Constitution had no ascertainable relation to economic groups or classes, but was the product of some abstract causes
remote from the chief business of life—gaining a livelihood.

Suppose, on the other hand, that substantially all of the merchants,
money lenders, security holders, manufacturers, shippers, capitalists,
and financiers and their professional associates are to be found on
one side in support of the Constitution and that substantially all or
the major portion of the opposition came from the non-slaveholding
farmers and the debtors—would it not be pretty conclusively demonstrated that our fundamental law was not the product of an ab-
straction known as "the whole people," but of a group of economic
interests which must have expected beneficial results from its adoption?

Beard's second chapter, "A Survey of Economic Interests in
1787," is the foundation of the entire work. It rests ultimately,
as does the work as a whole, on three assumptions. The first,
which Beard states explicitly, is that "the whole theory of the
economic interpretation of history rests upon the concept that
social progress in general is the result of contending [economic]
interests in society." Hence, he states, one must at the outset
identify the economic classes and social groups that existed in
the United States in 1787 and determine which of them could
expect to gain and which to lose from the overthrow or from
the maintenance of the legal-political-constitutional arrangements prevailing under the Articles of Confederation. This he
proceeds to do, in the form of an admittedly superficial survey.
The validity of the survey hinges on the second assumption (one
that he makes throughout the work), namely that the economic
conditions of the period were reliably depicted, at least in general, in the existing body of historical literature on the subject—

most of it in the Fiske "Critical Period" tradition.[4] The third assumption is less vital to the chapter but basic to the work: that it is valid to formulate categories of economic interests in advance of making the survey.

In view of the critical importance to Beard's work, and to the present one, of his survey of economic interests, it will be useful to outline his findings briefly. He first divides all property into two major classes, realty and personalty. Owners of realty he subdivides into three subgroups of farmers. The largest agrarian group consists of the small farmers, who, for working purposes, are substantially all assumed to have lived in inland, frontier areas, and who are identified in general as the "debtor class," responsible for the insurrections of the period and the "innumerable schemes for the relief of debtors." A smaller group of farmers consists of the wealthy manor lords of the Hudson, whom Beard classifies as persons fundamentally anti-personalty and politically in sympathy with the small "farmer-debtor" hordes. The third agrarian element comprises the slaveholding planters of the South, a group which, says Beard, differed from its New York counterpart in two respects: first, it included "many who were rich in personalty, other than slaves," and thus had greater "identity of interest" with northern merchants than with other farmers; secondly, it was in fear of slave revolts.

The small farmer-debtors, Beard continues, were adversely affected by the Constitution, immediately and directly, in that it expressly closed the avenues of escape from debt through state legislation, and established a general government strong enough to prevent them from ever rising again in armed insurrections. The Hudson valley manor lords were likewise ad-

---

[4] Traditional accounts pictured the decade of the 1780's as a period of great economic depression and commercial stagnation, during which financial chaos had set in, certificates of public debt having become virtually worthless and state legislatures, under the control of demagogues and hordes of dishonest debtors, having inundated the country with millions of dollars of worthless paper money. Most of these evils were assumed to have resulted from the weakness of the Congress under the Articles of Confederation. Beard (pages 47–48) considers the possibility that this picture might be largely the fictitious creation of contemporary propagandists and later historians, but proceeds to accept the picture explicitly as generally sound, and implicitly as a working hypothesis.

versely affected by the Constitution, but for more complex reasons. This class had taken "advantage of its predominance to shift the burden of taxation from the land to imports." The Constitution deprived states of the power to levy import duties, which meant that its adoption would again place the burden of state taxes on the land owned by the manor lords.[5] The slaveholders in the South, where no such shift in the basis of taxation had taken place, were not, according to Beard, adversely affected. Though the new Constitution "subjected them to regulation devised immediately in behalf of northern interests," it contained several "overbalancing compensations" for the southern planters.

Beard now turns his attention to personal property interests. These he divides into four major classes: money, public securities, "manufacturing and shipping," and western lands held for speculation.[6] All four groups, he asserts, were suffering from the conditions prevailing under the Articles of Confederation—indirectly from the lack of an effective general government, directly from the attacks the state legislatures made on personalty. The Constitution was designed for the relief of these suffering economic interests.

In Chapter Three, "The Movement for the Constitution," Professor Beard asks two questions: Were any interests adversely affected by existing legal-economic conditions? Were the leaders in the movement for the Constitution so affected? The first of these questions he assumes to have been answered

[5] In the introduction to his 1935 edition Beard revises somewhat his position regarding the landed aristocracy of New York. Citing Thomas C. Cochran's doctoral thesis, Beard says that some of the lords held public securities and were thus in favor of the establishment of adequate federal revenues via the Constitution.

[6] The classification of manufacturing and shipping as a single interest is Beard's. He apparently realized later that it was illogical to consider these two quite different interests as one, for later in the book he separates them. That is, in the first five chapters, in which he lays the foundations for his economic interpretation, he classifies the four "suffering personalty interests" as 1) money, 2) securities, 3) shipping and manufacturing, and 4) western lands, but in his final conclusions he shifts and without preparation for the reader describes the four interests as 1) money, 2) securities, 3) manufactures, and 4) trade and shipping. *Economic Interpretation*, 324.

with reasonable accuracy by his previous survey of interests. A reasonably accurate answer to the second he assumes could be derived from a study of the correlation between the activities and the economic interests of the leaders in the several attempts made between 1781 and 1786 to amend the Articles of Confederation. Assuming further 1) that the economic interests of such leaders remained substantially the same throughout these years and 2) that given individuals were consistent in their advocacy of change, Beard then makes a sketchy correlation survey. Quoting from primary sources in six instances and from secondary sources in six others, he cites three petitions for change that were presumably sponsored by persons whose chief economic interests were among the adversely affected forms of personalty, and names twenty-one individuals presumably having such interests who on one occasion or another advocated an amendment to the Articles of Confederation.[7]

In his fourth chapter Beard considers "Property Safeguards in the Election of Delegates to the Philadelphia Convention of 1787." The point of the chapter is that the delegates were selected indirectly, through state legislatures, rather than directly, by the people. At this stage Beard commits himself to a contradiction in assumptions which he never quite resolves. Whereas he assumed earlier (Chapter Two and elsewhere) that most legislatures were under the domination of agrarian-debtor interests in 1787, he now assumes that the selection of delegates by the legislatures facilitated the choice of persons representing the suffering personalty interests.[8] Assuming further that legal qualifications for voting in the several states were actually enforced, Beard then makes a state-by-state survey of the property qualifications for voting and officeholding and finds that

[7] About some of the individuals Beard is mistaken. For example, on page 55 he lists King, Ellsworth, and others as public security holders in 1783. As is shown in Chapter 3 below, these men held no securities until later.

[8] He could have resolved this simply, by assuming further that the state legislatures were at this particular moment temporarily in the hands of men representing personalty interests. Such a theory has been advanced for some states by later students—for example, by Robert L. Brunhouse, in his *Counter-Revolution in Pennsylvania, 1776–1790* (Harrisburg, 1942).

various such restrictions were in effect, some of them very
stringent ones.[9]

Chapter Five, a survey of the "Economic Interests of the
Members of the Convention," is the second vital factual keystone in the edifice Beard constructed. Drawing data from two
classes of sources (biographies, both full-length studies and
briefer sketches; and primary sources, principally the manuscript records of the Loan of 1790, which show security holdings, and the *Census of 1790*, which shows slaveholdings),
Beard examines the property holdings of each of the fifty-five
delegates who attended the Philadelphia Convention. He concludes that forty of them "represented through [their] personal
possessions" personalty in the form of public securities, fourteen
in the form of lands held for speculation, twenty-four in the
form of money at interest, eleven in mercantile, manufacturing,
and shipping property, and fifteen in slaves. The significance
Beard sees in these facts is closely connected with two assumptions he makes in this chapter. At the outset he reduces his
possible findings to an either-or proposition when he states,
"The only point here considered is: Did they represent distinct
groups whose economic interests they felt in concrete, definite
form through their own personal experience with identical
property rights, or were they working merely under the guidance of abstract principles of political science?" The conclusion
of the chapter is based on the assumption that a quantitative
breakdown of such property holdings is unimportant; that is
to say, Beard does not take into consideration the relative values
of the various forms of property making up the total property
holdings of each delegate.[10]

[9] This survey introduces another but quite related contradiction. That is,
if only persons with large amounts of property could participate in politics,
how could the unpropertied masses be ruling? Beard partially resolves this
question when he points out that ownership of real estate was very widely
distributed in 1787.

[10] That is, he makes no distinction between, say, a planter who had land
and slaves worth $20,000 and incidentally a few dollars in securities, and a
financier who had invested most of his resources in securities. Each is classified
as a security holder, and no weight is attached to the relative importance of

By the end of this chapter one important element of Beard's technique is clear. In each of these early chapters he begins by stating the ideal procedures for the execution of the tasks he sets for himself, and announces that he intends, for practical reasons, to confine himself to a superficial treatment in search of clues and general outlines. As he proceeds into new areas, chapter by chapter, he summarizes the conditional findings and postulations of preceding chapters and assumes, for working purposes, that such tentative findings are established facts.

The next three chapters rest, in the main, on a single assumption: that the *Federalist* essays and other contemporary propagandistic documents and expressions of opinion are reliable sources on the nature of the Constitution and the contest over its ratification. In Chapter Six Beard analyzes the Constitution as essentially an economic document. This brilliant essay is replete with subtle assumptions, points of logic, and philosophical abstractions. Chapter Seven surveys the "Political Doctrines of the Members of the Convention," almost exclusively on the basis of their utterances on the floor of the Convention. The keystone of this chapter is the assumption, partly substantiated by documented facts, that there was *in the minds of the individuals concerned* a connection between aristocratic or republican or other non- or anti-democratic systems of political philosophy and economic class thinking.

Chapter Eight, which consists of two parts, deals with the problem of ratification. In the first part Beard concludes that the procedure for securing ratification—namely through special conventions rather than by legislative action or popular referendums—was largely a tactical device to facilitate ratification in the face of what promised to be a difficult struggle. In the second part, a running survey of the formal process of ratification, in which he considers the states in a north-to-south geographical order rather than in the order in which they ratified, he con-

the securities of each. This practice is consistent with Beard's explicit concentration on the significance of holdings of various forms of property as giving the delegates experience with the tribulations of each, rather than as inspiring them to act in certain ways out of self-interest.

cludes that the expectation of difficulty in achieving ratification
was well founded: that ratification was accomplished in five
states contrary to the will of the people; in one state with unseemly haste, where there were indications that the popular will
had been thwarted; in one state where the popular will was
doubtful; and in six states without any noteworthy resistance—
in four of them quickly, in two slowly.

Chapter Nine, containing much the same methodological and
logical assumptions as the earlier chapters, is a survey of the
"Popular Vote on the Constitution." Using ingenious calculations as a means of projecting a paucity of known facts into a
larger estimate, Beard conjectures that about 160,000 persons
voted in the election of delegates to the several state ratifying
conventions, and that of these not more than 100,000 favored
ratification.[11] The smallness of the vote, he asserts, made it possible for representatives of personalty interests to achieve ratification in the face of the fact that in the general population they
were greatly outnumbered by representatives of agrarian interests. This assertion rests upon the assumption that the great
majority of the adult males who did not participate in the elections were agrarian in their interests, and that virtually all men
having personalty interests did participate.

Chapter Ten is a survey of the "Economics of the Vote on
the Constitution," and it presents the third vital set of facts in
the work. Proceeding by states from north to south (but omit-
ting Rhode Island), Beard does four things in this chapter,
basing his findings principally on Orin G. Libby's study of the
geographical distribution of the vote,[12] several secondary accounts of ratification, and the manuscript records of the funding of the war debts. First, he shows that the geographical dis-

[11] After a survey based on tabulations from all discoverable voting records
preserved in the archives of the thirteen states and of all votes recorded in
extant newspapers of the period, it is my conclusion that Beard's estimate
of the total vote was remarkably accurate.

[12] Orin Grant Libby, *Geographical Distribution of the Vote of the Thirteen
States on the Ratification of the Federal Constitution, 1787–1788* (Madison,
1894). Apart from interpretation, Beard's work actually added only two things
to this earlier study by Libby: biographical data on the fifty-five delegates
to the Philadelphia Convention and information on the public security holdings of various individuals.

tribution of the vote demonstrates, in general, that the contest was largely one of coastal versus interior sections. Significance is attached to this distribution by the assumption that the coastal regions were dominated by commercial, creditor, and anti-paper-money interests, and the interior regions by agrarian, debtor, and paper-money interests. Second, in terms of individuals, he shows that in one state, Pennsylvania, twenty-eight of the forty-six Federalist delegates owned various forms of personalty other than securities, and that the interests of thirteen of the twenty-three anti-Federalists were primarily agricultural. Except for security holdings he enumerates the economic interests of no other individuals. Third, he lists, but does not tabulate, individual security holders among the proponents of ratification in seven of the thirteen states. His lists, when tabulated, indicate that 167 delegates who voted for ratification—25 per cent of the 667 such delegates in these states, or 15 per cent of the 1,111 such delegates in the thirteen states—were holders of varying amounts (mostly not particularized) of public securities of one form or another. Sixty-six of the 167 delegates listed as security holders lived in Connecticut. Finally, Beard concludes that these data indicate that the contest over ratification was fundamentally a conflict between economic classes.

Chaper Eleven is an analysis of various contemporary comments which bear out, at least in part, Beard's analysis of the nature of the contest over ratification. This chapter rests on the same assumptions as Chapters Six, Seven, and Eight.

One additional observation must be made. As a basic feature of his entire work Beard uses what might be called a presentist frame of reference. That is to say, he assumes, consciously or unconsciously, that various questions, terms, and concepts which were current and had special meaning when he was writing had been current and had had the same meaning in the eighteenth century—such terms, for example, as "masses," "radicals," and "conservatives," and the concepts of urban working classes and modern political parties. To some extent he uses the same frame of reference in analyzing his source materials; for example, he assumes that account books depicting the operations in securities under Hamilton's funding plan can be interpreted in terms of twentieth-century accounting practices.

In general, historians have concerned themselves with Beard's assumptions and his logic. Such an approach is inevitably fruitless, for when Beard's logic is challenged his defenders can always counter by pointing to Beard's data on the economic interests of the delegates to the Philadelphia Convention and on the distribution of security holdings among the leaders in the contest over ratification. Furthermore, to make Beard's methods the question of first concern is to obscure and leave unexplored the question of whether a partially or wholly non-Beardian economic interpretation may not be valid.

Beard's thesis can be tested by two valid procedures. It must be tested by both of them, but care must be taken to keep them separate, for a combination of the two is not logically valid.

1. One may make the assumptions Beard made and use the methods he prescribed. This means that one asks, and seeks to answer, the questions Beard asked and sought to answer, by operating, so far as possible, within the framework of his own "broad outlines." His work was "frankly fragmentary," and he left it for other students to fill in the details. Until this has been done, Beard has not been fully tested, for his array of facts is otherwise inexplicable.[13]

2. Or one may question the validity of Beard's assumptions, his methodology, and the questions he posed. This must also be done if, upon testing the Beard thesis inside its own framework, it is found wanting. It must be done in order to answer basic related questions—those pertaining to the possibilities of a more rigorous economic interpretation, non-Beardian, pluralistic rather than monistic.

The first objective of the present work is thus to subject Beard's thesis to the most careful scrutiny, to fill in the details, on his own terms, in the framework of his own assumptions, method-

---

[13] This is not to overlook the fact that data, particularly selected data, can be organized in misleading ways. The point is that until more facts are brought together, no close approximation of their most meaningful order of arrangement is possible.

ology, and questions—in short, to discover whether the details are compatible with the broad outlines he sketched.

If under such scrutiny the Beard thesis should prove to be inadequate beyond repair—if the Beardian "old tire" is beyond patching—one can move 1) in the direction of a more tenable economic interpretation and, should this prove partially or wholly inadequate, 2) in other directions. With respect to the latter it is possible only to summarize the verifiable facts brought out in the course of the present study with a view to discovering clues as to the paths that may lead to an understanding of the making of the Constitution.

Now, in exploring the possibility that a different economic interpretation of the Constitution may be valid, it may develop that such economic interpretation is 1) entirely valid, 2) entirely invalid, or 3) partially valid. Should either of the first two possibilities prove to be the case, it would not mean that economic interpretation is or is not universally applicable, but only for this specific series of events. From the point of view of exploring the usefulness of economic interpretation in historical analysis, the period under study could be filed as one in which certain conditions prevailed and which could be compared with other periods whose salient characteristics were similar. If, on the other hand, it should develop that not even the most carefully drawn economic interpretation can "explain" all the circumstances, but that it does seem to "explain" some of them, then one must turn one's attention to these particular circumstances. By focusing attention upon these and subjecting them to the most rigorous analysis along every reasonable line of investigation it may be possible to learn something fundamental about the economic interpretation of history.

Unless economic interpretation proves entirely valid here, some broader questions about the making of the Constitution will remain unanswered. For suggestions as to the answers to these broader questions one must consider what approaches promise the most fruitful areas for further exploration.

Thus the basic aims of the present work come to focus upon four questions:

1. Is Beard's thesis regarding the making of the Constitution compatible with the facts?

2. If Beard's thesis is not tenable in the light of the facts and if his assumptions, methods, and the questions he poses are seen to be inadequate, can another economic interpretation of the Constitution be advanced as a tenable thesis or hypothesis?

3. What conclusions, if any, on methodology and on the entire concept of economic interpretation of historical phenomena can be drawn from this analysis?

4. If it is found that no economic interpretation explains the historical event under examination here—the making of the United States Constitution—what are the main avenues of investigation that must be followed in order to arrive at a closer approximation of the truth? That is, what positive conclusions can be drawn and where does one go from here?

PART TWO: THE PHILADELPHIA CONVENTION

II

Political Factions and Geographical Areas Represented in the Convention

THE several geographical areas, the political factions, and the economic interests represented in the Philadelphia Convention may be set forth and analyzed in three ways. The first is to scrutinize all the delegates elected—whether they served or declined to serve—in terms of the areas from which they came and the political factions with which they were identified in state affairs. The second is to examine the property holdings and means of gaining a livelihood of the fifty-five men who shared in the writing of the Constitution. The third is to look at their votes and conduct in the Convention itself to ascertain whether men of similar economic backgrounds tended to act together, and whether the members of given interest groups manifested the same measure of satisfaction with the finished product.

Each of these approaches throws light on the economic and political complexion of the Convention. Accordingly the analysis of the Convention which follows is divided into three chapters, each of which is devoted to one of the aspects named. The present chapter summarizes the political and geographical characteristics of the delegations selected to represent the several states in the Convention,[1] both those who served and those who declined to do so.

Delegates to the Convention were selected by the state legisla-

[1] In this section on the areas and factions represented in the Convention, no documentation will be offered except for specific votes cited. The affiliations of the delegates and the areas they represented are derived from a multitude of sources, all of which are cited in the more individualized sketches in Chapter 3. The analysis of the areas and factions that existed in the several states is drawn from an even greater variety of sources. This analysis is elaborated and thoroughly documented in Chapters 5, 6, and 7.

tures as delegates-at-large—that is, a delegate represented his state as a whole rather than a particular part of it. But each state was made up of several areas—much as a city has its various neighborhoods—which were partly the result of topographic and other geographical variations and partly manifestations of historical, ethnic, social, and economic variations. In the 1780's, before the advent of mechanically powered vehicles and significant turnpike roads, avenues of transportation, most often rivers, were the most important factor in determining these internal neighborhoods or areas in the various states. In speaking here of the geographical characteristics of delegations, it is these informal areas rather than formal political subdivisions of states that is meant.

NEW HAMPSHIRE

THE principal geographical areas in New Hampshire from which delegates could have been sent were four: 1) the Piscataqua River region; 2) the Merrimac River valley and the towns that traded with Newburyport by way of the Merrimac; 3) the Connecticut River valley; and 4) the semi-isolated northern half of the state. In the hills and mountains between these several areas were a large number of isolated towns.

State politics in New Hampshire involved two major factions and a number of minor factions. The major factions were 1) the Langdon faction, a state particularist group, based in Portsmouth and the Merrimac valley, and 2) the John Sullivan faction, a militant group of nationalizers with scattered bases, mainly in the Piscataqua region. Among the more important of the lesser factions were the former residents of the state of Connecticut, now living in the Connecticut valley of New Hampshire, who might be called the George Atkinson faction, and the Samuel Livermore faction, based in the semi-isolated northern half of the state.

Two delegates were elected to the Convention from New Hampshire who declined to attend: John Pickering of Portsmouth in the Piscataqua region, a member of the Langdon faction; and Benjamin West of Charleston in the Connecticut valley area, who belonged to the Sullivan faction.

The two delegates chosen to represent New Hampshire who did attend the Convention were John Langdon and Nicholas Gilman. Langdon, who lived in Portsmouth, was the head of the faction that bore his name. In the state he was a particularist, and as a legislator he had voted for paper money and debtor relief.[2] He was, however, personally and through business connections associated with Robert Morris and ultra-nationalistic friends in Philadelphia and was inclined to vote with them in the Convention.

Gilman, a resident of Exeter, represented the Merrimac area. (Exeter is closer to Portsmouth, but it traded via the Merrimac with Newburyport.) He was independent politically; though friendly to Sullivan, he was somewhat localistic in his views.

The elected delegation, then, represented all three major non-isolated areas (two delegates were sent from the Piscataqua region) and both major political factions (two delegates were associated with the Langdon faction).

MASSACHUSETTS

MASSACHUSETTS was made up of nine major geographical areas: 1) Boston and its immediate environs; 2) the interior towns connected most directly with Boston by the Boston Post Road and tributary roads; 3) the Essex-Salem area; 4) the Newburyport-Merrimac area; 5) the District of Maine; 6) the Plymouth-Cape Cod area; 7) the towns surrounding Rhode Island in the southeastern part of the state; 8) the Connecticut valley; and 9) the Berkshire Hills.

There were only two major political factions: the John Hancock, a faction of moderate state particularists, and the James Bowdoin, a strong nationalistic faction. Three smaller factions were allied with the Bowdoin faction—the Samuel Adams, Theodore Sedgwick, and Benjamin Lincoln factions. All the other subfactions were ordinarily allied with Hancock; the most important of these were the Benjamin Austin and Cushing factions.

Of the five delegates elected in Massachusetts one did not at-

[2] "Journal of the House of Representatives," September 14, December 25, 1786, in Albert Stillman Batchellor, ed., *Early State Papers of New Hampshire*, 20:696, 759 (Manchester, 1891).

tend the Convention: Francis Dana of Cambridge, in the Boston Road area. Though an independent, Dana was personally friendly toward John Hancock.

The four delegates who did attend the Convention were Rufus King, Elbridge Gerry, Nathaniel Gorham, and Caleb Strong.

King had lived in and can be thought of as a representative of both Newburyport and Maine. Both areas and King personally leaned toward state particularism, and they supported the Hancock faction. King and the areas were not inflexible in their convictions, however.

Gerry, who resided in Marblehead in the Essex-Salem area, was a close personal and political friend of Samuel Adams. Gerry and the area in general were supporters of Bowdoin because of his vigorous action on state governmental problems. They were, however, moderately state particularistic in outlook.

Gorham, of Charleston in the Boston area, was also a Bowdoinite. The area, however, was divided in its loyalties, about sixty per cent of the inhabitants being supporters of Hancock. Paradoxically, the area was strongly nationalistic despite its support of Hancock.

Strong, of Northampton in the Connecticut valley, was an intimate of Theodore Sedgwick and a supporter of Bowdoin and was moderately nationalistic. The area, too, supported the Bowdoin faction and was, in the main, nationalistic.

The total elected delegation from Massachusetts, then, represented the Newburyport-Merrimac, the Essex-Salem, the Boston and Boston-interior, the Connecticut valley, and the Maine area. The major areas unrepresented were the Rhode Island area, the Plymouth-Cape Cod area, and the Berkshire Hills. Both major factions were represented, Hancock and his allies by two delegates, Bowdoin and his allies by three.

RHODE ISLAND

RHODE ISLAND refused to send official delegates to the Convention. A group of Providence merchants, however, were unofficially represented by James Varnum, who stayed in Philadelphia for the duration of the Convention, keeping his sponsors informed as best he could and acting as a sort of lobbyist for the Providence interests.

CONNECTICUT

CONNECTICUT was comprised of five main geographical regions: 1) the New Haven area; 2) the New London area; 3) the Connecticut valley; 4) the northeast interior area; and 5) the northwest interior area.

Politically the state was divided into two principal factions along the line of special economic interests: a continental creditors faction, headed by Jeremiah Wadsworth and a number of his friends, and a state creditors faction, headed by William Williams, Joseph Hopkins, and James Wadsworth.

One delegate elected in Connecticut, Erastus Wolcott of East Windsor in the Connecticut valley, a member of the continental creditors faction, declined to attend the Convention.

Three elected delegates attended the Convention: Roger Sherman, William Samuel Johnson, and Oliver Ellsworth.

Sherman, the mayor of New Haven, was loosely associated with the state creditors faction and was personally a creditor of the state. New Haven was a principal base of the state creditors faction.

Johnson, of Stratford in the New Haven area, was politically independent and inactive in state politics, but was personally a creditor of the state.

Ellsworth, who lived in Hartford in the Connecticut valley, was a continental creditor and an active partisan in the continental creditors faction.

The total elected Connecticut delegation comprised two delegates from the New Haven area and two from the Connecticut valley. The New London, northeast interior, and northwest interior areas were unrepresented in the Convention, but both major factions were represented.

NEW YORK

ONLY two sections of New York were as yet settled: the area around the City, including Long Island and Staten Island, and the Hudson valley, including fringe settlements north of Albany toward Lake Champlain and west of Albany on the Mohawk.

The two major political factions were the state particularistic George Clinton faction, which was supported by a great majority of the citizens of the state, and the nationalistic Philip Schuyler faction, which was little more than a group of aristocrats around which had gathered the small opposition to Clinton.

All three delegates elected from New York sat in the Convention, though none of them attended full time: Alexander Hamilton, Robert Yates, and John Lansing.

Hamilton, a resident of the City, was the son-in-law of Philip Schuyler and the most vocal leader of the Schuyler faction. As a state legislator he had voted for debtor-relief measures.[3]

Yates, of Albany in the Hudson valley, was an officeholder and political leader in the Clinton faction.

Lansing, the appointive mayor of Albany, was also a legislative leader in the Clinton faction; he had voted for debtor relief.[4]

Both major areas and both major factions were thus represented, the Hudson valley and the Clinton faction by two delegates, the City and the Schuyler faction by one delegate.

NEW JERSEY

NEW JERSEY's topography divided the state into three parallel areas lying at a southwest-to-northeast angle across the state. Historically and economically, however, the line of division, cutting across topography, ran from southeast to northwest. The area northeast of that line corresponded to the colonial "East Jersey"

---

[3] Two debtor-relief bills came before the legislature while Hamilton was a member: a measure staying executions on debts owed British merchants and a measure virtually abolishing imprisonment for debts. Hamilton voted for both. *Votes and Proceedings of the Assembly of the State of New York*, January, 1787, Session (New York, 1787), March 8, 14, 1787.

[4] Lansing voted for the stay law on March 14, 1787. *Ibid.*

patents and fell within the New York economic orbit; the area on the other side of the line corresponded to the colonial "West Jersey" patents and fell within the Philadelphia economic orbit. It is these two areas of East and West Jersey that must be considered in connection with regional representation in the Philadelphia Convention.

The two principal political factions in the state were an outgrowth of the east-west division, namely, the East Jersey and the West Jersey faction. Despite local differences on continental questions, both groups were essentially nationalistic in outlook.

Two delegates were chosen in New Jersey who declined to attend the Convention. Both were from East Jersey: Abraham Clark of Essex County, the most important of the leaders of the East Jersey faction, and John Neilson of New Brunswick, who was also politically active for that faction.

Five delegates were chosen who attended the Convention: David Brearley, William C. Houston, William Livingston, William Paterson, and Jonathan Dayton.

Brearley, who lived in Trenton in West Jersey, was chief justice of the New Jersey Supreme Court, and as such was not very active in politics on behalf of the West Jersey faction.

Houston, of Trenton, was an active West Jerseyite.

Livingston, of Elizabeth in East Jersey, was governor of the state and was politically a middle-of-the-road leader, popular with both factions.

Paterson, of New Brunswick in East Jersey, supported his faction only lukewarmly and was not very active politically.

Dayton, who also lived in New Brunswick, was active in politics and was a close disciple of Abraham Clark, the East Jersey leader. As a member of the state legislature Dayton had voted for a law staying executions on debts.[5]

The total elected delegation included five members from East Jersey and two from West Jersey. As originally constituted, however, before there were any resignations or additions, the delegation consisted of two members from each area. In terms of polit-

---

[5] *Votes and Proceedings of the General Assembly of the State of New Jersey,* 12th Assembly, 1st Session (Trenton, 1786), October 31, 1786.

ical factions, the total elected delegation consisted of four East Jerseyites, one independent, and two West Jerseyites.

PENNSYLVANIA

PENNSYLVANIA consisted of numerous geographical divisions, which for present purposes may be reduced to the four main areas which could have been represented in the Philadelphia Convention: 1) Philadelphia and the Liberties; 2) the interior counties, including those on the Delaware River, which fell within the Philadelphia economic orbit; 3) the Susquehanna valley; and 4) the western area.

There were two well-organized political parties in the state, the so-called Anti-Constitutionalist or Robert Morris party, and the Constitutionalist or anti-Morris party. The Morris group was probably the strongest group of nationalizers on the continent. The anti-Morris group was strongly state particularistic.

All delegates elected in Pennsylvania attended the Convention: Robert Morris, James Wilson, Gouverneur Morris, George Clymer, Thomas Fitzsimons, Thomas Mifflin, Benjamin Franklin, and Jared Ingersoll.

Morris, from Philadelphia, was the head of the Anti-Constitutionalist or Morris party.

Wilson, also of Philadelphia, was a leader in the Morris party and an intimate personal friend of Morris.

Gouverneur Morris was a New Yorker residing in Philadelphia at this time. He was a leader in the Morris party and an intimate personal friend of Robert Morris.

Clymer, of Philadelphia, was an active member of the Morris party, but less close to or dependent upon Morris than were Wilson and Gouverneur Morris.

Fitzsimons, also of Philadelphia, leaned toward the Morris party but was often independent of it; he was not of the Morris inner circle.

Mifflin, who lived outside the city in Philadelphia County, was an independent in politics who wavered between the Morris and the Constitutionalist party, leaning toward the latter.

Franklin, of Philadelphia, was an independent who leaned strongly toward the Constitutionalist party, of which he was often counted a member.

Ingersoll, also of Philadelphia, was a Constitutionalist.

Thus the delegation included seven representatives from Philadelphia and one from the area immediately adjacent to the city. The Susquehanna valley and the west were unrepresented. The Morris faction was represented by four delegates and two independent sympathizers with the faction; the Constitutionalist party was represented by two delegates, one of whom was an independent with Constitutionalist sympathies. For all practical purposes, however, the Constitutionalist party might have been unrepresented, for none of its leaders was present and it was greatly outnumbered by its opponents.

DELAWARE

DELAWARE consisted of three geographical areas: the relatively advanced area around the Brandywine and its tributaries, in northern New Castle County; the Nanticoke River area in the southwest corner of the state, together with the western fringe of the state, which were in every way except in political boundaries a part of Maryland's Eastern Shore; and the remainder of the state, comprising the eastern portion of the state from the Brandywine area on the north to the Maryland border on the south, and unified by connections to the Delaware River and Delaware Bay.

There were no well-defined major political factions in the state, but many small political groups. Probably the most important of these were two opposing groups. One was a clique, based mainly in New Castle County and consisting chiefly of persons having Philadelphia connections, that had gathered around George Read and, to a lesser extent, John Dickinson. The other was an opposing group that had developed in lower Sussex County, at the center of which was the Mitchell family. The great majority of the population was connected only with small, shifting local cliques or family groups, or had no connections with any faction. Virtually all political groups in the state favored a stronger national union.

All the delegates chosen in Delaware attended the Philadelphia Convention: John Dickinson, George Read, Gunning Bedford, Jacob Broom, and Richard Bassett.

Dickinson lived outside Dover, but his closest connections were with New Castle County. He was a leader, though not a very active one, of the Dickinson-Read quasi-faction and was also intimately associated with and had been a leader of the Morris faction in Philadelphia.

Read, of the town and county of New Castle, was an active leader in the Dickinson-Read quasi-faction and he had occasional connections with the Morris faction in Philadelphia.

Gunning Bedford, Jr., of New Castle County, was unimportant politically and was not strongly attached to either of the two more important political groups.

Jacob Broom, of Kent County, was an independent in politics.

Bassett, a resident of Dover in Kent County, was an independent.

Thus the Delaware delegation consisted of three members from Kent County and two from New Castle County. The southwestern part of the state was not represented. Two delegates belonged to the Dickinson-Read group and three were independents. The Mitchell faction was unrepresented.

MARYLAND

THE principal geographical areas in Maryland were 1) the Eastern Shore; 2) the Susquehanna area; 3) the upper Western Shore (the Baltimore area); 4) the lower Western Shore; 5) the lower Potomac; and 6) the middle Potomac and western Maryland.

The four major factions in Maryland politics were the Charles Carroll faction, the Charles Ridgely faction (these two factions were closely allied in 1787), the Samuel Chase faction, and the Daniel of St. Thomas Jenifer faction (the latter two factions were closely allied in 1787). There were several other small factions in the state, composed largely of family connections, but most of them were allied with one of the above-named factions. The Carroll faction was consistently nationalistic. The others vacillated; in 1787 only the opportunistic Chase faction was strongly state particularistic.

Five delegates elected in the state declined to attend the Philadelphia Convention: Charles Carroll of Carrollton, in the upper Western Shore area, was the head of the Carroll faction; Gabriel Duvall, of Prince George County in the lower Potomac area, supported the Ridgely faction; Thomas Sim Lee, of Frederick town in the middle Potomac and western Maryland area, was a member of the Carroll faction; Thomas Stone, of Charles County in the lower Potomac area, was a member of the Jenifer faction; and Robert Hanson Harrison, also of Charles County, was allied with the Carroll faction.

Five delegates elected in Maryland attended the Convention: James McHenry, Daniel Carroll, Daniel of St. Thomas Jenifer, Luther Martin, and John Francis Mercer.

McHenry lived in Baltimore, in the upper Western Shore area. He was semi-independent in politics, but sympathized and was closely associated with Charles Ridgely and Charles Carroll.

Daniel Carroll, of Prince George County in the lower Potomac area, was a cousin of Charles Carroll and a member of the Carroll faction.

Daniel of St. Thomas Jenifer lived in Charles County on the lower Potomac. He was the leader of his own faction and intendant of the revenues of Maryland, the state's most important administrative office, and was allied politically with the Chase faction.

Luther Martin had residences and connections in Worcester County and Annapolis, in the Eastern Shore and lower Western Shore areas, respectively. He was the attorney-general of Maryland and an important figure in the Chase faction.

John Francis Mercer lived on the West River in Anne Arundel County, lower Western Shore, and was a member of the Chase faction.

The elected delegation included representatives from the Eastern Shore, upper Western Shore, lower Western Shore, lower

Potomac, and middle Potomac and western Maryland areas. The Susquehanna area was not represented. All four major political factions were represented.

VIRGINIA

VIRGINIA embraced six areas east of the Blue Ridge Mountains: the 1) Potomac, 2) Rappahannock, 3) York, 4) Upper James, 5) Lower James, and 6) Roanoke river valleys (the latter area extended into the interior from the Roanoke River to form Virginia's "Southside"); and three areas west of the Blue Ridge Mountains: 1) the Valley, 2) Trans-Alleghany, and 3) Kentucky.[6]

The political factions in the state were the Lee, Henry, Jefferson, and Randolph factions (the four of which controlled about seventy-five per cent of the voting power of the state and all of which were particularistic) and several independent factions.

Three delegates were chosen in Virginia who declined to attend the Philadelphia Convention: Patrick Henry of Prince Edward and Henry counties (the Roanoke area), the head of the Henry faction; Richard Henry Lee of Westmoreland County on the Potomac, the head of the Lee faction; and Thomas Nelson of Hanover on the York, the leader of an independent faction allied with the Jefferson faction.

Seven delegates from Virginia attended the Convention: George Washington, of Mount Vernon on the Potomac, who was connected with no faction in state politics but had a considerable personal following everywhere.

George Mason, of Fairfax County on the Potomac, leader of an independent faction.

James Madison, of Orange County on the Rappahannock, allied with the Jefferson faction, but often acting independently, who had nationalist sympathies.

James McClurg, of Williamsburg in the Lower James area, who was not active in state politics.

---

[6] The terms "Lower James" and "Upper James" as used here refer respectively to the upper and lower forks of the river. This was the eighteenth-century usage. Trans-Alleghany was what became West Virginia.

George Wythe, also of Williamsburg, member of the Jefferson faction.

John Blair, of York County on the York River, who had no factional connections and, as a judge, was inactive in politics.

Edmund Randolph, of Richmond in the Upper James area, leader of the Randolph faction.

The total elected delegation included three members from the Potomac area, two each from the York and Lower James areas, and one each from the Rappahannock, Upper James, and Roanoke-Southside areas. None of the three areas west of the Blue Ridge was represented. All four major factions and three independent factions were represented. Two delegates had no important political factional connections.

NORTH CAROLINA

NORTH CAROLINA was composed of six principal areas: 1) Albemarle Sound, including the navigable parts of the Chowan and Roanoke rivers (the upper tidewater); 2) Pamlico Sound, including the navigable parts of the Tar-Pamlico and Neuse rivers (the central tidewater); 3) the Cape Fear region (the lower tidewater); 4) the northeast piedmont, an extension of the Virginia Roanoke-Southside area; 5) the southwest piedmont; and 6) the area west of the mountains (most of which was Tennessee).

There were four principal political factions east of the mountains, those of Richard Caswell, Alexander Martin, Willie Jones, and Samuel Johnston, and a number of lesser factions. Most of the inhabitants of the western area were divided into two factions, one of which, led by John Tipton, opposed separate statehood, and the other, led by John Sevier, favored it.

Two delegates chosen in North Carolina, Richard Caswell and Willie Jones, declined to attend the Philadelphia Convention. Caswell, who lived in Lenoir County in the central tidewater area, was the head of the Caswell faction. Jones, who headed the Jones faction, had "home plantations" at both Halifax and Roanoke, and can be considered a representative of both the upper tidewater and the northeast piedmont.

Five delegates from North Carolina attended the Convention: William Blount, Alexander Martin, Hugh Williamson, Richard Dobbs Spaight, and William R. Davie.

Blount lived in Pitt County in the central tidewater area, but he had established important connections in Tennessee and was to move there shortly after the Convention; he may be considered at least a sympathetic representative of Tennessee. He had connections with the Caswell faction and with both Tennessee factions, but cannot be considered a "member" of either. As a state legislator he had voted for laws preventing the collection of debts due British merchants.[7]

Martin lived in Danbury, Stokes County, in the northeast piedmont. He headed the Martin faction, which was allied with the Caswell and Jones state particularist factions.

Williamson, of Edenton in the upper tidewater area, was an independent in politics.

Spaight, of New Bern in the central tidewater area, was not closely connected with any faction, but he was sympathetic with the Caswell and Jones factions.

Davie lived in Halifax, in the upper tidewater region at the foot of the northeast piedmont. He was associated with the Johnston faction, but only loosely. Like Blount, he had voted for laws preventing the collection of British debts.[8]

The total delegation elected in North Carolina thus included members from the upper tidewater, the central tidewater, northeast piedmont, and (in a limited way) the west. The lower tidewater and the southwest piedmont were not represented. All major factions in North Carolina proper were represented.

SOUTH CAROLINA

THE three general geographical areas in South Carolina were the low country, the middle country, and the up country.

The four major political factions in state politics, each corre-

---

[7] Digest of the proceedings of the House of Commons of North Carolina, printed in the *Maryland Journal and Baltimore Advertiser*, August 6, 1784.
[8] *Ibid.*

sponding to an economic interest group, were the low country plantation aristocrats, the factors of foreign merchants (these two factions were allied in 1787), the middle country planters, and the South Carolina merchants (the latter two factions were allied in 1787). A fifth major element in the population, the up country planters and farmers, displayed little interest in state politics.

One delegate chosen in South Carolina declined to attend the Convention: Henry Laurens of Charleston and Mepkin, in the low country. A retired merchant and a member of the planter aristocracy, Laurens was no longer very active in state politics.

The four members from South Carolina who did attend the Convention were all recruited from the planter aristocracy: John Rutledge, Charles C. Pinckney, Charles Pinckney, and Pierce Butler.

Rutledge, who maintained residences in Charleston and at his low country plantation, was the head of the Rutledge subfaction, which headed the planter aristocracy.

C. C. Pinckney maintained residences in Charleston in the low country and in Orangeburg in the middle country, where his plantations were located. Pinckney ranked high in the aristocracy, but he had business connections with and was friendly to the merchants' faction.

Charles Pinckney, who maintained residences in Charleston and at his middle country plantation in Orangeburg, headed a rising subfaction of the aristocracy which was soon to challenge and supplant the leadership of the Rutledge faction. He had close political connections with the middle country planters.

Butler maintained a residence in Charleston and one at his low country plantation. His political connections were with the planter aristocracy.

All four delegates who attended the Convention had supported paper money and debtor-relief laws.[9]

It is difficult to generalize about the South Carolina delegation. All five elected delegates were of the low country aristocracy, but the four delegates who attended the Convention also furnished

---

[9] See the analysis of individual economic interests in Chapter 3 and the discussion of South Carolina in Chapter 6.

partial representation to the middle country and the South Carolina merchants. Neither the factors nor the up country planters and farmers, however, were represented in any way.

GEORGIA

ONLY three general areas in Georgia had been settled by 1787: the Atlantic Coast–Savannah City area; the Savannah River valley; and Georgia's "west," an area extending west and northwest from Augusta for about eighty miles.

The important political factions in the state were the McIntosh faction, the Walton faction, and a third faction which might be described as the Yankee or Georgia Newcomers faction.

Two of the six delegates chosen in Georgia declined to attend the Convention: George Walton of Augusta in the Savannah valley area, head of the Walton faction, and Nathaniel Pendleton of Glynn County in the Coast-City area, whose connections were with the McIntosh faction.

The four delegates who did attend the Convention were William Houstoun, William Pierce, William Few, and Abraham Baldwin.

Houstoun, of Savannah, was associated with the McIntosh faction.

Pierce, also of Savannah, was associated with the Walton faction, although he was personally friendly with Lachlan McIntosh. Pierce had voted for paper money in the state legislature.[10]

William Few, of Augusta in the Savannah valley area, was a leader in the Yankee or Georgia Newcomers faction.

Baldwin, of Wilkes County in the west-piedmont area, was also a leader in that faction. He and Few had both supported a general debtor relief law that was introduced in the state legislature early in 1785.[11]

The total elected Georgia delegation thus included members from all three major areas and all three major factions.

[10] *Journal of the General Assembly of the State of Georgia*, August 10, 1786, MS in the Georgia Department of Archives and History, Atlanta.
[11] *Ibid.*, February 9, 1785.

To summarize, the delegations elected to the Philadelphia Convention included members from thirty-nine of the fifty-five major geographical areas in twelve states; Rhode Island sent no delegates. Four of the sixteen unrepresented areas were in the immediate vicinity of Rhode Island, in Massachusetts and Connecticut. The six major areas in the mountain and transmontane regions of Pennsylvania, Virginia, and South Carolina, and the Berkshire areas in Massachusetts and Connecticut were likewise unrepresented. With these exceptions, delegates were elected from virtually every major geographical area in the United States.

Politically, thirty-one of the thirty-four major factions in twelve states were represented by delegates. Thirteen, or about a fourth, of the delegates who actually attended the Convention had supported and voted for debtor-relief measures in their respective legislatures. This was approximately half the delegates who had served in the legislatures since the end of the war and who consequently had had an opportunity to help pass or defeat such measures. Careful examination of the journals of the several legislatures reveals that only three delegates, all of them from Delaware (Jacob Broom, George Read, and Richard Bassett), had consistently voted against such laws in their state legislatures.

Together, then, the delegations constituted an almost complete cross-section of the geographical areas and shades of political opinion existing in the United States in 1787. In a clear majority, however, were the advocates of a stronger union than that existing under the Articles of Confederation, as the first vote taken in the Convention was to demonstrate. Only one state's delegation, that of New York, was clearly dominated by members of a state particularist faction, though the delegations from North Carolina and Virginia included strong state particularist elements, as did that of Maryland. The dominant state particularist faction in Rhode Island refused to send delegates.

III

The Economic Interests of the Fifty-Five Delegates Attending the Convention

IN HIS survey of economic interests represented in the Philadelphia Convention, Professor Beard considered the delegates in alphabetical order. This arrangement was of no methodological significance, and inasmuch as a state-by-state presentation will facilitate additional analysis, that order of presentation will be followed in this chapter.

NEW HAMPSHIRE: JOHN LANGDON AND NICHOLAS GILMAN

JOHN LANGDON was the archetype of the personal property interest. The son of a prosperous farmer, he had been apprenticed in a countinghouse, after which he had gone to sea. By the time of the Revolution he had accumulated a sizeable amount of property, and his economic rise during the war was spectacular. Partly through shipbuilding and supplying food for the troops, and more through privateering and daring blockade-running, he had amassed a fortune and emerged from the war as one of the wealthiest men in New Hampshire.[1]

Immediately after the war he settled down to run a large mercantile business, his special field being trade with the French West Indies, to which he exported livestock and lumber and from which he imported sugar and rum. Since there was no restriction on this trade at either end, and since the ports with which he traded were

---

[1] See the biographical sketch of Langdon by his grandson, John Langdon-Elwyn, in Albert Stillman Batchellor, ed., *Early State Papers of New Hampshire*, 21:804 ff.; William G. Saltonstall, *Ports of Piscataqua* (Cambridge, 1941); and advertisements and notices in the Portsmouth *New Hampshire Gazette*, particularly for July, 1783.

insatiable markets for his products, his business was uniformly prosperous throughout the 1780's. Indeed, the trade was so routine that Langdon turned most of it over to subordinates while he devoted a large measure of his personal attention to political activities.[2]

Langdon's operations in financial paper were perhaps even more successful. As early as 1781 he was the Portsmouth agent for the Bank of North America of Philadelphia, in which he owned five shares having a total par value of $2,000. By the end of the war he had become the local agent for the financial operations of the powerful Robert Morris of Philadelphia. In December of 1783 he added to his agencies that of the new Bank of Massachusetts, in which he held four shares having a total par value of $2,000. When Hamilton's funding plan went into operation, Langdon owned $389.61 of the New Hampshire war debt, $26,572.78 in continental securities, and $959.25 in Connecticut state securities.[3]

NICHOLAS GILMAN, on the other hand, was a relatively small operator. The son of a prosperous proprietor of a general store in Exeter, he had worked in the store until 1776, when he entered the army, and again upon his return until the store was sold in 1785. He now entered public life as a delegate to Con-

[2] John Langdon Papers, in the Historical Society of Pennsylvania. Langdon's advertisements in the Portsmouth *New Hampshire Gazette* and *New Hampshire Spy* indicate the nature of his business. On the volume and nature of New Hampshire's trade with the French West Indies, see Jeremy Belknap, *History of New Hampshire* (3 vols., Boston, 1792), vol. 3, *passim*. Merrill Jensen's *The New Nation* (New York, 1950), 200–202, gives a general picture of that trade. For a translation of the French *arrêt* which established the commercial regulations that made the French West Indies trade a prosperous one for American exporters of lumber and livestock, see the Annapolis *Maryland Gazette*, March 24, 1785. My tabulation by months, 1781–1789, of newspaper announcements of vessels entering and clearing Portsmouth to and from the French West Indies reveals how stable the trade was.

[3] Lawrence Lewis, Jr., *A History of the Bank of North America* (Philadelphia, 1882), 143; N.S.B. Gras, *The Massachusetts First National Bank of Boston, 1784–1934* (Cambridge, 1937), 539; *New Hampshire Gazette*, July 31, 1781, January 18, March 29, December 20, 1783; and Records of the Loan of 1790, vol. 249, folio 35 (Subscription Register, Assumed Debt of New Hampshire); vol. 242, folio 4 (Journal of the Domestic Debt, 1791–96); vol. 495, folio 128 (Journal of the Connecticut Debt), all in Old Loan Records, in the Fiscal Section of the National Archives.

gress, and until his death in 1814 devoted his time almost exclusively to politics.[4]

Nicholas left most of the family business to his brother, John Taylor Gilman, and he seemed content to live on his modest patrimony and his salaries from public office, though he probably joined his brother in occasional business ventures. The Exeter tax rolls reveal that he owned his house but no mercantile, manufacturing, or farm property.[5]

Gilman owned a small amount of the public debt of New Hampshire, $1,024.94 face value, which he exchanged for new United States securities under the Loan of August 4, 1790, Hamilton's scheme for assuming and funding the war debts.[6] Gilman's paper profit from appreciation of his securities—that is, the extent to which, in Beard's language, he was a "direct economic beneficiary from the adoption of the Constitution"— amounted to about $500, or roughly $10 a month from 1787 to 1791. This estimate is made by the following method. New Hampshire public debt certificates sold in 1787 for approximately 2s. 6d. on the pound, or 12½ per cent of their face value; his approximate $1,000 in securities were thus worth

[4] William A. Robinson's biographical sketch of Gilman in the *Dictionary of American Biography;* biographical sketches in Batchellor, ed., *State Papers of New Hampshire,* 20:803 ff., and *Biographical Directory of the American Congress.* The last sketch refers to the store as a "counting house"; the nature of the business it transacted is revealed in advertisements in Portsmouth and Newburyport newspapers of the 1770's and early 1780's. For an announcement of the death of Gilman's father and the sale of the store, see the advertisement in *Fowle's New Hampshire Gazette and General Advertiser* (Portsmouth), January 21, 1785.

[5] Exeter Town Records, in the Microfilm Collection of Early Town Records, in the New Hampshire State Library. The originals of these records, which have also been consulted, are in the New Hampshire State Historical Society.

[6] Vol. 249, folio 32 (Subscription Register, Assumed Debt of New Hampshire). Professor Beard states that Gilman had securities "to the amount of $5400.67 . . . $6654.79 . . . and $11,021.95" (pp. 93–94), but he is mistaken. The first two figures he derived from the Nicholas Gilman Papers in the Manuscripts Division of the Library of Congress, a study of which shows that the securities were owned by the estate of Gilman's father, also named Nicholas. For the largest figure Beard cites "Ledger C, Treasury 6%" (vol. 42, folio 368, of the Records of the Loan of 1790). Examination of this entry reveals that the securities it refers to were first acquired by Gilman in 1798, eleven years after the Convention.

$125.[7] For these Gilman was to receive, under the terms of the Loan of 1790, new securities of the following sums and denominations: four-ninths of the total of old securities held, or $444.44, in six per cent bonds; three-ninths, or $333.33, in three per cent bonds; and two-ninths, or $222.22, in six per cent bonds on which interest was deferred for ten years. In the spring of 1791, when Gilman funded his securities, the market price of the six per cent bonds was seventeen shillings on the pound (85 per cent of face), making his six per cents worth $378; the market price of the three per cent bonds was nine shillings per pound (45 per cent of face), making his three per cents worth $150; his deferred six per cents, which also sold at 45 per cent of face, were worth $100. Thus the total market value of the new securities was approximately $628, or about $503 more than they had been worth in 1787.[8]

MASSACHUSETTS: RUFUS KING, NATHANIEL GORHAM, ELBRIDGE GERRY, AND CALEB STRONG

RUFUS KING, of Newburyport, was the son of a Maine farmer and part-time storekeeper. His inheritance had been insufficient to pay for his education, which had been financed largely through loans from a friend of his father's. When he was admitted to the bar in Newburyport in 1780, King quickly cleared up his debts by practicing there full time until 1784 and intermittently for three years thereafter, when he was not in New York as a delegate to Congress.[9]

In 1786 King married Mary Alsop, daughter of wealthy New Yorker John Alsop, import merchant and president of

[7] Gilman to John Sullivan, September 3, 1787, in Isaac W. Hammond, ed., *Miscellaneous Provincial and State Papers, 1725–1800,* 18:790 (Manchester, 1890).

[8] Market quotations from *American State Papers* (38 vols., Washington, 1832–1861): *Finance,* 1:231. Price fluctuations were recorded in the newspapers of the larger American cities throughout the 1790's. Late in 1792 the price of all securities, riding the crest of a speculative bubble which soon collapsed, temporarily rose about 35 per cent above these figures.

[9] Charles R. King, *Life and Correspondence of Rufus King* (6 vols., New York, 1894–1900), 1:2, 4, 30. See also the sketch of King by Claude M. Fuess in the *Dictionary of American Biography* and the sketch in the *Biographical Directory of Congress.*

the New York Chamber of Commerce. Thenceforth, though he spent a great part of his time in public life, King was drawn closer, both socially and professionally, into the New York mercantile world, and in 1788 he moved to New York City.[10]

Sometime before 1791 King invested $3,000 in twelve shares of the Bank of New York.[11] Aside from this, most of the capital he acquired from 1786 to 1788 he apparently invested in the New York public debt, and in 1791 he funded over $10,000 of these securities.[12] This was not, as might at first appear, necessarily a violation of King's declared abhorrence of speculators, for the purchase of New York securities was a conservative investment, regardless of whether or not a new government was established. Furthermore, the appreciation after 1787 was small, for New York had funded its debt and its share of the national debt in 1786, and the state made regular interest payments until relieved of the burden in 1790. After 1786 funded New York securities could not be bought anywhere for much less than ten shillings on the pound; hence King's paper profit was only about $1,300 in four years.[13]

[10] King, ed., *Rufus King*, 1:132.

[11] Henry W. Domett, *A History of the Bank of New York, 1784–1884* (New York, 1884), 135.

[12] Records of the Loan of 1790, vol. 22, folio 14; vol. 25, folio 60 (Ledgers of Assumed 6% Stock); vol. 32, folio 14 (Ledger, New York Assumed Debt); all in Old Loan Records, in the National Archives.

[13] On New York's funding program, see the discussion of ratification in New York, pages 283–310 below. This program was bitterly opposed by Hamilton, who feared that it would make the welfare of public creditors contingent on the welfare of the state government, which indicates that "Hamiltonianism" was by no means original with Hamilton. The funding of all debts on the national level had been talked of in various circles as early as 1781.

On the success of New York's program, see the letter of Philip Schuyler, Hamilton's father-in-law, in the Poughkeepsie *Country Journal* of March 10, 1789. Prices of New York securities in 1785, when talk of the funding plan had just begun, had ranged from 5s. 6d. to 5s. 9d. on the pound; "Honestus," in the New York *Daily Advertiser*, March 31, 1787. After the funding in 1786 New York securities were never less than 10 shillings; see quotations in various New York newspapers. See also the debates in the New York Assembly as recorded in the New York *Daily Advertiser*, March, 1787. The prices of United States securities in 1791, cited above in the remarks on Gilman, average out at roughly 63 per cent of face value. King's $10,000 of securities therefore cost him no less than $5,000 in 1786–88, and their market value appreciated to about $6,500 in 1791.

NATHANIEL GORHAM, of Charlestown, son of a packet boat operator and father of eight children, had been trained as a mechanic. His house was "hardly a fine one" and in 1772 had a £200 mortgage against it. Gorham gradually became acquainted with and interested in shipping, and began to accumulate some property, but in 1775 his entire fortune of £786 9s. in various forms of property was wiped out by the ravages of the British armies. Somehow he managed to make a fresh start, and during the war he engaged in privateering and speculating with a vengeance. Before the close of hostilities he had made a tidy fortune in much the same manner as John Langdon had done. Unlike Langdon, however—but like many of the Massachusetts war-rich—Gorham was unable to manage his money well, and from the end of the war until his death in 1796 his career was a story of progressive dissipation of his wealth through unsuccessful ventures.[14]

Gorham's ultimate bankruptcy was a direct, albeit surprising, result of the financial consolidations effected under the Constitution; in a sense he sat in the Convention and helped write the order for his own execution. Under a scheme which had been planned for some time and was formally consummated early in 1788, he and his partner, Oliver Phelps, contracted to buy the lands owned by Massachusetts in western New York. The terms of the contract called for three annual payments in state consolidated notes totaling £300,000, Massachusetts current ($1,-000,000). With these securities selling for 3s. 6d. on the pound in 1787, Gorham and Phelps expected that the lands would cost them about $175,000 net in specie. Upon the establishment of Hamilton's funding system, however, the securities quadrupled in price, and the increased obligation bankrupted the two partners. Scores of speculators in western lands, including Hamil-

---

[14] Available information on Gorham is fragmentary. General information is obtainable from Timothy Thompson Sawyer's *Old Charlestown: Historical, Biographical, Reminiscent* (Boston, 1902), 189 ff.; James F. Hunnewell, *A Century of Town Life: A History of Charlestown, Massachusetts, 1775–1887* (Boston, 1888), 117, 157; and the *Biographical Directory of Congress*. A loose running account of Gorham's mercantile career can be pieced together from his advertisements in Boston newspapers.

ton's close friend William Duer, were bankrupted in exactly the
same fashion.[15]

ELBRIDGE GERRY, one of the three men who refused to sign
the Constitution, and a leader of the opposition to its ratification in Massachusetts, was a wealthy and powerful Marblehead
merchant. Secure in his wealth, having inherited from his
father a vast mercantile business which he increased before and
during the war, Gerry was nonetheless probably one of the real
sufferers from the commercial conditions prevailing during the
period of the Confederation. Marblehead's economy was built
on fishing and whaling and the British West Indies trade, which
were the chief targets of British postwar commercial restrictions. Gerry was also a large holder of western lands. Indeed,
except in opposing the Constitution, Gerry fits Professor Beard's
description of suffering personalty interests in every way and on
a large scale.[16]

Gerry was the largest holder of public securities in the Convention, owning well over $50,000 in continental and various
state securities. A sizeable portion of this amount consisted of
original loans made by Gerry during the war, but most of it
had been acquired during the 1780's, partly in payment for
goods and partly, doubtless, through speculative investment.[17]

[15] Accounts of the Phelps-Gorham purchase may be found in William G.
Sumner's *The Financier and Finances of the Revolution* (2 vols., New York,
1891), 2:253 ff., and Ellis Paxson Oberholtzer's *Robert Morris, Patriot and
Financier* (New York, 1903), 302. The original contract terms are stated in the
Journal of the House of Representatives of the General Court of Massachusetts,
March 31, 1788, MS in the Massachusetts Archives. Massachusetts consolidated
notes had sold at 5 shillings and varied little until the Shays uprising in the
fall of 1786; see quotations in the Boston *Massachusetts Centinel*, especially
July to September, 1786. In 1786 they fell off sharply to 3s. 6d., where they
remained until after the Convention. Henry Knox Papers, vol. 20, No. 148, item
dated July 26, 1787, in the Historical Society of Massachusetts. After the Convention the price rose steadily until it reached about 15 shillings on the pound
in mid-1790.
[16] Benjamin Austin, *Life of Elbridge Gerry* (2 vols., Boston, 1829, 1830);
John Sanderson, *Biographies of the Signers of the Declaration of Independence*
(1846 edition, Philadelphia), 144 ff.; A. M. Dyer, *The Ownership of Ohio Lands*,
68, cited in Beard, *Economic Interpretation*, 99.
[17] Records of the Loan of 1790, vol. 279, accounts 582 and 795 (Subscription
Register, Assumed Debt of Massachusetts); vol. 282, folios 324, 931 (Register
of Certificates for Debts Due by the U.S. in the State of Mass.); vol. 283,
folio 1 (Register of Interest Certificates, 1786); vol. 284, folio 6 (Account of

CALEB STRONG, the son of an "ancient and honorable family of Northampton," was a prosperous country lawyer. He served as county attorney for Hampshire County from 1776 to 1800, but never attained any great prominence at the Massachusetts bar. When, in 1783, he was offered a position on the state supreme court, he declined it on the ground that his "fortune was too narrow to permit such a loss of income as an acceptance of this office would have entailed." He doubtless enjoyed, however, a steady albeit limited income from the modest fees he earned from time to time for drawing up writs and miscellaneous legal documents for the litigious farmers of western Massachusetts.[18]

Probably most of his personal property was invested in public securities. During the 1780's he purchased £3,271, Massachusetts current ($10,903), in Massachusetts consolidated notes, which he funded under the Loan of 1790.[19]

CONNECTICUT: WILLIAM SAMUEL JOHNSON, OLIVER ELLSWORTH,
AND ROGER SHERMAN

WILLIAM SAMUEL JOHNSON, of Stratford, was the son of Samuel Johnson, a wealthy clergyman. From his father he inherited, in 1749, £8,000 sterling, and his wife inherited £4,000 from her father. Trained in the law at Yale, Johnson made enough money from his practice before the war to finance a few unsuccessful ventures in shipbuilding and exporting of horses. He also owned a small iron mine in Kent, which earned him £12 annually, and an ironworks that never quite broke even.[20]

Certificates of Liquidated Debt); vol. 622, folio 142 (Subscription Register, Domestic Debt, 1790–91 Pennsylvania Loan Office); vol. 630, folio 60 (Journal of the Continental Debt, 1790–91); all in Old Loan Records, in the National Archives.

[18] Henry Cabot Lodge, "Memoir of Hon. Caleb Strong, LL.D.," in the *Proceedings of the Historical Society of Massachusetts*, 1:290–316 (Boston, 1874). Strong's close friend Theodore Sedgwick had a law practice much like his own, and much can be learned about that practice from study of the Theodore Sedgwick Papers in the Historical Society of Massachusetts.

[19] Records of the Loan of 1790, vol. 280, account 1284 (Subscription Register, Assumed Debt).

[20] George C. Groce, Jr., *William Samuel Johnson: A Maker of the Constitution* (New York, 1937), 38, 41–44.

At the outbreak of the war Johnson disposed of all his investments and his fortune underwent considerable shrinkage thereafter. So serious, indeed, was his plight in the 1780's that his property in the town of Washington and in New Milford was sold for nonpayment of taxes a year before the Philadelphia Convention.[21]

Only in the 1790's, while he was president of Columbia College (in which post he served from 1787 to 1800), did Johnson regain his former financial position. When he died in 1819, his estate was worth nearly $90,000.[22]

Johnson had invested £968 ($3,227) in loans to the state in 1784, but such postwar debts were not covered by the assumption plan of 1790. And despite the fact that he was primarily an investor in pure personalty, there is no evidence that Johnson owned any other public securities in 1787.[23]

OLIVER ELLSWORTH, of Hartford and East Windsor, was a familiar American "type," the self-made small-town lawyer with a finger in many economic pies. The son of a farmer, Ellsworth married above his station, worked at part-time jobs to supplement the meager income he derived from his practice (a total of three pounds in the first three years of his marriage), tenaciously hung on to every penny, invested shrewdly, and by sheer determination and work acquired a reputation and a large

[21] *Ibid.*; public notices in the Hartford *Connecticut Courant*, December 2, 1785, January 23, 1786.
[22] Groce, *Johnson*, 44.
[23] *Ibid.*, 120. Beard (p. 118) says Johnson "carried on extensive operations through his son Robert Charles Johnson . . . who was speculating extensively." Beard is very confused here, and the jumble of facts is difficult to untangle. For Johnson's personal holdings, Beard cites Ledger B, NY Office, Deferred 6%, 1790, folios 10, 152, 457. The first of these was an acquisition of securities in 1793, the third was the transfer of these securities to his son, and the second was a transaction in the name of Robert Charles Johnson; none were securities owned by Johnson prior to 1793, six years after the Convention.
Beard cites six other entries for Robert Charles Johnson, all of them in the same disarray. R. C. Johnson is listed on the books for several large transactions, but none of the entries were for securities which could have belonged to the younger Johnson before December, 1791. The nature of the entries indicates not that young Johnson was "speculating extensively," but that he was apparently acting as a broker for wealthier clients. William Samuel Johnson had acted as a broker for many years prior to the Revolution, and the son may well have entered that business under the guidance of his father.

estate. Every small town in America knows his type—uncultured, unimaginative, and proud of always having more money at the end of a year than he had had at the beginning.[24]

Ellsworth dabbled in everything that looked promising; he never missed a chance to earn a dollar and never let a dollar lie idle. He loaned money and occasionally bought land and houses. In 1784–1785 he invested about $530 in depreciated continental securities having a face value of approximately $4,217 (which, with accrued interest, had a face value of $5,985 when Ellsworth funded them in December, 1791), and, in typical fashion, he fought in state and national politics to protect his investment. The securities ultimately appreciated to a market price of roughly $3,770, a gain of $3,240—the equivalent of a monthly gain of $45 for six years. This and the original outlay of about $530 would hardly seem large enough to write a Constitution to protect, but the appreciation was a one hundred per cent annual return on the original investment, and Ellsworth would have so viewed it. Such men as Ellsworth—whom Gerry, for example, could have bought and sold twenty times over—are inclined to go to greater extremes in the protection of their property than those who are more secure in their wealth.[25]

ROGER SHERMAN, the canny old mayor of New Haven, had had a varied economic life. In his younger years he had worked as a farmer, surveyor, shoemaker, and lawyer until he had accumulated enough money to buy, with his brother William, a small store in New Milford. That was in 1750; by 1761 he was worth about £300, and he removed to New Haven, where he

[24] William G. Brown, *The Life of Oliver Ellsworth* (New York, 1905), 12, 22–23, 34. The brief anecdotal biography of Ellsworth in Kenneth Bernard Umbreit's *Our Eleven Chief Justices* (New York, 1938), 79–110, is excellent.

[25] Beard cites for Ellsworth's holdings Ledgers A, B, and C, Folio 21 in each, recording the sums of $2,660.98, $1,995.75, and $1,330.50, respectively. I found only Ledger A, Assumed 6% Stock (vol. 495 of the Records of the Loan of 1790) in the National Archives, but there is no doubt that the now-missing volumes contained the information Beard cited. Four-ninths of the total of $5,985 is $2,660; and $1,995 and $1,330 are one-third and two-ninths respectively, in accordance with the terms of the Loan of 1790. Ellsworth's purchase price is estimated on the basis of a price of 2s. 6d. per pound, the rate throughout the country in 1784–1787 for unfunded continental certificates (popularly known as "balloon notes").

opened another small store, devoting himself "to the sale of provisions and general merchandise, including books, in which occupation he was very successful." This store he turned over to a son in 1772.[26]

Sherman invested almost all his property in the revolutionary cause, and he was almost ruined by depreciation of his securities after the war. Throughout the 1780's he trembled on the brink of insolvency, but his local prestige and reputation for honesty kept him out of debtors' prison. His plight was desperate, however. His large family was a constant drain on his resources; "his eldest sons John and William proved business failures, [and] his son Isaac . . . had been involved in his brother William's mercantile collapse." In 1786 Sherman's property in New Milford was sold for nonpayment of taxes, and "by 1789 the work of his daughters had been necessary . . . to eke out the family income." [27]

In 1792, only a year before his death, Sherman's investment in the Revolutionary War debt was finally repaid when he funded $7,729 at the Connecticut loan office. The securities gave each of his heirs paper worth about $600, if no allowance is made for his debts.[28]

NEW YORK: ALEXANDER HAMILTON, JOHN LANSING, JR., AND ROBERT YATES

ALEXANDER HAMILTON's career and finances are too well known to require lengthy restatement here. A brilliant lawyer and financier, son-in-law of the wealthy head of the New York aristocracy, Philip Schuyler, Hamilton could easily have made a great fortune. Instead he devoted himself fanatically to public life, almost totally neglecting his family and private economy.

---

[26] Roger S. Boardman, *Roger Sherman, Signer and Statesman* (Philadelphia, 1938), 53–54, 71.

[27] *Ibid.*, 279, 296; public notice in the *Connecticut Courant*, January 23, 1786.

[28] Records of the Loan of 1790, vol. 495, folio 28 (Ledger A, Assumed 6% Stock). See note 25 above; the statement regarding the missing volumes applies also to Sherman's securities.

He was perpetually in debt, and despite his wife's large inheritance he died bankrupt.[29]

Acutely conscious of the necessity, in his sensitive position under the new government, of remaining above reproach, Hamilton acquired no public securities except the $800 worth of three per cent securities which he apparently bought in 1791.[30] He also owned a share and a half, worth $375, in the Bank of New York.[31]

JOHN LANSING, JR., of Albany, who walked out of the Convention after six weeks and who strenuously opposed the Constitution, was one of the patricians of the Hudson. Besides his enormous estate at Lansingburgh he had a lucrative law practice in Albany and was mayor of that city; he owned 40,000 acres of land in Schoharie County and probably more elsewhere. He has been described at "perhaps the wealthiest man in his party" (the Clinton–anti-Federalist faction), a party not without a number of other very wealthy men.[32]

Lansing owned over $7,000 in public securities, but this was an insignificant part of his fortune.[33]

ROBERT YATES, who also walked out of the Convention, was

[29] The Hamilton bibliography is too extensive to cite here. The most important item is the ten volume *Works of Alexander Hamilton* edited by Henry Cabot Lodge (New York, 1903). Biographies by Lodge, Claude G. Bowers, and Nathan Schachner and the *Reminiscences* of his son, John A. Hamilton, have been consulted for data on Hamilton's economic interests. Schachner, in his *Alexander Hamilton* (New York, 1946), 432, says that at the time of Hamilton's death the sale of his estate would have brought about $40,000, and that his debts far exceeded this sum.

[30] Various accusations have been made, both by contemporaries and by later historians, that Hamilton speculated in securities. Hamilton denied the charge, claiming that he owned only the $800 worth referred to above. *Works of Hamilton*, 8:268. His name is not recorded on the books of the Treasury Department or those of any of the state loan offices. It is true that Schuyler and many of Hamilton's friends made a great deal of money on securities (some of them were also bankrupted), but it is also true that they made money in many other enterprises in which Hamilton did not share.

[31] Domett, *Bank of New York*, 132.

[32] Ernest W. Spaulding, *New York in the Critical Period* (New York, 1932), 237.

[33] Records of the Loan of 1790, vol. 32, folio 97 (Ledger, New York Assumed Debt), in the National Archives. The exact sum was $7,311.82. Various members of the Lansing family held larger amounts.

related to Lansing by marriage. His family was one of high station, and he himself had received a classical education and studied law under William Livingston. He had a comfortable estate
and a lucrative practice, and when in 1777—at thirty-nine—he
accepted an appointment as a judge of the New York Supreme
Court, he observed that the rewards of his practice "held out
to him strong inducements to decline its acceptance." The
salary was relatively small; during the war it was paid in paper,
and one year his salary after depreciation was just sufficient "to
purchase a pound of green tea for his wife." Despite these comfortable beginnings, Yates lived modestly and after 1777 apparently supported himself largely by dipping constantly into
his capital; "he died poor." [34]

Yates owned no public securities, but some of the more active members of his family were security holders. [35]

NEW JERSEY: DAVID BREARLEY, WILLIAM PATERSON, WILLIAM
C. HOUSTON, JONATHAN DAYTON, AND WILLIAM LIVINGSTON

DAVID BREARLEY, of Trenton, was educated at Princeton and
trained in the law. He engaged briefly in private practice, served
a short time in the army, and in 1779 became chief justice of
the New Jersey Supreme Court. This post he held until 1789,
when he became a judge of the United States District Court.
He died in 1790. [36]

Brearley, grand master of the New Jersey Masonic Lodge,
"was not a wealthy man"; apparently he lived largely on the
modest salary of his judicial office. "Although hardly a brilliant
figure, he was capable and respected." [37] He had no money in

---

[34] Biography of Yates, appendix to Senate Document 728, 60th Congress,
2d Session, p. 205; the same sketch is printed in the 1821 edition of Yates's
notes on the Convention, *Secret Proceedings and Debates of the Federal
Convention*.

[35] Consult vols. 548, 549, 22, 25 and 32 of the Records of the Loan of 1790,
in the National Archives.

[36] Sketches of Brearley by Edmund Alden in the *Dictionary of American
Biography*, Richard P. McCormick in his *Experiment in Independence* (New
Brunswick, 1950), 256–257, and Eli Field Cooley in his *Genealogy of Early
Settlers of Trenton and Ewing* (Trenton, 1883), 15–16.

[37] McCormick, *Experiment in Independence*, 257.

shipping, manufacturing, or western lands. He had "at stake" one continental loan office certificate with a face value of $12.45 and a market value, at the time of the Convention, of about $2.49.[38]

WILLIAM PATERSON was the son of an Irish immigrant who brought him to America in 1747, when he was two years old. His father had become an itinerant peddler and had made enough by 1775 to establish a small store in Princeton. Paterson was educated at Princeton and trained in the law. He began practicing in 1770, but his income in four court sessions was only fifteen shillings, four pence, and after two years he went into a store with his brother, practicing law only part time. After 1779, when he became the state's attorney-general, he again devoted himself fully to the law.[39]

In 1779 Paterson bought Raritan Plantation, a confiscated loyalist estate, for £12,300, continental currency, for which he paid only about £250 in specie. This handsome bargain Paterson was in danger of losing upon the adoption of the Constitution. He had no other investments, and he was probably in and out of debt during the 1780's. "His large practice brought him a good income, but he had yet to make his fortune." He owned no public securities.[40]

WILLIAM CHURCHILL HOUSTON, who left the Convention after one week because of illness, was a professional officeholder. He was born on a small farm in North Carolina and was educated at Princeton, where he served as professor of mathematics and natural philosophy from 1768 to 1783. Meantime he studied

[38] Records of the Loan of 1790, vol. 595, account 2984 (Register of Public Debt Certificates, 1783–86), in the National Archives. The market price of these securities ranged from 3 shillings to 7 shillings and stood at 4 shillings at the end of 1786.

[39] Gertrude S. Wood, *William Paterson of New Jersey, 1745–1806* (Fair Lawn, N. J., 1933), *passim*.

[40] *Ibid.*; McCormick, *Experiment in Independence*, 257. See pages 32–33 of the latter work for an account of the real return to the state in hard money from the sale of confiscated estates. The loss of such investments was threatened by the Constitution because of the clause making treaties part of the "supreme law of the land"; the Treaty of Paris, 1783, had provided for the return of such estates. As it happened, the United States Supreme Court finally ruled that such estates should be returned (Martin v. Hunter's Lessee, 1 Wheaton 304), but this was after Paterson's death.

law and in 1781 was admitted to the bar in Trenton, but he practiced only a few weeks.[41]

Houston had a knack for acquiring minor but well-paying government jobs. He was receiver of the continental taxes in New Jersey from 1782 to 1785. In 1783 he became clerk of the New Jersey Supreme Court, "an especially lucrative post." Within three days after his death in 1788 "a host of competitors" rushed to apply for his job.[42] Houston apparently had no important economic interests aside from officeholding, and he held no public securities.

JONATHAN DAYTON was the youngest man in the Convention, born in 1760. He was the son of a wealthy merchant, General Elias Dayton. He was graduated from Princeton at sixteen, studied law, and was admitted to the bar. He served in the army throughout the war, was captured, released, and finally discharged in 1783. Then, at twenty-three, his business life began.[43]

Dayton's rise was spectacular. With his mercantile connections, legal ability, and inclination to engage in daring speculative ventures, he rapidly became a spectacular financial operator. In 1786 he held $4,014 in continental loan office certificates, but beginning in 1787, probably even during the Convention, he speculated extensively in public securities.[44]

Immediately after the Convention, in October, 1787, Dayton became involved in the biggest financial deal of his life. John Cleves Symmes formed a syndicate of many of New Jersey's

[41] Sketches in *The South in the Building of a Nation*, edited by Julian A. C. Chandler and others (13 vols., Richmond, 1909–1913), 11:518 ff.; *Biographical Directory of Congress* (1927 edition), 1117.

[42] For a colorful description of the "officeholding class" in New Jersey, see McCormick, *Experiment in Independence*, 97–98.

[43] Biographical sketch by W. L. Whittlesey in the *Dictionary of American Biography*, 5:166; *Biographical Directory of Congress* (1927 edition), 891; McCormick, *Experiment in Independence*, 258–259.

[44] Records of the Loan of 1790, vol. 595, accounts 2200, 2580, 3395–3396 (Register of Public Debt Certificates, 1783–86), in the National Archives. In 1790 Dayton also funded $1,411 in his own right under the Loan of 1790. McCormick (*op. cit.*, 259n) says Dayton was speculating in certificates in September, 1787, and that he subscribed over £11,000 in state securities to the funding loan of 1791 in New Jersey. Whether the latter were his own or those of the syndicate is not clear.

prominent men to buy a million acres of land on the Miami
River in Ohio and to lead a settlement of New Jersey emigrants
there. The purchase price was $666,666.67, of which one-
seventh was payable in army bounty rights and the balance in
specie or public securities. Dayton's task in the venture was to
buy and manipulate securities for the syndicate. In this he was
eminently successful; he managed to acquire about $190,000 in
public securities with an investment of probably no more than
$75,000 cash, and military warrants of an equal face value. The
Symmes group, like other such groups, encountered difficulties
as a result of the advanced price of certificates in 1792, but
through the skillful manipulations of Dayton—then an influential member of the House of Representatives and soon to become speaker—the terms of payment were eased, and they were
able to avoid calamity.[45]

WILLIAM LIVINGSTON had retired to New Jersey in 1772
after a turbulent but successful career as a radical leader in New
York politics. An aristocrat by birth and a democrat by inclination, Livingston was elected the first governor of New
Jersey in 1776 and held the office until his death in 1790.[46]

Livingston was not the eldest son and had therefore not inherited the vast family estate, but he developed a solid legal
practice and was fairly wealthy upon his retirement. In 1772
he made a statement of his property which indicated that it
amounted to £8,512, New York current ($21,000). Nearly
half the fortune was erased during the next year, however, because of the failure of his debtors. By the time of the Convention "he had seen his estate dwindle during the war as a result
of currency depreciation and the confiscation by Vermont of
the extensive holdings he had there." He owned his home and

---

[45] McCormick, *Experiment in Independence*, 230–232; *American State Papers:
Public Lands*, 1:104–106, 118, 129; Beverly W. Bond, ed., *The Correspondence
of John Cleves Symmes* (New York, 1926); Records of the Loan of 1790, in
the National Archives, records for all states and the Treasury Department,
passim.
[46] Theodore Sedgwick, *Memoir of the Life of William Livingston* (New
York, 1833), *passim*.

some good land in New York State, but little else. He owned no public securities.[47]

PENNSYLVANIA: ROBERT MORRIS, JAMES WILSON, GOUVERNEUR MORRIS, GEORGE CLYMER, THOMAS FITZSIMONS, THOMAS MIFFLIN, BENJAMIN FRANKLIN, AND JARED INGERSOLL

ROBERT MORRIS was known as the "Great Man," both to his friends and to his enemies. The real financial giant of the period—his brain would have made two of Hamilton's—Morris has rarely been rivaled in economic and political power in the history of the United States. The power he held in the 1780's may be compared to that of the House of Morgan in the early twentieth century, which means that no one knows exactly how great it was. Probably J. P. Morgan would have had to add the secretaryship of the treasury and the control of Tammany Hall to match Morris' power.[48]

Despite the extent and complexity of his investments, it is possible to get a fairly clear notion of Morris' economic affairs at the time of the Convention. He was born in Liverpool and came at an early age to Philadelphia, where he was apprenticed in the countinghouse of Charles Willing. When he was seventeen (in 1750) his father died, leaving him about $7,000, and on reaching his majority Morris and his inheritance became full partners in the firm of Willing and Morris. The firm's business was "lucrative and extensive" before 1776 and increased greatly during the war, at which time a third partner, John Swanwick, was added. During the war Morris was superintendent of finance ("the Financier of the Revolution"), in which capacity he was instrumental in the formation of the Bank of North

---

[47] *Ibid.*, 158; Lucius Q. C. Elmer, *The Constitution and Government of the Province and State of New Jersey* (Newark, 1872), 57–59; McCormick, *Experiment in Independence*, 257–258.

[48] The standard biographies of Morris, neither of which is satisfactory, are Ellis P. Oberholtzer's *Robert Morris, Patriot and Financier* (New York, 1903) and William G. Sumner's *The Financier and the Finances of the American Revolution* (2 vols., New York, 1891). A third, Clarence L. Ver Steeg's *Robert Morris, Revolutionary Financier* (Philadelphia, 1954), is valuable, but it concentrates almost exclusively on Morris' career during the war.

America, of which his partner, Thomas Willing, was the perennial president. At the time of the Convention Morris personally owned 106 shares of the Bank, having a par value of $42,400 and a market value of about $38,000; between them the three partners held 320 shares.[49]

In 1784 Morris negotiated a three-year contract with the French Farmers-General to supply twenty thousand hogsheads of tobacco annually to France, a contract which gave him a paper monopoly of the French tobacco trade. In actual fact, however, though Morris was able to force down the price of tobacco in Virginia temporarily from forty shillings to twenty-two shillings per hundredweight, Virginia merchants learned to circumvent the law and get tobacco into France themselves, and the price in Virginia ultimately rose to a level above that at which Morris had contracted to deliver. Therefore he probably only broke even in the venture, if he did that well.[50]

In the field of shipping Morris' record was as follows. The firm departed from the usual patterns of trade, such as sending American goods to England in direct exchange for British manufactures, and concentrated instead on importing wines and luxury goods and on seeking new markets for American products. From 1784 to 1787 eleven vessels, with a total capacity of 1,975 tons, which belonged to the firm or to Morris personally cleared Philadelphia for foreign ports. In addition the firm sent a vessel to the Orient in 1783, and in 1787, entirely with his

[49] See Oberholtzer, *Robert Morris*, 4–9. Figures regarding the Bank are tabulated from lists of stockholders in Lawrence Lewis, Jr., *A History of the Bank of North America* (Philadelphia, 1882), 133–147. These are lists of subscribers to the stock offerings of 1781 and 1784, but it is improbable that Morris sold any of his shares before 1787. On the distribution of ownership of the Bank in 1787 see the speech Morris made in the Pennsylvania General Assembly, in the Philadelphia *Evening Herald* of January 20, 1787. The market price of Bank stock had fallen from above par to 94 per cent of par in mid-1786, and to 90–92 per cent of par at the end of 1787. See Lewis, *Bank of North America*, 66–67; *Evening Herald*, January 19, 1788.

[50] For details of the contract see Jensen, *The New Nation*, 202–204, and Lewis C. Gray, *History of Agriculture in the Southern United States to 1865* (2 vols., Washington, 1933), 2:603–604. Regarding the difficulties Morris faced in carrying out the contract, see the manuscript Naval Officer Returns in the Virginia State Library and the William Hemsley Papers Relating to the Tobacco Business, 1784–1786, in the Manuscripts Division of the Library of Congress.

own money, Morris equipped two of his vessels with freight and sent them to the Far East, one to India and one to China. He was the first American to finance such a venture single-handed. Only three vessels belonging to the partnership—two brigs and a ship, with a total capacity of 430 tons—were engaged in foreign commerce during the period, but Morris was the sole owner of a 130-ton brig and three ships having a total tonnage of 1,030.[51]

In 1786 Morris was the owner of £4,193, Pennsylvania current ($11,181.33), in continental loan office certificates, which he funded under Pennsylvania's act of March, 1786, providing for the state's assumption of its share of the national debt.[52]

Morris' biggest venture, one that ultimately bankrupted him and sent him to debtors' prison, was land speculation. He owned very little land in 1787; it was not until two years later that he started his speculations on a grand scale. "He owned at different times, in tracts which he bought and rapidly sold again, almost the entire western half of New York. . . . In 1794 he sold more than three million acres to the Holland Company." In 1795 "Morris and his partners owned 932,621 acres in Virginia . . . 717,249 acres in North Carolina, 957,238 acres in South Carolina, 2,314,796 acres in Georgia, and 431,045 acres in Kentucky." All these lands were purchased largely with public securities, and for this reason he and his partners appear in the records of the Loan of 1790 as owners of securities in every state, totaling a sum running well into six figures. The great rise of security prices in 1791–1792 broke him, as it broke many others.[53]

At the time of the Convention, Morris' personalty—his purely liquid assets, including his share of the partnership—was roughly as follows: in the Bank, $52,000 par, $47,000 market value; in Pennsylvania loan office certificates, $11,000 par, $4,500 market

[51] Customs House Papers, in the Historical Society of Pennsylvania, *passim.* Morris' vessels were the ships *Commerce, Cincinnatus,* and *Alliance* and the brig *Catherine.*

[52] New Loan Certificates, vol. B, accounts 8237, 11673–11676, and 11690, and vol. C, page 11, in the Public Records Division of the Pennsylvania Historical Commission.

[53] Oberholtzer, *Robert Morris,* 301–304, 314.

value; in shipping, $20,000; and probably $100,000 in goods.[54]

Against these "quick" assets, however, must be balanced his quick liabilities. Morris was the greatest single debtor of the United States government; had he been called upon to pay his debts to the government in 1787, he would probably have been bankrupted immediately.[55] But this does not alter the fact that he was, in terms of personal property, the richest man in America, and that the value of the property over which he exercised direct or indirect control probably ran as high as two million dollars.

JAMES WILSON, the celebrated constitutional theorist, had a lucrative practice as the leader of the Pennsylvania bar. He was Robert Morris' attorney and intimate associate. Morris was extremely wealthy and Wilson aspired to beome so, and at times acted almost as a lackey to Morris.[56]

Wilson had a number of investments in his own right, but few of them seem to have turned out well. In 1780 he subscribed to £5,000 worth of the stock of the wartime Bank of Pennsylvania, and upon the incorporation of the Bank of North America in 1781 he invested $2,000 in five shares of its stock. He owned one vessel, the *Peggy and Nancy*, a second-hand, sixty-

[54] The estimate of the ships' value is based on their cost when new. Ships were sold by the ton; in 1787 white oak vessels were selling for £5 to £5 10s. per ton, and live oak and cedar vessels for £6 10s. to £7. Philadelphia *Pennsylvania Mercury and Universal Advertiser*, August 10, 1787, and various other newspapers, under "prices current." Pennsylvania loan office certificates were selling at 8 shillings per pound on the same day. The value of stock in trade is estimated from the lists of cargoes in the Customs House Papers in the Historical Society of Pennsylvania.

[55] Jensen, *The New Nation*, 381, citing the Arthur Lee Papers, Harvard University Library. Lee was a bitter political enemy of Morris, and his account may not be altogether reliable; he stated that Morris' debt to the United States was $691,584, "but the kind of money is not indicated." Jensen also cites the Revolutionary War Documents in the National Archives as showing that "the one who owed the government the most money was Robert Morris," but he does not state the amount.

[56] Charles Page Smith's *James Wilson, Founding Father, 1742–1798* (Chapel Hill, North Carolina, 1956), and the six unpublished volumes of Burton A. Konkle's Life and Writings of James Wilson, in Konkle's possession, are the only full-length biographies of Wilson. See also the biographical sketch by Julian P. Boyd in the *Dictionary of American Biography* and the sketches in Sanderson, *Biographies of the Signers* (1831 edition), 3:259 ff., and John B. McMaster and Frederick D. Stone, *Pennsylvania and the Federal Constitution, 1787–1788* (Philadelphia, 1888).

ton schooner which he purchased early in 1787 for the West Indies trade. With Robert Hooper of New Jersey he owned 15,848 acres of undeveloped land in Northumberland County, Pennsylvania.[57]

Wilson's biggest venture during the 1780's was a project for the development of extensive "rolling and slitting mills, Grist Mills, saw Mills, and a Forge" at the falls of the Delaware River, thirty miles from Philadelphia. His brother-in-law, Mark Bird, a Berks County merchant, was his partner in the enterprise. It was a highly speculative undertaking, the site having been chosen less because of its location at good water power than because Wilson expected Trenton ultimately to become the permanent capital of the United States. On the advice of Morris, Wilson and Bird sought a loan of a half million florins from a Dutch mercantile firm to finance the enterprise. Failing in this, they turned to the Bank and to various individuals. The scheme collapsed in 1787 and Bird went into bankruptcy. Wilson avoided formal bankruptcy, and he had his practice to fall back on, but he was heavily burdened with debts.[58]

In a desperate attempt to recover his fortune Wilson plunged increasingly into land speculations, which sank him ever deeper into debt. After 1790 he became involved in the infamous Yazoo land frauds. He made nothing in these ventures, however, and he was hounded by creditors from 1786 until the end of his life. A year before his death in 1798 he had no assets and owed $46,578 to a single company. Indeed, he was limited in his circuit riding as an associate justice of the United States Su-

[57] Lewis, *Bank of North America*, 19, 135; entries dated May 22 and July 5, 1787, in "Outward Entries," Customs House Papers, in the Historical Society of Pennsylvania.

[58] Draft of a letter from Wilson and Bird, January 16, 1785, and letter of E. Blaine to Wilson, February 15, 1785, both in the "Letters" volume of the James Wilson Papers in the Historical Society of Pennsylvania; *Evening Herald*, May 12, 1787 (notice of Bird's bankruptcy); William Hamilton to Jasper Yeates, October 8, 1786, in the volume entitled "Correspondence, 1781–1788" in the Yeates Papers, in the Historical Society of Pennsylvania. Hamilton was one of the creditors of Wilson and Bird, and he pressed Yeates, his attorney, to sue for collection; the sum owed him was about £2,000. Wilson was also personally indebted to Hamilton for a large amount; see Hamilton to Yeates, October 11, 1787.

preme Court because his entry into any of several states would have resulted in his imprisonment for debt.[59]

GOUVERNEUR MORRIS was a member of the New York landed aristocracy, only transiently a Pennsylvanian. Since he was not the eldest son, he did not inherit the magnificent family estate "Morrisania" but instead received a patrimony of £2,000. He had a lifelong ambition to own the place, however, and ultimately, "by the aid of loans and accommodations he became possessed of this estate." Well-educated and trained as a lawyer, he built up a solid practice in New York City before the war.[60]

During the war Morris began a close relationship with Robert Morris (there was no blood relationship). Brilliant in financial matters and daring by nature, he was soon as close to Robert Morris as Wilson was, perhaps closer. Though he carried out a number of important functions for Robert Morris, doubtless being well rewarded therefor, he seems to have had little other property. He supposedly "had already laid the foundations of a fortune" by 1787, but when he had the opportunity in 1781 to buy stock of the Bank, he was able to subscribe to only one share—$400—and he had no mercantile property, no lands except the debt-laden family estate, and no public securities.[61]

GEORGE CLYMER was a substantial and respected Philadelphia merchant, a partner in the firm of Meredith and Clymer. His investments, though not vast, were large and varied. He does not appear in customs house records as a shipowner, but his advertisements in Philadelphia newspapers attest to a thriving import-export business, and he occasionally ventured into ship-

[59] Charles H. Haskins, *The Yazoo Land Companies* (New York, 1891), 83; *State Papers: Public Lands*, 1:141; Arthur C. Bining, *Pennsylvania Iron Manufacturing in the Eighteenth Century* (Harrisburg, 1938), 171.

[60] Anne Cary Morris, ed., *Diary and Letters of Gouverneur Morris* (2 vols., New York, 1888), *passim;* Jared Sparks, *Life of Gouverneur Morris* (3 vols., Boston, 1832), *passim.*

[61] Lewis, *Bank of North America*, 134. The nature of Gouverneur Morris' association with Robert Morris is set forth entertainingly in Jensen, *The New Nation, passim.* Roosevelt (*Morris*, 167) says Morris owned an interest in an ironworks on the Delaware River, but it was none of the larger ones; Morris' name does not appear as an owner of vessels in the extant customs records of any American port, nor does it appear in any newspaper advertisements of goods for sale or in the Records of the Loan of 1790.

building. In 1780 he subscribed £5,000 to the temporary Bank of Pennsylvania, and the next year $2,800 to the Bank of North America. Meredith and Clymer funded £1,060 ($2,826.67) in continental loan office certificates under the Pennsylvania assumption act of 1786, and Clymer personally funded $12,-584.42 in various public securities under the Loan of 1790.[62]

THOMAS FITZSIMONS was another leading Philadelphia merchant who, like Robert Morris and Clymer, had large and varied interests. A successful merchant of long standing, he was one of the founders of the Bank and a director from its inception until 1803, president of the Philadelphia Chamber of Commerce, and president of the Insurance Company of North America from its establishment in 1790 until his death in 1811.[63]

Fitzsimons' mercantile business was large, and immediately after the Convention he followed Robert Morris' example and sent his own vessel to Canton. He subscribed to only two shares of the Bank, but he funded £3,118 ($8,314.67) in continental loan office certificates under the Pennsylvania act of 1786; he retained only $2,668.10 in securities until the funding Loan of 1790 went into effect, however. After 1790 he was one of Morris' partners in the latter's land speculations. His fortune was much impaired by the collapse of those ventures, but he survived without bankruptcy.[64]

[62] Henry Simpson, *The Lives of Eminent Philadelphians* (Philadelphia, 1859), 211; Sanderson, *Biographies of the Signers* (1831 edition), 3:147; Philadelphia *Pennsylvania Packet* and Philadelphia *Evening Herald*, 1783–1789, *passim;* New Loan Certificates, vol. C, p. 44, in the Public Records Division of the Pennsylvania Historical Commission; Records of the Loan of 1790, vol. 631, folio 158 (Journal "B" of the Continental Debt, 1791), in the National Archives; Lewis, *Bank of North America*, 133; McMaster and Stone, *Pennsylvania and the Federal Constitution*, 705.

[63] Biographical sketches in McMaster and Stone, *Pennsylvania and the Federal Constitution*, 706 ff., and Simpson, *Lives of Eminent Philadelphians*, 372–373.

[64] "Outward Entries, September 1, 1786 to December 29, 1787," in Customs House Papers, in the Historical Society of Pennsylvania; Lewis, *Bank of North America*, 120, 133; *Pennsylvania Packet*, January 12, 1785; Philadelphia *Freeman's Journal, or the North-American Intelligencer*, January 11, 1786; New Loan Certificates, vol. B, account 6401, in the Pennsylvania Historical Commission; Sumner, *Financier and Finances of the Revolution*, 2:294; Register of Certificates of Public Debt Presented to the Auditor of the Treasury, Book A, in Records of the Loan of 1790, in the National Archives. Beard garbled his account of Fitzsimons' security holdings in a way that is very misleading. He says (page 92) that Fitzsimons had $12,000 "nominal value" of certificates,

THOMAS MIFFLIN's economic career was a fabulous one. Born of wealthy parents in Philadelphia—the only Pennsylvania delegate besides Clymer, incidentally, who was born in the state—he had an undistinguished political career before the Revolution. He became quartermaster-general of the Continental Army in 1775 and later was accused of having misused government funds in a highly unethical, albeit legal way. In 1782, to hush the rumors, he published his amazing wartime economic autobiography. According to this account, Mifflin's private investments were as follows: [65]

In 1775 he had inherited a fair fortune. He joined the army and lost much in his absence because many debts due him were paid in continental currency. Of the remainder, $13,800 was invested by his brother Jonathan in a loan to the United States. A further large sum remained in Jonathan's hands until 1778, when he first "put it to interest."

In the fall of 1776 Mifflin invested with others in four vessels, one of which was lost almost immediately, wiping out Mifflin's share of £250 in that vessel. His share of the £2,401 8s. 2d. remaining investment comprised almost his total fortune; it was a daring gamble, but it paid handsomely. The other three vessels made large profits. The brig *Delaware*, on its maiden voyage to St. Eustatia in June, 1777, brought a clear profit of £3,952 6s. 11d. to each owner! Including this sum, the total return to Mifflin for his share in the investment was £6,107 15s. 4d.

In November, 1777, Mifflin sold for £2,500 cash a farm in Loudon County, Virginia, which he had bought in 1770 for

but he fails to point out that only $2,668.10 was allowed on Fitzsimons' claims, the certificates being of a variety that had been subjected much earlier to a scale of depreciation. Beard also says that he held other securities, and that his operations extended "beyond his state," citing the Records of the Loan of 1790, vol. 44, folio 335, and vol. 42, folio 300. Both of these are securities Fitzsimons acquired in 1797, ten years after the Convention; one was for $97, the other for $390.

[65] This amazing document is printed in the *Pennsylvania Packet* of February 7, 1782. The statement can only be superficially checked against various public documents, but the figures given for profits realized from individual voyages during the war were not highly unusual. Charges against Pennsylvania public officials were considerably more common than official corruption. The statement seems to me to be too detailed and too frank to be fictitious. There may be minor misstatements, but by and large it appears to be reliable.

£900. In December, 1777, when he resigned from the quarter-master generalship, he received £1,627 10s. as his pay. In March, 1778, he received £659 12s. 6d. for his share of the voyage of the schooner *Rattlesnake*, and in August, 1778, he got £4,200 for his share of the second voyage of the brig *Delaware*. In May, 1778, he sold his shares in two of the vessels, the *Rattlesnake* and the brig *General Lee*, to Blair McClenachan for £7,250 cash. In the spring of 1778 he purchased shares in three more vessels at a cost of £1,850, but he sold them in June at a small profit, before they went to sea. The *Delaware*, on its fourth voyage, was taken by the enemy.

In January, 1779, he advanced £400 in specie for the outfitting of three small vessels, two of which he later sold, leaving as his stock in trade a small share in the ship *Flora*.

These items, plus his pay as an officer (£560 12s. 6d. in final settlement notes due and paid May, 1779) and his commission of 5 per cent on £60,000 of supplies sold to the troops, constituted his income from 1775 to 1780. The total was over £23,000 sterling, or about $102,000.

Mifflin concluded his statement with a summary of the real estate he owned at the time (1782): a house in Philadelphia, his patrimony; 1,230 acres in Cumberland County, purchased in 1769; two small lots in New Jersey, across from Philadelphia, purchased in 1773; a country seat, five miles from Philadelphia, for which he was to pay a relative £60 during the remainder of her life; a third interest in three houses, a lot, and some ground rents in Philadelphia, inherited by his wife; a 620-acre tract in Cumru Township, Berks County, which he bought from June, 1777, to December, 1778, for £9,109 10s. continental currency; and 400 acres in the same township, bought in January, 1779, for £5,000 in continental currency, or £625 specie, on which he still owed half the purchase price.

Mifflin seems to have retired from most economic activity after 1782. He owned fourteen shares of the Bank with a face value of $5,600, but he owned no shipping, no western lands, and no manufacturing property, though he was keenly interested in the promotion of manufactures. By 1786 his $13,800 investment in continental loan office certificates had dwindled to £948 5s. ($2,528.67), and by 1789 he had disposed of it all. Apparently he chose to devote the remainder of his days to comfortable living and politics; he was governor of the state from 1790 until a year before his death in 1800.[66]

Of BENJAMIN FRANKLIN—printer, scientist, inventor, statesman, philosopher, and citizen of the world—little needs to be said. At the time of the Convention he was an enfeebled man of eighty-one. During his long and eventful life he had accumulated, according to one biographer, an estate worth $150,000, mostly in realty. During his absence from the country as minister to France, from 1776 to 1785, Franklin was able to escape the economic problems that existed in America, but he was dragged into politics immediately upon his return by those who sought to capitalize on his prestige. Prestige, indeed, was about all he had left, except for substantial amounts of real estate and £3,037 10s. ($8,100) in continental loan office certificates, which he funded in 1786 under Pennsylvania's law for that purpose. Franklin died a year and one month after the government under the Constitution went into operation.[67]

JARED INGERSOLL, of Philadelphia, was the son of a loyalist, Jared Ingersoll of Connecticut, a former royal official. After attending Yale College he studied law at the Middle Temple in London, where he was during the first years of the war. Upon his return in 1778 he started his law practice. Shortly thereafter

[66] The negative statements are based on newspapers and customs house records, the affirmative on Lewis, *Bank of North America*, 144–146; New Loan Certificates, vol. A, accounts 1229–1230, in the Pennsylvania Historical Commission; and Records of the Loan of 1790, vol. 610, folio 48 (Register of Pennsylvania Loan Office Certificates, 1788) in the National Archives.

[67] The Franklin bibliography is enormous. For the estate of his estate see John Bigelow, *Life of Franklin* (3 vols., New York, 1894), 3:470; for his public securities, see New Loan Certificates, vol. A, account 469, in the Pennsylvania Historical Commission. Franklin wrote in February, 1788, that he had loaned £3,000 to the old Congress in 1776, receiving certificates promising 6 per cent interest, "but I have received no interest for several years, and if I were now to sell the principal, I could not get more than 3s. 4d. for the pound which is but a sixth part"; Albert H. Smyth, *Writings of Franklin* (10 vols., New York, 1905–1907), 9:635, quoted in Beard's introduction to the 1935 edition of his *Economic Interpretation*, xiv. Franklin was either senile or was deliberately trying to deceive someone, for his certificates sold for eight shillings on the pound, and interest had been paid punctually since 1786.

he married the daughter of Charles Pettit, who was a wealthy merchant, manufacturer, and dealer in public securities, but an advocate of state sovereignty and a bitter enemy of Robert Morris. Ingersoll's connections were therefore with the "wrong" merchants in Philadelphia.[68]

Ingersoll's rise as a lawyer was apparently slow, possibly because of the politics of his father-in-law; in 1791 he sought to be admitted to practice before the United States Supreme Court, but his application was rejected on the ground that he was not of sufficient professional stature. Later he became attorney and personal advisor to the great mercantile prince Stephen Girard, and thereafter rose to eminence and became one of the leading practitioners before the Supreme Court.[69]

In 1787 Ingersoll had, besides a wealthy father-in-law, a moderately successful practice, a fourth interest in a 30-ton sloop in the coasting trade, and little else. He owned no public securities.[70]

DELAWARE: JOHN DICKINSON, GEORGE READ, RICHARD BASSETT, GUNNING BEDFORD, JR., AND JACOB BROOM

JOHN DICKINSON was a lawyer-farmer, wealthy by the standards of his state at the time. He was born into a substantial farming family living in Dover, received a legal education at the Middle Temple in London, and thereafter practiced law in Philadelphia. He married the daughter of a wealthy merchant, and while at his insistence his wife gave her inheritance to a relative, the connection did his legal career no harm. Almost from the time he began practice in 1757 and until the outbreak of the war Dick-

[68] Sketches of Ingersoll in Simpson, *Lives of Eminent Philadelphians*, 596; *Biographical Directory of Congress* (1927 edition), 1137–1138; scattered information about Ingersoll in Lawrence Henry Gipson, *Jared Ingersoll: A Study in American Loyalism* (New Haven, 1920) and Robert L. Brunhouse, *The Counter-Revolution in Pennsylvania, 1776–1790* (Harrisburg, 1942); information about Pettit in the latter volume, in Philadelphia newspapers, and in the journals of the Pennsylvania legislature, *passim*.

[69] Charles Warren, *The Supreme Court in United States History* (2 vols., New York and Boston, 1922), 1:545; Gipson, *Jared Ingersoll*, 364.

[70] The vessel, the sloop *Betsy*, was owned with another Philadelphian and two citizens of Connecticut; see entry dated September 25, 1786, in "Outward Entries, September 1, 1786 to December 29, 1787," in Customs House Papers, in the Historical Society of Pennsylvania.

inson was one of Philadelphia's leading attorneys. He became prominent before the Revolution and rose to great power in Pennsylvania politics during the war, being closely allied with that "Great Man," Robert Morris—some even said that he was the actual head of the Morris faction—and he continued to exercise great influence there until 1785.[71]

In 1785 Dickinson returned permanently to his estate near Dover and a life of semi-retirement. He became a gentleman farmer and rarely engaged in law thereafter. Most of his surplus capital seems to have been invested in real estate in Philadelphia, New Jersey, and Delaware; apparently he sold most of his Philadelphia and New Jersey real estate to his brother Philemon. He owned no public securities or mercantile property, and he had severed business connections with the Philadelphia merchants, although he was, of course, still intimate with them. His annual income in 1787 and 1788 was estimated at £1,510, Delaware currency ($4,026), probably about a third of what it had once been.[72]

GEORGE READ was one of the six sons of a "wealthy citizen of Dublin," Ireland, who had removed to Maryland. Read studied law in Philadelphia and about 1753 began practice in New Castle. He surrendered all claim to his father's estate, saying that he had received his share through his education. His practice never brought him more than "a moderate income," which he supplemented with his salaries as an occasional public official and the produce of a small farm. In 1787 his annual income was

[71] Charles Janeway Stille, *The Life and Times of John Dickinson* (2 vols., Philadelphia, 1891), *passim;* James T. Adams' sketch of Dickinson in the *Dictionary of American Biography; Biographical Directory of Congress*. For an account of Dickinson's political activities in Philadelphia see Brunhouse, *Counter-Revolution in Pennsylvania, passim,* and various Philadelphia newspapers, particularly the *Freeman's Journal,* throughout January, 1783.

[72] Stille, *John Dickinson;* Beard, *Economic Interpretation,* 87–88; New Castle County Lists, Dover Hundred and Christiana Hundred, and Kent County Lists, Dover Hundred, for 1787 and 1788, in Tax Assessment Lists, in the Delaware Hall of Records, Dover. Delaware was unique in having an income tax at this time, and it had no direct property taxes. In accordance with long usage, incomes were assessed at twenty per cent of their actual amount. Since Dickinson's income was assessed for taxes at £302, his real income must have been about £1,510. For a good contemporary description of the Delaware system of taxation, see *Amercan State Papers: Finance,* 1:429.

£550 ($1,467), and he owned $341.53 face value of public securities and two shares of stock (par $800) in the Bank of North America.[73]

RICHARD BASSETT was the adopted son of a wealthy planter-lawyer, a Mr. Lawson. He was trained in law in Philadelphia and began practicing in Delaware about 1770. His income from the law was modest, but he inherited 6,000 acres of the vast plantation Bohemia Manor, in Maryland, which was sufficient to provide for all his needs. He also owned residences in Dover and Wilmington.[74]

Bassett was converted to Methodism in 1779 by no less a person than Francis Asbury, and he continued to be filled with "religious enthusiasm" for most of the rest of his life. He even used his beautiful estate for the promotion of early Methodist camp meetings. Bassett's income in 1787 was only £200 ($533), on which he managed to live in comfort. He owned no public securities and practiced very little law.[75]

GUNNING BEDFORD, JR., styled himself "Junior" to avoid confusion with a cousin of the same name who was prominent in Delaware. He was graduated from Princeton in 1771, studied law in Philadelphia, and began practice in Dover in 1779. He removed to Wilmington late in the war and practiced there until 1784, after which he never again practiced privately. He

[73] Sanderson, *Biographies of the Signers* (1831 edition), 3:351 ff.; *Biographical Directory of Congress* (1927 edition), 1447; New Castle County Lists, New Castle Hundred, in Tax Assessment Lists, in the Delaware Hall of Records; Records of the Loan of 1790, vol. 919, account 166 (Register of Public Debt Certificates), in the National Archives; Lewis, *Bank of North America*, 147.

[74] *Papers of the Delaware Historical Society*, vol. 29 (1900); biographical sketch of Bassett by Edmund K. Alden in the *Dictionary of American Biography;* William Pierce's sketches in *Documentary History of the Constitution,* 103.

[75] Kent County Lists, Murderkill Hundred, 1787, in Tax Assessment Lists, in the Delaware Hall of Records, and the sketches cited in the preceding note. Beard credits Bassett with being an owner of public securities, citing vol. 44, folio 26, and vol. 42, folio 33, of the Records of the Loan of 1790, but examination shows these to be accounts of the years 1796 and 1797, for $100 and $630, respectively, and there is no record of earlier ownership. Bassett's name does not appear anywhere else in the records of the Treasury Department nor in those of the loan offices of Maryland, Pennsylvania, and Delaware, all in the National Archives.

became attorney-general of the state in 1784, a position he filled for five years, and then became a federal district judge, in which capacity he served until his death in 1812.[76]

Bedford supplemented the modest salaries he received as a public servant by operating a farm which he purchased late in 1787. In addition he owned $2,874 face value of public securities, largely continental, which he had acquired for about $360. This had been a very wise investment, albeit a daring one for Bedford to have made when his annual income did not exceed £100 ($267).[77]

JACOB BROOM was the son of a blacksmith turned farmer, a man of "considerable substance in real estate, silver, and gold." He was not the heir under his father's will, but he was, on a small scale, a successful farmer himself. His annual income from the two farms he owned in 1787 was about £275 ($733). By thrift and prudent management he was usually able to reserve a part of this income for small investments in the form of interest-bearing loans. The modest size of his nonagricultural investments is indicated by his holdings of public securities: one certificate of $2.78 and one of $38.80 face value.[78]

[76] Edmund K. Alden's biographical sketch of Bedford in the *Dictionary of American Biography; Biographical Directory of Congress* (1927 edition), 685; and a longer sketch in *Papers of the Delaware Historical Society*, vol. 29 (1900). Beard fell into the error of confusing Bedford, Jr., with his cousin. He states (page 77) that Bedford became governor in the 1790's and was interested in banking; this was the elder Bedford.

[77] Records of the Loan of 1790, vol. 624, folio 55 (Journal of the Assumed Debt of Pennsylvania, 1791–1795), and vol. 631, folio 293 (Journal of the Continental Debt), in the National Archives. Bedford's salary as attorney-general is not precisely determinable. The salary of the governor was £200 and that of the justices of the Supreme Court of Delaware £90. *Votes and Proceedings of the House of Assembly of the Delaware State*, 1785, January 17, 1785. In most states the attorney-general's salary was less than that of the justices. Even the assessment records preserved in Dover confuse the two Bedfords. A listing for Christiana Hundred, where Bedford, Jr., was buried, includes an entry for him, £20, or an approximate annual income of £100.

[78] Sketch of Broom in *Papers of the Delaware Historical Society*, vol. 51 (1901); New Castle County Lists, Christiana Hundred, 1787, and Kent County Lists, Murderkill Hundred, 1787, both in Tax Assessment Lists, in the Delaware Hall of Records; Records of the Loan of 1790, vol. 919, accounts 53 and 595 (Register of Public Debt Certificates, 1784–1787), in the National Archives; *Abstracts of Wills in New Castle County, 1732–1800* (Delaware Historical Society, 1911).

MARYLAND: JAMES MCHENRY, DANIEL CARROLL, DANIEL OF ST.
THOMAS JENIFER, LUTHER MARTIN, AND JOHN FRANCIS MERCER

JAMES MCHENRY was born in Ireland, there received a classical
education, and emigrated to Baltimore in 1771 at the age of
eighteen. His father established a mercantile business there with
McHenry's brother John and achieved "considerable financial
success." The father died in 1782, leaving both sons financially
independent. John remained in mercantile affairs until the mid-
1780's.[79]

McHenry studied medicine under Dr. Benjamin Rush in
Philadelphia and served as army surgeon during the war. Apparently he never practiced medicine privately after the war;
"his easy financial circumstances did not force him to earn a
livelihood." His only known economic activity after the war
consisted of a few real estate transactions with his brother. He
never engaged in business, and he held no public securities.[80]

DANIEL CARROLL was a wealthy member of the old Maryland
planter aristocracy. He owned a large estate in Prince George
County, much of which was in what became the District of
Columbia, he held fifty-three slaves, and his chief economic interest was tobacco farming. He was one of the original promoters of the Potomac Company, and in 1783 he purchased the
confiscated house and lot of a Baltimore Tory for £2,630, an
investment that was jeopardized by the Constitution. He held
only an insignificant amount of public securities, $226.51,
roughly equivalent to the value of one of his slaves.[81]

[79] Bernard C. Steiner, *The Life and Correspondence of James McHenry*
(Cleveland, 1907), *passim;* Philip A. Crowl, *Maryland during and after the
Revolution* (Baltimore, 1943), 112. After the elder McHenry's death John
McHenry formed a partnership with one McElderry. *Maryland Journal and
Baltimore Advertiser,* August 31, 1784. He became seriously ill in 1787, occa-
sioning James McHenry's departure from the Convention. At that time he
was no longer in business. He died in 1790, leaving his entire estate to James.

[80] Steiner, *McHenry,* 4. In 1797 McHenry held more than $6,000 in public
securities which he had acquired sometime in the 1790's. Records of the Loan
of 1790, vol. 45, folio 22 (Maryland Loan Office 1790–97, 3%), in the National
Archives.

[81] Matthew P. Andrews, ed., *Tercentenary History of Maryland* (4 vols.,
Baltimore, 1925), 4:908; *Biographical Directory of Congress* (1927 edition),
790; John T. Scharf, *History of Western Maryland* (2 vols., Philadelphia,

DANIEL OF ST. THOMAS JENIFER, like Carroll, was a member of the old aristocracy of Maryland. He owned at least twenty slaves and "was possessed of unusual wealth for the time and made his home on his large estate, known as 'Stepney,' in Charles County." William Pierce observed that "from his long continuance in single life, no doubt but he has made the vow of celibacy. He speaks warmly of the ladies notwithstanding." He was well known for the parties he gave at his beautiful plantation.[82]

In addition to being a successful planter Jenifer was an expert in governmental finance and had a great talent for obtaining and holding public offices. Prior to the Revolution he had been "Proprietor's Agent and Receiver-General in charge of proprietary revenues." Beginning in 1782, as intendant of the revenues and financial agent for the state, he was the most powerful and best-paid officer in the Maryland government. In this capacity Jenifer was responsible for the handling of all public securities in the state; he did not, however, own any securities himself.[83]

LUTHER MARTIN, one of the outspoken opponents of the Constitution, was a man of humble origins. His parents and their nine children lived in near poverty. Martin, the third child, somehow obtained an education, and taught school from 1763 to 1770. "His means were scanty, and he was then, as ever after, in pecuniary stress. . . . He ran into debt, and when he stopped school-teaching to devote his whole time to study law, he was arrested on five different warrants of attachment." He was admitted to the

1882), 1:679; Crowl, *Maryland during and after the Revolution*, 49; *Census of 1790, Heads of Families, Maryland*, 86; Records of the Loan of 1790, vol. 622, account 213 (Subscription Register, Domestic Debt [Pennsylvania Loan Office], 1790–91), in the National Archives.

[82] Sketches in Crowl, *Maryland during and after the Revolution*, 28–29; *Biographical Directory of Congress* (1927 edition), 1148; Pierce's sketches in Farrand, *Records of the Federal Convention*, 3:93; *Biographical Cyclopedia of Representative Men of Maryland and the District of Columbia* (Baltimore, 1879); biographical sketch of Jenifer by Mary W. Williams in the *Dictionary of American Biography*.

[83] *Ibid.* The records of the intendant's office are preserved in the Maryland Hall of Records. Beard (page 117) reports that Jenifer's "son," Daniel Jenifer, Jr., held $6,000 in securities; this is of course another instance of mistaken identity, for Jenifer never married.

bar in 1771, and "his income soon reached the large sum . . . of £1,000 per year"; his spare hours he spent managing a salt mine at Accomac. After the war his annual income rose as high as $12,000.[84]

His biographer records, however, that "next to intemperance, gross carelessness in money matters seems to have been his pervading fault." He accumulated a large estate but dissipated his money; once he offered $40,000 in land as security for a loan of only $1,200 in cash.[85]

Though Martin was a misfit in the Maryland aristocracy, Samuel Chase secured for him in 1778 the office of attorney-general of Maryland, a post he held for more than a quarter century. He dabbled in various speculative mercantile enterprises, and he invested £3,150 in confiscated loyalist property, some of it in partnership with the powerful merchant Charles Ridgely, Jeremiah Townley Chase, a lawyer, and Samuel Chase, a merchant-lawyer politician. His home was doubtless spacious and comfortable, for in 1790 he owned six house slaves. He also owned $4,355.73 in public securities.[86]

JOHN FRANCIS MERCER, who joined Luther Martin in strong opposition to the Constitution both during and after the Convention, was born in Virginia and was educated at William and Mary College. He studied law with Jefferson, and in 1781 left his large tobacco plantation in Marlborough (Stafford County) in the hands of overseers and began to practice law in Williamsburg. While serving as a delegate to Congress from Virginia he married the daughter of a wealthy Maryland family. Shortly thereafter "his wife inherited Cedar Park in Maryland," and in 1785 he removed to that estate.[87]

[84] Henry P. Goddard, *Luther Martin, the "Federal Bull-Dog"* (Baltimore, 1887), *passim.*

[85] *Ibid.*, 38–39.

[86] *Ibid.*; Crowl, *Maryland during and after the Revolution*, 48, 50, 63, 128; Records of the Loan of 1790, vols. 941, 945, 937, folio 60 in each (Stock Ledgers A, B, and C, Public Debt, 1790–97), in the National Archives.

[87] Biographical sketch of Mercer by Mary W. Williams in the *Dictionary of American Biography*; *Biographical Cyclopedia of Maryland*, 443; *Census of 1790, Heads of Families, Maryland*, 41; James M. Garnett, "John Francis Mercer," in the *Maryland Historical Magazine*, 2:191 (1907); Crowl, *Maryland during and after the Revolution*, 112.

By the time of the Convention, when Mercer was only twenty-eight, he had already accumulated a sizeable fortune. In addition to large plantations in Virginia and Maryland he had a good law practice in Maryland and owned $7,236.45 in public securities of the United States.[88]

VIRGINIA: GEORGE WASHINGTON, GEORGE MASON, JAMES MADISON, JAMES McCLURG, GEORGE WYTHE, JOHN BLAIR, AND EDMUND RANDOLPH

GEORGE WASHINGTON is usually assumed to have been the richest man in America. While this may be disputed, there is no doubt that he had a tremendous fortune in land and slaves. Indeed, there is no question that he was land- and slave-poor. Of his extensive landholdings large parts had been granted to him by grateful states for his war services, and another large part had been bought with borrowed money. A typical instance of his craving for land is an episode that occurred after the war. While traveling in upstate New York with Governor George Clinton he saw a beautiful woodland, and though he had no cash, was already burdened with debts for land purchases, and was unlikely ever to see the land again, he arranged to borrow $6,000 from Clinton and bought it on the spot.[89]

Washington seems to have had almost an aversion to pure per-

[88] Records of the Loan of 1790, vol. 945, folio 72 (Stock Ledger C, Public Debt, 1790–97), in the National Archives. This is a 3 per cent book. Since original funders were given one-third of their new securities in three per cent certificates under the terms of the Loan of 1790, and since Mercer was given $2,412.15 in three per cents, his total holding must have been $7,236.45. He had miscellaneous smaller holdings, which are recorded in other volumes.

[89] The best biography of Washington is Douglas Southall Freeman's multi-volume work, but unfortunately the sixth volume, finished by others and published in 1954, after Freeman's death, lacks both the detail and the quality of the previous volumes, and it sketches the postwar eighties and nineties only superficially. Washington's will, estimating the property he owned in 1799 at $530,000, is published in Jared Sparks, *Life of Washington* (Boston, 1842), Appendix IX. Washington's evaluation of his lands was, in my opinion, somewhat too high. The Clinton episode is from Ernest W. Spaulding's *His Excellency George Clinton* (New York, 1938), 231–233. It took Washington about four years to repay the sum he had borrowed to purchase this land. Ultimately, however, he made a profit on the deal by selling the land in small parcels.

sonalty; of the $64,000 in securities Congress gave him to pay for his personal expenses during the war—he had accepted no salary— he sold almost all at depreciated rates and had only £158 left to fund in 1790. Indeed, he had to borrow £10,000 to cover his expenses when he went to New York City to become president.[90]

GEORGE MASON, another of the outspoken opponents of the Constitution, was a wealthy member of the Virginia aristocracy who combined extensive commercial ventures with his tobacco and wheat planting. He had married Anne Eilbeck, the "only child and heiress" of a rich Maryland merchant, and after the war his son was often in Europe handling mercantile affairs for him.[91]

Mason's will, read upon his death in 1792, reveals the vast size of his fortune. It included 15,000 acres "of the very best land in the Potomac region," 60,000 "of the finest acres in Kentucky, some three hundred slaves, more than fifty thousand dollars' worth of other personal property, and at least thirty thousand dollars of debts due on his books, while his own indebtedness was absolutely nothing." His holdings of public securities were apparently only nominal, and those of his son totaled only $1,400.[92]

JAMES MADISON, "Father of the Constitution," was much better versed in the theory of money than successful in its acquisition. Constantly in public life as he was, he depended on salaries, gifts from his father, and loans or gifts from friends as a means of subsistence. His own estate consisted of 560 ill-kept acres in Orange County, valued at $725, six adult slaves and three slave children, and five horses. He had been trained in the law, but he never practiced his profession, and when he finally retired from politics

[90] George Bancroft, in his *History of the Formation of the Constitution of the United States of America* (2 vols., New York, 1882), 2:411, quotes a letter from M. Otto, the French emissary, in which Otto claims to have a letter from Washington complaining "of being obliged to sell at a rate of twenty for one the certificates which Congress sent to him." This is extremely doubtful, for the price of the securities never fell that low. For his holdings in 1790 see the Records of the Loan of 1790, vol. 1113, folio 79 (Virginia Loan Office, Register of Assumed Debt), in the National Archives.

[91] Kate Mason Rowland's *The Life and Correspondence of George Mason* (2 vols., New York, 1892) remains the best biography of Mason, but see also H. D. Hill, *George Mason*.

[92] Rowland, *George Mason*, 2:368; Records of the Loan of 1790, vol. 1118, account dated September 30, 1791 (Register of the Assumed Debt of Virginia), in the National Archives.

he came to learn that he was not a very skillful farmer. Usually detached from the hard world of economic reality, Madison owned no personalty, held no paying job, and owned no public securities.[93]

JAMES MCCLURG was "the son of Dr. Walter McClurg, a wealthy citizen and noted physician." He studied at William and Mary College, then went abroad to study medicine at Edinburgh, Paris, and elsewhere. On his return from Europe in 1773 "he located at Williamsburg, where . . . in a very short time he made his way to the head of his profession in that state, a position which he held for fifty years." [94]

McClurg was one of the wealthiest men, in terms of personalty, in his part of Virginia. His land and slaveholdings were insignificant, but he was well supplied with money and he was one of the largest holders of securities in the Convention, being the owner of $31,740.67 face value in public securities of Virginia and of the United States. He was also later an investor in the stock of the first Bank of the United States and one of its directors.[95]

GEORGE WYTHE had inherited a comfortable estate in his youth which he had entirely dissipated before his thirtieth birthday. He then settled down to study law, began practice, and made a comfortable living until the outbreak of the war. At that time he emancipated most of his slaves, settled half of his estate on a nephew, and sold the other half on a long-term installment-payment contract. In 1777 he became a judge of the Virginia Court of Chancery and two years later was made chancellor of Virginia.[96]

In 1787 his annual income included £300 ($1,000) salary as

[93] For a list of Madison's property in 1788, see Orange County Land Books, 1782–1792, and Personal Property Books, 1782–1789, in the Tax Returns Collection, in the Virginia State Library.

[94] For one of the few sketches of McClurg see Howard A. Kelly and Walter L. Burrage, *American Medical Biographies* (3 vols., Baltimore, 1920), 2:124 ff.

[95] Records of the Loan of 1790, vol. 1112, folio 51 (Virginia Loan Office, Register of Assumed Debt) and vol. 1118 (Register of Public Debt), under dates November 23 and December 21, 1790, in the National Archives; Beard, *Economic Interpretation*, 130. Beard incorrectly places the total of McClurg's securities at $26,819. McClurg funded in three separate transactions, one for $4,367.31, one for $2,072, and one for £7,590 (Virginia currency, in which six shillings made one dollar) or $22,771.35, a total of $31,740.66.

[96] Sanderson, *Biographies of the Signers* (1846 edition), 4:172; *Biographical Directory of Congress* (1927 edition), 1734.

chancellor, approximately £30 ($100) from the installments he received on the purchase price of property he had sold, and £28 ($93.33) from rent on two lots in Williamsburg. The next year his property consisted of the two town lots in Williamsburg, three slaves, and £484 1s. 10d. ($1,613.78) face value of Virginia public securities.[97]

JOHN BLAIR was a member of a respectable and prosperous family. After receiving his education at the Middle Temple in London he returned to America and practiced law for twenty years prior to the Revolution. In 1778 he became a judge of the Virginia Court of Appeals, was promoted the next year to a judge of the Court of Chancery and served in that office until 1789, and then became an associate justice of the United States Supreme Court, where he sat until 1796, four years before his death.[98]

In addition to his modest salary as a judge Blair received £36 a year in rentals. In 1788 his property included 1,128 acres in James City County, valued at £479 8s.; ten lots in Williamsburg (yielding the above-mentioned £36 rental), where he also had twelve slaves and two horses; 430 acres, valued at £198, in York County, where he made his home and where he owned eleven adult and three minor slaves and two horses. He also held public securities of Virginia with a total face value of $10,795.83 and a market value of approximately $2,500.[99]

EDMUND RANDOLPH was a member of one of the leading families of Virginia. A well-educated man, an eminent lawyer, governor of his state, and first attorney-general of the United States, he was nonetheless beset with economic difficulties. As a delegate

[97] Williamsburg City Land Book, and Williamsburg City Personal Property Book, 1788, in the Tax Returns Collection, in the Virginia State Library; Sanderson, *Biographies of the Signers* (1846 ed.), 4:183–184; Records of the Loan of 1790, vol. 1112, folio 91 (Virginia Loan Office, Register of Assumed Debt), in the National Archives.

[98] Earl G. Swem's biographical sketch of Blair in the *Dictionary of American Biography;* Charles Warren, the *Supreme Court in United States History* (3 vols., Boston, 1923), 1:38 and *passim.*

[99] James City County Land Book; Williamsburg City Land Book; Williamsburg City Personal Property Book; York County Land Book; and York County Personal Property Book; all for 1788, in the Tax Returns Collection, in the Virginia State Library; Records of the Loan of 1790, vol. 1113, folios 2–3, 135, and vol. 1118, transaction of September 29, 1791 (Virginia Loan Office, Register of Assumed Debt), in the National Archives.

to Congress in 1782 he complained to Madison of his lack of funds, saying, "I surely do not commit an unpardonable sin in reprehending my father for not handing down a fortune to me." [100]

In 1784 he finally did inherit something. He "became heir to Peyton Randolph's estates; but he also became the heir to a patrimony of debts, gathered on their way to the heir, which, with the ten thousand pounds to be paid his sisters, was a heavy burden. . . . Randolph derived little benefit from his uncle's bequest; the produce of the land scarcely sufficed to support the increasing number of negroes." He had had to borrow money from his brother-in-law to go to Richmond when he became governor, and he mortgaged his home to obtain funds to go to New York to become attorney-general.[101]

In 1788 his property consisted of a half interest in four town lots and 464 acres in Henrico County, his share of which was worth £118, and he owned outright 130 acres in the county, valued at £43; 1,500 acres, valued at £818, in James City County; eighteen town lots in Williamsburg, renting for £35 annually, and twelve adult and four minor slaves in Williamsburg; and 401 acres, worth £214, in York County. He also owned $13,832.81 in Virginia public securities. Despite the fact that these securities appreciated in value from about $3,450 to about $8,900 as a result of the adoption of the Constitution, and despite his great need, Randolph disapproved of the Constitution and refused to sign the document.[102]

NORTH CAROLINA: HUGH WILLIAMSON, RICHARD DOBBS SPAIGHT, WILLIAM BLOUNT, WILLIAM R. DAVIE, AND ALEXANDER MARTIN

HUGH WILLIAMSON was as accomplished a citizen as North Carolina could have sent to the Convention: a physician, scientist,

[100] Moncure Daniel Conway, *Omitted Chapters in History Disclosed in the Life and Papers of Edmund Randolph* (New York, 1888), 45.

[101] *Ibid.*, 50, 385 ff.

[102] Henrico County Land Book Alterations, 1786; and James City County Land Books; Williamsburg City Land Books; York County Land Books; Williamsburg City Personal Property Book; all for 1788, in the Tax Returns Collection, in the Virginia State Library; Virginia Loan Office, Register of Assumed Debt, vol. 1113, folio 86, in Old Loan Records, in the National Archives.

philosopher, and statesman. He was born in Pennsylvania, studied divinity at the College of Philadelphia and was a Presbyterian minister for two years, and then served the college for three years as a professor of mathematics. He then turned to medicine, studying in Edinburgh and Utrecht, and returned to Philadelphia to practice until 1773. He next went to Europe on an astronomical expedition, from which he returned in 1776, settling in North Carolina. In 1777–1778 Williamson was engaged, with his brother, in an attempt to carry on a wartime trade with the West Indies. When the naval campaigns there threatened to destroy all such trade, Williamson joined the army as surgeon-general of the North Carolina troops and served in that capacity until 1782. Much of his time during the next decade was devoted to politics.[103]

When not politically engaged during the 1780's, Williamson practiced medicine, and apparently his practice was substantial and rewarding. He dabbled in various investments—he owned about $2,600 face value (about $300 market value) in North Carolina and continental securities, and he owned some western lands —but his major source of income was his medical practice.[104]

RICHARD DOBBS SPAIGHT was the young son of a wealthy family of planters in North Carolina. His father had been secretary of the colony under the crown, and his uncle had been governor of the colony. He was sent abroad for his education and studied in Ireland and the University of Glasgow until 1778, when he returned home to join the army. After the war he left his estate largely to overseers while he engaged in continental and state politics. Spaight was a member of Congress at twenty-four and was only twenty-nine at the time of the Convention.[105]

[103] Samuel A. Ashe and others, *Biographical History of North Carolina* (6 vols., Greensboro, 1907), 5:458 ff.; Louise I. Trenholme, *The Ratification of the Federal Constitution in North Carolina* (New York, 1932), 74–75; *Biographical Directory of Congress* (1927 edition), 1709.

[104] Records of the Loan of 1790, vol. 1243, folio 3 (Loan Office, North Carolina), vol. 622, account 425 (Subscription Register, Domestic Debt, 1790–91 [Pennsylvania Loan Office]), and vol. 630, folio 213 (Journal of the Continental Debt, 1790–1791), in the National Archives; and the sketches cited in the preceding note.

[105] John H. Wheeler, *Sketch of the Life of Richard Dobbs Spaight* (Baltimore, 1880), *passim*.

Spaight's land, all inherited, was valued at £6,500, and he owned seventy-one slaves. His interests were almost exclusively agricultural; he had no mercantile or other business connections, and he owned no public securities.[106]

WILLIAM BLOUNT's primary interests were planting, land speculation, and the development of the west. One of thirteen children of a successful farmer, Blount had a substantial tidewater plantation in his own right, and his brothers engaged in planting, law, and mercantile pursuits. On his plantation Blount owned thirty slaves, but by 1787 his attention was focused chiefly upon his Tennessee lands. Soon after the Convention he moved to Tennessee, where he served as territorial governor from 1792 until 1796, when he became a United States senator. He had not served long in the Senate when he was expelled for his part in inciting an Indian uprising against the Spanish.

The exact magnitude of his land speculations in 1787 is not clear. He had acquired only 5,000 acres of Tennessee lands in his own name, but much more was acquired for him by agents and held in their names. His recent biographer gives the impression that Blount's dealings in the 1780's were enormous, but he cites no figures. The first definite figures given are for 1794 or thereabouts, by which time Blount had increased his holdings greatly, to nearly a million acres.[107]

WILLIAM R. DAVIE, an impetuous, ambitious young lawyer, had been reared and educated by an uncle. He had been admitted to the bar in 1780, but instead of beginning practice he had sold his inheritance "to raise a troop of cavalry and two companies of

---

[106] William C. Pool, "An Economic Interpretation of the Ratification of the Federal Constitution in North Carolina," in the *North Carolina Historical Review*, 27:131 (April, 1950); *Census of 1790, Heads of Families, North Carolina*, 130. Beard lists Spaight as a holder of securities in an "old account," citing MS Ledger E, Treasury, 3% (vol. 45 of the Records of the Loan of 1790), folio 308. Examination of this account reveals that it refers to securities acquired by Spaight in 1799, twelve years after the Convention. Beard says, in his economic biography of Spaight, that he "seems to have taken no share in the public security transactions," but then in his summary he lists Spaight among the holders. *Economic Interpretation*, 143, 150.

[107] William H. Masterson, *William Blount* (Baton Rouge, 1954), *passim*; Pool, "Economic Interpretation of Ratification in North Carolina," in the *North Carolina Historical Review*, 27:451 (October, 1950); *Census of 1790, Heads of Families, North Carolina*, 33, 147.

mounted infantry," which he commanded as a major. After being thrice wounded he was discharged in 1783, and then he began his practice. Thus he had disposed of his estate and was in only the fourth year of practice at the time of the Convention.[108]

His rise in the law profession was rapid, however, and "he quickly accumulated a large estate." Exactly how large it was in 1787 is difficult to ascertain. In 1789 he refused an appointment as a federal district judge on the ground that "the salary was so poor he could not afford it." But by 1790 he owned thirty-six slaves, and at about that time he acquired an excellent plantation at "Tivoli" in South Carolina. He owned no securities and apparently had no practice with North Carolina merchants.[109]

ALEXANDER MARTIN was a farmer, lawyer, and governor by occupation and a poet and playwright by avocation. He was born in New Jersey, educated at Princeton, and trained in the law. In 1772 he began practicing in North Carolina, but his practice must have been small, confined as it was to tiny Guilford Court House, more than two hundred miles inland from navigable water and the avenues of commerce. He converted his income into land and slaves, and by 1790 his plantation was occupying forty-seven slaves and producing enough to ensure him "ample means." Having been a colonel in the continental ranks at the time of the battles of Brandywine and Germantown, and having fared well as a farmer, Martin enjoyed great prestige among his backwoods neighbors, and they twice elected him governor and once United States senator. He was essentially a man of rather modest agrarian interests, however, and he held neither public securities nor, so far as known, any other personalty except his slaves.[110]

[108] J. G. de Roulhac Hamilton, _William Richardson Davie_ (Chapel Hill, 1907); William J. Peele, _Lives of Distinguished North Carolinians_ (Raleigh, 1898), 69.

[109] Hamilton, _Davie_, 17; Peele, _North Carolinians_, 69; Ashe, _Biographical History of North Carolina_, 6:88; _Census of 1790, Heads of Families, North Carolina_, 64; Pool, "Economic Interpretation of Ratification in North Carolina," in the _North Carolina Historical Review_, 27:139-140 (April, 1950).

[110] Ashe, _Biographical History of North Carolina_, vol. 3; _Census of 1790, Heads of Families, North Carolina_, 168. On Martin as a poet and playwright see Roger Powell Marshall, "A Mythical Mayflower Competition: North Carolina Literature in the Half-Century Following the Revolution," in the _North Carolina Historical Review_, 27:188 (April, 1950).

SOUTH CAROLINA: JOHN RUTLEDGE, CHARLES COTESWORTH PINCKNEY, CHARLES PINCKNEY, AND PIERCE BUTLER

JOHN RUTLEDGE had been one of the most able and possibly the most successful lawyer in the American colonies. He had received his legal training in England and had begun practicing in 1761, at the age of twenty-two, when his family was verging on bankruptcy. Fifteen years later, at the outbreak of the Revolution, he had brought the family out of its difficulties and had become the richest lawyer in the colony, standing now at the head of the South Carolina aristocracy. His fortune at that time comprised money, slaves, and fourteen parcels of real estate, nine consisting of city property and five of plantations. The *assessed* value of his estate was £70,000 sterling (about $325,000), and the annual cash income he received from his practice was over £9,000 (about $40,000).[111]

Rutledge lost heavily as a result of his leadership of the Revolutionary cause in South Carolina. His entire estate was confiscated by the British army of occupation in 1780, and he regained very little of it after the war. He made no attempt to practice law after he became president of South Carolina in 1776, and his only income was his salary of $2,500 as chancellor justice (equivalent to chief justice), which office he held after 1784. The new state of Franklin gave him 25,000 acres of land in recognition of his services in the Revolution, "but this land was never more than a tax burden," and the title to it ultimately proved to be invalid. "From time to time, in a very poor market, he sold pieces of real estate, including much of his city property in Charleston, to satisfy insistent creditors." He even mortgaged one of his parcels of real estate to borrow paper money from the state, under its paper-money act of 1786. The 243 slaves he held in 1790 were apparently more of a burden than an asset. Though still physically and mentally strong at the time of the Convention, Rutledge was

[111] Richard Barry, *Mr. Rutledge of South Carolina* (New York, 1942), 149–150. Barry says that Rutledge held sixty slaves at that time. I believe, but have been unable to verify, that Barry overlooked Rutledge's slaveholdings in Beaufort, where in 1790 he held 217 slaves.

financially broken and debt-ridden, and he was living on a vanishing capital.[112]

CHARLES COTESWORTH PINCKNEY's economic career somewhat resembled Rutledge's. Born into the aristocracy, he was trained in law in England and was admitted to the bar in 1770. This was nine years later than Rutledge's entrance into practice, but an enormous patrimony helped him catch up with Rutledge. His practice was substantial, and by the beginning of the war he owned two hundred slaves and was dividing his time between law and the administration of his plantations. His property was confiscated by the British in 1780, and only his land was returned to him after the war. Hence he was forced to assume a great debt in order to buy new slaves. In 1784 his debts were so pressing that he sold all his Charleston property in order to save his plantation at Orangeburg.[113]

About 1786, however, thanks to a good rice crop, Pinckney's fortunes took a turn for the better. His plantations began to show a profit, and his law practice soon brought him as much as 4,000 guineas (nearly $20,000) a year. Though his recovery was not complete by 1790, only seventy of his slaves having been replaced by that time, he was probably free from debt, and he owned over $15,000 face value of continental and state securities.[114]

CHARLES PINCKNEY, like his cousin Charles Cotesworth Pinckney and Rutledge, combined planting with a law practice. Born in 1757, he reached maturity during the war and was thus deprived of the opportunity to be educated in London. He was ad-

[112] *Ibid.*, 304; Loan Office: Appraisals, Certificates, and Plats, May 10, 1786, manuscript file in the South Carolina Archives, Columbia; *Census of 1790, Heads of Families, South Carolina*, 10, 42; Charleston *Royal South Carolina Gazette*, November 27, 1780.

[113] James Herring, ed., *National Portrait Gallery of Distinguished Americans* (4 vols., Philadelphia, 1854), vol. 4; James B. O'Neall, *Biographical Sketches of the Bench and Bar of South Carolina* (2 vols., Charleston, 1859), 2:134 ff.; Charles G. Singer, *South Carolina in the Confederation* (Philadelphia, 1941), 19; Charleston *Royal South Carolina Gazette*, November 27, 1780; Charleston *South Carolina Gazette*, January 22, 1784.

[114] Herring, *National Portrait Gallery*, vol. 4; O'Neall, *Bench and Bar of South Carolina*, 134 ff.; *Census of 1790, Heads of Families, South Carolina*, 38, 97; Records of the Loan of 1790, vol. 1258, folio 38 (Journal of the Assumed Debt, South Carolina) and vol. 1259, folio 68 (Journal of the Public Debt, South Carolina), in the National Archives.

mitted to the bar in 1779. The state was then occupied by the British and the next year Pinckney was taken prisoner. His economic life began in 1783 with a mass of obligations.[115]

Pinckney was fortunate, however, in his marriage to the daughter of a prominent merchant. This connection saw him through the difficult early years, and he ultimately rose to eminence in the South Carolina bar. By 1788 his income was over $5,000 a year. In 1790 he owned 111 slaves, including those inherited by his wife, but he held no public securities.[116]

PIERCE BUTLER, like his colleagues in the South Carolina delegation, was a planter-lawyer, and his economic career during and after the war closely paralleled theirs, despite the fact that he was a newcomer to the South Carolina aristocracy. An Irishman of noble ancestry, he was sent to Boston as a British army officer, but resigned his commission in 1773 and moved to South Carolina, where he quickly made a place for himself in the colony's economic and social life. He was considered sufficiently important by the British to be included among the victims of their original confiscation order of 1780, whereby they declared confiscate the property of the top twenty "nabob" revolutionaries in South Carolina, the élite of the colony's aristocracy. At war's end he found his property devastated and many of his slaves gone.[117]

[115] O'Neall, *Bench and Bar of South Carolina*, 2:141 ff.; *Biographical Directory of Congress* (1927 edition), 1413–1414.

[116] O'Neall, *Bench and Bar of South Carolina*, 2:141 ff.; Pinckney Family Papers, in the Manuscripts Division of the Library of Congress, volumes dealing with Charles Pinckney. Barry, in his *Mr. Rutledge*, page 311, says that by 1787 Pinckney's income was "three or four times" the salary of Rutledge, which would mean from $7,500 to $10,000 a year, but the Pinckney Family Papers in the Library of Congress indicate a real income of considerably less than that. The slaveholdings are recorded in *Census of 1790, Heads of Families, South Carolina*, 34, 40, 97.
Professor Beard understates Pinckney's slaveholdings, setting the number at fifty-two, which included only the slaves Pinckney held on a single plantation in St. Bartholomew's Parish. Beard is also mistaken in listing Pinckney as a holder of more than $14,000 in public securities. *Economic Interpretation*, 139. His citation is MS Loan Office, S. C., 1791–1797 (vol. 1258 of the Records of the Loan of 1790), folio 221. Examination of that account reveals that it refers to securities acquired by Pinckney in 1793, six years after the Convention.

[117] Robert L. Meriwether's biographical sketch of Butler in the *Dictionary of American Biography; Biographical Directory of Congress* (1927 edition), 770; Barry, *Mr. Rutledge*, random notes scattered through pages 306–314; Charleston *Royal South Carolina Gazette*, November 27, 1780.

To restore his financial strength Butler went to Holland immediately after the war, mortgaged all his land, and negotiated a large loan from a Dutch mercantile firm. He thus avoided the high postwar interest rates and credit prices in restocking himself with slaves. The big debt he had contracted almost ruined him, however, when two successive rice crops failed. Although his creditors were prevented from seizing his property by the emergency measures against such executions passed in 1786 by the South Carolina legislature, of which Butler was a member, he entered the Convention in 1787 as a debtor in rather desperate circumstances. His recovery began with the excellent rice crop of the fall of 1787, however, and by 1790 he was apparently in good condition once more.[118]

In 1790 his slaves on two plantations numbered 143. He had no public securities, but in 1792 he became one of the original stockholders and directors of the first Bank of the United States.[119]

GEORGIA: ABRAHAM BALDWIN, WILLIAM FEW, WILLIAM PIERCE, AND WILLIAM HOUSTOUN

ABRAHAM BALDWIN was the son of a blacksmith in Connecticut, head of a family of "working-class intellectuals." The elder Baldwin went into debt to educate his children—so heavily that it was only after his father's death in 1787 that Baldwin managed to retire these obligations. Baldwin graduated from Yale College in 1772, subsequently studied theology and was licensed to preach in 1775, and taught divinity at Yale until 1779. He then entered the army as a chaplain and served until the end of the war in 1783. He had studied law while in the army and was admitted to the bar of Connecticut in 1783. The next year he moved to Augusta,

---

[118] Most of the information about Butler's loan and his economic plight after the war is derived from John Lewis Gervais' letter to Leonard DeNeufville, April 13, 1786, in the Gervais and Owen Personal Misc. File, in the Manuscripts Division of the Library of Congress, and from the Miscellaneous Pierce Butler Papers, in the South Carolina Historical Society, Charleston.

[119] *Census of 1790, Heads of Families, South Carolina*, 10, 34; Beard, *Economic Interpretation*, 81–82. Beard overlooked the 112 slaves Butler held on his Beaufort plantation.

Georgia, practiced law for a year, and then entered politics.[120]

His biographer says, "There is no evidence (which has been sought for) that he was interested in any agricultural or business enterprises in Georgia, or engaged in land speculation, or enjoyed any considerable practice at the bar. He inherited no patrimony, and his income was largely derived from his official salaries," which were three dollars a day in the Georgia legislature and six dollars a day as a delegate to Congress, two positions which he filled for several years. "With this meagre income Baldwin's private life must have been one of extreme frugality and simplicity." [121]

A contemporary writer of doubtful veracity said that Baldwin supplemented his income while in Congress by working as the hired keeper of a boardinghouse in New York; at any rate, he probably supplemented it in various ways, and he invested wisely. He was as shrewd with his money as he was in his politics. About a year before the Convention he acquired about $2,500 face value of continental securities in Connecticut, an investment which cost him little more than $300 in cash, but which appreciated to nearly $1,600 market value by the end of 1791. He was also the holder of nine shares of the stock of the Bank of New York, having a par value of $500, on which he still owed more than half.[122]

WILLIAM FEW was the son of a poor Maryland farmer who had moved to North Carolina when William was a child. Later William hired out as a bricklayer and also worked on the family farm, but the farm was eventually swallowed up by debts. In 1776 he removed to the new frontier country of Georgia, where he quickly rose to leadership among his fellow farmers. At the end of the war he decided to enter law, and he educated himself for the profession by reading law treatises between stints of plowing. He began practicing shortly afterward, and slowly, through

[120] Henry C. White, *Abraham Baldwin* (Athens, Georgia, 1926), *passim*; *Biographical Directory of Congress*, 664.

[121] White, *Abraham Baldwin*, 189.

[122] Philadelphia *Independent Gazetteer, or the Chronicle of Freedom*, February 16, 1788; Records of the Loan of 1790, vols. 495–497 (Connecticut Loan Office, Ledgers A, B, and C, Assumed Debt), folios 135–136 in each, in the National Archives; Domett, *Bank of New York*, 133.

determination and native intelligence, began to rise above his origins. Ultimately he became moderately wealthy.[123]

At the time of the Convention Few said that his "pecuniary prospects were very flattering," but he was still a farmer of modest means. He had expanded his Wilkes County farm to include 1,150 acres, mostly undeveloped, and he had bought another 1,150 acres of wild land in Franklin County. Both these parcels were acquired from the state at three shillings an acre, representing a total cost of £345 ($1,533.33). In addition Few owned $640.57 in public securities, having a market value in 1787 of about $80.[124]

WILLIAM PIERCE was a bankrupt merchant. Except that he was born in Georgia in 1740, only eight years after the founding of the colony, almost nothing is known of his life before the Revolution. Since he lived in Savannah and owned neither land nor slaves, it is a reasonable conjecture that his family was one of artisans, mechanics, or tradesmen. Pierce served with distinction in the war, being discharged in 1783 as a major, with a sword and special citations from Congress.[125]

In 1783 Pierce went into an import-export business and organized the firm of Pierce, White, and Call. Less than a year later the firm was dissolved, but Pierce was enabled to make a fresh start through his marriage at this time to the daughter of Edward Fenwick. His wife brought a dowry that was sufficient for the or-

[123] "Autobiography of William Few," in the *Magazine of American History,* 7:352 ff.; *Biographical Directory of Congress* (1927 edition), 964.

[124] The sketches cited in note 123, above; Land Grants, Wilkes County, 1783, pp. 13, 15, 33, in the Georgia Department of Archives and History; Records of the Loan of 1790, vol. 1313, folio 25, vol. 1305, folio 16 (Journals of the Georgia Loan Office), and Register of Certificates of Public Debt Presented to the Auditor of the Treasury, Book A, in the same Records, in the National Archives. Beard says Few presented a certificate of 1779 having a "nominal" value of $2,170. Though technically true, the statement is misleading, for the certificate had been scaled down during the war to a face value of $114.80. Beard is also misleading when he says that Few was "involved in the Yazoo land deals." Few's involvement in that affair consisted of instigating the investigation which resulted in a nullification of the fraudulent grants.

[125] Charles C. Jones, Jr., *Biographical Sketches of the Delegates from Georgia to the Continental Congress* (Boston, 1891), 155 ff.; *Biographical Directory of Congress* (1927 edition), 1412; Albert Berry Saye, Georgia's Delegates to the Federal Convention of 1787: Who They Were and What They Did, manuscript master's thesis, 1935, in the library of the University of Georgia.

ganization of a new firm, William Pierce & Company. Pierce did
well for a time, establishing a connection with Jared Ingersoll's
wealthy father-in-law, Charles Pettit, in Philadelphia, and getting
a share of the rice trade through his friendship with the aristocratic planter Lachlan McIntosh. In the fall of 1785 a temporary
decline in the European rice market hurt his business, and having
neither the skill of an experienced merchant nor any reserve capital, he was never quite able to recover. He was forced to leave
the Convention in mid-July and go to New York in an attempt
to save his business, but his efforts failed; in 1788 he went bankrupt. Pierce died in 1789, leaving a mass of personal debts.[126]

WILLIAM HOUSTOUN was a young member of the relatively
new but wealthy planter aristocracy in Georgia. Members of his
family had been high royal officials in the colony, and he was educated in law at the Inner Temple in London, though his training
was cut short by the outbreak of the war. Several members of his
family were loyalists, but Houstoun was an active patriot.[127]

Like the South Carolina delegates, Houstoun combined planting with the practice of law. The loss of the manuscript records
of the first census in Georgia precludes knowledge of how many
slaves he owned, but that his plantation was a large one is evidenced by the fact that in 1782 he purchased a 500-acre confiscated estate for £750 and the 2,500-acre confiscated estate of
Patrick Houstoun for £25,000. The terms of the sale, stipulating
payment half in specie, half in certificates of Georgia's war debt,
depleted Houstoun's liquid resources, and despite the extent of
his property he was plagued by debts for some years. As a delegate to Congress in 1785 he wrote that he wanted to return home
but could not do so because he "had exhausted every shilling of
his own, had been compelled to borrow from time to time, and at

---

[126] This account of Pierce's experiences as a merchant is pieced together
from several sources, secondary and primary: the biographical sketches cited
above; advertisements and notices in the Savannah *Gazette of the State of
Georgia*, 1783 *passim*, February 12, December 11, 1784, October 13, 1785, 1786–
1788 *passim;* and Pierce's letter to Charles and Andrew Pettit, April 1, 1785, in
the Dreer Collection of Letters of Members of the Federal Convention, in the
Historical Society of Pennsylvania.

[127] Jones, *Delegates from Georgia*, 155 ff.; *Biographical Directory of Congress*, 1118; Saye, Georgia's Delegates to the Federal Convention (MS.).

the moment he was so exceedingly pressed and so much involved that it was impossible for him to think of moving till he could receive a pecuniary relief sufficient to extricate him; meanwhile he was perplexed in finding means for his support." Houstoun held no public securities, was in debt, and lacked liquid capital, and the bulk of his property was jeopardized by the Constitution. Even so, he was the richest member of the Georgia delegation.[128]

* * *

The biographical data presented above permit the following generalizations as a more precise characterization of the economic interests of the delegates than that presented earlier by Professor Beard.

I. Professional and Other Callings of the Members of the Convention

A. *Thirty-four of the delegates were lawyers.* Of these,
    Eight derived all or the greater part of their incomes from their practice, which practice was largely with merchants in interstate and foreign commerce: King, Hamilton, Dayton, Wilson, Gouverneur Morris, Ingersoll, Charles C. Pinckney, and Charles Pinckney. We return to these men shortly.
    Thirteen were "country lawyers," practicing largely with farmers and others having realty interests, and they derived all or the greater part of their incomes from their practice: Strong, Ellsworth, Lansing,* Paterson, Read, Bassett,* Mercer,* Davie,* Alexander Martin,* Dickinson,* Houstoun,* Few,* and Randolph.* Nine of them, those marked with asterisks, were also farmers on varying scales; that is, they combined farming with law practice to gain their livelihoods.
    Ten received all or most of their incomes in the form of salaries for public office: Yates, Brearley, Houston, Livingston, Bedford, Luther Martin, Wythe, Blair, Rutledge, and Baldwin.

[128] Sale-Book of Confiscated Estates, Chatham County, Liberty County, 1782–1785, purchases of June 13 and June 19, 1782, in the Georgia Department of Archives and History, Atlanta; Houstoun to Samuel Elbert, April 2, 1785, quoted in Edmund C. Burnett, *The Continental Congress* (New York, 1941), 629.

Three of the lawyers, Johnson, Madison, and Sherman, were trained in law but did not make their livelihoods from it.

B. *Eighteen of the delegates were farmers.* Of these,

Sixteen conducted large-scale agricultural operations as planters or farmers: Lansing, Bassett, Carroll, Jenifer, Mercer, Mason, Randolph, Spaight, Blount, Davie, Alexander Martin, Charles Pinckney, Charles C. Pinckney, Butler, Houstoun, and Washington. All of them except Lansing and Bassett owned slaves. In addition, Luther Martin, Madison, Wythe, Blair, and Rutledge owned slaves.

Two conducted farming on a small scale: Broom and Few.

C. *Fifteen of the delegates were engaged in or associated with mercantile activity.* Of these,

Eight were the lawyers named earlier who received all or the greater part of their incomes from law practice and had as clients, largely or exclusively, merchants in interstate and foreign commerce. Two of these, Wilson and Ingersoll, themselves owned shares in small vessels.

Seven were merchants engaged in commerce, interstate and foreign, four of whom (those marked with asterisks) owned vessels: Langdon,* Gorham, Gerry,* Robert Morris,* Clymer, Fitzsimons,* and Pierce.

D. *The primary interests of the delegates* were as follows:

Including lawyers whose practice was primarily or exclusively concerned with farming or other realty interests, twenty derived all or almost all of their income from the soil; that is to say, their interests were primarily realty-agrarian, as opposed to personalty: Strong, Ellsworth, Lansing, Paterson, Read, Bassett, Mercer, Davie, Alexander Martin, Few, Carroll, Mason, Randolph, Spaight, Blount, Butler, Houstoun, Washington, Broom, and Dickinson.

Including lawyers whose incomes were derived largely or exclusively from mercantile clients, thirteen had interests that were primarily mercantile—that is, in personal property as opposed to real property: King, Hamilton, Dayton, Wilson, Gouverneur Morris, Ingersoll, Langdon, Gorham, Gerry, Robert Morris, Clymer, Fitzsimons, and Pierce.

Two derived their incomes almost equally from agricultural pursuits and the practice of law with mercantile clients: Charles Pinckney and Charles C. Pinckney.

Twelve derived all or the greater part of their income from salaries in public offices: Yates, Brearley, Houston, Livingston, Bedford, Luther Martin, Wythe, Blair, Rutledge, Baldwin, Gilman, and Jenifer.

Two derived all or almost all of their income from their practice as physicians: McClurg and Williamson.

Three had retired from active economic pursuits with substantial fortunes: Franklin, McHenry, and Mifflin. The estates of all three men consisted primarily of realty, but the latter two had made their fortunes in mercantile pursuits.

Three are loosely classifiable as pensioners: Sherman, Johnson, and Madison. Sherman's income was derived from his own labor, salaries as a public official, and occasional practice of law as well as the contributions made by his children. Johnson's income was derived from a multitude of small realty and personalty investments, occasional law practice, and from his son. Madison's income came from official salaries and from loans and gifts from friends and his father. All three men were in rather trying economic circumstances.

II. Investments and Property Holdings of the Delegates

A. *Lands Held as Investments*

Substantially all the men owned their residences, and five (Gouverneur Morris, Madison, Blair, Dickinson, and Mifflin) owned nonproductive country estates.

Eight men held town lots and/or houses, exclusive of their residences and mercantile property: McHenry, Carroll, McClurg, Wythe, Blair, Randolph, Rutledge, and Mifflin.

Twelve held undeveloped lands for "speculation," that is, lands they did not use or intend to use for farming: Gerry, Lansing, Washington, Williamson, Blount, Franklin, Mason, Dayton,* Fitzsimons,* Robert Morris,** Wilson,** and Gorham.** The three whose names are marked with double asterisks went bankrupt from their land speculations as a result of the adoption of the new system, and the two marked with single asterisks suffered considerable reductions in their fortunes for the same reason.

B. *Property in Manufacturing Investments*

Three delegates, Ellsworth, Wilson, and Johnson, held investments in manufacturing property. Both Ellsworth's and Johnson's had a value of less than £100 sterling, and that of Wilson was in bankruptcy.

C. *Property in Money and Banking*

Probably every member of the Convention loaned as well as borrowed money at one time or another. The following twelve men had property in the form of banking capital or money at interest on a scale sufficient to be a significant investment:

DELEGATE	BANK STOCK AT FACE VALUE	DELEGATE	BANK STOCK AT FACE VALUE	PRIVATE LOANS
King	$3,000	Mifflin	$800	
Hamilton	375	G. Morris	400	
R. Morris	52,000	Baldwin	2,250	
Wilson	2,000	Langdon	4,000	
Clymer	2,800	McClurg		amt. unknown
Fitzsimons	800	Mason		$30,000

D. *Property in Public Securities*

This property is summarized in the table on the following page. All figures are rounded, of course, and the market values given are merely estimates, based on the market prices of the securities held by the delegates, as quoted in various Philadelphia newspapers by kinds of holdings: Virginia "Final Settlement Notes," Pennsylvania "Loan Office Certificates," "Balloon Notes," etc. The prices of all securities were generally higher in Philadelphia than in any other city in the country.

| DELEGATE | FACE VALUE | APPROXIMATE MARKET VALUE | | APPRECIATION OR PAPER PROFIT |
		1787	DECEMBER 1791	
Gerry	$50,000	$10,000	$32,500	$22,500
McClurg	32,000	6,500	20,800	14,300
Langdon	28,000	3,500	18,200	14,700
Clymer	15,500	6,350	10,100	3,750
C. C. Pinckney	15,000	2,500	9,750	7,250
Randolph	13,800	3,450	8,900	5,450
Robert Morris	11,000	4,500	7,150	2,650
Strong	11,000	2,200	7,150	4,950
Blair	10,800	2,500	7,100	4,600
King	10,000	5,000	6,300	1,300
Fitzsimons	8,300	3,300	5,400	2,100
Franklin	8,100	3,250	5,250	2,000
Sherman	7,800	1,000	5,000	4,000
Mercer	7,200	2,150	4,600	2,450
Lansing	7,000	3,500	4,550	1,050
Ellsworth	6,000	750	3,800	3,050
Dayton	5,500	1,000	3,600	2,600
Luther Martin	4,400	1,300	2,850	1,550
Bedford	2,900	360	1,875	1,515
Williamson	2,600	300	1,700	1,400
Mifflin	2,500	1,000	1,600	600
Baldwin	2,500	300	1,600	1,300
Wythe	1,600	350	1,050	700
Gilman	1,000	125	625	500
Few	650	80	425	345
Washington	500	75	325	250
Read	350	50	225	175
Carroll	225	90	150	60
Broom	40	10	25	15
Brearley	15	5	10	5
Total	$266,275	$65,495	$172,610	$107,115

A few things about these statistics should be pointed out. Thirty, or a little over half, of the delegates held securities in varying amounts; it is of interest to compare this figure with the analogous figures for members of the ratifying conventions, both friends and enemies of the Constitution. See Chapters Five, Six, and Seven below.

More will be said later about the behavior of these interests in the Convention. It may be pointed out here, however, that five of the men who either refused to sign the finished Constitution or walked out of the Convention (Gerry, Randolph, Mercer, Lansing, and Luther Martin) were among the largest holders of securities in the Convention. Had they sold their securities in Philadelphia as the Convention opened, the proceeds would have been sufficient to buy all the securities owned by forty-five of the remaining fifty delegates.

E. *Agricultural Property*

At least thirty-one of the members owned lands being used at the time for farming, in most cases by the owners themselves: Lansing, Bassett, Carroll, Jenifer, Mercer, Mason, Randolph, Spaight, Blount, Davie, Alexander Martin, Charles C. Pinckney, Charles Pinckney, Rutledge, Butler, Houstoun, Washington, Broom, Few, Dickinson, Read, Yates, Livingston, Franklin, Wythe, Blair, McClurg, Williamson, McHenry, Mifflin, and Madison. The nineteen slaveholders were listed earlier.

F. *Adversely Affected Interests*

The Constitution, according to Beard, promised to affect favorably investments in vacant lands, money, manufacturing, and public securities; and to have no unfavorable effect on agricultural property as such. Beard asserted that it affected debtors unfavorably; in addition, two forms of property were affected adversely by the making of the Constitution, if only for a short time. Eighteen members of the Convention had interests in such property or were debtors:

Four had purchased confiscated property: Paterson, Carroll, Luther Martin, and Houstoun.

Five were speculators in lands who contracted to buy in depreciated public securities: Robert Morris, Wilson, Gorham, Dayton, and Fitzsimons.

Thirteen members, including four who had also purchased confiscated estates or lands for securities, were debtors for significant amounts; their condition ranged from acute embarrassment to desperation and outright bankrutcy: Sherman, Rutledge, Robert Morris, Wilson, Luther Martin, Pierce, Washington, Madison, Randolph, Butler, Houstoun, Charles Pinckney, and Charles C. Pinckney.

* * *

A word may be said about the relative weights of the various kinds of property in the total holdings of members of the Convention. These holdings were diverse and valuable, but the most common and by far the most valuable were farmland and slaves. The 569 slaves owned by the four delegates from South Carolina were probably worth half again as much as the total public security holdings of all the other members. The slaves and farmlands owned by the delegates from Virginia and Maryland were worth far more than the mercantile, banking, and manufacturing property owned by all the other delegates.

The economic interests represented by the members may be viewed in another way. Thirteen of the delegates had voted in state legislatures for various debtor-relief measures, and thirteen others had interests that were adversely affected by the making of the Constitution. Four more not included in either of these groups opposed the Constitution. Of the remaining twenty-five delegates, only nine made as much as a thousand dollars in four and a half years by the appreciation of their security holdings.

It is clear that Professor Beard's assertion that the members of the Convention were a "consolidated economic group" with an "identity of personalty interests" cannot be accepted without a large number of qualifications.

IV

Economic Interests and Votes in the Convention

ANY analysis of the relationship between personal economic interests and political behavior in the Convention must necessarily be tentative. For one reason, as the data in the preceding chapter reveal, the interests represented by given delegates do not always permit of placing them in mutually exclusive categories—a delegate might not only have been a farmer but he might also have had a large investment in public securities; or he might have been a merchant who was likewise a debtor in desperate straits. For another and perhaps more important reason, the delegates in the Convention did not vote as individuals but by states, with the result that, except for the most prolific speakers, their conduct as individuals is somewhat obscured.

Despite these obstacles, however, certain observations may be made with respect to the connection between economic interests and political outlook. If, to be consistent with Beard's system, all the merchants and their attorneys, together with the larger holders of public securities, are considered as one group, and all the farmers, debtors, country lawyers, and holders of state offices who held no securities, mercantile property, or other significant personalty are considered as another, the delegates can be divided into two quite different camps with respect to their economic interests. The first group could be styled the "Personalty Group," the second the "Realty Group." The lines of division would then fall as follows:

STATE	PERSONALTY GROUP	REALTY GROUP
N. H.	Langdon and Gilman	None
Mass.	King, Gerry, Strong, and Gorham	None
Conn.	Sherman and Ellsworth	Johnson
N. Y.	Lansing and Hamilton	Yates
N. J.	Dayton	Paterson, Livingston, Brearley, Houston
Pa.	Clymer, Fitzsimons, Franklin, Ingersoll, Mifflin, Wilson, Robert Morris, and Gouverneur Morris	None
Del.	Bedford	Bassett, Dickinson, Read, and Broom
Md.	Luther Martin and Mercer	Jenifer, Carroll, and McHenry
Va.	Randolph, McClurg, Mason, Blair, and Wythe	Washington and Madison
N. C.	Williamson	Alexander Martin, Blount, Davie, and Spaight
S. C.	C. C. Pinckney	Charles Pinckney, Rutledge, and Butler
Ga.	Pierce and Baldwin	Few and Houstoun

Perhaps a few of the delegates could be classified otherwise, but it would not greatly change the basic alignment. Johnson could perhaps be shifted to the personalty group, but his state of Connecticut is already so classified. Dickinson likewise could be shifted, on the grounds of his earlier associations, but that would not change the Delaware majority. Wythe could be shifted on the ground that his public security holding was too small to have influenced his stand on issues, but since Wythe was absent most of the time the question is a purely academic one. McHenry could conceivably be transferred from the realty to the personalty group. This shift alone would change the complexion of a delegation. It would have little effect on the present analysis, however, since McHenry, too, was frequently absent—more than half the time the Convention was in session.

The table indicates that the personalty interests were in a clear majority in the Convention: thirty-one members as against twenty-four in the realty group. More important for immediate purposes, it will be seen that all the states except Maryland were decisively dominated by one group or the other (Georgia, split 2–2 in the table, must be regarded as a personalty state because Houstoun attended only for the first week or two). Seven were personalty states: Massachusetts, New Hampshire, Connecticut, New York, Virginia, Pennsylvania, and Georgia; four were realty states: New Jersey, Delaware, North Carolina, and South Carolina.

If the economic interests represented by the delegates were the dominating element, or even one of several dominating elements, in the making of the Constitution, one would expect to find an alignment inside the Convention along the above lines. Not on all issues, of course, for there were necessarily issues on which no economic interests were at stake or on which such interests conflicted; nor should one expect to find these exact alignments on any particular issue, for parliamentary strategy also had its effect. In general, however, as votes on all issues piled up in the day-to-day business of the Convention, the basic, underlying pattern of voting behavior should show the personalty states standing on one side, the realty states standing on the other, and Maryland vacillating between these two groups.

The table on the next page puts this proposition to the test. The figures cited are from the Convention votes as recorded in Madison's notes and the official journal of the Convention. A glance at the table indicates that there were distinct voting patterns in the Convention, but that they hardly coincided with the personalty and realty interest groups as listed above. The most conspicuous alignment is that of the extreme northern states with the extreme southern states: New Hampshire, Massachusetts, North Carolina, South Carolina, and Georgia. This alignment is shown in the tabulation below, in which the per-

	New Hampshire	Massachusetts	Connecticut	New York	New Jersey	Pennsylvania	Delaware	Maryland	Virginia	North Carolina	South Carolina	Georgia
New Hampshire	......	177-242 73.1%	159-262 60.6%	none	130-222 58.5%	154-258 59.6%	133-251 52.9%	121-260 46.5%	150-262 57.2%	150-244 61.4%	171-260 65.7%	161-256 62.8%
Massachusetts	177-242 73.1%	......	219-401 54.6%	46-106 43.3%	178-352 50.5%	245-399 61.8%	214-388 55.1%	182-390 46.6%	244-401 60.8%	252-391 64.4%	254-399 63.3%	233-391 59.5%
Connecticut	159-262 60.6%	219-401 54.6%	......	47-106 44.3%	224-361 62.0%	214-415 51.5%	218-408 53.4%	220-410 53.6%	221-421 52.4%	222-401 55.3%	220-419 52.5%	220-409 53.7%
New York	none	46-106 43.3%	47-106 44.3%	......	55-93 59.1%	44-104 42.3%	56-105 53.3%	44-97 45.3%	50-106 47.1%	51-104 49.0%	48-106 45.2%	53-103 51.4%
New Jersey	130-222 58.5%	178-352 50.5%	224-361 62.0%	55-93 59.1%	......	193-356 54.2%	226-350 64.5%	194-353 54.9%	171-361 47.3%	173-352 49.1%	163-359 45.4%	196-357 54.9%
Pennsylvania	154-258 59.6%	245-396 61.8%	214-415 51.5%	44-104 42.3%	193-356 54.2%	......	220-403 57.0%	204-404 50.4%	275-415 66.2%	212-396 53.5%	201-413 48.6%	206-404 50.9%
Delaware	133-251 52.9%	214-388 55.1%	218-408 53.4%	56-105 53.3%	226-350 64.5%	220-403 57.0%	......	215-386 55.7%	212-408 51.9%	190-398 48.9%	189-406 46.5%	182-398 45.7%
Maryland	121-260 46.5%	182-390 46.6%	220-410 53.6%	44-97 45.3%	194-353 54.9%	204-404 50.4%	215-386 55.7%	......	227-410 55.3%	180-392 45.9%	167-408 40.9%	192-399 48.1%
Virginia	150-262 57.2%	244-401 60.8%	221-421 52.4%	50-106 47.1%	171-361 47.3%	275-415 66.2%	212-408 51.9%	227-410 55.3%	......	262-401 65.3%	235-419 56.0%	245-409 59.9%
North Carolina	150-244 61.4%	252-391 64.4%	222-401 55.3%	51-104 49.0%	173-352 49.1%	212-396 53.5%	190-388 48.9%	180-392 45.9%	262-401 65.3%	......	261-400 65.2%	256-392 65.0%
South Carolina	171-260 65.7%	254-399 63.3%	220-419 52.5%	48-106 45.2%	163-359 45.4%	201-413 48.6%	189-406 46.5%	167-408 40.9%	235-419 56.0%	261-400 65.2%	......	294-409 71.8%
Georgia	161-256 62.8%	233-391 59.5%	220-409 53.7%	53-103 51.4%	196-357 54.9%	206-404 50.9%	182-398 45.7%	192-399 48.1%	245-409 59.9%	256-392 65.0%	294-409 71.8%	......

* The table reads like the conventional mileage chart. The sets of two figures on the first line following the name of the state at the left represent a comparison of its voting record with that of the states given at the head of the several columns. The first figure indicates the number of times the two states voted on the same side of issues, and the second the total number of times they voted on the same issues. The percentage given on the second line is the ratio of the first to the second figure above—that is, the percentage of the total number of issues voted upon by the two states that elicited the same vote from both of them.

centages represent, as in the table on page 96, the proportion of the issues voted upon by two states that elicited the same vote.

	New Hampshire Per Cent	Massachu-setts Per Cent	North Carolina Per Cent	South Carolina Per Cent	Georgia Per Cent
New Hampshire . . .	. . .	73.1	61.4	65.7	62.8
Massachusetts	73.1	. . .	64.4	63.3	59.5
North Carolina	61.4	64.4	. . .	65.2	65.0
South Carolina	65.7	63.3	65.2	. . .	71.8
Georgia	62.8	59.5	65.0	71.8	. . .

Considered as a unit, the bloc voted with Connecticut 55 per cent of the time; with New York 47 per cent; New Jersey 51 per cent; Pennsylvania 54 per cent; Delaware 49 per cent; Maryland 45 per cent; and Virginia 59 per cent of the time.

A second alignment was Delaware and New Jersey, and a third was Pennsylvania and Virginia. Delaware and New Jersey tended to vote with the northern states on most issues, but on less than half the issues did they vote with their fellow realty states, the Carolinas. Pennsylvania and Virginia split on only a third of the issues they both voted upon; when they did, Pennsylvania voted with the personalty states to the north and Virginia with her realty neighbors to the south. New York, a personalty state, voted more than half the time only with Delaware and New Jersey, realty states, and Virginia, a personalty state. Maryland and Connecticut acted as two lone wolves, Maryland opposing the basic five-state bloc and voting only with her neighbors, and Connecticut barely tending to break even with everyone, though voting consistently with personalty-dominated New Hampshire and realty-dominated New Jersey.

In short, the voting patterns of the state delegations in the Convention by no means followed the lines of a basic economic cleavage into realty and personalty interests.

A second way to test alignments inside the Convention affords a considerably closer view. Though delegates voted by states, it is possible to ascertain how individuals voted on a number of key issues. One source of data is Professor Max Farrand's monumental *Records of the Federal Convention*, in which he gives an attendance list, a record of the dates on which given delegates were known to be absent from the Convention. Recorded speeches, motions, and other expressions of attitude reveal how given individuals voted on given issues. Further, Madison and some of the other delegates who took notes in the Convention occasionally recorded the votes of individual delegates. By a process of elimination the attitudes of a remarkably high percentage of the delegates on specific issues can be ascertained.

On June 8, for example, the Convention voted on a motion that the national legislature in the contemplated new government be given an absolute veto power over any and all state laws which it judged improper; this was a test of the extent of extreme nationalism in the Convention. Gerry spoke out strongly against this proposal, but since Massachusetts voted as a state in favor of it, delegates Gorham, King, and Strong, all in attendance, must have voted for it. Ellsworth of Connecticut had made a strong speech a few days earlier in favor of a similar proposal, but since his state voted against it, Sherman and Johnson must both have voted no. It is probable that Hamilton of New York voted for the motion, since it was in his original plan and, according to Yates, he had voted for it a week earlier. Since New York's vote was negative, Yates and Lansing must both have voted against the motion; Lansing's opposition is attested by his condemnation of the idea in his later report to New York's Governor Clinton. Of the New Jersey delegation, Dayton and Houston were absent; the state voted no, which means that at least two of the three attending delegates voted no, and that it is a two-to-one probability that any of the three voted against it. Further, since the New Jersey delegation was indecisively split on only one of the 361 votes it cast in the entire Convention, it is quite likely that all three opposed the motion. Delaware's vote was divided: Madison records that Broom was absent, that Dickinson and Read voted for the proposal, and that Bedford and Bassett voted against it. Four members of the Maryland delegation, McHenry, Martin, Carroll, and Mercer, were absent; the remaining delegate, Jenifer, cast the state's vote against the proposal. Virginia's vote is recorded by Madison: Mason and Randolph were against the motion; McClurg, Blair, and Madison were in favor of it; and Washington abstained from voting. Of the North Carolina delegates, Blount was absent, Williamson spoke against the proposal, and at least two of the remaining three, Spaight, Davie, and Martin, must also have opposed the measure since the state's vote was cast against it. Charles Pinckney of South Carolina favored the proposal, being the author of the motion; since his state voted against it, it follows that Rutledge, Charles C. Pinckney, and Butler all opposed it. Baldwin of Georgia was absent, and all three of Georgia's remaining delegates undoubtedly voted against the motion. This may be inferred from the fact that on the three occasions when the motion came up (with Georgia voting against it each time), the four Georgia delegates were in and out of the house in such combinations as to make it a certainty that all of them voted no on the question at least once. Neither of New Hampshire's delegates was in attendance.

In this manner the vote of every delegate can be, at least inferentially, accounted for on this issue, except, unfortunately, the votes of Pennsylvania's eight delegates. Only two of these, Wilson and Gouverneur Morris, spoke out on any great number of the issues. It is probable that some of the delegates were occasionally absent from the house, but their residence in Philadelphia makes it impossible to determine whether any of them had gone home for a week or so, as delegates from other states sometimes did. Thus whereas the votes of delegates from other states on a number of issues can be ascertained by these methods, those of the Pennsylvanians cannot.

For the purpose of testing the proposition that the personalty interests in the Convention were a consciously cohesive faction, however, it is not necessary to know how individual Pennsylvanians cast their votes. The Pennsylvania delegation was exclusively one of personalty interests, so that however much dissension there may have been inside the delegation—indications are that there was very little—the vote of the state was invariably on the side of those interests. If, therefore, the proposition is sound, delegates representing personalty interests would have tended, with few exceptions, to have sided with Pennsylvania on a great majority of the critical and fundamental questions voted upon. By the same token, delegates representing realty and agrarian interests would have voted against Pennsylvania.

On sixteen such key questions there is internal evidence of the probable votes of individual delegates. These votes are depicted in the table on pages 102–103. In general, all sixteen questions bear directly upon Gouverneur Morris' classic statement of the "great question" (September 17), "shall there be a national Government or not?" [1]

On the basis of the summaries at the right of the table, indicating the number and percentage of votes in agreement with Pennsylvania's, the delegates may be divided into three more or less distinct categories. The first consists of twenty-six delegates who voted with Pennsylvania on a majority or all of the issues; exactly half of them were primarily or exclusively representatives of the personalty interests, and the other half representatives of realty and agrarian interests. A second category comprises the fourteen men who manifestly did not side with Pennsylvania; none of them voted with Pennsylvania on more than half the questions. Seven of these were representatives of the personalty interests, seven were representatives of the realty interests. The third group, numbering six, was indecisive; these delegates voted with Pennsylvania on just over half the issues. Four of them were representatives of the realty interests, two of the personalty interests.

The conclusion is inevitable, then, that in so far as can be ascertained from the votes of individual delegates, no alignment

[1] Six of the votes pertain to the fundamental issue whether sovereignty should continue to remain in the hands of the states or should be transferred to a new general government, five relate to restrictions on state governments, three are on economic clauses in the Constitution, one concerns the process of ratification, and one is on a proposal to make the Constitution unamendable. The votes may be found in Max Farrand's *The Records of the Federal Convention of 1787* (3 vols., New Haven, 1911), 1:130–147 (Vote 30, Detail of Ayes and Noes), 162–173 (Vote 34), 369–382 (Vote 74); 2:84–96 (Vote 203), 116–128 (Vote 228), 245–256 (Vote 268), 352–365 (Vote 336), 380–395 (Vote 345), 434–444 (Votes 387, 391, 392, 393, 394), 445–456 (Vote 399), 457–470 (Vote 415), 621–640 (Vote 559).

of *personalty interests* versus *realty interests* existed in the Convention.

A third test bears more directly on economic matters. At the heart of Professor Beard's interpretation of the Constitution as an economic document is a statement that the critical economic features of the instrument were certain positive grants of power and certain negative clauses, restrictions against attacks on property. Specifically, the most important positive features were the grant to Congress of exclusive power to regulate commerce and to fund the war debt. The key negative clauses were those prohibiting the issue of paper money by states and declaring that states could pass no laws impairing the obligation of contract—that is, laws staying executions for debts or making fiat money or goods legal tender for debts.

An analysis of the attitudes revealed while these four significant features of the Constitution were in the process of adoption should, therefore, throw additional light on the question whether the delegates were creating a system to promote and protect special interests "which they felt in definite, concrete, form." Each of the features is considered briefly in the following paragraphs.[2]

At first almost every delegate was agreed that the new government should have the power to regulate and levy duties on commerce. The working out of the details of the subject, however, revealed basic conflicts of interests and differences of opinion almost sufficient to break up the Convention.

Two limitations on congressional control of commerce did find their way, after bitter struggles, into the finished Constitution: the temporary restriction against regulation of the slave trade and the prohibition of duties on exports. Three other important proposals were the subject of intense controversy in the Convention. On August 28 Massachusetts, Connecticut, Pennsylvania, Maryland, Virginia, South Carolina, and Georgia voted against Madison's proposal to make absolute the restric-

---

[2] In the following analysis, dates are cited in the text. As readers will have access to different editions of the journals and notes of the Convention, this seems the most suitable form of documentation.

Votes of Delegates in Agreement with and Votes Opposed to Those of the Pennsylvania Delegation on Sixteen Key Issues

X—vote in agreement with Pennsylvania; o—vote opposed to Pennsylvania; P—personalty; r—realty

Vote of:	1	2	3	4	5	6	7	8	9	10	11	12	13	14	15	16	Total Votes Cast	In Agreement with Pennsylvania No.	Percentage
Pennsylvania	N	Y	N	N	N	N	N	N	Y	Y	N	N	Y	N	Y	N			
McClurg (P)	X	X	|	|	|	|	|	|	|	|	|	|	|	|	|	|	5	5	100
Hamilton (P)	X	X	|	|	|	|	|	|	|	|	|	|	|	|	|	|	3	3	100
Houston (r)	|	|	X	|	|	|	|	|	|	|	|	|	|	|	|	|	1	1	100
Langdon (P)	|	|	X	X	X	X	X	X	X	|	X	o	X	X	X	X	13	12	92.3
Gilman (P)	|	|	X	|	X	X	X	X	X	|	X	o	X	X	X	X	13	12	92.3
Dayton (P)	|	|	X	X	X	X	X	X	|	o	o	X	X	X	X	X	12	11	91.6
Gorham (P)	X	|	X	X	X	X	X	X	o	o	X	X	X	X	X	X	15	12	80
Washington (r)	X	X	X	X	X	X	X	X	o	X	o	X	X	o	X	X	15	12	80
Madison (r)	X	|	X	X	X	o	X	X	X	X	o	X	X	X	X	X	16	12	75
King (P)	X	X	o	X	X	X	X	X	X	X	o	o	o	X	X	X	15	11	73.3
Livingston (r)	o	X	X	X	X	X	X	o	|	o	o	X	X	o	X	X	14	10	71.4
Brearley (r)	o	o	X	|	X	X	o	X	|	o	o	X	o	X	X	X	14	10	71.4
Few (r)	X	o	X	X	X	X	o	X	|	X	o	X	o	o	X	?	14	10	71.4
Dickinson (r)	o	o	X	X	X	X	o	o	X	o	o	X	X	o	X	X	13	9	69.2
C. Pinckney (r)	o	X	X	|	o	X	X	o	o	o	X	o	o	X	X	X	16	11	68.7
Blair (P)	X	X	X	X	X	X	X	X	X	X	X	o	o	o	X	X	16	11	68.7
Baldwin (P)	|	X	X	X	o	X	o	X	o	X	o	X	X	o	X	X	15	10	66.6
Read (r)	o	o	o	o	X	o	o	X	|	X	o	o	X	X	X	?	15	10	66.6

Name	Votes	Total	Aff.	%
Blount (r)	× | | × × × × × ? × × × ? ∘ | | | ∘ ∘ | ∘ | × × | × | | |	12	8	66.6
Strong (P)	× | | × × × × × ∘ × ∘ ∘ ∘ ∘ | | | × × | | ∘ ∘ | ∘ ∘ | |	6	4	66.6
Pierce (P)	∘ | | ∘ × × × × × ∘ ∘ ∘ × × × | | × × | | ∘ ∘ | × ∘ | |	3	2	66.6
Williamson (P)	× | | × × ∘ ∘ ∘ × ∘ ∘ ∘ × × ∘ | | ∘ ∘ | | ∘ ∘ | ∘ ∘ | |	16	10	62.5
Spaight (r)	∘ | | ∘ ∘ × × × ∘ × × × ∘ ∘ × | | × × | | × × | × × | |	16	10	62.5
Rutledge (r)	× | | × × ∘ ∘ ∘ ∘ × × × ∘ ∘ × | | × × | | ∘ × | ∘ × | |	16	10	62.5
C. C. Pinckney (P)	× | | × × × × × ∘ ∘ ∘ × × ∘ | | ∘ ∘ | | | ∘ ∘ | | ∘ | |	16	10	62.5
Butler (r)	× | | × × × × × × × × × × × | | × × | | | × ∘ | × ∘ | |	16	10	62.5
Broom (r)	× | | × × × × × ∘ ∘ × × × ∘ | | ∘ ∘ | | | ∘ ∘ | ∘ ∘ | |	14	8	57.1
Carroll (r)	∘ | | ∘ ∘ ∘ ∘ ∘ × ∘ ∘ ∘ × × ∘ | | ∘ ∘ ∘ | | ∘ ∘ ∘ |	14	8	57.1
Jenifer (r)	× ∘ | × × × × × ∘ × × ∘ ∘ ∘ × × | × × × | | ∘ × | ∘ | ∘ |	16	9	56.2
Randolph (P)	| × | ∘ ∘ × × × × × × × × × ∘ | × × ∘ | ∘ ∘ | | ∘ | | |	16	9	56.2
Bedford (P)	| × | × × × × × ∘ ∘ × × ∘ ∘ ∘ × | ∘ ∘ × × × × | | ∘ ∘ | |	15	8	53.3
Bassett (r)	∘ ∘ × ∘ ∘ ∘ ∘ ∘ ∘ × × × × × × ∘ ∘ | ∘ ∘ ∘ × ∘ × | ∘ ∘ ∘ | |	15	8	53.3
Ellsworth (P)	| × ∘ ∘ ∘ ∘ ∘ ∘ | | ∘ ∘ ∘ ∘ × ∘ ∘ ∘ ∘ ∘ ∘ ∘ ∘ | ∘ ∘ | | |	14	7	50
Davie (r)	| × × × ∘ ∘ ∘ ∘ ∘ | × × ∘ ∘ ∘ × × ∘ ∘ × ∘ × × | × ∘ | | |	6	3	50
Lansing (P)		2	1	50
Johnson (r)		16	7	43.7
Sherman (P)		16	7	43.7
A. Martin (r)		7	3	42.8
Paterson (r)		5	2	40
Houstoun (r)		5	2	40
Mason (P)		16	6	37.5
McHenry (r)		11	4	36.3
Yates (r)		3	1	33.3
Gerry (P)		15	4	26.6
L. Martin (P)		11	2	18
Mercer (P)		2	0	0
Wythe (P)		—	—	—

tion against state import duties. On the next day Maryland, Virginia, North Carolina, and Georgia voted for a proposal so to tie the hands of Congress that no laws respecting commerce could be passed without a two-thirds majority of both houses. This proposal, which would have prevented the adoption of the first national commercial system and almost every major tariff bill passed before the Civil War, was also favored by South Carolina, though all the South Carolinians except Charles Pinckney voted against it, in keeping with the bargain they had made for northern support on the slave trade. Finally, on September 15, a spectacular last-ditch proposal was made which might have destroyed the entire commercial system being established. This proposal, which would have removed from congressional control all import and export duties levied by states, had the support of Virginia, North Carolina, and Georgia, and half the Pennsylvania delegation.[3]

This conflict over the proposal to grant to Congress exclusive power over commerce was partly one of personal interests, partly one of state and sectional interests, and partly one of opinions based on little more than abstract philosophy. Every state except New Hampshire voted for at least one of the three crippling proposals mentioned above, two states voted for two of them, and two others voted for all three. All but a handful of the delegates present voted for at least one of them; only Gilman, Langdon, Madison, possibly Washington, and perhaps two or three others voted consistently to give Congress exclusive power over commerce.

One would expect that if there was unanimity on any issue in the Convention, it would have been on the payment of the war debts, because of the large number of security holders among the delegates. On the contrary, however, there was much disagreement, and the discussions were, in a way, a preview of the great debates that were to take place in Congress over the adoption of Hamilton's funding plan in 1790. With

[3] Probably Fitzsimons, Mifflin, Franklin, and Ingersoll voted for it, judging by the expressed attitudes of Clymer, Gouverneur Morris, and Wilson and the pre-convention expressions of Robert Morris.

one minor exception nothing was said in the Convention on the subject of the debts until thirty days before adjournment.[4] At that time, on August 18, the report of the Committee of Detail, summarizing the Convention's expressed sentiments, revealed, among other things, that no provision regarding the debt had been made. Thereupon, Madison and Charles Pinckney moved that a catch-all committee be set up to consider a number of miscellaneous additional powers. Pinckney, who was not a security holder, included in his list a power "to secure the payment of the public debt." Rutledge, who likewise owned no securities, added a motion that power to assume the war debts of the states should also be considered by this committee.

The question of the public debt was discussed intermittently for a week, at the end of which the clauses in the Constitution respecting public obligations were agreed upon. During the week's debate twenty-two men made their attitude on the subject more or less clear. Eight of them expressed strongly the sentiment that all public creditors should be taken care of, and fourteen expressed reservations regarding the payment of all or parts of the public debt.

Gerry, the largest holder of securities in the Convention, was the most outspoken champion of public creditors, urging that Congress be expressly required to pay the national debt, and favoring the assumption of state debts (August 18, 21, 22, 25). King, a large holder of the public debt of New York, spoke strongly in favor of assumption (August 18), and Sherman, a creditor of Connecticut, argued in behalf of specific requirements for the payment of both national and state debts (August 18, 25). Rutledge and Charles Pinckney, neither of whom held any securities, were advocates of the assumption of state debts (August 18).[5] Gouverneur Morris, who held no securities, was almost as emphatic as Gerry in his insistence that the new Congress be specifically required to pay the public debt.

[4] King had mentioned the possibility of assumption of state debts on July 14.
[5] Pinckney and Rutledge were being attentive to the interests of their state. South Carolina had an enormous war debt, it was a creditor of Congress for a large amount, and its citizens owned very little continental debt. See the account of ratification in South Carolina, pages 202–235 below.

On the other hand, Ellsworth, who held continental but no state securities, was against the assumption of state debts, but he urged that it be specifically required that continental debts be paid (August 18, 25), which was exactly coincident with his personal interests. John Langdon, the third largest public creditor in the Convention, voted against assumption of state debts and argued against any special provisions for any public creditors, saying that he "wished to do no more than to leave the creditors in the statu quo" (August 18, 25). Gilman, another security owner, joined Langdon in voting against assumption (August 18) and any special provisions for continental creditors (August 25). The Delaware delegation present, including Bedford, Broom, and Read, all holders of securities, and Bassett, who held none, voted against assumption (August 18). The New Jersey delegation present, including Dayton, a substantial security holder, Brearley, a nominal security holder, and Livingston, who held no public paper, joined Delaware in voting against assumption (August 18). Randolph, one of the larger creditors in the Convention, Mason, only nominally a public creditor, and Johnson, not a holder of securities, expressed sentiments similar to Langdon's that no special provisions should be made for public creditors, and they were all against expressly requiring Congress to pay the public debt (August 25). Butler, not a creditor, joined the latter delegates, and he stated further that he was against making "payment as well to the Bloodsuckers who had speculated on the distresses of others, as to those who had fought & bled for their country" (August 23, 25).

Thus four men—Gerry, King, Sherman, and Ellsworth—were obviously working ardently for the interests represented by their own investments. Except for these four, neither public creditors nor non-creditors evinced anything like consistent attention to the personalty interests they represented.

With respect to the negative clauses—the restrictions against attacks on property by state legislatures—it was observed earlier that a fourth of the delegates had voted for just such "attacks." It is therefore not surprising to find that when the clauses forbidding paper money and establishing the sanctity of contracts came up for a vote on August 28, many of the delegates opposed the prohibition of such legislation.

The vote against paper money was overwhelming: only Virginia opposed the restriction and Maryland was divided. Of the five Virginians present, at least three must have voted against the restriction. Mason and Randolph had expressed extreme disapproval of paper on August 16, but Madison had indicated his unwillingness to have it cut off altogether. If the Virginia vote was split, then, it must have been Washington, Madison, and Blair who opposed the restriction and Mason and Randolph who favored it, though it is conceivable that the latter two may also have voted in the negative.[6] Apparently the distribution of Maryland's split vote was McHenry and Martin against the restriction, Carroll and Jenifer for it. In addition to these five (or seven) opponents of the restriction, two other delegates expressed similar sentiments: Gorham, in the debate, and Mercer, who was not present but who had declared himself "a friend of paper money" on August 16. Thus from seven to nine delegates opposed this protection of property.

There was considerably more opposition to the contract clause. Rufus King's motion that there be "a prohibition on the States to interfere in private contracts" immediately evoked a barrage of criticism. After some discussion the Convention approved a substitute motion, made by Rutledge, from which King's proposal was deliberately omitted and which provided instead only that *ex post facto* laws and bills of attainder be prohibited. The votes of individuals are indicated in the table above, as issue number 10. Though the votes of a dozen or so men are only highly probable, not certain, it appears from recorded statements and a process of elimination that no fewer than twenty-seven of the thirty-eight delegates present voted for Rutledge's motion to scrap the sanctity-of-contracts clause.[7]

[6] See the debates of August 16 and Madison's footnote thereto; a careful reading would seem to indicate that the Virginia delegation tended to split on the question in this manner.

[7] King's contract clause was restored at the very end of the Convention by the Committee on Style, and it slipped through without debate in the dying

They were Dayton, Livingston, Brearley, Madison, William-son, Blount, Spaight, Butler, Charles and Charles C. Pinckney, Rutledge, Baldwin, Few, Dickinson, Read, Bassett, Bedford, Broom, Clymer, Robert and Gouverneur Morris, Franklin, Fitzsimons, Mifflin, Ingersoll, Langdon, and Gilman.

If one adds to this list the six delegates who opposed the restriction on paper money but who favored the contract clause, it is apparent that at least thirty-three of the forty-one delegates whose attitudes are ascertainable [8] voted against one or both of the critical constitutional safeguards against attacks on property. Eighteen of the thirty-three belonged to the "Personalty Group," fifteen had realty-agrarian interests. Of the eight who voted for both restrictions, five were men having personalty interests, three had realty-agrarian interests.

There remains a fourth and final criterion of Professor Beard's proposition that the members of the Philadelphia Convention were significantly influenced in their deliberations by the personal property interests they represented. This criterion is the relation between the economic interests of the delegates and their attitudes toward the finished Constitution.

To attempt to ascertain with what measure of satisfaction each member viewed the Constitution is, unfortunately, to work with too nebulous a subject. That some of the delegates—for example, King, Wilson, and Madison—were enthusiastic about the finished product is obvious both from their utterances in the Convention and from their later conduct. That others were lukewarm toward it or even signed it against their better judgment is also obvious. Blount signed only after the style of the signatures was changed from one indicating individual approval to one merely attesting that the state delegations present unanimously approved the Constitution.[9] McHenry was "opposed to many parts of the system" but was prepared to support it

moments of the Convention. Only in this manner was it worked into the Constitution at all. Since Gouverneur Morris was the chairman of this committee, it may be a mistake to place him among those voting for Rutledge's motion.

[8] King and Gerry were momentarily out of the house when the votes came up, but they both favored both restrictions.

[9] Madison's notes, September 17.

because it was amendable. "I distrust my own judgment," he said.[10] Franklin said there were many parts he did not approve and would never approve.[11] Dayton considered the Constitution defective and derided those who thought it would be a panacea for the nation's ills.[12] Some delegates thought the Convention had gone too far; others, Hamilton among them, that it had not gone far enough. But the attitudes of too few individuals are known, and the shades of opinion are too ephemeral, to be subjected to systematic scrutiny.

Some progress in this direction can be made, however, by considering the interests of those definitely opposed to the new system. Suppose the Convention had been a ratifying convention; in that event, at least seven members would have voted against the adoption of the Constitution: Gerry, Lansing, Yates, Mercer, Luther Martin, Randolph, and Mason.

These seven men constituted almost an all-star team of personalty interests. All except Martin were members of high rank in their local aristocracies; all except Yates had very large incomes. Two of them were lawyers with large mercantile clienteles, three had large mercantile interests. Three had extensive landholdings in the west. Mason was the largest private creditor in the Convention, Gerry the largest public creditor. Five of the group were among the larger public security holders in the Convention: they held approximately a third of all the securities owned by the delegates, in terms of both market and face value, and they made more than $31,000 by the appreciation of those securities after the establishment of the new government. The market value of their securities in 1787 was sufficient to have bought the security holdings of forty-three members of the Convention—all but five—and Mason's money at interest would have bought the remainder with $5,000 to spare.

On this basis one could venture to argue, speciously, and almost make a convincing case of it, that the internal conflict in the Philadelphia Convention lay between the men of considera-

[10] McHenry's notes, September 17.
[11] Madison's notes, September 17.
[12] Dayton to Symmes, October 22, 1788, in Beverly W. Bond, ed., *The Correspondence of John Cleves Symmes* (New York, 1926), 260.

ble personalty interests, who opposed the Constitution, and men having realty-agrarian interests, a band of debtors, and a few men having modest personalty interests, who favored the Constitution.[13]

Professor Beard made no attempt at a systematic analysis of the role of economic interests inside the Philadelphia Convention. Instead, he predicted what such an analysis would show if it were made: "A thorough treatment of material forces reflected in the several clauses of the instrument of government created by the grave assembly at Philadelphia would require a rewriting of the history of the proceedings in the light of the great interests represented there."[14]

The foregoing analysis would seem to indicate that anyone wishing to rewrite the history of those proceedings largely or exclusively in terms of the economic interests represented there would find the facts to be insurmountable obstacles.

[13] Of the thirty-nine signers of the Constitution, twenty were men whose primary interests were in the form of personalty, nineteen had primarily realty-agrarian interests. If the six men in the personalty group who were debtors in a desperate plight and/or speculators in lands who suffered from the funding of the debts under the Constitution are shifted to the realty-agrarian group, the group takes on a quite different complexion. Then only fourteen of the thirty-nine signers would have belonged to the class for whose benefit, according to Professor Beard's thesis, the Constitution was written. The remaining twenty-five belonged to the group comprising farmers, men with realty interests, debtors, and immediate losers. Thus, to carry further the analogy of the Philadelphia Convention to a ratifying convention, only 36 per cent of the thirty-nine men favoring the Constitution are classifiable as members of the personalty interests group, whereas 86 per cent of those who would have voted against the Constitution are so classifiable. The seven opponents held two and a half times as much in securities (face value) per capita as the thirty-nine proto-Federalists, and their holdings of other forms of personalty were also more than twice as much per capita as those of the proto-Federalists.

[14] Beard, *Economic Interpretation*, 153.

PART THREE: RATIFICATION

V

Ratification in States Generally Favorable to the Constitution

T WO months before the Philadelphia Convention completed its work on the Constitution a movement was under way in New York to prevent its ratification. But crafty politicians inside the Convention were not to be caught napping. Conscious as they were of their role as statesmen creating a new system of government, as practical politicians they never forgot that the forthcoming struggles over ratification were to be tremendous political battles. Thus, in the Convention, even as they debated principles and haggled over details, they were writing into the Constitution the first provision in their future political strategy. This was Article VII, the process of ratification: *The ratification of the Conventions of nine States, shall be sufficient for the Establishment of this Constitution between the States so ratifying the same.* Harmless enough on its face, this provision stacked the deck in the forthcoming contest and virtually assured ratification.

This seventh article, together with the complementary resolutions sent to Congress and to the several states, reveals the nature of the contest, at least in the minds of Federalist strategists.[1] Economic interest groups and classes would view the Constitution along various lines; propagandists would claim

---

[1] It hardly needs to be repeated here that the choice of the name "Federalists" by the friends of the Constitution was in itself a bit of political strategy. The Federalists were really nationalists on the issue of ratification. The real federalists were those who preferred the confederation existing under the Articles to the general government proposed by the Constitution. Nonetheless the labels "Federalist" and "anti-Federalist" stuck, and wherever the terms are used in this work "Federalists" refers to advocates of ratification, "anti-Federalists" to opponents of ratification.

that all men of virtue were on their side, and that all their opponents were scoundrels; and theoreticians would analyze the
contest in countless ways, each partially on a sound basis. But
it was *states*, as such, which had to be won, and the design of
Article VII and the strategy of the Federalists were geared to
this fact.

The key words in Article VII are "Conventions," "nine
States," and "the States so ratifying." The decision to circumvent the state legislatures, through the medium of specially
elected ratifying conventions, was made in the realization that
ratification would be much more difficult, perhaps impossible,
if the Constitution had to overcome the machinations and pit-
falls and roadblocks to which it might be subjected in the legislatures.[2] The strategic importance of the provision that the
Constitution would become binding on the states which had
ratified, after the requisite number had so approved, is equally
clear: it would give the friends of the new system a strong
means of pressuring obstinate states into ratifying.

To put the Constitution into operation the friends of ratification had to win nine of the thirteen states; its enemies had to
win only five to prevent it. The postwar history of the states
indicates that there was more to this than meets the eye. The
states were, for all practical purposes, free, sovereign, and independent; that is, each had to solve its own problems with its
own resources. Obviously the states were not equally equipped
to do so. Some were pitifully weak, others had a measure of
strength, and some were really strong. Since it is only the dissatisfied that seek change, it was a fair assumption that states
would be inclined to come under the new roof pretty much in
direct proportion to the degree of success they had achieved as
sovereign states.

Considered in this light, the contest over ratification takes on
new meaning. Even a superficial view would seem to indicate,

---

[2] This feature had philosophical as well as practical aspects. In point of
legal theory, ratification by state legislatures would be no more binding than
any other laws and could be repealed by subsequent legislatures. Ratification
by the people of the states in conventions would create a supreme law, a fundamental constitution that would supersede all acts of legislatures.

what thorough study confirms, that five states were hopelessly unequipped to cope with their problems alone: Delaware, New Jersey, Connecticut, Georgia, and Maryland. These states could be counted on to ratify quickly and with little opposition. Of the remaining eight states, ratificationists had to win only four, their opponents five. Federalist chances of capturing the requisite four were excellent. South Carolina, though strong, had suffered wartime losses from which she had not recovered. Massachusetts, though potentially among the strongest, was rent with internal strife and was sorely pinched by postwar commercial conditions. Pennsylvania's inherent strength was dissipated in bitter factional struggles between Philadelphia and the rest of the state. New Hampshire, extremely provincial and probably able to go it alone, was likewise full of dissension. These four states could be brought to ratify, over some resistance, by high-pressure propaganda and careful political manipulation. Only New York, a budding giant, Virginia, the veritable Prussia of the Confederation, Rhode Island, whose strength belied her size, and North Carolina, an unknown quantity, remained. Each of them was using its great natural advantages to make a success of its own affairs, and each had shown a strong disposition to oppose measures designed to strengthen the Union. Once the new government was established, however, it would be difficult for even these states to remain outside.[3]

[3] There is nowhere a precise contemporary forecast of the contest along these lines. Yet valuable suggestions are contained in various sources, among others the correspondence of Madison and of Hamilton, both published and unpublished, in the Library of Congress; the David Henley Papers in the Manuscripts Division of the Library of Congress; the Knox Papers in the Historical Society of Massachusetts; and the Bryan Manuscripts in the Historical Society of Pennsylvania. Newspapers, except those of Philadelphia, New York, and the weak states, are fairly accurate barometers of public opinion on the eve of the contest. The extent of the propaganda activities carried on by the two sides is a measure of how difficult politicians considered their task to be in the several states.

In general, pre-campaign opinon may be summarized as follows. Almost everyone was agreed that in the five weaker states ratification would be achieved easily. New Hampshire was expected to ratify, albeit with some dissent, and there was genuine surprise in all camps when the state's convention postponed a decision in February, 1788. South Carolina was expected to ratify because of the special status of slaves under the Constitution and because members of the two leading families of the state's aristocracy, the Rutledges and

The primary purpose of the following analysis of the contests over ratification is to test the validity of Professor Beard's class-struggle interpretation, and the emphasis will be upon a comparison of the economic interests of the men on both sides of the issue. As proposed at the outset, the analysis will be cast in Beard's own terms, and his classifications of interest groups will be used in so far as it is possible to do so. For two reasons, however, the analysis will be divided into three parts, one for the states in which there was little opposition to ratification (Delaware, New Jersey, Georgia, Connecticut, and Maryland), one for the states that ratified with some difficulty (Pennsylvania, Massachusetts, South Carolina, and New Hampshire), and one for the states that held out until after the Constitution was in effect (Virginia, New York, North Carolina, and Rhode Island). This method has the advantage that it will result in a chronological narrative instead of a catalog, for the divisions correspond closely though not exactly to the order in which the states ratified. In addition, the method may, of itself, throw some further light on the true nature of the contest. The present chapter deals with the first group of states, those in which ratification encountered little opposition.

DELAWARE

DELAWARE was prepared to ratify the Constitution even before the document was completed. When, in June, 1787, the legislature had completed the business of its regular session, it adjourned until August 29, at which time it reconvened in special session for the express purpose of acting as quickly as possible on the recommendations of the Philadelphia Convention. The special session lasted only one day. The legislators heard the report of Richard Bassett (a member of the legislature as

the Pinckneys, had signed the document. Ratification in Massachusetts and Pennsylvania was expected to be difficult, with hair's-breadth margins deciding the issue. Virginia and New York were considered definitely disposed to reject the Constitution, and the highest powered barrages of propaganda were directed at those states. North Carolina was a mystery, but it was generally expected to follow Virginia's lead. Rhode Island, it was expected, would not ʰatify, at least at the outset.

well as of the Convention) that the Constitution would be ready in about a month, and adjourned until October. The calling of a ratifying convention was delayed because of a dispute over the riotous October elections in Sussex County, but on November 7, without a dissenting vote, the legislature provided for special elections for a ratifying convention. These elections were held three weeks later, at which time each county elected ten delegates. It appears that despite the rapidity with which these events took place, a large number of voters turned out. The ratifying convention apparently went through the formalities of organization and of reading and discussing the Constitution, then voted on the question without further ado. The vote was unanimous, 30 to 0 in favor of ratification, and on December 7 Delaware became the first state to approve the new Constitution.[4]

No one was surprised by Delaware's speed and the unanimity of the convention's delegates. The little state had had a brief taste of independence, and that was more than enough. The very attempt of the Three Lower Counties to exist as a quasi-sovereign republic was tragi-comical.

Delaware did not have the necessary physical resources and advantages, nor had it evolved far enough economically, to compensate for its limited area and population in the struggle for sovereign existence. Every strong feature was accompanied by a related weakness. In upper New Castle County it had all the requisites for an extensive milling industry except that wheat must be imported from Pennsylvania because of an insufficiency of good land in Delaware. In the central and northern parts of the state, where the soil was a rich clay, the farms were small and the land was crowded, and in the southern parts, where there was an abundance of land, it was hardly worth farming. Internal transportation was excellent; not only did the state have a fair road system but almost every farm was within

[4] *Votes and Proceedings of the House of Assembly of the Delaware State*, May, August, and October sessions, 1787 (3 vols., Wilmington, 1787–1788). No journal of the ratifying convention was printed. Delaware's resolution to ratify is in Charles C. Tansill, ed., *Documents Illustrative of the Formation of the Union* (Washington, 1927), 1009.

a dozen miles of one of its many navigable streams. What was lacking was a good port. Wilmington, which had good road connections with Chester and Lancaster counties in Pennsylvania, had an otherwise good harbor which was much too shallow for large craft. New Castle had an ample depth of water but poor tides. The upper part of the state was logically a natural appendage to Pennsylvania, from which Delaware had but recently been completely separated. The southwestern and western parts of the state were logically an appendage to the Eastern Shore of Maryland, with which many Delawareans wanted the state to become politically united.[5]

Strangely enough, the 1780's were in most respects a decade of good times in Delaware. Its commerce and industry flourished. Milling increased so rapidly after 1783 that land on creeks suitable for millsites cost more than £100 an acre. In 1786 over 20,000 barrels of superfine flour, more than double the output of a normal prewar year, was exported from Wilmington; this export alone was worth about $130,000 in Wilmington. In 1789 the Brandywine mills turned out 50,000 barrels of superfine flour, consuming as much wheat as was exported from Philadelphia in that year. Fifteen large full-time mills, owned by eleven Delawareans, produced the great bulk of this flour.[6]

Commerce increased just as rapidly. Most of Delaware's trade had always been carried on through Philadelphia, but after the war a state self-consciousness began to develop. When Pennsylvania enacted a high tariff schedule in 1785, an all-out effort was made to free Delaware trade from its dependence on Philadelphia. Wilmington and New Castle were made free ports, and Delaware merchants began to take advantage of their

---

[5] John A. Munroe, Delaware in the Revolutionary Era, 1775–1815, *passim*, typescript doctoral dissertation, 1947, in the library of the University of Pennsylvania. This work has been published in a somewhat revised form as *Federalist Delaware* (Philadelphia, 1954). Delaware and Pennsylvania had had separate legislatures since 1704, but had shared a single governor until 1776.

[6] Munroe, Delaware in the Revolutionary Era (MS.), 208; Johann D. Schoepf, *Travels in the Confederation, 1783–84* (translated from the German and edited by Alfred J. Morrison, 2 vols., Philadelphia, 1911), 1:378; William Winterbotham, *An Historical, Geographical, and Philosophical View of the United States of America, and of the European Settlements in America and the West Indies* (New York, 1796), 2:466.

geographical position. They capitalized, for example, on the fact that at Wilmington the Delaware River froze over about two weeks later and thawed about two weeks sooner than at Philadelphia. By the end of the decade, though Delaware still depended on Philadelphia for its imports from Britain, it had moved a long way toward substantial independence in its other trade. Wilmington had eleven vessels in the West Indies trade, six in trade with Ireland, and nearly twenty in the coasting trade.[7]

Farmers, though not a part of this boom, shared in its benefits. Prices of their crops were up, costs of imports were down, and import and excise duties, formerly paid by Delawareans for the benefit of the Pennsylvania treasury, were now paid only on imports from Britain. Only a few of the larger wheat farmers were really thriving, but most farmers managed to do better than break even.

Delaware's financial record, too, was relatively good. Specie taxes levied for the six years ending January, 1787, totaled $298,000, a little more than a dollar a year per capita, hardly an oppressive burden. Though all its taxes were direct property taxes—reckoned on the basis of income—the state collected 71 per cent of its specie levies, an unusually high percentage of collection for the times. Despite the relative lightness of the tax load, Delaware kept pace with its financial obligations until 1787, when it virtually suspended fiscal legislation pending the outcome of the Philadelphia Convention. It had paid, in specie, all the interest due on its major debt, the certificates issued in 1782 to compensate soldiers for depreciation of the war paper money with which they had been paid. It had retired most of its other debts, owing only a little more than $32,000, and it had paid more than 65 per cent of its congressional requisitions.[8]

[7] Munroe, Delaware in the Revolutionary Era (MS.), 237 ff. Statistics on Delaware's trade for 1789 are given in *American State Papers: Commerce*, volume 1, and Timothy Pitkin, *Statistical View of the Commerce of the United States of America* (New Haven, 1835).

[8] *Votes and Proceedings of the House of Assembly of the Delaware State* (published in Wilmington after each session, 1784–1789). See particularly the committee reports dated January 17 and February 5, 1785, January 27, 1787, January 30, 1788, and January 30, 1789. Delaware had also levied during the

Nevertheless Delaware could expect considerable financial gain from the creation of the new government. The tax load would be cut greatly, for, exclusive of sums spent for carrying on the war, more than 72 per cent of Delaware's expenditures during the above-mentioned six-year period had been made for obligations which the new Congress would now assume: interest on war debts, continental requisitions, and payment of Delaware's delegates to Congress. Almost all the state's indebtedness (except its overdue requisitions) would also be assumed by the new government. Further, since the major portion of new congressional taxation was expected to fall on imports, Delaware's share of the new taxes would be comparatively light. Finally, though the amount of continental debt owned in Delaware was small, only $45,000, the debt was widely held, and many persons would each receive a few dollars when it was funded.

Economic considerations thus may have played a part in Delaware's speedy ratification: a few would profit directly from the formation of the new government—chiefly the large commercial millers, who could expect better prices for their flour, and the few large holders of continental debt—and all citizens would get a small bonus, by way of a small tax reduction. But economic factors were obviously minor. The one overwhelming consideration was the ultimate folly of an attempt by little Delaware to exist permanently as an independent republic.

While the absence of opposition in the Delaware ratifying convention precludes comparison of the economic interests of contending groups, a brief survey of the interests of the delegates is of some worth. If, as Beard has suggested, the movement for ratification was dominated by personalty interests, opposed by farmer–debtor–paper-money groups, then one would

period a total of $60,000 of taxes payable in indents (certificates issued for interest due on continental loan office certificates), of which 63 per cent was collected. In 1787 the state levied no direct taxes, but only an excise on imported liquors and a tax on carriages. A repetition of this action in 1788 put the state in financial difficulty for a brief period.

All the above figures are converted into dollars from original figures in pounds as given in the *Votes and Proceedings:* £1 Delaware currency was worth $2 2/3 Spanish milled dollars, 7s. 6d. was worth $1.00.

expect the Delaware convention to have been dominated by the former group, and the latter to have been largely unrepresented. Actually the convention was a fair cross section of the political, social, national, and economic groups of the state, without any of Beard's "dynamic elements" which supposedly facilitated ratification.

Below are given the occupations, annual incomes, and public security holdings (face value) of the thirty men in the Delaware ratifying convention, all of whom voted in favor of adopting the Constitution.[9]

One of the delegates, Nicholas Way (New Castle County), was a physician. His annual income was $667; he owned no securities.

One of the delegates, Richard Smith (Kent County), was an associate justice of the state supreme court and a farmer. His annual salary as a judge was $187 and his annual income as a farmer was $533; he owned no securities.

Five were lawyers: Gunning Bedford, Jr., and Gunning Bedford, Sr., who had $1,493 annual income between them; Kensey Johns, who had an annual income of $3,133 (these three delegates were from New Castle County); Richard Bassett, who was also a substantial landowner, and who had an annual income of $533; and Nicholas Ridgely, who had been admitted to the bar only four months before the convention, and who had an annual income of $200 (Bassett and Ridgely were from Kent County). None of these delegates held any public securities.

The remaining twenty-three delegates were all farmers. Their names, the counties they represented, their annual incomes, their security holdings, and occasional other data follow:

John James (New Castle), a substantial landowner; annual income $1,133; owner of $401.61 in public securities.

James Latimer (New Castle), a retired judge, apparently with some milling and mercantile interests; $1,465 income; $45.84 securities.

[9] The following information is gleaned from a variety of sources. Incomes are calculated at five times the assessments for 1787–1788, as recorded in the Tax Assessment Lists in the Delaware Hall of Records at Dover. (See Chapter 3, note 72, above.) Figures in the manuscript lists are here converted from pounds and shillings into dollars and cents. Security holdings are from the Records of the Loan of 1790, vol. 919, accounts 17–20, 34–35, 68–70, 81, 151, 190, 205–209, 223–224, 228, 487–488, and 525 (Register of Public Debt Certificates, 1784–87), in the National Archives. There is no record of holders of the state debt, but all of this except $4,800 was owed to one man. See *Votes and Proceedings*, January 30, 1789. Biographical sketches and lists of lawyers and doctors are given in John Thomas Scharf's *History of Delaware*, 1:471–472, 523–538; (Philadelphia, 1888); in *Historical and Biographical Papers of the Delaware Historical Society*, particularly the first fifteen volumes or so; and in

Solomon Maxwell (New Castle), $360 income; $1,027.40 securities.

Thomas Watson (New Castle), $467 income; no securities.

James Black (New Castle), $160 income; $160.59 securities.

Thomas Duff (New Castle), landowner and justice of the peace; $267 income as a farmer, varying and unknown income as a justice of the peace; no securities.

George Truitt (Kent), $267 income; no securities.

James Sykes (Kent), a substantial landowner; $1,067 income; no securities (not to be confused with his son, James, Jr., a physician).

Daniel Cummins (Kent), $40 income; no securities.

Joseph Barker (Kent), $200 income; no securities.

George Manlove (Kent), $213 income; no securities.

Edward White (Kent), $240 income; no securities.

Allen McLane (Kent), a petty officeholder as well as a farmer; $160 income; no securities. McLane's chief interest and ambition was to hold public offices; under the Federalists he received numerous minor appointments.

Thomas Evans (Sussex), $87 income; no securities.

William Hall (Sussex), $120 income; $676.50 securities.[10]

John Ingram (Sussex), $213 income; no securities.

John Jones (Sussex), a substantial landowner; $400 income; no securities.

Israel Holland (Sussex), also a justice of the peace; $133 income as a farmer plus a varying and unknown income as a justice of the peace; no securities.

William Moore (Sussex), also a justice of the peace; $160 income as a farmer plus a varying and unknown income as a justice of the peace; no securities.

Isaac Cooper (Sussex), also a justice of the peace; $120 income as a farmer plus a varying and unknown income as a justice of the peace; no securities.

John Laws (Sussex), $333 income; no securities.

Woodman Stockley (Sussex), $40 income; no securities.

Thomas Laws (Sussex), also an undersheriff; $40 income as a farmer plus an unknown income as undersheriff; no securities.

various other secondary works. None of the men is mentioned as a merchant in the available sources: private merchants' papers, customs records of Pennsylvania, and Philadelphia and Wilmington newspapers. Men who were neither merchants, millers, doctors, nor lawyers, nor known to be practitioners of any other profession, are assumed here to have been farmers.

[10] No explanation has been found for the relatively large security holdings of Black, whose holdings equaled his annual income, or of Maxwell and Hall, whose holdings totaled three and five times their annual incomes, respectively. Either they had made some shrewd speculations—a distinct possibility, for continental securities in Delaware had sold as cheaply as eight for one at the end of the war—or they had some income which escaped the eyes of the tax assessors.

In summary, the convention was primarily one of small farmers, of whom sixteen had annual incomes between $40 and $267, six also held minor public offices, and five held public securities. One of the delegates was also a state legislator at the time, eight more had previously served in the legislature. Two of the delegates had voted for an issue of paper money in 1786, two had voted against such an issue. Only one of the delegates was a member of the Society of the Cincinnati.[11]

NEW JERSEY

NEW JERSEY put the ratification movement into high gear when, also unanimously, it approved the Constitution on December 18. In the eleven intervening days since Delaware's ratification, Pennsylvania, to be considered later, had also ratified. New Jersey was thus the last of the three states—all of them in the Delaware Valley—that ratified before the end of 1787.

The Constitution had been little discussed during the annual contests for the legislature early in October, 1787, probably because most of the campaigning had been done by the time the Constitution was completed. It is noteworthy, in view of Beard's assertion that "New Jersey was among the states which pushed through ratification of the Constitution without giving the agrarian party time to organize its forces," that twenty-five of the twenty-eight legislators from the counties that had voted for an issue of paper money in 1786 were re-elected, and that the paper-money faction retained control of both houses. Numerous petitions favoring speedy ratification were signed even before the legislature convened, and Governor William Livingston recommended that a convention be called as soon as possible. Accordingly the legislature, without a dissenting voice, called for elections of delegates on the fourth Tuesday in November

---

[11] Those voting for paper money were Moore and Holland, those against it were Bedford, Sr., and McLane; *Votes and Proceedings*, January 28, 1786. The lone member of the Society of the Cincinnati was McLane. Henry Hobart Bellas, "History of the Delaware State Society of the Cincinnati," in *Historical and Biographical Papers of the Delaware Historical Society*, vol. 13 (Wilmington, 1895).

and set the second Tuesday in December for the opening of the convention.[12]

The outcome of the elections was never in doubt. So far as known, only one pamphlet and two newspaper articles were printed on the subject; all favored ratification, indicating that there was not enough vocal opposition in New Jersey to warrant a pro-Constitution propaganda campaign. The elections were held quietly, beginning November 27, and on December 11 the delegates convened. After a week's discussion the Constitution was put to a vote and, to the surprise of no one, was unanimously approved.[13]

The reason for this prompt action is not difficult to find: like Delaware, New Jersey was hopelessly unequipped for political independence. Its motives were, if possible, even stronger than those of Delaware, for it could expect, in addition to obvious long-term gains, immediate relief from staggering burdens which it faced at the moment.[14]

New Jersey's economy was diversified and, for the most part, essentially sound. Diversified agriculture formed the basis of that economy. The climate and the limited supply of good land precluded the rise of great estates, but farmers were able to grow more than enough for their own use, and by marketing their surpluses, mainly wheat, in New York and Philadelphia they managed to be generally prosperous. Agriculture was supplemented by a multitude of manufactures. Though the indus-

[12] *Votes and Proceedings of the General Assembly of the State of New Jersey*, 12th Assembly, 1st Session, 21–24; Richard P. McCormick, *Experiment in Independence* (New Brunswick, 1950), 262–264; Beard, *Economic Interpretation*, 271.

[13] *Minutes of the Convention of the State of New Jersey, Holden at Trenton the 11th Day of December 1787* (reprint, Trenton, 1888). The newspaper articles were those by "Cassius" in the Elizabeth Town *New Jersey Journal and Political Intelligencer* of October 31, 1787, and "A Jerseyman," reprinted from the *Trenton Mercury* (no longer extant) in the *Pennsylvania Packet* of November 15, 1787.

[14] What follows, unless otherwise documented, is derived largely from McCormick's *Experiment in Independence*, particularly pages 252–279. This is the only secondary study used without reservation in the present work. After reading pertinent monographs on the states and on ratification and after giving extensive study to manuscript and printed sources for each of the thirteen states, I am of the opinion that it is the only study of the period which can be accepted virtually without qualification.

trial revolution had not yet arrived in New Jersey, there were nearly twelve hundred manufacturing establishments in the state, ranging from the eighty forges and the eight great iron furnaces to the hundreds of grist mills and sawmills which were usually operated by one to three men.[15]

New Jersey had one great weakness, however, which made all independent political action ineffective. This was its lack of a good port. Had the natural harbors of either the Hudson or the Delaware been on the Jersey side of those rivers, the state, with its central location and its good internal transportation facilities, would have been a great economic power. Instead it was dependent upon New York and Philadelphia, a barrel tapped on both ends, so to speak. In 1784 only some 350 men in the state were engaged in trade, of whom probably four-fifths were tradesmen who depended on New York and Philadelphia for their goods. Only a handful of merchants and ship-owners had vessels in direct trade with Europe, and the total number of vessels owned in the state (mostly small sloops and schooners in the coasting and the West Indies trade) only slightly exceeded 200.[16]

Toward the end of the war New Jersey's economy underwent a temporary boom which lasted until late in 1785, when it began to languish. Apparently credit had been overextended, and trade, following declines in New York and Philadelphia, sank into a torpor. The iron industry was in the doldrums, farm prices were declining, and, to add to the farmers' troubles, the Hessian fly began in 1786 to devastate his wheat fields. There was no classic crash and depression, but rather a general atrophy of the whole economy.

[15] McCormick's *Experiment in Independence,* 127–133, gives an excellent summary of manufacturing in the state. A list of all manufacturing establishments, by counties, as of November, 1784, was published in *Votes and Proceedings,* 9th Assembly, 1st Session, p. 33. A second such list, for 1789, is in *Votes and Proceedings,* 13th Assembly, 1st Session, pp. 32–33.

[16] The figures on ships, merchants, and tradesmen are from *Votes and Proceedings,* 9th Assembly, 1st Session, p. 33. New Jersey had almost no mercantile classes. Compare the above figures with those for Rhode Island, which had between three and four times as much shipping and only a third as many people—in other words, from ten to twelve times as much shipping per capita.

The heart of New Jersey's troubles was financial. The state had made a valiant effort to maintain public credit, having assumed the payment of interest on most of the nearly $2,500,000 in continental debt owned in the state, as well as its own state debt of $788,000. To do so it had levied taxes totaling $116,691 annually in addition to its levies for ordinary expenses. This sum was not in itself a staggering one, but since New Jersey was already paying heavy import duties to New York and Pennsylvania for substantially all its imports, it constituted a second tax burden. An excise tax, which was tried only once, would have placed so great a load on trade that all economic activity above the barter level would have been virtually suspended. Thus almost all taxes were direct levies on real property.

The article in the Constitution that promised relief from this burden was the one lodging in Congress the exclusive power to levy import duties. This would not only place public creditors on a sounder footing but, more important, would bring tremendous relief to New Jersey's taxpayers. This promised relief, particularly for the thousands of small farmers who were saddled with the major part of the burden, was the economic consideration that contributed most to New Jersey's overwhelming support of ratification.

A number of intangibles supplemented this important economic consideration to produce New Jersey's enthusiastic reception of the Constitution. Professor Beard's theory that the promised sanctity of contracts induced public and private creditors to support ratification may have some little validity, but it is difficult to measure, for the agrarian, paper-money faction in New Jersey was almost precisely identifiable with the public-creditor interest, both in terms of geographical location and in terms of personnel. Of more importance was the desperate fear of many old Whigs in the state that the success of the Revolution was at stake, New Jersey having failed so completely in its effort to go it alone. In them the feeling that the Constitution was the last hope of saving the Union was real and strong. Probably more important than either of these factors was New Jersey's acute consciousness of its vulnerability in war, for the state had probably suffered more than any other as a battleground of the Revolution.

Thus the movement for ratification in New Jersey was a spontaneous one springing from a wide variety of groups, a variety amply demonstrated by the economic backgrounds of the members of the ratifying convention. The convention was a fairly representative cross section of the economy of the state. The thirty-eight members of the convention are listed below with salient economic facts about each.

One member, John Neilson, was a merchant and owner of four vessels in overseas trade. He was both a debtor and a creditor, owing money to his connections abroad and being owed money in turn by his local customers. He was one of the twenty-two original New Jersey subscribers to the stock of the Society for Promotion of Useful Manufactures (S.U.M.). Apparently he held no public securities.[17]

Another member, John Stevens, Sr., was a wealthy capitalist, an investor in both real and personal property. His lands were valued at £62,500 ($166,667), and he had invested in numerous small manufacturing ventures. He had held over $20,000 in continental loan office certificates in 1784, and in December, 1787, his son owned $28,000 in final settlement notes, but by the time the debts were funded in 1790 Stevens himself owned only $1,505.94 in continental securities and no state securities.[18]

Two of the delegates were physicians: John Beatty and Eli Elmer. In 1786 Beatty held $350 in commissary certificates and by 1791 had in-

[17] McCormick, *Experiment in Independence*, 109–110 and notes.

[18] *Ibid.*, 268 and notes; Records of the Loan of 1790, vol. 597, folio 114 (Ledger of 3% stock), in the National Archives.

Records of continental debt holdings in New Jersey are incomplete, but they are adequate for determining almost all holdings at the time of the convention and at the time funding took place in 1790–1791. The Ledger of 3% Stock is the only record of the funding of continental debt, but since three per cents constituted one-third of the new certificates exchanged for old ones under the terms of the act of August 4, 1790, total holdings can be readily calculated. Certificates held in 1786 and 1787 can be almost completely determined from the Records of the Loan of 1790. Volume 595 (Register of Public Debt Certificates, 1783–86) includes the $917,000 of quartermasters' and commissaries' certificates held in the state up to 1786. Volume 594 (Register of Loan Office Certificates Presented for Interest Payment, 1786–88) records the interest paid on the $1,121,000 of loan office certificates held in the state, and principals of holdings can be calculated by multiplying interest payments by 16 2/3. Only for the soldiers' final settlement notes, which amounted to something over $400,000, is it impossible to ascertain holdings as of 1786 or 1787, and these are covered by the Ledger of 3% Stock for 1791.

Holdings of state securities can be determined only for 1791, from the record of Subscriptions toward a Loan . . . Payable in Certificates of the Debt of the State of New Jersey, in the New Jersey Historical Society.

creased his holdings of continental debt to $707. Elmer was also an erst-
while agent for John Cleves Symmes and the Miami Land Company.[19]

Three of the delegates were engaged in iron manufacturing: Thomas
Reynolds, John Jacob Faesch, and Thomas Anderson. All three also held
public securities: Reynolds, $108 in quartermaster's notes; Faesch, $6,273
in the same; and Anderson, $321 in these notes and, in 1791, $1,760 in
state securities.[20]

Two of the delegates were college presidents: Jacob Hardenbergh of
Queen's College (Rutgers) and John Witherspoon of Princeton. Neither
of them held securities or had any other significant economic interests.[21]

Four of the delegates were lawyers: Richard Howels, David Brearley,
Robert Ogden, and Frederick Frelinghuysen. Brearley was also chief
justice and Howels was soon to succeed William Houston as clerk of the
supreme court. Brearley owned $12 in continental securities in 1786, and
Frelinghuysen held $269 in that year, which he had increased to $1,008
by 1791.[22]

The remaining twenty-five delegates, as nearly as can be ascertained,
were farmers and landowners. They were neither great landowners nor
poor farmers, but most of them were men of substantial estates: John
Fell, Peter Zabriskie, Cornelius Hennion, John Chetwood, Samuel Hay,
David Crane, Benjamin Manning, Elisha Lawrence, Samuel Breese,
William Crawford, George Anderson, Joshua M. Wallace, Benjamin
Whithall, Andrew Hunter, Whitten Cripps, Edmund Wetherby, Jesse
Hand, Jeremiah Eldredge, Matthew Whilden, Joshua Corshon, William
Windes, William Woodhull, David Potter, Jonathan Bowen, and Robert
Hoops.

Fell was a retired merchant who still had some limited mercantile
connections. Hunter was a minister as well as a farmer. Corshon was
also sheriff of Hunterdon County. A handful of the farmers held small
amounts of personalty in addition to their farms. In 1791 Fell owned
three shares of stock in the Bank of New York, worth $750, and $275
in state securities. Hunter also owned state securities having a face value
of $789. Chetwood funded $84 worth of continental securities in 1791;
Crane owned $271 in continental certificates in 1786 which he had dis-
posed of by 1791; and Manning owned $210 in such securities in 1786,

[19] McCormick, *Experiment in Independence*, 268 and note; Register of Public
Debt Certificates, vol. 595, accounts 3018 and 4961, in Old Loan Records in
the National Archives.
[20] McCormick, *Experiment in Independence*, 130, 268; Records of the Loan
of 1790, vol. 595, accounts 1414–1420, 2285, 2287, 2289, 2506, and 4597 (Register
of Public Debt Certificates), in the National Archives.
[21] McCormick, *Experiment in Independence*, 268; John E. Pomfret's sketch
of Witherspoon and Oral S. Coad's sketch of Jacob Rusten Hardenbergh in the
Dictionary of American Biography.
[22] McCormick, *Experiment in Independence*, 268 and notes; Edward Q. Keas-
bey, *The Courts and Lawyers of New Jersey, 1661–1912*, vol. 2 (New York,
1912); Records of the Loan of 1790, vol. 595, account 2984, and vol. 597, folio
91, in the National Archives.

which he funded in 1791. Corshon is listed as a holder of three per cents in 1791, but the amount is not indicated in the extant sources.[23]

GEORGIA

GEORGIA continued the series of ratifications begun by the weaker states when, on January 2, 1788, it became the third state to ratify unanimously. Ratification there was an emergency measure, for even as the convention was meeting in Augusta the state militia was mustering for defense of the state against an expected attack by the Creek Indians.

From start to finish the ratification movement in Georgia was dominated by the proximity and hostility of the Indians. As late as June, 1787, politicians were hotly debating whether any further powers should be granted to Congress, but such arguments were dropped in July when the Creeks began hostilities on the frontier. In October the legislature was called into emergency session to prepare for war. The Constitution, promising national help against the Indians, was locally thought of simply as one of several measures that would provide for the defense of the state, and thus a bill calling for a ratifying convention passed without recorded debate or dissent.

Elections for the convention were held concurrently with elections for the new legislature, in the first week of December. A short-lived newspaper debate between friends and enemies of the Constitution began in mid-November, but it quickly degenerated, as did most political arguments in Georgia, into personal feuds. There was doubtless some opposition to the Constitution in the state, and had it not been for the conclusive argument that the Indians were threatening the very survival of the inhabitants, ratification would probably not have been unanimous. Election returns are available only for Chatham County (Savannah), where half again the normal number of voters turned out. Though candidates did not campaign as

[23] McCormick, *Experiment in Independence*, 268 and note; *Biographical Directory of Congress* (1927 edition), 960; Domett, *A History of the Bank of New York, 1784–1884* (New York, 1884), 134; Records of the Loan of 1790, vol. 595, accounts 2033, 2698, 3502, and vol. 597, folios 69 and 74, in the National Archives.

friends or enemies of the Constitution, the two elected delegates got twice as many votes as the losing candidate, a man of known anti-Constitution leanings. To the west, where the Indians virtually lurked in the bushes overlooking the polling places, there was almost almost no opposition. The convention met on the fourth Tuesday in December and, after a week of little more than formal proceedings, voted unanimously for ratification.[24]

Georgia had less economic motive for ratifying the Constitution than any of the other states in which ratification was achieved without serious opposition. Though the state was raw and immature, it was enjoying a tremendous boom in the 1780's, and had it not been for the Indian problem it might have been disposed to decide that it could handle its problems alone.

Georgia consisted of three distinct areas of settlement, each of which had well-defined social and economic characteristics. One of these was an area on the Atlantic coast. Socially and ethnically heterogeneous and capable of being divided, for more minute studies, into three subareas, this coastal region was populated by English Anglicans near Savannah, Scotch Presbyterians near Darien, and German Lutherans around Brunswick. But the dominance of the area's economy by rice-producing, slave-manned plantations and the resulting aristocratic social structure and outlook gave the area a large measure of unity. The state's metropolis was in this area, and most of the merchants, factors, and lawyers lived there. The second area was along the Savannah River, below the fall line at Augusta. Here two social groups

[24] Journal of the Assembly of the State of Georgia, September Session, 1787 (MS.), in the Georgia Department of Archives and History; Savannah *Gazette of the State of Georgia*, July–December, 1787. Arguments published in the *Gazette* began with a piece against the Constitution by "A Georgian" in the issue of November 15 and continued with sundry articles on November 22 and 29.

The election returns were printed on December 6. The vote for the candidates for the convention was as follows: William Stephens, 272, Joseph Habersham, 251, and Thomas Gibbons, Sr., 124. Gibbons' voting record as a legislator and his bitter article against the amendment to the Articles of Confederation that would grant Congress the power to levy an impost (*Gazette*, October 13, 1785, under the signature "T. G.") clearly mark him as an anti-nationalist. The total number of votes cast in the election was apparently 365; in ordinary elections during this period the number was usually between 250 and 275.

were dominant, transplanted New Englanders and recently arrived Scotch-Irish. Farms ranged from small establishments
without slaves to a few great plantations, but most of the population consisted of small slave-owning farmers who aspired to
become great tobacco planters. Though almost a postwar settlement, the area was already producing tobacco worth nearly as
much as the rice crop of the coast. The third area was the upper
Savannah and Piedmont frontier region, a wild, as yet largely
subsistence-farming area which was teeming with new settlers.
Lumber and skins, both harvested in the process of clearing new
land, were the only marketable commodities produced in the
area.[25]

The state enjoyed an astonishing boom during the postwar
decade. Its population doubled in the eight years after 1782, the
frontier area alone growing from about 15,000 to more than
42,000 inhabitants during this period. Exports from Savannah
increased from an average of about £75,000 in the five years
before the war to more than £150,000 sterling ($666,667) in
1789. Additional products amounting to about £35,000 a year
were carried overland for export from Charleston. The greatest
increase in production was in tobacco, which, though hardly
cultivated at all until after the war, amounted by 1789 to more
than £40,000 ($167,778) annually. Maritime activity increased
even more rapidly. In 1784, the first full year of peace, 144
vessels measuring about 8,700 tons cleared from Savannah; three
years later 354 vessels measuring about 24,000 tons cleared the
port. At the beginning of the period almost all the state's trade
was carried in bottoms belonging to Britain or the British West
Indies; at the end of the decade more than a third of it—a greater
tonnage than the total at the beginning—was carried in Georgia-

[25] Information for this sketch has been assembled from a variety of sources.
Distribution of population is derived from Stella M. Sutherland's *Population
Distribution in Colonial America* (New York, 1936); distribution of property
is compiled from the manuscript Tax Digests, by counties, in the Georgia Department of Archives and History; religious data are from the maps showing
distribution of religions in 1776 in Charles O. Paullin's *Atlas of the Historical
Geography of the United States*, edited by John K. Wright (Washington,
1932); miscellaneous additional data are derived from the *Gazette* and elsewhere.

owned bottoms. In virtually every respect Georgia's economy during the period was marked by uninterrupted expansion and prosperity.[26]

Nor were Georgia's finances, though often confused and disorderly, a source of fundamental difficulty during the period. A large amount of confiscated loyalist property was sufficient to retire the state's war debts, and through an ingenious plan adopted in 1782 a war debt of more than a million dollars was funded while taxes were kept at a minimum. The confiscated property, approximately equal to the state debt, was sold on an installment plan, purchasers paying seven per cent interest. The state debt was then funded at six per cent interest. The one per cent surplus income was applied to the state's civil expenses. Despite confusion in administration and occasional embezzlement of funds, the system worked, and the legislature was able to meet the state's obligations while levying direct taxes amounting to only about £5,000 a year and collecting nominal import duties of about the same amount. In 1786 a paper-money issue of £50,000 was authorized to finance the Indian war that was expected, but the war did not immediately materialize and less than £20,000 was actually issued. This circulated at about par until the time when it was called in and destroyed. Only in answering requisitions of Congress was Georgia lax, but no one in Georgia was particularly concerned about such laxity until the Indian uprisings began in 1787. Public creditors in the state were apparently kept satisfied, for they published no propaganda

[26] Prewar commercial figures are from Samuel Hazard, ed., *United States Commercial & Statistical Register*, vol. 1, no. 1, pp. 4–5 (Philadelphia, 1839); figures for 1789 are from *American State Papers: Commerce*, 1:157–172; ship movements are tabulated from entrances and clearances recorded in the *Gazette* from 1783 to 1789. Tonnage has been estimated by multiplying the number of vessels of each kind of rigging which entered and cleared at Savannah by the average size of vessels of each kind of rigging which entered and cleared at Charleston, as recorded in the Manifests of Export Cargoes, in the South Carolina Historical Commission at Columbia. A good description of the state's trade, particularly its internal navigation, may be seen in the Philadelphia *Pennsylvania Evening Herald* of May 17, 1786. The overland trade from Augusta to Charleston is described in the *Gazette* of November 27, 1783, and January 20, 1784. Population figures are from Sutherland, *Population Distribution*, Evarts B. Greene and Virginia D. Harrington, *American Population before the Federal Census of 1790* (New York, 1932), and the *Census of 1790*.

in the newspapers and they presented no petitions to the Assembly.[27]

It is impossible to compile complete economic biographies of the members of the Georgia ratifying convention because the records for individual Georgians collected for the Census of 1790, from which slaveholdings could have been ascertained, are no longer extant. But enough data are available to permit compilation of the occupations and personal property holdings of most of the men. These data show that as a group these men had almost none of the personal property interests which Beard says were the dynamic elements in the ratification:

Two of the delegates were physicians: Nathan Brownson (Effingham County) and James Powell (Liberty County). Brownson owned a small plantation in Liberty County and 3,825 acres of unoccupied land in Washington County. He had been governor in 1781–1782. Powell owned 575 acres of Washington County land which he had purchased from the state in 1784 for three shillings an acre.[28]

Two of the delegates were lawyers: William Few and William Stephens (Chatham County). Few, whose interests have been sketched earlier,[29] was the only security holder in the convention. Stephens, who also dealt in real estate, owned $600 in Savannah town lots, and had purchased for £100 a confiscated estate in Richmond County.[30]

Three of the delegates were merchants: Edward Telfair (Burke County), John Wereat (Richmond County), and Robert Middleton (Greene County). Telfair owned upwards of $22,000 in Savannah mercantile property in 1793, and 1,000 acres of Washington County land, and he had purchased confiscated town property in Augusta for £750. He had been governor in 1786, and was to serve in this capacity again from 1789 to

---

[27] The funding act of 1783 is printed in Allan D. Candler, ed., *Colonial Records of the State of Georgia* (25 vols., Atlanta, 1904–1915), vol. 19, part 2. The best accounts of the operation of the system are the annual reports of the Finance Committee of the Assembly, in Journals of the General Assembly, July 21, 1783, January 26, February 14, 1784, January 12, 1785, February 7, 1786, January 20, 1787, and January 29, 1788, in the Georgia Department of Archives and History.

[28] Orders for Certificates of Land Issued in 1781–83, p. 18; List of Persons Petitioning for Land in 1784, p. 25; Nathan Brownson File; all three manuscripts in Georgia Department of Archives and History. For a sketch of Brownson see the *Biographical Directory of Congress* (1927 edition), 750.

[29] Above, pp. 83–84.

[30] Above, pp. 83–84; Sale-book of Confiscated Estates, 1782–85; Sale in Augusta, September 13–14, 1785, p. 3; Tax Digest, Chatham County, 1793; William Stephens File; all three manuscripts in the Georgia Department of Archives and History; *Gazette*, March 13, 1783.

1793. He was trained as a lawyer but did not practice.[31] Wereat sold his prewar holdings of wharves, sawmills, and lots in Savannah to practice law and engage in minor mercantile activity in Augusta after the war. His private affairs were much neglected during the years 1783–1793, while he held the powerful office of state auditor. He also owned £905 in confiscated Savannah town property and 575 acres of vacant land in Washington County. He served as the state's chief executive in 1778–1779.[32] Middleton had sold his mercantile business in 1783 to move to the frontier. There he took up 862½ acres of land and engaged in farming and occasional trading. He later acquired more than 60,000 acres of western lands, title to which was examined and cleared when the Yazoo frauds were being investigated.[33]

One of the delegates was a full-time officeholder: Henry Osborne (Camden), the state commissioner of Indian affairs. Osborne became a Superior Court judge in 1790 and was impeached a year later for election frauds.[34]

Ten of the men were planters: Thomas Daniell (Greene), Colonel Jenkin Davis (Effingham), Joseph Habersham (Chatham), Captain George Handley (Glynn), Christopher Hillary (Glynn), Jared Irwin (Washington), George Mathews (Wilkes), John Elliott (Liberty), John Milton (Glynn), and Jacob Weed (Camden). Daniell settled on the frontier in 1784, bringing his six children and 17 slaves from South Carolina. He took up 1,000 acres of land in Washington County.[35] Davis owned 2,050 acres of vacant land and a plantation in Effingham County.[36] Habersham was the owner of a 281-acre rice plantation, various smaller plots, 67 slaves, and 1,000 acres of western land.[37] Handley had been

[31] Tax Digests, Chatham County, 1793, p. 55; Land Grants, 1784, Washington and Franklin Counties (hereafter cited as Washington and Franklin Land Grants), 232; Book of Bonds, Bills of Sale, Deeds of Gift, and Powers of Attorney, 1783–1792, pp. 191–192; Sale-book of Confiscated Estates, 1782–85: Richmond County, 2; all four manuscripts in the Georgia Department of Archives and History; E. M. Coulter, "Edward Telfair," in the *Georgia Historical Quarterly*, 20:99–124 (June, 1936).

[32] Sale-book of Confiscated Estates, 1782–85: Chatham County, 9; Washington and Franklin Land Grants, 259; both manuscripts in the Georgia Department of Archives and History; Mary Granger, ed., *Savannah River Plantations* (Savannah, 1947), 405.

[33] List of Persons Petitioning for Land Grants in 1784, p. 12; House Journal, 1797, p. 342; both manuscripts in the Georgia Department of Archives and History; *Gazette*, August 28, 1783.

[34] Henry Osborne File, in the Georgia Department of Archives and History.

[35] Thomas Daniell File; Washington and Franklin Land Grants, 52, 287; both in the Georgia Department of Archives and History.

[36] Jenkin Davis File; Washington and Franklin Land Grants, 52, 287; both in the Georgia Department of Archives and History.

[37] Tax Digest, Chatham County, 1793, p. 27; Washington and Franklin Land Grants, 107; both manuscripts in the Georgia Department of Archives and History; printed return of Little Ogechee District, in the *Gazette* of September 20, 1787.

granted a 750-acre estate in Glynn County for his war services and bought two confiscated plantations costing £3,737 10s. He also owned 1,670 acres of western land. Handley became governor of Georgia in 1788.[38] Hillary was the purchaser of extensive confiscated property. He had bought seven confiscated plantations totaling 2,000 acres and four confiscated slaves, the total sale price of which was £2,170. He also owned 560 acres of western land.[39] Irwin had left his plantation in Burke County in 1784 to become a pioneer planter on the frontier. He owned a confiscated plantation in Burke and 2,287½ acres in Washington County. He later became governor, and during his tenure he signed the Rescinding Act erasing the Yazoo frauds from the statute books.[40] Mathews was another back-country planter and was the governor of the state. His plantation in Wilkes County consisted of 400 acres.[41] Of the property of Elliott, Milton, and Weed no information was found except that they were planters. Milton was Georgia's secretary of state from 1777 to 1799.[42]

Three of the delegates were small farmers: John King (Wilkes), James McNeil (Richmond), and John Rutherford (Washington). King's 250-acre farm was a bounty received for his service as a private during the war. He purchased another 400 acres from the state in 1784.[43] McNeil owned 600 acres of new land, most of which was not yet under cultivation.[44] Rutherford owned a 450-acre farm which he had received as a bounty for war service. In 1783 and 1784 he also acquired 1,300 additional acres of vacant land for £195, for which he was still indebted to the state.[45]

[38] George Handley File; Sale-book of Confisficated Estates, 180, and Sale of September 13–14 in Augusta, 6; Washington and Franklin Land Grants, 118; all in the Georgia Department of Archives and History.

[39] Book of Bonds, 1783–1792, pp. 169–170; Sale-book of Confiscated Estates, 185, Effingham County, 5, Burke County, 3, Glynn and Camden Counties, 2; Washington and Franklin Land Grants, 270; Orders for Certificates of Land Issued in 1781–83, p. 7; all in the Georgia Department of Archives and History.

[40] Jared Irwin File; Sale-book of Confiscated Estates: Burke County, 4; Washington and Franklin Land Grants, 124, 128; all in the Georgia Department of Archives and History.

[41] Land Grants, Wilkes County, 1784, p. 21, in the Georgia Department of Archives and History; *Biographical Directory of Congress* (1927 edition), 1298.

[42] Miscellaneous information has been derived from a variety of sources, including the John Elliott File in the Georgia Department of Archives and History and occasional references to the men in the *Gazette* and in various correspondence files. Milton was secretary of the Georgia chapter of the Society of the Cincinnati.

[43] John King File; Land Grants, Wilkes County, 15; both in the Georgia Department of Archives and History. There were five John Kings in the state at the time, one of whom, apparently not the ratifier, purchased a confiscated estate for ninety pounds.

[44] James McNeil File; Land Grants, Wilkes County, 4; both in the Georgia Department of Archives and History.

[45] List of Persons Petitioning for Land in 1784, p. 28; Land Grants, Wilkes County, 59; Washington and Franklin Land Grants, 200; all in the Georgia Department of Archives and History.

Three of the delegates were frontiersmen who earned their livings by acting as occasional Indian agents, doing some trapping, and hunting for their provisions. These were James Maxwell (Liberty), James Seagrove (Camden), and Florence Sullivan (Wilkes).[46]

No data were found for two of the delegates, Robert Christmas (Greene) and Henry Todd (Burke).

William Few, with only a nominal holding, was the only owner of public securities in the convention. Four of the members—Handley, Hillary, Mathews, and Milton—were members of the Society of the Cincinnati. Three, Elliott, Maxwell, and Powell, had voted against the paper-money issues of 1786, and three others, King, McNeil, and Osborne, had voted for that issue. Six of the members had been or were to become governors—Wereat, Brownson, Telfair, Handley, Irwin, and Mathews.[47]

CONNECTICUT

ON JANUARY 4, 1788, Connecticut became the fourth state to accept the Constitution without serious battle. Unlike the other three, however, it did not achieve ratification without eliciting some real opposition. The vote in the ratifying convention was 128 to 40. Superficially it would seem to be this overwhelming majority that needs to be explained, but actually it is the opposition that requires explanation.

The campaign for ratification in Connecticut had begun in August with three kinds of newspaper propaganda. The first to appear was standard Federalist propaganda eulogizing the members of the Philadelphia Convention and exploiting the popularity of George Washington and Benjamin Franklin. Then a rumor was circulated that a movement to establish an American monarchy was gaining widespread strength, and that only the Philadelphia Convention could head it off. Finally, a series of personal attacks was launched against the potential leaders of the opposition in the state. The campaign, a classic instance

[46] James Maxwell, James Seagrove, and Florence Sullivan files, in the Georgia Department of Archives and History.

[47] *Gazette,* October 21, 1784, February 15, 1787; Journal of the General Assembly, August 4, 10, 1786, in the Georgia Department of Archives and History.

of the use of high-pressure propaganda, was executed with masterly precision and not without some rather sordid techniques. Whether the campaign was really necessary is open to question. True, the ratificationists were never completely sure of victory until after the ratifying convention met, and hence they preferred, to use a twentieth-century political term, to run scared. But by November, 1787, when the legislature announced the call for a ratifying convention, it was obvious that there was almost no opposition to the Constitution.[48]

Late in December special town meetings were held for the election of delegates. Unfortunately there is no way of arriving at even a loose estimate of the popular vote on the Constitution, since most delegates, strangely enough, were elected without instructions. Apparently the special meetings were for the most part orderly and well attended. The ratifying convention itself met at Hartford at the end of December. There was some suspense as the convention opened, since no one could be sure where the sympathies of individual delegates lay, but it proved to be a particularly colorless convention, lacking the chicanery and parliamentary jockeying that often characterized meetings of deliberative bodies in Connecticut. Oliver Ellsworth made long and able speeches on behalf of ratification, but the most significant speeches were the brief ones of the erstwhile antinationalist leaders of the state. The drama of the convention came in the first few days as, one by one, these leaders made

---

[48] The campaign may be traced in the Hartford *Connecticut Courant and Weekly Intelligencer*, the New London *Connecticut Gazette and Universal Intelligencer*, the Middletown *Middlesex Gazette*, and the New Haven *Connecticut Journal*.

The propaganda campaign in Connecticut is worthy of study by anyone who would understand the subsequent nationwide campaign, for Connecticut served as something of a testing ground for Federalist propaganda. That this is so, and that it is one of the reasons for the intense campaign in Connecticut, cannot be doubted by anyone who will read the extant newspapers of each of the various states for the period 1787–1789, in the order in which the states ratified. Another reason for the intensity of the campaign was the peculiar political situation in Conecticut. Though the people of the state were enthusiastically in favor of ratification, it may have been in the power of two men, Joseph Hopkins and William Williams, to have blocked ratification in the convention. Personal enmity between the Connecticut Federalist leaders and these two men prevented the Federalists from approaching them directly, hence the circuitous popular campaign.

their positions known. Almost all had reservations, but almost all announced that they favored ratification. On January 4 the question was put to a formal vote, which stood more than three to one in favor of unconditional ratification.[49]

The economic background of Connecticut's nationalism and its enthusiastic support of the Constitution are not difficult to assess. The state was in an economic trap, occasioned largely by its quasi-sovereign status; only through a change in that status could it escape from the trap.[50]

Since before the war Connecticut had lacked sufficient good farmland to support its inhabitants. With a rapidly increasing population and a virtually static farm output, it was greatly overpopulated by the mid-eighties, despite the great exodus to Vermont and the west. The state, having an abundance of skilled and semi-skilled labor, of small, convenient water powers, and of potential surplus capital in the form of continental and state debt owned by a multitude of Connecticut citizens, was ripe for manufacturing. The logical policy for it to follow was 1) to promote manufacturing through bounties, protective duties, and the various other mercantilist devices and 2) to release its potential capital for investment by funding both forms of debt.

But at the moment Connecticut's principal staple was livestock, especially horses, and the vessels of its large mercantile fleet had been designed especially for transporting animals to the West Indies. They were not entirely suitable for transport-

[49] Debates in the convention are reported in Elliott's *Debates*. The formal proceedings were reported in the various local newspapers. An account which is valuable for its factual details, but which misses the drama of the convention because of lack of understanding of the general history of Connecticut during the postwar decade, is Bernard C. Steiner's "Connecticut's Ratification of the Federal Constitution," in the *Proceedings of the American Antiquarian Society*, 25:70–127 (1915).

[50] The following analysis is based upon study of various manuscripts in the Connecticut Archives at Hartford, particularly vol. 5, "Finance and Currency," and vol. 2, "Industry"; the New Haven Port Records in the Fiscal Section of the National Archives; the invaluable pamphlet series *Tercentenary Publications in the History of Connecticut* (published by the Connecticut Tercentenary Commission, 1936); the various contemporary newspapers; and numerous state and local histories, particularly such antiquarian works as, for example, William C. Fowler, *History of Durham, Connecticut* (Hartford, 1866) and John L. Rockey, ed., *History of New Haven County* (2 vols., New York, 1892).

ing other staples, either on coasting or on transoceanic voyages, and the state's economy operated on too slim a margin to permit building a new fleet for any risky ventures. Hence Connecticut had no substantial share of the carrying trade and was dependent upon New York for its foreign imports. This dependence upon New York meant that it was not in a position to regulate its own commerce. The profits exacted by New York merchants and the New York state impost made the levy of further duties by Connecticut impracticable. Even had such protective duties been levied, the proximity of Long Island and Rhode Island made smuggling too easy to resist.

This inability to control its commerce vitiated the quasi-mercantilist legislative program that had been enacted in Connecticut between 1784 and 1786. Unable to levy duties on imports successfully, the state was without an adequate source of revenue for the discharge of its debts and the transformation of potential capital in the form of public securities into real capital. It attempted to levy both excise and direct taxes, but the excises were an oppressive, uncollectible second burden on vital consumer goods, and direct taxes were more than the poor and unproductive land could bear. Thus the state's fiscal policy aggravated rather than alleviated its problems, and the economy suffered a sort of creeping paralysis.

A single example will suffice to illustrate the problem. Jeremiah Wadsworth of Hartford owned more land and more commercial and manufacturing property than any other man in the state, and he held many thousands of dollars in public securities. Yet in 1785 and again in 1787 parcels of his real property were sold at public auction—along with that of hundreds of others—because of nonpayment of taxes! In short, he was losing part of his landed property to the state because of his inability to pay the taxes it levied for the purpose of paying the interest due him on another kind of property. Wadsworth's was a fantastic situation, but it was a common one in Connecticut.[51]

The new Constitution would be a magic wand to Connecti-

[51] *Connecticut Courant*, public notices of October 24, 1785, and January 8, 1787.

cut. The import duties heretofore collected in New York for the exclusive benefit of that state, as well as duties collected in other entrepôts, would, under the Constitution, be collected by the new general government for the benefit of all the states. With the income from these duties the new government would assume and fund both continental and state debts. By thus relieving Connecticut of its principal financial burden, it would virtually obviate the need for state taxes, and by funding the debt it would transform public securities into a surplus of fluid capital. The public securities owned in Connecticut were worth, in terms of 1787 prices, about $650,000; by 1791 this same paper was worth more than $1,850,000—a net gain in liquid capital of more than $1,200,000.[52] This princely sum was to liberate the state's commerce and form the basis of insurance companies, banks, and other pure capital operations as well as make possible the development of capitalistic manufacturing. The Constitution would change Connecticut from one of the poorest of the "have-not" states into one of the richest of the "haves." Small wonder that most people in the state favored ratification.

To understand the motives of those who opposed the Constitution is more difficult. It would seem that potentially there were some elements of a class struggle in the Connecticut contest, but it did not materialize. Ratification was favored not only by most of the merchants and professional men, but by most of the poor farmers, debt-ridden or not. A number of the opponents were from extremely poor towns, but the majority of the poorer towns favored ratification, and in any event much of the opposition was centered in New Haven County, a commercial area. Thus while there were some potentialities for a conflict along the economic class lines suggested by Beard, such an interpretation is insufficient to explain more than a handful of votes.

[52] The state debts assumed had a face value of $1,600,000, and continental debts owned and funded in Connecticut amounted to $1,049,251.89 face value. Summary Volume 174A, in the Records of the Loan of 1790, in the National Archives. Values in 1787 are estimated on the basis of prices quoted in New York and Boston newspapers. Prices of securities were quoted in almost all newspapers in 1791; some figures are given in *American State Papers: Finance*, vol. 1, *passim*.

Another and more important factor had its roots in the post-war political history of the state.[53] In 1783–1784 Connecticut had reacted vehemently against the impost and other amendments to the Articles of Confederation that were proposed to enable Congress to fund the war debts. The philosophical basis for this opposition was the connection of the amendments with the so-called commutation plan, whereby officers of the continental army were to be retired with five years' full pay as a bonus. Almost simultaneously the Society of the Cincinnati was organized, and the three movements were considered one by many citizens of Connecticut. Connecticut's deep-seated fear of an aristocracy and its anti-militaristic traditions prompted vigorous opposition to the proposed amendments. The leadership of the opposition in the state, however, was comprised of a large group of state creditors, who were reluctant to surrender the impost to Congress because it would deprive the state of what was expected to be an easy source of revenue, and would thus favor continental creditors at their expense. Connecticut's later commercial and tax plight was not yet foreseen, 1783 and 1784 having been years of optimism.

The impost-commutation-Cincinnati issue soon died, but the group of anti-nationalists who had gathered about the state creditors expanded in three years into a powerful faction or, more correctly, a coalition of factions. In 1786 these factions were brought closer together by another conflict with continental creditors over the issue whether both forms of debt or only the state debt should be accepted in payment for Connecticut's western reserve lands. They were by degrees maturing into something like a political party, held together by a complex of personal, social, and purely political as well as immediate economic ties.

The group was led by three men, each of whom was a

[53] The succession of events narrated here has been traced in the extant Connecticut newspapers for the years 1783 to 1787, particularly in the semi-official accounts of the proceedings of the legislature. The meaning of events there related, however, cannot be understood unless the conduct of participants is correlated with their state and continental security holdings, as recorded in the Records of the Loan of 1790, in the National Archives.

state creditor having the support of a special group: William
Williams, Joseph Hopkins, and General James Wadsworth.
Williams, signer of the Declaration of Independence, was, like
the majority of his following, philosophically an Old Whig and
an advocate of state sovereignty. Hopkins headed the groups
primarily concerned with their state security holdings, though
Hopkins himself disposed of his securities before the Loan of
1790 was effected. General Wadsworth had acquired a powerful and lucrative office, that of comptroller of the finances. His
following, outside of his home town and adjacent areas in New
Haven County, consisted largely of veterans and others who
might be called a patronage faction, or a proto-officeholding
class.

Williams was intelligent enough to realize that Connecticut's
identity as a state could be preserved only by radical changes
in the federal system. Hopkins saw clearly that the new general
government could take care of state as well as continental creditors. Both of them had been badly frightened by Shays' Rebellion. Consequently both supported the Constitution and led
their followers with them. Wadsworth's group, however, failed
to see that the Constitution would bring any particular gains;
indeed, they faced the prospect that their offices would be reduced in number, prestige, and remuneration. These Wads-
worthians therefore opposed ratification and became the nu-
cleus of the forty anti-Federalists in the convention.

Extant records do not enable one to determine the precise
occupations and property holdings of all members of the Connecticut ratifying convention, but reasonably accurate descrip-
tions of most of the members can be compiled from the data
available.

The economic interests of those favoring ratification are
given below. The figures in parentheses represent the face value
of the public security holdings of the delegates. The letter *S*
designates state securities, the letter *C* continental securities,
both as funded under the Loan of 1790. *Old C* indicates ownership in 1783–1784 of continentals which were disposed of by

1791. Holdings are rounded off to the nearest dollar and are calculated on the basis of the fact that six per cents represented four-ninths of funded securities. The names of those who had owned property that had been sold for taxes are followed by the letters *P-T* in parentheses.

The economic interests of three of the delegates voting for ratification—Ellsworth, Sherman, and Johnson—have already been outlined. Of the remaining 125 so voting,

Twenty-nine of the delegates were lawyers. Little is ascertainable about the nature of their practices, but the following facts are available:

Two no longer practiced, being retired or semi-retired: Oliver Wolcott ($261 S) and Matthew Griswold ($51 C) (*P-T*).[54] Five were not practicing in 1787 because they were serving as judges of high state courts: Eliphalet Dyer of Windham ($616 C), Joseph Hopkins of Waterbury, Richard Law of New London ($153 S, $3,913 C), Daniel Sherman of Woodbury, and Jedadiah Strong of Litchfield.[55] One, Jesse Root of Hartford, was not engaged in private practice in 1787 because he was state's attorney for Hartford County.[56] Two were only part-time lawyers, deriving the greater part of their incomes from manufacturing ventures: Jedadiah Elderkin of Windham, owner of a powder mill, and John Phelps of Stafford ($2,700 C) (*P-T*), owner of an iron works.[57] Nine, judging from their locations and occasional hints in biographical sketches, were "country lawyers": Aaron Austin of New Hartford, Daniel Nathaniel Brinsmade of Washington, Daniel Everitt of New Milford, Samuel Beach of Cheshire, John Chandler of Newton, Moses Cleaveland of Canterbury ($2,052 S, $36 *Old* C), Jabez Fitch of Canterbury, Ephraim Root of Coventry ($7 *Old* C), and William Williams ($2,493 S) of Lebanon;

[54] William A. Robinson's sketch of Matthew Griswold and Stanley M. Pargellis' sketch of Oliver Wolcott in the *Dictionary of American Biography; Biographical Directory of Congress* (1927 edition), 1037, 1722; and sketches of both men in innumerable local histories; Records of the Loan of 1790, vol. 495, folio 70, and vol. 498, folio 193, in the National Archives.

[55] Richard M. Bayles, *History of Windham County* (New York, 1889), 140; *Biographical Directory of Congress* (1927 edition), 936, 1208, 1581; Rockey, *History of New Haven County*, 2:634; Dwight C. Kilbourn, *The Bench and Bar of Litchfield County, Conn., 1709-1909* (Litchfield, 1909), 142, 288. Judicial appointments have been traced in Leonard W. Labaree, ed., *Records of the State of Connecticut* (Hartford, 1945); see the index. Data on securities are from the Records of the Loan of 1790, vol. 495, folio 103, and vol. 498, folios 5 and 73.

[56] *Biographical Directory of Congress* (1927 edition), 1478; Dwight Loomis and J. Gilbert Calhoun, *The Judicial and Civil History of Connecticut* (Boston, 1895), 177.

[57] Loomis and Calhoun, *Judicial and Civil History of Connecticut*, 161; Labaree, ed., *Records of Connecticut*, 6:461; *Connecticut Courant*, September 17, 1787, January 21, October 6, 1788.

all but Austin, Cleaveland, and Williams were justices of the peace.[58]
Ten, judging from their places of residence and from hints in biographical
sketches, were lawyers with mercantile and maritime clienteles: Gideon
Buckingham of Milford, John Davenport of Stamford ($15,835 *S*,
$2,783 *C*), Pierrepont Edwards of New Haven, Samuel Huntington of
Norwich ($300 *C*), John Treadwell of Farmington ($1,741 *S*), Stephen
Mix Mitchell of Weathersfield ($4,000 *S*, $1,615 *C*) (*P-T*), Samuel H.
Parsons of Middletown ($25 *Old C*), Jonathan Sturges of Fairfield
($189 *S*), William Judd of Farmington ($2,241 *C*), and Asher Miller of
Middletown.[59]

Three of the delegates were judges of courts of record who apparently
had no legal training: Dyer Throop of East Haddam ($2 *Old C*), Erastus
Wolcott of East Windsor ($1,825 *S*, $104 *C*), and James Davenport of
Stamford ($18,972 *S*, $1,037 *C*).[60]

Ten were merchants directly engaged in interstate and foreign commerce: Thaddeus Burr of Fairfield ($3,854 *S*, $2,761 *C*), Hezekiah Fitch
of Salisbury, Jeremiah Halsey of Preston, Amasa Learned of New London,
Jedadiah Huntington of Norwich ($294 *Old C*, $6 *C*), Joseph Woodbridge of Groton, who owned three brigs and two sloops measuring a

---

[58] Kilbourn, *Bench and Bar of Litchfield County*, 41–42, 142–143, 231;
Rockey, *New Haven County*, 1:667; Jane Eliza Johnson, *Newton's History
and Historian, Ezra Levan Johnson* (Newton, 1917), 142; Bayles, *History of
Windham County*, 139. Sketches of Williams are numerous; see, for example,
Edward E. Curtis's sketch in the *Dictionary of American Biography*, Sanderson's *Biographies of the Signers*, 2:81–93, and the *Biographical Directory of
Congress* (1927 edition), 1708. Data on securities are from Records of the
Loan of 1790, vol. 491, folios 709 and 963; vol. 495, folios 106 and 107; vol. 498,
folio 127. I found no biographical sketches of Cleaveland and Root; in their
security accounts they are described as "Attorneys at Law." Justiceships of the
peace are recorded in Labaree, ed., *Records of Connecticut*, vol. 6; see the
index.

[59] Rockey, *New Haven County*, 2:244; *Biographical Directory of Congress*
(1927 edition), 881, 936, 1133, 1321, 1626; Loomis and Calhoun, *Judicial and
Civil History of Connecticut*, 160, 200; *History of Middlesex County* (published anonymously, New York, 1884), 32. No biographical sketch of Judd is
available, but some of his activities are recorded in the *Connecticut Courant* of
May 1, 1786, and April 7, 1788; he is described as an "Attorney at Law" in his
securities account. Data on securities are from Records of the Loan of 1790,
vol. 491, folio 135; vol. 495, folios 31, 43, 47, 64; vol. 498, folios 6, 94, 135, 150.
Parsons, who bought 24,000 acres of Western Reserve land in 1788, became an
extensive operator in Ohio lands and died bankrupt as a result of the appreciation of securities. See Labaree, ed., *Records of Connecticut*, 238n, and Archie
B. Hulbert, ed., *The Records of the Original Proceedings of the Ohio Company* (2 vols., Marietta, 1917); see the index.

[60] *History of Middlesex County*, 321; Henry R. Stiles, *The History and
Genealogies of Ancient Windsor, Connecticut* (2 vols., Hartford, 1892), 2:816;
Biographical Directory of Congress (1927 edition), 1722. Data on securities are
from the Records of the Loan of 1790, vol. 491, folio 933; vol. 495, folios 11,
57; vol. 498, folios 10 and 72. Judgeships are recorded in Labaree, ed., *Records
of Connecticut*, vol. 6 (see the index) and in the above sketches.

total of 615 tons, John Watson of East Windsor ($1,352 S, $936 C), Roger Newberry of Windsor ($394 S, $160 C) (P-T), William Hart of Saybrook ($6,772 S, $18,484 C), who owned several vessels operating in the livestock trade with the West Indies, and the renowned Jeremiah Wadsworth of Hartford ($17,676 S, $3,807 C) (P-T), a merchant, former president of the Bank of New York, shipowner, manufacturer, and financier.[61]

Three of the delegates were tradesmen (country storekeepers): Samuel Canfield of New Milford ($1,116 C), Wheeler Coit of Preston ($1,219 S, $9,000 C), and Isaac Huntington of Bozrah.[62]

Five were physicians: Hezekiah Brainerd of Haddam ($1,561 S, $3,176 C), Charles Phelps of Stonington ($1,865 C), Samuel Orton of Woodbury, Jeremiah West of Tolland, and Joshua Porter of Salisbury.[63]

Two were ministers: Robert Robbins of Colchester and Andrew Lee of Farmington.[64]

Two were tavernkeepers: Asa Barnes of Southington (P-T) and Epaphras Sheldon of Torrington.[65]

Of the remaining seventy-four delegates, all or virtually all, as nearly as can be ascertained, were farmers. Most of them can be identified as farmers from a multitude of sources more varied than those cited for

[61] Cornelia P. Lathrop, *Black Rock, Seaport of Fairfield, Connecticut, 1644–1870* (New Haven, 1930), 8–9, 165–166; Louis F. Middlebrook, *History of Maritime Connecticut during the American Revolution, 1775–1783*, 2:66, 109, 134 (Salem, 1925); *Connecticut Gazette*, May 21, 1784, April 6, 1789; Groton Rate Lists, 1783–84, in the Connecticut Archives, Hartford; Stiles, *Ancient Windsor*, 2:520, 777; *Connecticut Courant*, January 4, 1785, November 27, 1786, November 12, 1787; *History of Middlesex County*, 486; Edward E. Curtis' sketch of Wadsworth in the *Dictionary of American Biography*; *Biographical Directory of Congress* (1927 edition), 1654, and sketches of Wadsworth in many local histories. The richest source on Wadsworth is the collection of Wadsworth Papers in the Connecticut Historical Society at Hartford. Data on securities are from the Records of the Loan of 1790, vol. 491, folio 1023; vol. 495, folios 6, 24, 34, 63, 134; vol. 498, folios 13, 19, 27, 83, 143, 147.

[62] Records of the Loan of 1790, vol. 495, folio 111; vol. 498, folios 14, 140. All three men are identified as tradesmen in their security accounts (Huntington from vol. 498, folio 265, an account representing an acquisition of securities in 1796). Huntington was probably related to Samuel and Jedadiah Huntington of the adjacent town of Norwich.

[63] Orton and West are identified as physicians in the list of delegates given in Labaree, ed., *Records of Connecticut*, 6:550–552; Phelps in Richard S. Wheeler, *History of the Town of Stonington* (New London, 1900), 538; Porter in Chard Powers Smith, *The Housatanic*, 261; and Brainerd in his securities account. Security holdings are recorded in Records of the Loan of 1790, vol. 495, folio 58, and vol. 498, folios 18, 37.

[64] Both are identified by the title "Reverend" in Labaree, ed., *Records of Connecticut*, vol. 6; see the index.

[65] Herman R. Timlow, *Ecclesiastical and Other History of Southington, Connecticut* (Hartford, 1875), Appendix xx, p. 45; Samuel Orcutt, *History of Torrington, Connecticut* (Albany, 1878), 27.

the mercantile and professional delegates tabulated above. Most of them
were fairly substantial landowners, and most of them had small supplementary incomes from other sources. Fifty-two, for example, were justices of the peace.[66] No purpose can be served by listing their names,
but the individuals listed below should be mentioned specifically because
they held public securities: [67]

Isaac Foot of Stafford ($5 *Old C*)
Asa Witter of Canterbury ($1 *Old C*)
John Whitlessey of Washington ($3 *Old C*)
Wait Goodrich of Glastenbury ($6 *Old C*)
Daniel Miles of Goshen ($101 *Old C*)
John Chester of Weathersfield ($7 *Old C*)
Jabez Chapman of East Haddam ($15 *Old C*)
Asaph Hall of Goshen ($179 *S*)
Caleb Holt of Willington ($320 *S*)
Elisha Mills of Stratford ($4,509 *S*)
Ebenezer White of Chatham ($234 *S*)
Daniel Foot of Colchester ($254 *S*)
Phillip Burr Bradley of Ridgfield ($604 *S*)
Jeremiah Ripley of Coventry ($4,120 *S*, $720 *C*)
Joseph Moseley of Glastenbury ($1,008 *S*, $589 *C*)
William Noyes of Lyme ($4,662 *S*, $14,254 *C*)
Samuel Carver of Bolton ($42 *S*, $164 *C*)

In addition, three more farmers deserve mention because their property
was sold for taxes between 1786 and 1788: James Potter, John Beach, and
Elisha Pitkin.

The ranks of the opponents of ratification were filled with
persons of similar economic backgrounds, though a slightly
smaller proportion had personalty interests, less than half as
many were public security holders, and a slightly greater proportion were farmers.

Four of them were lawyers. Apparently none was practicing full
time, however, if any were practicing at all. James Wadsworth of East
Haven was the comptroller of the finances. Constant Southworth of
Mansfield was the promoter of a silk manufactory and other manufactures.
Daniel Hall of Durham ($5 *Old C*) and Daniel Perkins of Enfield (*P-T*)
bought and sold goods and real estate and both were interested in
manufactures.[68]

[66] See Labaree, ed., *Records of Connecticut*, vol. 6, index. Justices of the
peace were appointed by each session of the General Assembly.
[67] Records of the Loan of 1790, vol. 491, folios 91, 472, 506, 546, 700–703,
857, 897–898; vol. 495, folios 16, 49, 98, 103, 114, 160, 164, 179, 199, 211; vol.
498, folios 34, 70, 99, 132.
[68] Sketch of Wadsworth in the 1927 edition of the *Biographical Directory of
Congress*. Southworth's activities have been traced in vol. 5, "Industry," p.
237c and elsewhere, manuscript in the Connecticut Archives, and in news-

One was a judge of a court of record who apparently had no formal legal training: Noah Phelps of Simsbury.[69]

Two were merchants engaged directly in interstate and foreign commerce: John Elliott of Guilford and Samuel Osborne of Woodbridge. Osborne, who had been a purchaser for the army commissary department during the war, owed the state £1,126 for unsettled accounts in 1788.[70]

One, William Gold of Branford, was a physician.[71]

Two were ministers: Daniel Humphrey of Simsbury and David Brooks of Cheshire.[72]

One, Jonathan Gillet of Sharon ($211 S, $30 C), was a tavernkeeper.[73]

Two were surveyors: Josiah Coleman of Sharon and Elihu Marvin ($289 C) of Hebron.[74]

As nearly as can be ascertained, all or virtually all the remaining twenty-seven delegates were farmers. Their status as farmers was approximately the same as that of the farmers who favored ratification; that is to say, most of them were fairly substantial landowners, and most of them had small supplementary incomes from other sources. More than half of them held remunerative, appointive state offices, most of which were justice-ships of the peace. Two of them, Hezekiah Holcomb ($8 *Old C*) and Davis Todd ($37 *Old C*) were holders of public securities.[75]

The following is a summary of the occupational breakdown of the Connecticut ratifying convention.

papers—for example, the *Connecticut Gazette* of January 19, 1787; Fowler, *History of Durham*, 148, 187; Francis Olcott Allen, *History of Enfield, Connecticut* (3 vols., Lancaster, Pennsylvania, 1900), 3:2253. Security holdings are recorded in Records of the Loan of 1790, vol. 491, folio 7. The public notice of the sale of property is in the *Connecticut Courant* of December 26, 1785. Wadsworth's security holdings are problematical. It seems probable, judging from his political conduct and statements made by and about him during the controversies of 1783–84 and 1786, that he was a state creditor, but his holdings cannot be traced because the records do not distinguish between transactions of his own and those carried out on behalf of the state.

[69] See Labaree, ed., *State Records of Connecticut*, vol. 6, index under Noah Phelps. There is no reference to Phelps as a lawyer in any of the sources consulted.

[70] Rockey, *New Haven County*, 1:134 and elsewhere; Labaree, ed., *Records of Connecticut*, 6:487; occasional newspaper advertisements in the *Connecticut Journal*.

[71] Rockey, *New Haven County*, 2:212.

[72] *Ibid.*, 1:663; Timothy Green, *Register for the State of Connecticut, with an Almanack, for the Year of Our Lord 1786* (New London, 1785), 50.

[73] Charles F. Sedgwick, *General History of the Town of Sharon* (3d edition, Amenia, New York, 1898), 127; Records of the Loan of 1790, vol. 495, folio 91, and vol. 498, unnumbered account. The identity of the holder is not absolutely certain. Gillet apparently removed to Vermont in 1792.

[74] Sedgwick, *History of Sharon*, 119; Labaree, ed., *Records of Connecticut*, 6:170; Records of the Loan of 1790, vol. 498, folio 189.

[75] Records of the Loan of 1790, vol. 491, folios 629, 734.

OCCUPATION	RATIFIERS Per Cent	ANTI-RATIFIERS Per Cent
Lawyers	22.7	10.0
Judges	2.3	2.5
Merchants	7.8	5.0
Tradesmen	2.3	0.0
Physicians	3.9	2.5
Ministers	1.6	5.0
Tavernkeepers	1.6	2.5
Surveyors	0.0	5.0
Farmers or unknown . . .	57.8	67.5
	100.0	100.0
Security holders	35.1	15.0

MARYLAND

MARYLAND was the last of the states that ratified the Constitution without serious conflict. On April 26, 1788, its convention approved the instrument by a vote of 63 to 11. Meantime, in the three months since Connecticut's ratification, a sixth state, Massachusetts, had ratified after a titanic struggle, so that Maryland was the seventh state in the new Union.

Ratification in Maryland was attended by much sound and fury. Two of the state's delegates had walked out of the Philadelphia Convention before it ended and had returned home, noisily denouncing the Constitution. The October, 1787, elections for the General Assembly were a test of voter sentiment. Samuel Chase, who became the leader of the opposition in Maryland, found after delivering one or two speeches against the Constitution that his electorate was enthusiastically in favor of it. Accordingly, in their campaigns for election to the House of Delegates, he and his political allies soft-pedaled the ratification issue. After the elections, however, they began a propaganda campaign designed to prevent an unconditional ratification by Maryland.[76]

[76] Philip A. Crowl, *Maryland during and after the Revolution* (Baltimore, 1943), 76–77; *Votes and Proceedings of the General Assembly of the State of Maryland* (published at Annapolis in two parts, one for the Senate and one for the House, after each session), November Session, 1787.

When the legislature convened in November, the two houses heard a report from the delegates to the Philadelphia Convention. This consisted chiefly of Luther Martin's attack on the Constitution (later published as a tract under the title *The Genuine Information*) and James McHenry's able defense of the Constitution. Despite Martin's attack the Senate immediately resolved to call a convention of delegates "for their assent and ratification" of the Constitution. Elections were to be held in January and the convention was to meet during the first week of March. All delegates were to be required to have a minimum of £500 of property. The House, where Samuel Chase held sway, diluted the Senate's proposals by removing the property qualification, postponing the elections and the convention until April, and asking of the convention delegates only "their full and free investigation and decision." To prevent the delay which would have attended an intercameral dispute, the Senate acquiesced in the House's modifications.[77]

A bitter campaign ensued, in which the ratificationists used arguments that were philosophical in approach and their opponents cast arguments in a demonstrably hypocritical pseudo-democratic form.[78] About ten thousand voters, a considerably larger than normal number, turned out at the polls and gave the advocates of ratification an overwhelming victory. The popular vote in favor of ratification was about two to one, and the Federalists elected sixty-four candidates as against the opposition's twelve.[79]

The Federalists in the convention treated their opponents

[77] *Votes and Proceedings:* House, December 1, 1787, Senate, November 26, 1787.

[78] Philip A. Crowl, "Anti-Federalism in Maryland," in the *William and Mary Quarterly*, 3d Series, 4:446–469 (October 1947).

[79] These figures were arrived at as follows. a) The figure 10,000. The total number of votes cast in each county in the congressional elections of 1788 is known, as are the votes for candidates to the ratifying convention in six voting areas: the counties of Anne Arundel, Baltimore, Washington, Harford, and Montgomery and the town of Baltimore. It is assumed that these six places cast approximately the same percentage of the total vote in the two elections; from there the calculation was simple arithmetic. b) The margin of victory of two to one. About 45 per cent of the popular vote is known. It is assumed that the winning party carried the same percentage of the total vote in each area where it won and the vote is unknown as it did in the areas where it won and the vote is known.

with something approaching utter contempt. They sat quietly as Chase, Martin, and others delivered lengthy diatribes against the Constitution; not a single advocate of the Constitution spoke in its behalf. Rejecting every attempt of their opponents to postpone the decision, the majority simply waited until those opponents were physically exhausted, then called for an immediate ballot and approved the Constitution by a vote of 63 to 11. After a minor dispute over proposed amendments, the convention adjourned, and Maryland's ratification was formally transmitted to Congress.[80]

The reasons for Maryland's overwhelming vote for ratification are somewhat more intricate than those for ratification in the other states so far considered. Maryland, though small, was not "weak" in the tangible economic and political ways that Delaware, New Jersey, Georgia, and Connecticut were weak. It was richer, in terms of production for export, for example, than those four states combined.[81] Nonetheless it had fundamental internal weaknesses.

Maryland's weakness stemmed from a complex of economic and social factors. For decades its great staple had been tobacco, but for some years before 1788 the soil of the Eastern Shore, formerly the source of wealth of a tobacco-planting aristocracy, had been virtually exhausted. The tobacco lands in the upper parts of the Western Shore were likewise near depletion, as were most of the older areas on the Potomac, those nearest its mouth. Furthermore, throughout Maryland the tobacco planters had been milked almost dry for generations by British factors and merchants, and in Maryland the Revolution had been at least in part motivated by a desire to break the bonds of debt which held the planters. On the other hand, the tobacco lands of the piedmont zone of the Potomac and the wheat lands around Baltimore were still highly fertile, and the planters in

[80] The proceedings and some of the debates in the convention are published in volume 3 of Jonathan Elliot, ed., *The Debates in the Several State Conventions on the Adoption of the Federal Constitution* (5 vols., Philadelphia, 1861).

[81] In 1791 the combined exports from Delaware, New Jersey, Georgia, and Connecticut were valued at $1,350,000, and those of Maryland alone $2,239,000. *U.S. Commercial and Statistical Register*, 1:56, 100, 232, 332, 413.

both places were still rich and mighty. Meantime, for the past two decades, the town of Baltimore had been growing rapidly as a result of a tremendous commercial and manufacturing boom. It was fast becoming a "northern" urban area, and was rapidly filling the void of economic power left by the dethroned British. Thus Maryland had both a decaying, albeit in places still powerful and wealthy, landed aristocracy and a modern, booming urban center. The transition that was later to convert Maryland into a "border" rather than a "southern" state was already well under way.[82]

Despite the changing locus of economic power, however, political power was, under Maryland's constitution of 1776, lodged entirely in the hands of the planter aristocracy. Voting and officeholding were restricted by real property qualifications that were higher than in any other state, and most of the legislators, who were regularly returned to their seats in both houses, were members of a group of less than fifty families. Elected officials were normally neither instructed nor chosen on the basis of campaign issues. Instead, they enjoyed on most issues a great deal of discretionary power. The imposition of this oligarchical political system upon the dynamic, shifting economy of Maryland was the principal reason both for Maryland's weakness and for its enthusiastic acceptance of the Constitution.

Maryland's institutional, social, and economic systems lay at the roots of the attitudes of its people toward the Constitution in several ways. There were a few direct economic considerations. Most of the merchants and manufacturers of Baltimore supported the Constitution. It was an easy decision for them to make, for they were obviously not getting all that could be desired from the planter-dominated state government, and the new general government, if one could believe the propaganda emanating from Philadelphia and points northward, was to be

---

[82] Charles Barker, *Background of the Revolution in Maryland* (New Haven, 1940); Lewis C. Gray, *History of Agriculture in the Southern United States to 1860* (2 vols., Washington, 1933); Avery O. Craven, *Soil Exhaustion as a Factor in the Agricultural History of Virginia and Maryland* (Urbana, Illinois, 1926); Baltimore Import and Export Books, in the Customs Records in the Fiscal Section of the National Archives; Miscellaneous Naval Officer Returns, in Maryland Hall of Records, Annapolis.

the answer to the merchant's and artisan's prayer. The wheat-planting segment of the aristocracy stood to make definite gains from the proposed commercial treaty with Spain, in ways which will be elaborated in a later chapter. This factor was apparently somewhat neutralized by the fact that many in the aristocracy, wheat planters included, held western lands for speculation, and their interests in this respect were those of the westerners, who were opposed to the proposed Spanish treaty.[83] The absence of widespread opposition in Maryland makes it difficult to estimate the weight of these conflicting interests.

But at most the promise of tangible economic gains was manifestly insufficient to account for Maryland's overwhelming vote for ratification. The wheat planters and the personalty interests in Baltimore constituted only a fraction of the political power in the state. Furthermore, of the six political subdivisions in which urban interests and wheat planters were strongest—the counties of Baltimore, Harford, Anne Arundel, and Montgomery, Baltimore town, and the City of Annapolis—the anti-Federalists carried three. In those places the ratifiers elected only eight delegates, whereas their opponents elected all twelve of theirs and piled up more than half their popular votes there.[84]

The decision to ratify or not to ratify lay with the members of the slave-owning, tobacco-planting aristocracy, and the direct economic gains they could anticipate were negligible. In only one respect, the appreciation of public securities, did the Constitution offer any demonstrable gain, and public securities were an insignificant part of the total wealth of most of the planters who stood to benefit from it. For example, the *total* gain from the appreciation of securities held by the sixty-three delegates who voted for ratification in the convention was about equal to the value of the *average* slaveholdings of each of them.

[83] Merrill Jensen, "The Cession of the Old Northwest," in the *Mississippi Valley Historical Review*, 23:27-48 (1936). For a discussion of the effect of the Constitution and the Spanish treaty upon the interests of wheat farmers and westerners, see pages 366-367 below.

[84] Crowl, in his *Maryland during and after the Revolution*, 165-168, lists all known votes except those for Harford County, which may be seen in the *New York Journal* of April 24, 1788.

Besides, public creditors in Maryland already stood on fairly solid footing.[85]

The preponderating factor in the favorable reception of the Constitution by the Maryland aristocracy was a complex and nebulous one. The postwar political history of the state had demonstrated that the ultra-conservative defenses of the constitution of 1776 could be breached by a group skilled in rough-and-tumble political techniques. During the years 1784–1787 a faction of the aristocracy headed by Samuel Chase had attempted to seize political power in Maryland by a daring series of stratagems, most of which, quasi-democratic in approach, derived much of their strength from direct attacks on the aristocracy itself. The Philadelphia Constitution appeared just as the Chase faction had been temporarily forestalled by a hair's breadth in its most ambitious program, the creation of a paper-money state bank. When the ratifying convention met, the aristocracy had not breathed a relaxed, comfortable breath in three years.[86]

The Constitution offered a welcome escape. A vigorous new general government would, by its very existence, prevent further machinations on the part of the Chaseites (considered by the aristocracy to be little better than Shaysites), for much of their program was tenable only if Maryland retained its practical sovereignty. Furthermore, the relative power of the proposed new government was a symbol of law, peace, and good social order. Finally, the new order was symbolically akin to the old order cast off in 1776; that is, it was psychologically a substitute for the vanished external authority of the British crown.

Why, then, was there in Maryland any opposition to the Constitution at all? Professor Beard, basing his observations on the earlier work of Libby, concluded that "the opposition came

[85] Maryland's handling of her debts may be traced in the annual summaries in *Votes and Proceedings*. Data on the security holdings of the members of the ratifying convention will be given below. Baltimore and Annapolis newspapers rarely quoted security prices, but the prices at which they sold locally were occasionally printed in various Philadelphia newspapers.

[86] Crowl, *Maryland during and after the Revolution, passim;* Annapolis *Maryland Gazette*, 1785–1787.

from the rural districts and particularly from the paper money constituencies." The hordes of small farmer-debtors who had sought paper money as a cheap remedy for their indebtedness, Beard contended, opposed the Constitution because it cut off this fraudulent source of relief. This theory has been pretty thoroughly exploded by Philip A. Crowl, who has made a careful comparison of the votes on paper money in 1785 and 1787 with the votes on the Constitution in 1788:[87]

> Eleven counties, the majority of whose delegates voted *for* paper money in 1785, returned Federalist representatives in 1788; two counties whose delegates opposed paper money in 1785 voted against the Constitution in 1788; and seven counties whose delegates voted favorably on the paper-money bill of 1786 also voted favorably on the Constitution. A comparison of the votes on the Constitution of the individual members of the ratifying convention with the votes of the same men in the House of Delegates on the paper-money bills reveals the same disparity. Of the eleven men who voted in the House of Delegates on the paper-money bill of 1785 and later attended the ratifying convention of 1788, seven expressed their approval of *both* the Constitution and paper money, one voted against the Constitution and *against* paper money, and only three voted both against paper money and for the Constitution. Thirteen men who later attended the ratifying convention voted on the paper-money bill before the House of Delegates in 1786. Of these, three voted for paper money and against the Constitution, four against paper money and for the Constitution, but six voted favorably in *both* cases.

Crowl, in turn, has an alternative explanation. Most of the leaders in the fight against ratification, he states, had speculated heavily in the purchase of confiscated loyalist estates. They had sought paper money as a cheap means of retiring the debts they had assumed for these speculations, and they naturally opposed the Constitution because it cut off this source of relief. In 1780 a few others had written off prewar indebtedness to British merchants by payments of depreciated currency to the state, and they opposed the Constitution because it gave the Treaty

[87] Crowl, *Maryland during and after the Revolution*, 134.

of 1783 the status of supreme law, thus opening the courts to suits by former British creditors.[88]

There is one vital flaw in Crowl's reasoning, aside from the fact that as many ratificationists as anti-ratificationists in Maryland had purchased confiscated property. The paper-money bills introduced into the legislature by the Chaseites in 1785 and 1786–1787 provided that the paper to be issued could be used only for certain express purposes, among which payments due for confiscated property were not included.[89]

There was another consideration, however, which tends to support Crowl's reasoning in every respect except the paper-money nexus. In litigation before the Court of Appeals in Maryland since January, 1787, had been the question whether a particular form of public securities could be legally used for payment of debts due for purchases of confiscated property, and all executions were under suspension during the litigation. There was reason to believe that the court would hold that the securities were thus receivable, and a month after the ratifying convention adjourned, the court did so rule. These securities— the so-called specie certificates—had been obtainable on the open market at about forty per cent of par. It was reasonable to expect that the funding of debts by the new government would cause a rapid appreciation in the price of this paper to nearly its face value; as a matter of fact, the price had already begun to rise. Ratification of the Constitution would thus be detrimental to the interests of speculators in confiscated property in the same way it had conflicted with the interests of many speculators in vacant lands.[90]

Almost all the delegates in the convention who voted for ratification were of the planter aristocracy. Their economic interests may be summarized as follows:

Six were lawyers, all but one of whom operated large plantations, all of whom were members of the aristocracy, and none of whom derived the major part of his income from the practice of law. These were

[88] *Ibid.*, 127–129.
[89] See the abstract of the proposed law in the *Maryland Gazette* of January 11, 1787.
[90] *Maryland Gazette*, January 10, May 29, 1787.

Thomas Johnson (Frederick County), who also had an interest in western lands and confiscated property, but whose main estate was a plantation with 38 slaves; Richard Potts (Frederick), one of the few delegates voting for the Constitution whose public security holdings, $9,452 in continentals, were probably as valuable as his planting interest, a plantation with 22 slaves; Nicholas Carroll (Anne Arundel), who owned $1,543 of state securities and a 30-slave plantation; William Tilghman (Kent), a member of the Lloyd-Tilghman clan (which stood at the apex of the aristocracy), who owned a plantation and 37 slaves; George Plater (St. Mary's), who owned a vast 93-slave plantation and a nominal amount ($288) of state securities; and Alexander Contee Hanson (Annapolis), who neither practiced law nor owned a plantation, but apparently derived his income mainly from his salary as a judge of the general court.[91]

Two of the delegates, both from Baltimore, were physicians: John Coulter, who had no planting interest but whose property included four household slaves, and James McHenry, whose economic interests have been detailed in Chapter 3 above.[92]

[91] Sketches of Johnson, Potts, and Plater may be seen in the *Biographical Directory of Congress;* of Carroll and Hanson in John Thomas Scharf's *History of Western Maryland* (2 vols., Philadelphia, 1882), 1:380 ff.; and of Tilghman in Oswald Tilghman's *History of Talbot County, Maryland, 1661–1861* (2 vols., Baltimore, 1915), 1:368 ff. There is some confusion in the records about Tilghman. He practiced law in Talbot County, owned his slaves in Queen Anne's County, and illegally represented Kent County in the convention (several men on both sides illegally represented counties of which they were not residents). These three counties are all clustered on the Eastern Shore, hence such a situation was easily possible. There was only one other William Tilghman in the state, and he lived in Worcester County; hence it would seem that it must have been the one owning a plantation in Queen Anne's County who was the delegate.

For the slaveholdings, see *Census of 1790, Heads of Families, Maryland* (hereafter cited as *Census of 1790, Maryland*), 16, 64, 68, 99, 109. Data on Carroll's securities are from the Records of the Loan of 1790, vol. 73, folio 27 (Ledger, B Stock [deferred six per cents], Assumed Debt), and vol. 72, folio 27 (Ledger, C Stock [three per cents], Assumed Debt). Volume 74, representing six per cents, is missing, but since deferred six per cents and three per cents amounted to five-ninths of the funded debt, the entire holding can be calculated from these ledger entries. It is recorded directly in the journal entries in volumes 926 and 932. Data on Potts's holdings are from vol. 937, folio 9 (Ledger, A Stock [six per cents], Public Debt, 1790–97). This entry records four-ninths of the total funded holding; the remainder is calculated. Crowl (*op. cit.*, 126), lists Potts as owning $2,600 more than this figure, citing the Assumed Debt Journals, vols. 926 and 932, but these latter holdings were apparently acquired after 1791. On Johnson's speculations in land and confiscated property, see Crowl, *op. cit.*, 104n, 114n.

[92] I have been able to learn little about Coulter. He is described as a physician by Crowl (*op. cit.*, 135) and in miscellaneous references in the *Maryland Journal and Baltimore Advertiser.* His slaveholdings are given in *Census of 1790, Maryland*, 21. His other holdings, if any, are unknown. He is not listed as a shipowner in the Baltimore port records or as a security holder in the Records of the Loan of 1790, and he apparently bought no confiscated property.

One delegate, Benjamin Edwards (Montgomery), operated a mercantile house in Georgetown and a moderate-sized plantation with 17 slaves.[93]

Fifty-four of the delegates were planters. The planters may be subdivided according to personalty holdings as follows:

Three had an interest in vessels engaged in interstate and/or foreign commerce: Edward Lloyd (Talbot), Henry Hollingsworth (Cecil), and William Deakins, Jr. (Montgomery). Lloyd is sometimes credited with being the richest man in the state. His vast estate is worth describing in some detail: in 1783 he paid taxes on 260 slaves (305 by 1790), 147 horses, 799 sheep, 578 hogs, 571 horned cattle, 215,000 pounds of tobacco, 30 barrels of pork, 500 ounces of silver plate, a 60-ton schooner, 72 tracts of land under cultivation in Talbot County totaling 11,884½ acres, a 229-acre plantation in Anne Arundel County, and four plantations in Queen Anne's County, the sizes of which are unknown.[94] Hollingsworth owned a third interest in a 32-ton schooner and a plantation with 23 slaves.[95] Deakins was the co-owner with a Baltimore mercantile firm of a 170-ton ship in trade with Holland and owner of two small plantations with a total of twelve slaves. He was also a large security holder, having $3,326 in state securities and perhaps a larger amount of continental securities.[96]

Besides Deakins, seven of the planters owned public securities:[97] George Gale (Somerset), who had $4,262 in state securities (slaveholdings not ascertainable); John Gale (Somerset), $4,833 in continentals (slaveholdings not ascertainable); Charles Chilton (St. Mary's), $619 in continentals, 6 slaves; Richard Thomas (Montgomery), $3,461 in continentals, 54 slaves; Michael Jenifer Stone (Charles), $3,814 in continentals (slaveholdings not ascertainable); William Richardson (Caroline), $124

---

[93] Sketch in *Biographical Directory of Congress* (1927 edition), 935; *Census of 1790, Maryland*, 87. Edwards apparently owned no vessels, for his name does not appear in the incomplete records for the Port of Georgetown in the Naval Office Returns, in the Maryland Hall of Records.

[94] Tilghman, *History of Talbot County*, 1:181 ff.; *Census of 1790, Maryland*, 114.

[95] Miscellaneous Port Records: Baltimore Arrivals, 1786–8, in the Customs Records in the Fiscal Section of the National Archives; *Census of 1790, Maryland*, 43.

[96] Baltimore Arrivals, 1786–8, entry for November 26, 1787; *Census of 1790, Maryland*, 85, 94; Records of the Loan of 1790, vols. 72, 73, folio 23 in each. Crowl lists Deakins as the owner of another $7,000 worth of continentals, citing vols. 927 and 937–941–945. I did not find any references in these volumes to securities held by Deakins before 1791.

[97] Data on slaveholdings are from the *Census of 1790, Maryland*, 39, 86, 105. The names of some of the other delegates are listed in the census, but not as residents of the counties they represented, and identity is not certain. Data on securities are from vols. 72 and 73, folio 17 in each; vols. 937, 941, and 945, folios 16, 33, 41, 59, and 83 in each; and vol. 925, unnumbered page 21. Some of the totals as listed here vary slightly from those given by Crowl (*op. cit.*, 126). Crowl also lists Moses Rawlings and Isaac Perkins as security holders, but he does not cite folios, and I was unable to find any record of funding by these men.

continentals, 36 slaves; and John Stewart (Somerset), $2,102 in continentals (slaveholdings not ascertainable).

Three of the planters, besides Johnson, are listed by Crowl as investors in confiscated property: Abraham Faw (Frederick), who also owned a farm and two slaves; James Shaw (Dorchester), whose slaveholdings are not ascertainable; and Isaac Perkins (Kent), whose slaveholdings are not ascertainable.[98]

Thirty were substantial planters, most of whom owned far more slaves than the average holdings in their counties, but who, so far as known, owned no personalty in the form of shipping, manufacturing, goods, securities, or confiscated property. These delegates, with their slaveholdings, are listed below. (For convenience of documentation, the page reference in the *Census of 1790, Heads of Families, Maryland,* in which the delegates' slaves are recorded, is given in parentheses).

Richard Barnes (St. Mary's), 200 slaves [99]
Fielder Bowie (Prince George), 60 slaves (p. 92)
Gustavus R. Brown (Charles), 144 slaves on plantations in Charles and
    St. Mary's counties (pp. 47, 107)
Peter Chaille (Worcester), 22 slaves (p. 127)
Thomas Cramphin (Montgomery), 32 slaves (p. 88)
Matthew Driver (Caroline), 24 slaves (p. 36)
George Digges (Prince George), 105 slaves (p. 93)
Peter Edmondson (Caroline), 14 slaves (p. 37)
Samuel Evans (Cecil), 8 slaves (p. 43)
Robert Goldsborough, Jr. (Talbot), 41 slaves (p. 113)
William Granger (Kent), 15 slaves (p. 83)
Benjamin Hall (Prince George), 60 slaves (p. 95)
James Gordon Heron (Cecil), 10 slaves (p. 46)
William Hemsley (Queen Anne's), 45 slaves (p. 98)
James Hollyday (Queen Anne's), 62 slaves (p. 100)
Thomas Sim Lee (Frederick), 171 slaves on plantations in Prince
    George, Montgomery, and Frederick counties (pp. 66, 92, 95)
James Martin (Worcester), 33 slaves (p. 124)
William Morris (Worcester), 33 slaves (p. 124)
Moses Rawlings (Washington), 12 slaves (p. 117)
Joseph Richardson (Caroline), 8 slaves (p. 39)
Nicholas Lewis Sewall (St. Mary's), 39 slaves (p. 106)
John Parnham (Charles), 26 slaves (p. 522)
Henry Shryock (Washington), 7 slaves (p. 115)
Thomas Sprigg (Washington), 44 slaves (p. 121)

[98] All three men are listed as purchasers of confiscated property by Crowl (*op. cit.,* 103n). Faw's slaves are recorded in *Census of 1790, Maryland,* 67. Perkins is listed in *Census of 1790, Maryland,* but the figure for the number of his slaves was illegible in the original census schedules.

[99] Barnes is listed by Crowl (*op. cit.,* 137, 139) as owning "over 200" slaves, but he is not listed in the census as a slaveholder.

Osborne Sprigg (Prince George), 43 slaves (p. 97)
John Stevens (Talbot), 23 slaves (pp. 112–113)
John Stull (Washington), 10 slaves (p. 120)
James Tilghman (Queen Anne's), 50 slaves (p. 98)
Zephaniah Turner (Charles), 15 slaves (p. 54)
Donaldson Yeates (Kent), 6 slaves (p. 80)

Ten were apparently slave-owning planters whose slaveholdings, for various reasons, cannot be ascertained. These were John Chesley, Jr., Charles Grahame, Walter Smith, and Joseph Wilkinson (all of Calvert County), John Done (Worcester), Joseph Gilpin (Cecil), Nicholas Hammond and Daniel Sullivan (both of Dorchester), John Seney (Queen Anne's), and Henry Waggaman (Somerset).

One, William Paca, was elected as an anti-Federalist but voted for ratification. Paca, a former governor, lived in Queen Anne's County, but he represented Harford in the convention. He was a lawyer and a wealthy planter, owning 92 slaves on his Eastern Shore plantation. He had invested upwards of £2,000 in confiscated British property.[100]

The members of the convention who voted against ratification of the Constitution were of quite different economic backgrounds. Only three were planters, but most of them owned slaves and some plantations, and the rest were large owners and/or speculators in various kinds of personalty. Their interests were as follows:

Five of them were lawyers: Samuel Chase, Jeremiah Townley Chase (Anne Arundel), Luther Martin (Anne Arundel), John Francis Mercer (Harford), and William Pinkney (Harford). Samuel Chase lived in Baltimore but represented Anne Arundel County in the convention. He was a speculator in commodities, confiscated property (over £11,000 invested), shipping, money, and manufactures (one-eighth share in a large confiscated iron works).[101] Jeremiah Chase had a large law practice, mainly with Annapolis merchants, and owned a plantation and 28 slaves and had invested over £4,000 in confiscated property.[102] Martin's legal career and his investments in public securities ($4,355) and confiscated property (over

---

[100] *Census of 1790, Maryland*, 98; Crowl, *Maryland during and after the Revolution*, 96, 152–154.

[101] There is no adequate biography of Chase. There are sketches in the *Dictionary of American Biography* and the *Biographical Directory of Congress*, and Crowl gives valuable information. Much of his economic and political activity can be traced in contemporary newspapers and in the *Votes and Proceedings* of the two houses of the legislature.

[102] *Biographical Directory of Congress*, 804; *Census of 1790, Maryland*, 16; Crowl, *op. cit.*, 128.

£3,000) have been described above.[103] Mercer's career as a lawyer-planter and his investments, including $7,236 in public securities, have also been described above.[104] Pinkney was just beginning his brilliant career as a lawyer.[105]

One of the delegates—besides Chase—was a merchant, Captain Charles Ridgely (Baltimore County). Ridgely, the political boss of the county, was one of the richest men, in terms of personalty, in the area. He owned (partly outright, partly in shares) two ships, measuring 492 tons, in the European trade and a 75-ton brig and a 158-ton schooner in the European and West Indies trade. He had invested more than £11,000 in confiscated property and had organized a £40,000 syndicate to purchase a mammoth ironworks. He owned about $3,000 in public securities and several planta- tions employing a total of 117 slaves and 60 free laborers. Ridgely had owed £650 to British merchants before the war which he had cancelled by payment of depreciated currency to the state, but which he was forced to pay in full when the courts were opened for such suits under the Constitution.[106]

Three of the delegates were planters: Benjamin Harrison (Anne Arundel), who owned 35 slaves; Nathan Cromwell (Baltimore County), who owned 15 slaves; and Charles Ridgely of William (Baltimore County), who owned 6 slaves. Ridgely, cousin of his wealthy namesake Captain Charles Ridgely, had retired £3,273 in prewar debts with wartime cur- rency. A successful suit for the recovery of this sum tried in 1790 virtually bankrupted him.[107]

The backgrounds of two of the delegates, Edward Cockey (Baltimore County, and William Love (Harford) are obscure. Cockey owned 6 slaves, but there is no available evidence to indicate whether he and Love were planters.[108]

The economic status of the two sets of delegates may be summarized as follows:

[103] See above, pp. 69–70.
[104] See above, pp. 70–71.
[105] John J. Dolan's sketch of Pinkney in the *Dictionary of American Biog- raphy* and sketch in the 1927 edition of the *Biographical Directory of Con- gress*, 1414–1415.
[106] Baltimore Arrivals, 1782–84, in Customs Records, in the Fiscal Section of the National Archives; Records of the Loan of 1790, vol. 925, folio 3, and vol. 922, transaction dated May 14, 1788; *Census of 1790, Maryland*, 24. There is much interesting information about Ridgely scattered through Crowl's monograph. Ironically, according to my tabulations of votes as recorded in the *Votes and Proceedings*, the Chase faction and the Ridgely faction in the Assembly were bitterly opposed to each other on almost all issues until 1788.
[107] *Census of 1790, Maryland*, 10, 23, 24; Crowl, *op. cit.*, 128.
[108] *Census of 1790, Maryland*, 23.

Occupation	Federalists Per Cent	Anti-Federalists Per cent
Lawyer	9.5	45.4
Physician	3.1	0.0
Merchant	1.6	9.1
Planter	85.8	27.3
Unknown	0.0	18.2
Investments in:		
Shipping	6.3	18.2
Securities	17.4	27.3
Manufacturing	0.0	18.2
Confiscated property	7.9	36.3

This tabulation would seem to indicate that the nature of the struggle over ratification in Maryland was almost precisely the opposite of that depicted by Beard. Among the opponents the proportion of lawyers was nearly five times at large as among the ratificationists, the proportion of merchants six times as large, and the proportion of farmers less than a third as large. The proportion of investors in shipping was thrice as large, of investors in public securities half again as large, of investors in confiscated property four and a half times as large. Finally, over 18 per cent of them had investments in manufacturing, whereas no Federalists had such investments.

* * *

Each of the five states thus far considered ratified the Constitution with speed and almost with unanimity. This ease of ratification Professor Beard explains in two ways: that in some states the Constitution was pushed through before the "agrarian–paper-money forces" had time to organize their strength, and that, by implication, there were in all these states important suffering personalty interests which led and "furnished the dynamic element" in bringing about ratification against the wishes of a large portion of the inhabitants.

Neither of these explanations is valid. In no state was the

Constitution ratified without the consent of the farmers and a majority of the friends of paper money. In the three states that ratified unanimously most of the support for ratification came from farmers, in two of them (New Jersey and Delaware) from relatively small, slaveless farmers. In Maryland the support for ratification came mainly from the plantation aristocracy, the leaders of which owned very little "dynamic" personalty as compared with their agricultural property.

In one state, Connecticut, Beard's thesis partially accounts for the ratification; a large number of the friends of the Constitution there did hold public securities and other forms of personalty. It is only a partial explanation, however, for it takes no account of two important facts: that well over half the Federalist members of the Connecticut ratifying convention were farmers, and that as many, if not more, of the anti-Federalists in Connecticut owned "dynamic personalty" as did Federalists in the other four states.

Stated in positive terms, the ease of ratification in these five states may be attributed to the fact that the great majority of their inhabitants saw that definite, immediate, and substantial advantages would accrue to the states as such, as well as to themselves as individuals. The principal advantages seen by two of the states were essentially economic: New Jersey and Connecticut could anticipate great tax relief for their masses of farmers and positive economic gains for their personalty interests. The principal advantages seen by three of the states were essentially noneconomic. Delaware ratified primarily because it was tiny, weak, and exposed, and all its citizens recognized the advantages of pooling its paltry assets with those of the other states. Maryland ratified primarily because the aristocracy felt that the social order which gave it supremacy was insecure without the existence of a strong external authority. Georgia ratified primarily because of the imminent danger of an Indian uprising which it felt incapable of dealing with unaided.

VI

Ratification in States Divided
on the Constitution

THE five states considered in the preceding chapter were the weakest members of the Union. In them, as had been expected, ratification was accomplished with very little effort on the part of the Federalists.

A second group of states comprises Pennsylvania, Massachusetts, and South Carolina, fundamentally strong states that had certain characteristics which either sapped their strength or gave them the illusion that they were weak, and New Hampshire, a weak state that had certain characteristics which gave it the illusion of being strong. In each of these states ratification was expected to be attended with some difficulty. The Federalists were confident, however, that by concentrated effort the opposition to the Constitution in them could be overcome. This chapter deals with the contests over ratification in these states, in the order in which they ratified the Constitution.

PENNSYLVANIA

THE KEYSTONE STATE startled the continent and gave the ratification movement a great impetus when, on December 15, 1787, just a week after Delaware's ratification, its convention approved the Constitution by an overwhelming two-to-one majority.

Both the speed of ratification and the imbalanced vote in Pennsylvania are misleading if they are taken to mean that the state was enthusiastically favorable to the Constitution. In the main they merely reflect a highly organized campaign, executed

with unseemly haste and ruthless precision. The legislature had
been nearing the end of its session when the Constitution
was completed on September 17. Pennsylvania was the only
state with a formally organized statewide two-party system,
and at the moment its Republican party, a strong nationalist
group dominated by Robert Morris, was in control of the
Assembly. Rather than risk the issue with the new Assembly
to be elected in October, the Republicans had determined to
call a ratifying convention before adjourning. This almost
proved impossible, for the Philadelphia Convention had lasted
longer than had been expected, and it was not until September
27 that Congress formally submitted the Constitution to the
states. The congressional resolution arrived in Philadelphia by
special courier late on the 28th. Meantime the Assembly was
scheduled to adjourn on Saturday, September 29. The nineteen
members of the opposition party in the Assembly [1] now resorted to a desperate measure; they absented themselves from
the House, thus preventing a quorum. A large band of men was
dispatched to search the city, and two of the absent members
were found, seized, and dragged forcibly into the House. The
quorum thus achieved voted that an election be held in early
November for delegates to a convention that would begin on
November 21. [2]

Immediately the Federalist Republicans, employing some of
the most persuasive writers of the day—including James Wilson,
Tench Coxe, and Noah Webster—launched a powerful and
carefully planned propaganda campaign on behalf of the Constitution. They spared no efforts to win the support of the back
country, but they focused their campaign on the city and
county of Philadelphia, for in the decade after the Declaration
of Independence the party that controlled the ten seats of the

---

[1] The opposition party was sometimes styled the "Constitutionalist" party
and sometimes the "Radical" party. The term "Constitutionalist" designated
its advocacy of the state constitution of 1776. To avoid confusion the otherwise less accurate term "Radicals" will be used here.

[2] For a narrative of these events see Robert L. Brunhouse, *The Counter-
Revolution in Pennsylvania, 1776–1790* (Harrisburg, 1942), 200–202.

city and county dominated the state, party strength elsewhere being stable and almost equally divided.[3]

In the city the great merchants and men with other personalty interests fluctuated in their political affiliations, but at the moment about three out of five were Republicans. The decision on ratification rested with the multitudes of artisans, mechanics, and tradesmen in the city and the farmers around it. These lower classes, once strong backers of the "Radicals," had revealed their sympathies in the quorum fiasco. The Philadelphia anti-Federalists ran a strong ticket, heading it as a stratagem with Benjamin Franklin, but the Federalist victory was a smashing one, the average vote for candidates favoring ratification being 1,198 as against 160 for their opponents. In Philadelphia County the ratificationists elected all five delegates, and they unexpectedly picked up five delegates in normally Radical Northampton and Northumberland counties. Elsewhere the voting followed the usual patterns, but the elections in these three counties assured overwhelming approval of the Constitution in the ratifying convention.[4]

The convention dragged out for almost a month. The opponents of the Constitution managed to waste a week debating rules of procedure, after which their long-winded leaders discussed every detail of the Constitution at great length, and the Federalists, unlike their Maryland brothers, argued back. The arguments of John Smiley and William Findley, chief spokesmen for the opposition, interestingly enough were cast in a mold of theoretical republicanism, whereas those of James Wilson, spokesman for the ratificationists, were based on theoretical democracy. The debate finally ran its course and on

[3] This observation is made on the basis of my tabulations of all the votes cast in the Assembly from 1781 to 1790, as recorded in the *Minutes of the General Assembly of the Commonwealth of Pennsylvania* (Philadelphia, generally published by sessions). A complete file of these minutes is available in the Library of Congress microfilm collections. For a brief picture of the distribution of party strength in selected years, see Brunhouse, *Counter-Revolution in Pennsylvania*, 321–325.

[4] The election activities have been traced in the November, 1787, issues of various Philadelphia newspapers: *Freeman's Journal, Pennsylvania Packet, Evening Herald, Pennsylvania Gazette, Pennsylvania Mercury*, and others.

December 15 the vote was taken. Forty-six members voted for ratification, twenty-three voted against it.[6]

To account for this vote is an exceedingly complex undertaking. Here, however, the task is simply to examine Beard's personalty-versus-realty, economic interpretation of the conflict. No such examination can be validly made without reference to the history of Pennsylvania's economy and politics during the decade prior to the ratifying convention. Study of state politics of this period, even a cursory reading of the statutes, legislative journals, and debates in the Assembly, indicates clearly that both parties consistently sponsored legislation designed to promote the interests of merchants, manufacturers, and security holders as well as those of farmers. There were sharp disagreements, however, over the most effective and desirable means of promoting these interests and, more important, over the broader political implications of such promotion. Examination of the political activities engaged in on behalf of two of these interest groups sheds a great deal of light on the economic influences at work in the convention.

With respect to the commercial interests the two Pennsylvania parties agreed on most matters of policy: regulation, discriminatory tariffs, bounties, and the like. On one important issue, however, they disagreed bitterly. The Republicans were intimately associated with the Bank of North America—it was not mere coincidence that Robert Morris, the "boss" of the party, was also "boss" in the affairs of the Bank—and their public policy was geared to the assumption that the commercial activities of Philadelphia and the state could best be stimulated by the credit facilities of the Bank. The Radicals opposed the Bank on the philosophical ground that it was a monopoly and therefore inherently bad, and on the economic ground that the Bank's credit aided only a select group of the larger importing merchants, that at best it did nothing for and at worst impaired

⁵ Elliott's *Debates*, vol. 2 (1836 edition), contains the proceedings and debates of the Pennsylvania convention. See also the voluminous collections of newspaper and pamphlet literature on the subject in John Bach McMaster and Frederick D. Stone, eds., *Pennsylvania and the Federal Constitution, 1787–1788* (Philadelphia, 1888).

the interests of the other large merchants and those of the smaller merchants, the tradesmen, the artisans, the mechanics, and the manufacturers. They therefore advocated a state bank which would combine the features of a traditional land bank with various modern innovations, basing its paper not on land mortgages alone but also on commercial, manufacturing, and other personalty mortgages, the taxing power of the state, public securities, both state and continental, and specie reserves. The result of this political disagreement was that the state had both kinds of banks.[6]

This public policy, with generous assistance from the fundamentally sound and dynamic Pennsylvania economy, was eminently successful. During the 1780's the volume of trade was more than half again as large as it had been during the best years before the war. More than ever Philadelphia was America's entrepôt, despite new competition from New York and Baltimore, and its shippers were able to capture a substantial share of the southern carrying trade formerly held by Boston. True, the unprecedented boom in importing that they had enjoyed during 1783–1784 was followed by a leveling off in 1785 and, judging from price fluctuations, a considerable recession in the importing season of 1786, but by 1788 import activity was again at record levels. Exporting followed a similar pattern, though the fluctuations were less sharp, and the fall

[6] This was the basis of the "paper money" of Pennsylvania. That it was not an inflationary device designed by debtors to defraud creditors is evidenced by four principal facts. 1) The bank was conducted upon sound business principles, and its income later paid a large share of the state's administrative expenses. 2) Only the most solvent could borrow from it, on mortgages of debt-free property. 3) Its paper circulated at approximately the same price as did the paper of the Bank of North America. 4) It was intimately connected with the funding of state and continental debts in Pennsylvania. Its proponents in the city had made an effort two years earlier to organize a second private bank. When this was successfully blocked by the maneuvers of the Morris bank, they then worked for the establishment of this state bank which would operate in direct competition with the Bank of North America. For a running account of the attempt to establish a second bank, see the *Pennsylvania Packet* of January, 1784. For a crisp statement of the position of the advocates of the state bank, see the article signed "Colbert," in the *Pennsylvania Packet*, March 31, April 1, 1785. The account of the paper bank in Brunhouse's *Counter-Revolution in Pennsylvania*, pages 150–151, 170–171, is a muddled one. A better, though incomplete account is that in Jensen's *The New Nation*, 316–317.

exporting season of 1787 broke all previous records for Philadelphia shipping. Thus in the year the Constitution was formulated and at the moment the Pennsylvania ratifying convention was sitting, commercial prosperity in the state was near
an all-time peak. The Radical party claimed credit for this
prosperity; the Republicans seemed to pretend it did not exist.
The result was that commercial factors were more or less neutralized in the contest over ratification.[7]

The other group of interests to be considered are those of
the public creditors. On the issue of the handling of the public
debt the two parties were at opposite poles. It has generally
been assumed that the notion of buying the loyalty of the
wealthy—that is, tying their interests to those of government
by funding the public debt—was first put into practice in this
country by Hamilton and his friends. Actually such a program
was effected five years earlier by the Radical party in Pennsylvania, when, in creating its state bank, it not only funded the
state debts but also assumed Pennsylvania's share of the national
debt. The Republicans, realizing that this maneuver was designed to tie the interests and therefore the loyalty of public
creditors to the fate of the state government, fought the proposed funding-assumption scheme with much the same arguments
that were later used by the proto-Jeffersonians in opposing
Hamilton's funding and assumption scheme, despite the fact that

---

[7] The foregoing summary is based upon my tabulations and study of Philadelphia shipping, as recorded in the Philadelphia Customs House Papers in the
Historical Society of Pennsylvania and the Public Records Division of the
Pennsylvania Historical and Museum Commission. Unfortunately there is a
gap in the records of "Inward Entries" from May 1, 1785, to June 1, 1786. I
have supplied the number of vessels entering and clearing during this period,
and estimated their tonnages, from announcements of ship movements in the
Pennsylvania Packet, which gave full daily accounts of vessels entering and
clearing. For price fluctuations see Anne Bezanson, *Prices and Inflation during
the American Revolution* (Philadelphia, 1951). This study would seem to indicate that a definite recession took place just at this time.

Considerable study will be necessary before it can be determined whether
the recession was the result of "natural" causes such as over-importation, or
whether it was artificially induced for political and economic reasons by the
Bank's juggling of credit, and whether it was a result or a cause (or both) of
the agitation for the state bank. In my opinion these questions are of fundamental importance to an understanding of the history of Pennsylvania during
this period and of the formation of the Constitution.

they, like the later Jeffersonians, were often themselves holders of large sums of public securities. That this political device had the desired effect of inducing many public creditors to give their first loyalty to the state is manifest from the security holdings of the members of the ratifying convention.[8]

It may be objected that the interpretation here placed on these data is questionable in view of the fact that Philadelphia, where mercantile activity and public security holdings were heavily concentrated, voted by an overwhelming majority in favor of ratification. Such an objection would take no account of two important considerations. First, the leadership and the organization of the Radical party was made up of merchants, public security holders, and lawyers, as was that of the Republican party. For example, in 1784 the Radical delegation from Philadelphia in the General Assembly was exclusively one of merchants: Charles Pettit, William Moore, John Bayard, Frederick Kuhl, and William Will. Pettit, one of the principal leaders of the party, was also the owner of one of the largest ironworks in the state, and all five were large security holders (Moore held £17,776 in continental loan office certificates). Furthermore, the anti-ratificationist candidates who were defeated in Philadelphia in 1787—Pettit, John Steinmetz, William Irvine, and state treasurer David Rittenhouse—had similar interests.[9]

---

[8] A writer in the *Evening Herald* of March 8, 1785, said of the funding act that "to unravel the code of policy which it contains, requires no small share of sagacity and Machiavelian shrewdness." Some understanding of it may be reached by a careful reading and analysis of the arguments published in all the Philadelphia newspapers from 1784 to 1786, particularly the notes on the debates in the Assembly published in the *Evening Herald*. I have studied individual roles and attitudes further by correlating with them the security holdings of political figures and the loans granted them by the state bank. These fiscal data are recorded in New Loan Certificates, vols. A, B, C, and D, in the Public Records Division of the Pennsylvania Historical and Museum Commission, Harrisburg.

[9] New Loan Certificates, vol. A, accounts 225, 230, 263, 4915, 4919–4925, 5381–5383; vol. B, accounts 6177–6184; vol. C, accounts 37, 54; vol. D, accounts 19235–19241; all in the Public Records Division of the Pennsylvania Historical and Museum Commission; Frederick Kuhl's Day Book, in the Historical Society of Pennsylvania; advertisements in the various Philadelphia newspapers —for example, Steinmetz's in the *Freeman's Journal* of October 10, 1783, and Pettit's in the issue of October 13, 1784. Most of these men had been instru-

Secondly, in Philadelphia the decision lay with the mechanics, artisans, and tradesmen, for they far outnumbered the mercantile and moneyed groups. These producing classes were somewhat dissatisfied with the protective duties levied on their behalf by the state, and, more important, they were incensed at the Radicals because of the attempt the latter had made in 1786 to reduce Philadelphia's representation in the Assembly by removing mechanics from the lists of taxpayer-voters.[10]

Despite the fact that the influence of the commercial interests and that of public security holders—Beard's two most important "dynamics" in the movement for ratification—were effectively neutralized in the contest in Pennsylvania, there was one critically important economic element in the struggle. This was the status of the Bank of North America. The Radicals, not content with the establishment of their competing state agency, had tried to destroy the Bank in 1785 by repealing its charter. The Bank operated for a year under charters from other states, and then its Pennsylvania charter was restored with limitations. As the subject of continuous political controversy, however, its footing was tenuous. But the sanctity-of-contracts clause in the proposed new Constitution would be a guarantee forever against legislative interference in the affairs of the Bank. It was this, not the protection of individual private creditors, that was the real significance of that celebrated clause so far as Pennsylvania was concerned.[11] Every stockholder in the Bank, everyone who dealt regularly with the Bank, and everyone under the personal influence of Robert Morris could

mental in the movement for a second bank, and Pettit had drawn up the state's funding act.

[10] Brunhouse, *Counter-Revolution in Pennsylvania*, 192; *Minutes of the General Assembly*, 10th Assembly, 3d Session, September 7, 1786. After the Republicans were returned to power in the elections of October, 1786, the right to vote was restored to the mechanics.

[11] It was not until 1819 that the United States Supreme Court had the opportunity to rule that a corporate charter was a contract within the meaning of the contract clause. *Dartmouth College v. Woodward*, 4 Wheaton 518. In a very similar issue in Pennsylvania in 1784, however, involving an act of 1779 which amended the charter of the University of Pennsylvania, the State Council of Censors held just the opposite, that a corporate charter was not a contract. The opinion was written by Radical leader George Bryan. The decision is recorded in the Journal of the Council of Censors, 1784, vol. 2, pp. 520–526,

easily be moved to help establish a political system that would prevent tinkering by the state's politicians.[12]

But these economic considerations were only part of an intricate mixture of philosophical, religious, ethnic, social, and geographical considerations involved in the contest over ratification in Pennsylvania. Three of the most important such considerations may be mentioned. Two of these were basic philosophical differences between the two parties which, at the risk of oversimplification, may be termed 1) state sovereignty versus national sovereignty and 2) democracy versus republicanism. Both of these are extremely large concepts, involving contemporary labels the meanings of which unfortunately are often obscure, and both were very large issues involving a sizeable number of smaller issues. Many, perhaps most, voters aligned themselves with one party or the other because of its position on some of the lesser of the component issues, such matters, for example, as the wartime loyalty oath and persecution of the Quakers, the question of the charter of the University of Pennsylvania, the organization of the state militia, and the Society of the Cincinnati. 3) Related to both these philosophical bases of division, but not quite the same as either, was intrastate sectionalism and its most persistent manifestation, the demand for local self-government.

Some facts relative to the economic holdings of the contestants in Philadelphia have been cited. It remains to be shown whether the contest in the ratifying convention was, in Beard's terms, one between personalty and realty interests. The geographical distribution of the vote would seem to suggest a conflict between personalty and realty, for Federalists were elected from all counties on the lower Delaware as well as from the city. Beard's argument that this was the case is rather convincing. Basing his observations on fragmentary biographical

in the Public Records Division of the Pennsylvania Historical and Museum Commission.

[12] Thomas Smith, president of the Bank eighty years later, wrote in respect to the state's interference in the affairs of the Bank that "the political heresy of State rights was then, as now, rampant." Quoted in Lewis, *Bank of North America*, 149.

sketches of the sixty-nine members of the convention, he concluded that the several economic classes of delegates in the convention voted as follows: [13]

CLASS	FOR RATIFICATION	AGAINST RATIFICATION
Merchants	4	1
Lawyers	8	1
Doctors	2	—
Clergymen	2	—
Farmers	10	13
Capitalists	12	3
Total Classifiable . . .	38	18
Security holders . . .	19	0

A more careful examination, however, reveals a quite different makeup of the ratifying convention. The economic interests of the delegates were as follows.[14]

DELEGATES VOTING FOR RATIFICATION

One of the delegates, George Latimer (city of Philadelphia), was a merchant directly engaged in international trade. He also owned one share in the Bank of North America and a 102-acre tract in western Pennsylvania, which he was apparently holding for speculation.[15]

[13] Beard, *Economic Interpretation*, 273–281.

[14] Two sets of documents have been used to determine the security holdings of the members of Pennsylvania's convention. The first set consists of the records of the funding of continental debts under the state assumption act of 1786—the records entitled New Loan Certificates, cited in notes 8 and 9, above, which are preserved in the Public Records Division of the Pennsylvania Historical and Museum Commission. The second set comprises the Records of the Loan of 1790 in the Fiscal Section of the National Archives. The following volumes in the latter collection were useful: vol. 622, Subscription Register, Domestic [continental] Debt, 1790–91; vol. 624, Journal of the Assumed Debt, 1791–95; vol. 625, Ledger, 6% Stock, 1791–97; vol. 630, Journal of the Continental Debt, 1790–91; vol. 631, Journal of the Continental Debt, Journal "B"; vol. 54-2, Ledger, 6% Stock; vol. 610, Register of Loan Office Certificates 1788; vols. 611 and 612, Registers of Public Debt Certificates, 1785–87; vol. "X," Register of Loan Office Certificates, 1786–87; and vol. "W," Register of Certificates issued by John Story, 1785–86.

[15] Lewis, *Bank of North America*, 139; *Pennsylvania Archives*, 3d Series, edited by William H. Egle and G. E. Reed, vol. 26, p. 762. Beard lists Latimer as a security holder, citing "Journal B," which can refer only to volume 631. Despite a careful search, I found no indication of any original funding activities by Latimer in this or any other volume.

Four of the delegates were tradesmen—that is, owners of retail stores: [16]

Hilary Baker (Philadelphia County), a trader who dealt principally in iron wares.

John Boyd (Northumberland), co-owner of a country store. Boyd had also been the co-owner of a potash works which failed in the 1780's, and he owned $808 worth of public securities.[17]

William Wilson (Northumberland), Boyd's partner in the country store and the defunct potash works.

Benjamin Elliott (Huntington), whose principal occupation was farming, though he owned a country store. His farm consisted of 80 acres and 8 head of stock. He also owned 590 acres of vacant land and $10.30 in securities.[18]

Six of the delegates were "capitalists," owners of manufacturing establishments:

John Arndt (Northampton), proprietor of a grist mill and owner of a 148-acre farm and 10 head of livestock.[19]

Robert Coleman (Lancaster), proprietor of an ironworks.[20]

David Deshler (Northampton), proprietor of two grist mills, one in Salisbury Township and one in Allen Township, and owner of 410 acres of farmland in the two places. He also owned $15,432 face value of continental loan office certificates, though he funded only $7,550 of them under the state assumption program.[21]

Richard Downing (Chester), owner of a fulling mill, a grist mill, and a sawmill and of 400 acres of vacant land in Northumberland County.[22]

[16] Identification of occupations and other biographical information, unless otherwise documented, is derived from the sketches of the members in William H. Egle's "The Constitutional Convention of 1776: Biographical Sketches of Its Members," in the *Pennsylvania Magazine of History and Biography*, vols. 2 and 4 (1879, 1880) and the same author's "The Federal Constitution of 1787: Biographical Sketches of the Members of the Pennsylvania Convention," *ibid.*, vols. 10 and 11 (1886, 1887).

[17] Records of the Loan of 1790, vol. 613, account 7952; New Loan Certificates, vol. A, accounts 1606–1607; vol. B, accounts 8239–8241.

[18] *Pennsylvania Archives*, 3d Series, 22:328, 345, 354, 365; Records of the Loan of 1790, vol. 612, account 5136.

[19] *Pennsylvania Archives*, 3d Series, 19:368.

[20] Beard mistakenly lists Coleman as a security holder, citing the Register of Loan Office Certificates, 1788. This is vol. 610 of the Records of the Loan of 1790; folio 38 shows that Coleman owned $277.45 in securities which were transferred to John Bayard early in 1787, and folio 2 refers to $125 in certificates which Coleman sold to Lewis Brontz prior to 1787. Hence Coleman owned no securities when the convention met, and he acquired none later.

[21] *Pennsylvania Archives*, 3d Series, 19:24, 253; Records of the Loan of 1790, vol. 611, folio 100; New Loan Certificates, vol. A, accounts 296–298, 301, 303–314.

[22] *Pennsylvania Archives*, 3d Series, 12:428.

Sebastian Graff (Lancaster), co-owner of an iron forge. He also owned a 250-acre farm and 13 head of livestock.[23]

John Richards (Montgomery), an ironmaster who also owned a small shop and a 469-acre farm with 12 animals.[24]

Six of the delegates were lawyers:

Stephen Chambers (Lancaster).

David Grier (York), who funded $4,927 in securities in 1786. Grier was dead in 1791, but his executors funded $12,054 in his name in that year, signifying that Grier had been acquiring securities at about the time the convention met.[25]

Thomas Hartley (York), who also owned about a thousand acres of western lands.[26]

John Hubley (Lancaster), who owned $29 in securities.[27]

Jasper Yeates (Lancaster), who handled the affairs of the Robert Morris partnership—Willing, Morris, and Swanwick—in the Lancaster area. Yeates owned $17,375 in securities.[28]

James Wilson (city of Philadelphia), whose interests have been indicated above, pages 57–59.

Two of the delegates were physicians:

Enoch Edwards (Philadelphia County), who owned 300 acres of unoccupied land in Washington County, a 145-acre farm in Philadelphia County, and $5,729 in securities.[29]

Benjamin Rush (city of Philadelphia), who owned one share in the Bank of North America and $1,341 face value of securities.[30]

Two of the delegates were clergymen:

John Black (York), a Presbyterian minister who owned no real estate but who owned $443 in securities.[31]

F. A. Muhlenberg (Montgomery), the renowned clergyman-politician who was to become the first speaker of the United States House of

---

[23] *Ibid.*, 12:772; Records of the Loan of 1790, vol. 630, folio 252.

[24] *Pennsylvania Archives*, 3d Series, 16:625.

[25] New Loan Certificates, vol. A, accounts 3057–3059, 3062–3067; vol. B, accounts 10266–10271, 10273–10274; Records of the Loan of 1790, vol. 630, folio 251.

[26] Beard, *Economic Interpretation*, 277.

[27] Records of the Loan of 1790, vol. 610, folio 8.

[28] Yeates Papers, in the Historical Society of Pennsylvania; Records of the Loan of 1790, vol. 622, folio 2; vol. 624, folio 2; vol. 630, folio 1. The entries in volume 630 duplicate those in volume 622 except that interest is added. The larger figure is used here.

[29] *Pennsylvania Archives*, 3d Series, 16:538; 26:554; Records of the Loan of 1790, vol. 630, folio 80.

[30] Lewis, *Bank of North America*, 134; New Loan Certificates, vol. B, accounts 7439–7440.

[31] Records of the Loan of 1790, vol. 612, account 8880.

Representatives. Muhlenberg owned a small farm consisting of 56 acres and 5 animals.[32]

Nine of the delegates had other non-farming occupations and interests:

Samuel Ashmead (Philadelphia County), a semi-retired country gentleman whose estate was assessed at £1,174 ($3,131) in 1782. He owned $1,374 in securities.[33]

Stephen Balliet (Northampton), a tavernkeeper who owned a 262-acre farm and $1,871 in securities.[34]

George Gray (Philadelphia County), proprietor of a ferry operating across the Delaware River which, according to his political enemies, brought him a handsome income. Gray was also a substantial landowner, possessing 663 acres, 40 animals, and two slaves on four farms, and he owned parcels of real estate in Philadelphia.[35]

John Hunn (Philadelphia County), a former sea captain living in a state of semi-retirement on his farm. He also owned 400 acres of vacant land in Bedford County.[36]

Joseph Horsefield (Northampton), a saddler who owned no known real estate but who owned $3,696 in securities.[37]

Thomas McKean (city of Philadelphia), an erstwhile Radical political leader and the state's chief justice, a lawyer who was not engaged in private practice. McKean owned two valuable parcels of real estate in the Dock Ward in Philadelphia and 400 acres of vacant land in the western part of the state. He owned $5,581 in securities which he had funded in 1786 under the state assumption act, and by 1788 he had acquired an additional $1,772 in continental loan office certificates.[38]

Timothy Pickering (Luzerne), a non-practicing lawyer who at the moment was dabbling in a number of enterprises in the hope of making his fortune. He had connections with various groups of land speculators and sometimes acted as their agent.[39]

---

[32] *Biographical Directory of Congress* (1927 edition), 1343; *Pennsylvania Archives,* 3d Series, 16:644. A writer in the *Freeman's Journal* of October 10, 1783, attacked Muhlenberg's participation in politics and called him a "clergyman without religion."

[33] *Freeman's Journal,* October 10, 1783; *Pennsylvania Archives,* 3d Series, 16:101; Records of the Loan of 1790, vol. 622, folio 596.

[34] *Pennsylvania Archives,* 3d Series, 19:219; Records of the Loan of 1790, vol. 612, account 8233; vol. "X," no page number.

[35] *Freeman's Journal,* October 10, 1783; *Pennsylvania Archives,* 3d Series, 16:530, 581, 637, 710.

[36] *Ibid.,* 25:536.

[37] *Ibid.,* 19:203, 363; Records of the Loan of 1790, vol. 630, folios 22, 24. The security listing is duplicated, with accrued interest, in volume 630, folios 20–21.

[38] McKean Papers, in the Historical Society of Pennsylvania; Records of the Loan of 1790, vol. 610, folio 26; New Loan Certificates, vol. A, accounts 2745–2752; vol. C, account 99.

[39] William A. Robinson's sketch of Pickering in the *Dictionary of American Biography;* Beard, *Economic Interpretation,* 278. The Pickering Papers, in the Historical Society of Massachusetts, contain much additional data. Beard mis-

William McPherson (Philadelphia County), a former professional soldier who sought with little success to become a professional officeholder in the 1780's. In September, 1789, McPherson was appointed by Washington to the position of surveyor of customs in Philadelphia.

General Anthony Wayne (Chester), owner of a 360-acre farm in Eastown and various parcels of realty given him for war service. He received his largest gift from Georgia. There, with General Nathaniel Greene, he had bought confiscated estates costing £15,512. By a resolution of the House of Assembly of Georgia the two generals had been given a bonus which credited them with £9,000 on this property. Greene died in 1786 and Wayne was apparently still indebted for the balance. Wayne's financial affairs occasioned difficulty for him during the 1780's; in addition to the large debt he owed to Georgia, he was apparently still in debt for a loan of 50,000 guilders he had secured in Holland. He was interested in various other ventures, mainly dealings in vacant lands, but he does not appear to have profited from many of them. He moved to Georgia soon after the convention. He owned $3,600 in securities.[40]

Sixteen of the delegates were farmers:

John Allison (Franklin), whose large farm consisted of 757 acres, 15 animals, and three slaves, and who owned $32 in securities.[41]

John Barclay (Bucks), whose farming activity apparently prospered, for besides his 98-acre farm in Durham Township he owned real estate in Philadelphia and 400 acres of vacant land in Northumberland County, and three shares (par value $1,200) in the Bank of North America.[42]

Thomas Bull (Chester), who owned 432 acres, 11 animals, and one slave.[43]

takenly lists Pickering as a security holder, citing the Index to Funded 6's, which is a reference to volume 54-2, folio 150, of the Records of Loan of 1790. This account shows that Pickering acquired $335 in funded six per cents from John Nicholson on April 29, 1793; no reference is made to any securities owned before that time.

[40] *Pennsylvania Archives*, 3d Series, 12:396; Sale-book of Confiscated Estates: Chatham County, p. 3, in the Georgia Department of Archives and History; John L. Gervais to Leonard DeNeufville, April 13, 1786, in the Gervais and Owen Papers, in the Manuscripts Division of the Library of Congress; New Loan Certificates, vol. A, accounts 739–742.

[41] *Pennsylvania Archives* (see references in the index to series 3); Records of the Loan of 1790, vol. 611, folio 75.

[42] *Pennsylvania Archives*, 3d Series, 13:567; 25:73; Lewis, *Bank of North America*, 133, 139; Records of the Loan of 1790, vol. 630, folio 87. That Barclay was a farmer is not certain, but he did own the 98-acre farm, and he is not included in the extensive lists of early lawyers, merchants, tradesmen, and manufacturers published in J. H. Battle, ed., *History of Bucks County, Pennsylvania* (Philadelphia, 1887).

[43] *Pennsylvania Archives*, 3d Series, 12:519; Records of the Loan of 1790, vol. 624, folio 22. Beard (*Economic Interpretation*, 276) correctly points out that Bull had managed an iron furnace before the war, but he is mistaken in stating that Bull returned to that occupation after the war. No indication that he engaged in any activity besides farming appears in Egle's sketches, on which McMaster and Stone (cited in note 5) based their sketches, which in turn were the basis for Beard's.

Thomas Campbell (York), who owned a farm of 200 acres.[44]

Thomas Cheney (Chester), who owned 150 acres, 12 animals, and one slave.[45]

William Gibbons (Chester), who inherited a farm from his parents, the size of which is not ascertainable.

John Hannum (Chester), who owned 420 acres, 21 animals, and $16 in securities.[46]

James Morris (Montgomery), who owned 350 acres, 26 animals, and one slave.[47]

John Nevill (Washington), a frontier farmer who had acquired a great deal more land than he was able to farm. By April, 1788, his landholdings amounted to 2,493 acres. He also owned $776 in securities.[48]

Benjamin Pedan (York), who owned 307 acres and 8 animals.[49]

Jonathan Roberts (Montgomery), who owned 300 acres and 15 animals.[50]

Thomas Scott (Washington), who like Nevill was a frontier farmer who owned more land than he could farm. He also owned $127 in securities.[51]

Henry Slagle (York), who owned 400 acres and 23 animals.[52]

Abraham Stout (Bucks), who owned 250 acres and 12 animals.[53]

Henry Wynkoop (Bucks), who owned what was a very large farm for the area, consisting of 500 acres, 9 animals, and 6 slaves. Though not a

[44] *Pennsylvania Archives*, 3d Series, 21:803.

[45] *Ibid.*, 12:247.

[46] *Ibid.*, 12:381; Records of the Loan of 1790, vol. 612, account 4892. Beard errs in listing Hannum as a security holder. He cites "Ledger C, 3% Stock," which refers to vol. 646, folio 196, of the Records of the Loan of 1790. This entry shows that Hannum acquired $224.60 in three per cent stock from Andrew Potter on June 3, 1791, and that he had none before that time. The $16 of securities referred to here was an old continental loan office certificate which Hannum apparently sold before 1790, for he never funded that or any other securities under the Loan of 1790.

[47] *Pennsylvania Archives*, 3d Series, 16:67, 234. Beard incorrectly lists Morris as a security holder, citing the "Index to Funded 6 C." This citaton refers to vol. 54-2, folio 371, of the Records of the Loan of 1790, which shows Morris as the owner of $1,887.91 in 6 per cent securities. The entry, however, is one carried forward from an earlier entry in Ledger A, 6% Stock (vol. 636, folio 398). This is likewise an entry carried forward from an earlier entry, the original transaction (vol. 636, folio 337). The original transaction shows that Morris acquired the securities from Andrew Summers, Jr., on January 10, 1792, more than four years after the Pennsylvania ratifying convention.

[48] *Pennsylvania Archives*, 3d Series, 22:740; 26:592 ff.; Records of the Loan of 1790, vol. 611, folio 12.

[49] *Pennsylvania Archives*, 3d Series, vol. 21, Lists for Chanceford Township, 1782.

[50] *Ibid.*, 16:704.

[51] *Ibid*, 36:604, 606; Records of the Loan of 1790, vol. 612, account 7777.

[52] *Pennsylvania Archives*, 3d Series, 21:565, 718.

[53] *Ibid.*, 13:595.

lawyer Wynkoop was presiding judge of the Bucks County Court. He owned a $6 certificate of the public debt.[54]

Thomas Yardley (Bucks), whose farm was nearly as large as Wynkoop's, consisting of 400 acres, 15 animals, and 3 slaves. Yardley owned a public debt certificate having a face value of $2.56.[55]

DELEGATES VOTING AGAINST RATIFICATION

One of the delegates, Nathaniel Breading (Fayette), was a merchant engaged directly in international trade, a frontier capitalist who operated on a large scale. He regularly conducted a direct trade via the Ohio and Mississippi rivers with the Spanish at New Orleans, operated wholesale and retail stores and an iron furnace, and owned large quantities of western lands.[56]

One of the delegates, Joseph Heister (Berks), was the proprietor of a retail store. Heister operated a store in Reading, and had married the daughter of a Philadelphia importing merchant. He was the largest security holder in the convention; in 1786 he owned $17,152 in securities, and by 1788 he increased his holdings to $30,838, in which year he collected $4,254 in interest. He also owned large tracts of western land.[57]

Seven of the delegates were "capitalists," owners of manufacturing establishments:

Richard Bard (Cumberland), proprietor of a lumber mill. Bard also carried on extensive farming operations on a 545-acre farm with 21 animals and 3 slaves.[58]

John Bishop (Berks), who carried on extensive and varied manufacturing operations in a fulling mill, a sawmill, a grist mill, and two distilleries. His other personalty interests included western lands owned and held for speculation and $1,525 in securities. He also owned a 440-acre farm and 20 head of livestock.[59]

Jonathan Hoge (Cumberland), a liquor manufacturer who owned and operated two large distilleries. He also owned a 278-acre farm and 7 head of livestock and securities amounting to $286.[60]

[54] *Ibid.*, 13:536; Battle, ed., *History of Bucks County*, 256, 691–692; Records of the Loan of 1790, vol. 611, folio 64.

[55] *Pennsylvania Archives*, 3d Series, 13:531; Records of the Loan of 1790, vol. 611, folio 64.

[56] Franklin Ellis, *History of Fayette County, Pennsylvania, with Biographical Sketches* (Philadelphia, 1882), 650.

[57] Beard, *Economic Interpretation*, 279; Records of the Loan of 1790, vol. 630, folios 122, 309; vol. 631, folios 250, 298; vol. 610, folio 43; New Loan Certificates, vol. A, accounts 1775–1802; *Pennsylvania Archives* (consult index in Series 3).

[58] *Pennsylvania Archives*, 3d Series, 20:632.

[59] *Ibid.*, 18:605, and index to Series 3; Records of the Loan of 1790, vol. 611, folios 114–115; vol. 612, account 8693; vol. "X," unnumbered entry.

[60] *Pennsylvania Archives*, 3d Series, 20:556, 707; Records of the Loan of 1790, vol. 611, folio 13.

Abraham Lincoln (Berks), owner of a sawmill. He also owned 19 animals and 760 acres of land, a large part of which was probably timberland.[61]

Nicholas Lotz (Berks), owner of a sawmill near Reading and proprietor of a clothing business. He also owned a 153-acre farm. He funded $1,448 in securities under the funding plan of 1786, and by the end of 1788 he had acquired additional securities totaling $2,912.[62]

Adam Orth (Dauphin), an iron manufacturer, the owner and operator of Newmarket Forge. He also owned 746 acres of land, most of which was used to furnish wood for his furnaces, and a negro slave. He owned $300 in securities in 1786 and had acquired $51 more by 1788.[63]

John Reynolds (Cumberland), who owned two grist mills, a sawmill, and two distilleries. He also owned a 200-acre farm with 9 animals and 3 slaves. His other personalty holdings included several tracts of western land and $659 in securities.[64]

One of the delegates, John Andre Hanna (Dauphin), was "a successful lawyer at Harrisburg" who held $1,435 in securities.[65]

One of the delegates, Joseph Powell (Bedford), was a clergyman. He also owned a 150-acre farm and 14 head of livestock, and he had purchased several tracts of western land.[66]

Six of the delegates had other non-farming occupations and interests:

William Brown (Dauphin), who was engaged in various land-promotional activities and speculations. He owned $3,878 in securities in 1786, and had acquired an additional $6,767 in continental loan office certificates by 1788.[67]

William Findley (Westmoreland), a weaver by trade who also owned a farm of 250 acres and 13 animals. His real occupation was that of professional politician. He was speculating in public securities; in 1786 he owned only $75 in securities, but by 1788 had acquired $5,902 more.[68]

---

[61] *Pennsylvania Archives*, 3d Series, 19:687.

[62] Beard, *Economic Interpretation*, 279; *Pennsylvania Archives*, 3d Series, 18:572, 654; Records of the Loan of 1790, vol. 610, folios 39, 45; vol. 611, folio 114; vol. "X"; New Loan Certificates, vol. A, accounts 1954–1958.

[63] *Pennsylvania Archives*, 3d Series, 17:552; New Loan Certificates, vol. B, account 11073; Records of the Loan of 1790, vol. 611, folio 166.

[64] *Pennsylvania Archives*, 3d Series, 20:757 and index; Records of the Loan of 1790, vol. 611, folios 19, 59.

[65] Beard, *Economic Interpretation*, 279; Records of the Loan of 1790, vol. 630, folio 49.

[66] *Pennsylvania Archives*, 3d Series, 22:234 and index.

[67] William H. Egle, *History of the Counties of Dauphin and Lebanon* (Philadelphia, 1883), 426 and elsewhere; New Loan Certificates, vol. A, accounts 1, 2, 3, 60; vol. B, accounts 10, 391; vol. C, accounts 120, 126; Records of the Loan of 1790, vol. 610, folios 23, 24; vol. 611, folios 21, 23, 25; vol. 612, accounts 8976–9025.

[68] George Dallas Albert, *History of the County of Westmoreland, Pa.* (Philadelphia, 1882), 208 ff.; *Biographical Directory of Congress* (1927 edition), 966; Records of the Loan of 1790, vol. 624, folio 40; vol. 631, folio 223.

James Marshall (Washington), a county sheriff and land speculator. He owned 3,091 acres in western Pennsylvania and large tracts in western Virginia, and he held $421 in securities.[69]

James Martin (Bedford), who was engaged in miscellaneous promotional and speculative deals. He owned farms in Bedford and Washington counties which he rented and $10,858 in securities.[70]

John Smilie (Fayette), owner and operator of a 300-acre farm with 20 head of livestock, but like Findley a professional politician.[71]

John Whitehill (Lancaster), a tavernkeeper. He also owned a farm of 374 acres and 9 animals. His security holdings were modest, amounting to only $61.[72]

Six of the delegates were farmers:

John Baird (Westmoreland), who owned 100 acres and 9 animals and held $172 in securities.[73]

James Edgar (Washington), the size of whose farm was not ascertained.

John Harris (Cumberland), who owned 375 acres, 9 animals, and one slave. He funded $1,485 in securities in 1786.[74]

John Ludwig (Berks), who owned two farms with a total of 363 acres and 24 animals, and held $150 in securities.[75]

Robert Whitehill (Cumberland), who likewise owned two farms. One farm, in Cumberland County, consisted of 427 acres, 11 animals, and one slave; the other, in Lancaster County, consisted of 200 acres, 10 animals, and one slave. Just how much Whitehill's security holdings amounted to is not clear. In 1786 he funded $3,651 in securities. In 1791 he funded an additional $4,305 under the Loan of 1790, but on the same day he transferred this amount equally to three other men. It is probable that the entire second operation was conducted in their behalf.[76]

[69] Boyd Crumrine, ed., *History of Washington County, Pennsylvania* (Philadelphia, 1882), 226, 728; Records of the Loan of 1790, vol. 611, folio 18; vol. 612, account 5913.

[70] *Pennsylvania Archives*, 3d Series, 22:317, 415; Records of the Loan of 1790, vol. 54-2, folio 330. Only the $4,825 in 6 per cent stock of this original funding operation is recorded in volume 54-2. The remainder has been calculated on the basis of the fact that six per cents constituted four-ninths of the total amount funded.

[71] *Pennsylvania Archives*; consult index to 3d Series.

[72] *Ibid.*, 17:616, 725; New Loan Certificates, vol. A, account 4094; Records of the Loan of 1790, vol. 616, account 6561.

[73] *Pennsylvania Archives*, 3d Series, 20:714; Records of the Loan of 1790, vol. 622, folio 561.

[74] *Pennsylvania Archives*, 3d Series, 20:714; New Loan Certificates, vol. A, accounts 2713-2717.

[75] *Pennsylvania Archives*, 3d Series, 18:607, 676; Records of the Loan of 1790, vol. 610, folio 40.

[76] *Pennsylvania Archives*, 3d Series, 20:710; 17:738; Records of the Loan of 1790, vol. 630, folio 48; New Loan Certificates, vol. A, accounts 2718-2724; vol. B, accounts 10525-10526, 10528.

William Todd (Westmoreland), the size of whose farm was not ascertained. Todd owned $3,430 in securities in 1786.[77]

These data may be summarized as follows to show how the delegates lined up for and against ratification, considered from the point of view of their occupations and from the point of view of their investments and security holdings:

ECONOMIC CLASSIFICATION	VOTING YEA		VOTING NAY	
	No.	PER CENT	No.	PER CENT
Occupation:				
Merchant	1	2.2	1	4.3
Tradesman	4	8.7	1	4.3
Manufacturing capitalist	6	13.0	7	30.4
Lawyer	6	13.0	1	4.3
Physician	2	4.3	—	—
Clergyman	2	4.3	1	4.3
Miscellaneous	9	19.6	6	26.0
Farmer	16	34.8	6	26.0
Total	46	100.0	23	100.0
Investments in:				
Commerce	6	13.0	2	8.7
Manufacturing	8	17.4	8	34.8
Vacant lands	11	23.9	8	34.8
Securities	23	50.0	17	73.9
One or more of the above . . .	39	84.7	21	91.3
Security holdings:				
Combined, all delegates		$67,666		$70,852
Average per holder		2,942		4,167
Mean per holder		846		1,460
Average, all delegates		1,471		3,080

In short, the delegates on the two sides held about the same amounts of the same kinds of property, and they were engaged in similar occupations. The anti-Federalists were better endowed with holdings of most forms of personalty, particularly

[77] *Ibid.*, vol. B, account 10593; vol. C, accounts 86, 92, 94.

public securities. If the differences in the property holdings of the members are of any significance whatever, they tend to indicate that the exact opposite of Beard's thesis is more nearly the truth than the thesis itself.

MASSACHUSETTS

MASSACHUSETTS, still nursing the wounds in its body politic inflicted by Shays' Rebellion and the underlying troubles which had produced the insurrection, was a large hurdle for the Federalists. In the minds of some of its citizens the Rebellion had brought a reaction favorable to a stronger Union, but among at least as many it had occasioned the opposite reaction, and the delegates elected to the Massachusetts ratifying convention, though generally uninstructed, were thought to be hostile to the Constitution. The state sorely needed some kind of outside help, but its people, scarcely trusting one another and in no mood to trust outsiders, were split into bitter factions. Consequently Federalists everywhere held their breath as the Massachusetts ratifying convention assembled, and they did not breathe easily again until February 6, 1788, when, thanks to shrewd generalship in the convention, the delegates voted by the narrow margin of 187 to 168 to ratify the Constitution.

At the time the Philadelphia Convention had finished its work on the Constitution Massachusetts was preoccupied with its internal problems. The legislature, in the hands of a coalition of Shaysites and moderate Shays sympathizers who were determined to accomplish by legal means a redress of the grievances they had been unable to rectify by force of arms, was the object of popular attention.[78] The state's newspapers responded slowly

---

[78] Apparently it is not very generally recognized that Shays sympathizers captured control of the Massachusetts government in 1787. An example of their power is afforded by a view of the state Senate. In the spring elections of 1787 nineteen new members were elected and twenty-one incumbents were returned to their seats. Five of the new members had actually borne arms against the state in the insurrection, seven more later voted against the Constitution, and six of the remaining seven were avowedly friendly to the cause of the rebels (though some disapproved of the resort to violence). Several of the twenty-one re-elected incumbents had similar sympathies, and a half dozen more comprised Samuel Adams' faction, which was also in general sympathy

to the news of the completion of the Constitution: those outside Boston hardly mentioned it at all, and except for a short-
lived flood of distorted, pro-ratification "news" items originating in Philadelphia, nothing on the subject appeared in Boston
newspapers during September and October. After a complaint
was voiced in the legislature that in publishing only such matter
the Boston newspapers were being unfair to the opponents of
the Constitution, the discussions became more lively. Of the
three largest Boston newspapers, one, the *Centinel,* printed
arguments on both sides of the issue; a second, the *Gazette,* a
newspaper favorable to the faction headed by ex-Governor
Bowdoin, published chiefly pro-ratificationist propaganda; and
the third, the *American Herald,* spokesman for John Hancock
and his following, published chiefly anti-ratificationist propaganda.[79]

Hence it is somewhat surprising that when the legislature received reports from its delegates to the Philadelphia Convention
it issued, with no recorded debate or dissent, a call for a convention to consider ratification. Elections were set for the first
week in December, and the meeting of the convention for
January 9, 1788. Little is to be learned from study of the town
meetings that elected delegates, for only about two dozen of
the members of the convention were given instructions. It seems
likely, however, that a clear majority of the 355 delegates, perhaps as many as 200, were opposed to ratification.[80]

with the rebels' cause, though they deprecated the insurrection. See Theodore
Sedgwick to Nathan Dane, July 5, 1787, in the Sedgwick Papers, in the Historical Society of Massachusetts; Boston *Massachusetts Centinel,* June 2, 1787.
Also compare the repeated demands of the Shaysites, as published in the various Boston, Worcester, Springfield, and Northampton newspapers, with the
statutes enacted in Massachusetts in 1787 and 1788.

[79] Boston *Massachusetts Centinel, Boston Gazette,* and Boston *American Herald,* October–December, 1787, and January, 1788.

[80] Journal of the House of Representatives of the General Court of Massachusetts, 8th Court, 2d Session, manuscript in the Massachusetts Archives;
Massachusetts Centinel, December, 1787. Libby, in his *Geographical Distribution of the Vote,* 75–78, shows that twenty-five of the towns gave instructions
to their delegates. Samuel Bannister Harding, in his *The Contest over the
Ratification of the Federal Constitution in the State of Massachusetts* (New
York, 1896), 67n, quotes a member of the convention as predicting at the outset that there would be 192 votes against the Constitution and 144 for ratification.

The Federalists executed their campaign skillfully once the delegates began to arrive in Boston. They began by releasing, in the Boston newspapers and in pamphlets, a barrage of propaganda designed to appeal to the country members. In the convention, to gain opportunity for backstage maneuvering as well as for argument on the floor, they induced the convention to debate each clause of the Constitution separately. Because John Hancock and Samuel Adams remained silent and because Elbridge Gerry, who had removed from his home town, Marblehead, where his greatest political strength lay, had been defeated as a candidate for the convention, the Federalist delegates had a definite edge in forensic talent. This combination of newspaper propaganda and convention debates doubtless won over many of the lukewarm opponents of the Constitution.[81]

The Federalists' most important maneuvers, however, took place off the convention floor. Sam Adams, a staunch friend and political ally of Gerry, was publicly noncommittal. Privately he had expressed strong reservations about the Constitution, even though most of his income was apparently derived from interest on his public security holdings. To win Adams' support, a mass meeting of the mechanics and tradesmen of Boston and environs was staged at the famous Green Dragon Inn two days before the convention met. The participants in this meeting, numbering nearly four hundred, adopted a set of strong resolutions in favor of the Constitution. This was enough for Adams, and he announced that he would support ratification.[82]

Adams' influence was small, however, as compared with that of John Hancock. Hancock, a strong advocate of states' rights on personal and political as well as philosophical grounds, had it in his power to throw the convention's vote either way. To

[81] A number of accounts of the proceedings of the convention have been published: Elliott's *Debates* (1854 edition), vol. 2; a contemporary edition, published by the Boston newspaper firm of Adams and Nourse in 1788, *Federal Convention of Massachusetts*; a revised edition published in 1808 by Oliver and Munroe, Boston publishers, *Massachusetts Constitutional Convention, 1788*; and an edition published by the state in 1856, *Massachusetts Convention, 1788*.

[82] *Massachusetts Centinel*, January 9, 1788; Harding, *The Contest in Massachusetts*, 95–97. Harding says that Adams' enthusiasm for the contest was dampened by the death of his son at the time the convention was meeting.

enlist Hancock's support the Federalists promised to support him for the vice-presidency or, if Virginia did not ratify in time to qualify Washington, even for the presidency. Nothing could have appealed to Hancock more, and he gave his support to ratification. After a month of maneuvers and debates the Federalists felt strong enough to call for a vote, and by a majority of only 19 of the 355 delegates the Constitution was approved.[83]

In the ratifying convention, as in much of the postwar history of Massachusetts, conflicts between economic classes were of at least superficial influence. To understand the influences and their limitations, it is necessary to review some of the features of the state's postwar economic and fiscal plight.

During the 1780's Massachusetts' economy was undergoing fundamental readjustments. Certain external conditions had deranged the patterns of the state's commerce and necessitated basic changes in traditional commercial methods: the closing of the British West Indies to American bottoms, the prohibitive tariff that Britain imposed on imported whale oil, and Virginia's creation of a mercantile fleet which greatly reduced Massachusetts' share of the tobacco-carrying trade. The difficulties that Massachusetts faced as a result of these developments were aggravated by two internal changes. First, the personnel of the commercial community underwent basic changes, occasioned by the departure during the war of a large number of loyalist merchants and the rise, through privateering, of a new rich group who were as yet largely inexperienced and insecure in their wealth.[84] Second, the seaboard towns, principally Boston, lost their source of agricultural exports and much of their in-

[83] Rufus King to Henry Knox, February 1, 1788, in Charles R. King, *Life and Correspondence of Rufus King* (6 vols., New York, 1894–1900), 1:319; Harding, *The Contest in Massachusetts*, 85–87.

[84] Probably more than three-fourths of the mercantile community in Boston left the state as loyalists. "An Act to prevent the return to this state of certain persons therein named," published in the *Boston Gazette* of September 1, 1783, lists 54 persons described as merchants, 18 as mariners, 11 as traders, and 4 as shopkeepers. Sixty-six more were called "Esquire," probably half of whom were merchants, since royal officials and country gentlemen were listed separately as such. About 150 merchants were active in Boston after the war, no more than 20 of whom had been active as merchants before the war.

ternal trade after the war. The wheat farmers of the Connecticut valley, who before the war carried their crops by sled to
Boston for export, began in the 1780's to do most of their trading via the river with Hartford and New York City.[85]

Another major change in Massachusetts' economy after the
war was a boom in manufacturing activity. Exclusive of sperma-
cetti works, distilleries, and shipbuilding, which had been the
state's principal manufacturing enterprises before the war, there
were 2,397 factory establishments in Massachusetts by 1786.
The value of goods they annually produced for export during
the late 1780's was three times as great as the total annual production of all New England before the war.[86] Thus there was
during the postwar decade an enormous growth in the relative
importance of manufacturing and a comparable decline in the
importance of shipping.

As a result of all these economic changes various economic
groups in the state, most of them new and insecure classes,
clamored for political action on their behalf, and few of them
were able to appreciate legislation designed for other groups
or the general good. There was, in short, a marked growth of
economic self-consciousness.

The fiscal policy of the state and the problems it faced during
the 1780's perhaps did as much as these economic changes to
foster conflicts between economic groups. These matters were

[85] See the *Boston Gazette* of February 9, 1767, for evidence that most of the
wheat grown in the Connecticut valley at that time was being exported to
Boston by sled and thence to foreign markets. Postwar wheat exports from
Boston amounted to only a fraction of what they had been prior to 1776. See
"Account of the Exports and Clearances of the Port of Boston for the Years
1787 and 1788," in the Massachusetts Miscellaneous Collection in the Manuscripts Division of the Library of Congress. My tabulations of ship movements
reported in newspaper announcements indicate that during the months of
April to December the number of clearances was about the same as it had
been before the war, but that the period January to March, which had formerly been a busy exporting season, was now a slack one.

[86] Data on manufacturing are derived from "Evaluations and Taxes," vol.
163 in the Massachusetts Archives. Prewar exports from New England reached
an all-time high in 1771, when they totaled £150,381 sterling (about $667,000).
Samuel Hazard, ed., *United States Commercial and Statistical Register*, vol. 1,
number 1, pp. 4–5 (Philadelphia, February 13, 1839). During the 1780's postwar
exports from Massachusetts, a large part of which consisted of manufactured

handled with little foresight and less justice. The state was dilatory in taking any action with respect to its war debts, and upon returning from the war many of its soldiers were forced to sell, for as little as fifteen cents on the dollar, the securities and notes in which they had been paid. When the state funded its debts in 1784, it made insufficient allowance for the inflated wartime prices at which some of the securities had been issued, and Massachusetts was saddled with a debt in excess of five million dollars. The annual tax load was over a million dollars, far more than the state's direct-property and poll-tax system could reasonably bear. As taxes mounted, so did complaints. The most vocal dissidents were the ex-soldiers, who protested that a soldier who had been paid a hundred pounds in securities upon his discharge had been forced to sell them for less than twenty pounds, and that by 1786 annual taxes of nearly the sum he had realized were being levied to support principal and interest payments on those securities. As time passed the gulf between security holders and taxpayers broadened, particularly during the governorship of James Bowdoin, 1785–1787.[87]

Thus by the time the issue of ratification came before the people of Massachusetts, conditions were such that it might well have been decided on economic grounds. Shipping interests welcomed the Constitution, for the new general government it created could enact legislation to counter Britain's commercial restrictions. Furthermore, though it was not talked of publicly, it may have been that some Massachusetts shippers hoped to gain a larger share of the southern carrying trade through legislative restrictions against Britain, and that the talk of "retalia-

goods, were worth, in terms of prices at the places of export, well over four million dollars annually. My calculations for Boston are derived from the source cited in note 85; for Salem, from "Abstract of Imports Previous to 1792," in the Customs Office Records, Port of Salem, in the Fiscal Section of the National Archives; for Beverly, from Beverly Customs Office Records, in the Beverly Historical Society; and for all other ports from newspaper reports of vessel movements.

[87] The state's fiscal activities have been traced in the Journal of the House of Representatives, in the Massachusetts Archives. For an example of the complaints of the veterans see the article signed "A Member of the Hatfield Convention," in the Northampton *Hampshire Gazette*, November 1, 8, 1786.

tion" was merely a blind. Security holders likewise could enthusiastically endorse the Constitution, for it would remove the
payment of principal and interest from a hostile state legislature.
Many other propertied men who feared Shaysism may also have
supported the Constitution.

Yet it is not safe to oversimplify the issues. For one reason,
shippers and security holders constituted only a fraction of the
voting population. The number of security holders, in particular, declined rapidly after 1786 from thousands of small holders
to a few hundred large holders. Even if it is assumed that a few
shippers and security holders could control the votes of their
towns, there remains the fact that the towns in which there
were virtually no security or shipping interests far outnumbered
towns having such interests. Two students have recently asserted
that of 246 such "personalty-less" towns in Massachusetts
proper, 142 voted through their delegates to oppose the Constitution and 104 voted in favor of the Constitution. In the district of Maine 19 such towns voted for ratification and 22
against it.[88]

Thus according to these students' classifications more than
four of every five delegates in the convention represented such
non-personalty towns, and of these 57 per cent voted against
ratification of the Constitution, 43 per cent in favor of it. If
these figures are even approximately correct, a class-struggle
interpretation of the contest over ratification can have no meaning, even if the personalty "class" had been unanimous in support of ratification.

There are other limitations to an economic interpretation of
the contest over ratification in Massachusetts. The anti-Federalists in the convention expressed opposition to the Constitution
on the grounds that it included no bill of rights, that it required
no religious tests of officeholders, and that it tolerated slavery,
and on numerous other political and philosophical grounds, but

[88] Oscar and Mary F. Handlin, "Radicals and Conservatives in Massachusetts
after Independence," in the *New England Quarterly*, 17:343 ff. (September,
1944).

none on the ground of the economic and fiscal implications of its adoption. It seems reasonable to assume that if the delegates from interior Massachusetts, never reluctant to express their real sentiments on any issue, had objections to the Constitution that were consciously derived from economic considerations, they would have said so. One leading Federalist in the convention, Rufus King, attributed most of the opposition to lack of information and a prejudice which later came to be called anti-intellectualism.[89] Again, John Hancock had considerable influence among men who had commercial and public security interests and who would have followed him either way. When he cast his lot with the Federalists he doubtless persuaded many such men to vote for ratification, and thus a purely political act gave a seemingly economic coloring to the decision of some members of the convention.

It is perhaps sound to make the following general statements about the contest in Massachusetts. A substantial number of delegates who believed that their interests would be improved by the adoption of the Constitution voted for it for that reason, and some who feared they would suffer direct or indirect economic losses as a result of its adoption voted against ratification for that reason. On the other hand, a large number of delegates who could expect to derive economic gain from the adoption of the Constitution voted against ratification. A large number favored ratification on philosophical or political grounds, and an even larger number opposed it on similar grounds. It is quite likely that in Massachusetts, where the ideals of the Revolution were strong, many favored the Constitution because they considered it the fulfillment of the Revolution, while others, paradoxically, opposed it because they considered it counter-Revolutionary.

Only careful study of the economic status of the persons involved in the contest will reveal to what extent an economic

[89] Harding, *The Contest in Massachusetts*, 76–78. See also the speeches of anti-Federalists Benjamin Randall and Amos Singletary there quoted. Singletary was a substantial security holder.

class-struggle interpretation is valid. The following data are the results of such a study.

It is impossible, of course, to learn the occupations and economic interests of the voters who elected delegates in the town meetings. One can, however, make some reasonable estimates of the economic interests and occupations of the adult male population as a whole in the towns that voted for and in the towns that voted against the Constitution. By using the tax evaluations of 1786 as a basic source for the number of places of employment of various kinds, estimates have been made by the following method. Two adult males are allotted to each retail and wholesale store except those in Boston, Newburyport, and Salem, where three is the figure used. The number of sailors is estimated as one for every ten tons of shipping, which was the approximate average in all New England ports for which records are extant. Six workers are allowed for each manufacturing establishment; this figure includes an allowance for all manufacturing labor and personnel whether directly employed in the establishment or not, including such various self-employed craftsmen as carpenters, coopers, tailors, bakers, printers, and others. Finally, professional and miscellaneous groups, such as ministers, physicians, lawyers, country gentlemen, and professional officeholders are estimated at the rate of one for every nine adult males whose primary interests and occupations were in pursuits other than farming. All the remaining adult males are assumed to have been farmers.[90]

When this method is applied to the towns in Massachusetts proper which voted for the Constitution and those that voted against it, the following distributions of occupational groups are obtained:

[90] I worked out this method after making a study of port records, contemporary estimates, and the tax lists of some 650 New England towns, with some assistance from certain valuable secondary studies, notably William B. Weeden's *Economic and Social History of New England, 1620–1789* (2 vols., Boston, 1891) and Victor S. Clark's *History of Manufactures in the United States, 1607–1860* (3 vols., New York, 1929). The results were tested against all tabulations of the distribution of occupations that were available, and the ratios proved to be reasonably accurate.

	IN TOWNS VOTING AYE		IN TOWNS VOTING NAY	
OCCUPATION	No.	Per Cent	No.	Per Cent
Professional and mis- cellaneous	1,804	4.9	1,018	3.0
Commercial	4,542	12.3	1,792	5.3
Maritime	4,923	13.3	233	0.7
Manufacturing . . .	6,623	17.9	7,297	21.7
Farming	19,063	51.6	23,359	69.3
Total adult males .	36,955	100.0	33,699	100.0

If these estimates are reasonably accurate, and if the several groups were represented in the town meetings in the same proportions as in the adult male population, three of the five interest groups favored ratification by varying margins. The group comprising professional and miscellaneous occupations supported the Constitution by nearly two to one; the commercial group by two and a half to one; and the maritime group by more than twenty to one. It should be noted, too, that while among the opponents of ratification a considerably larger proportion were farmers than was the case among those favoring it, about 45 per cent of the farmers in the state favored ratification, and more than half the persons favoring ratification were farmers.

More valid bases of comparison are the occupations and economic interests of the 355 members of the ratifying convention, and these can be determined with more precision:

OCCUPATIONS OF DELEGATES WHO VOTED FOR RATIFICATION

Twenty of the delegates who voted for ratification were merchants engaged directly in interstate and foreign commerce, at least thirteen of whom were also engaged in shipping in their own vessels: [91]

[91] Charles Francis Swift, *History of Old Yarmouth* (Yarmouth, 1884), 178; Duane H. Hurd, *History of Plymouth County, Massachusetts, with Biographical Sketches* (Philadelphia, 1884), 11, 157; Duane H. Hurd, *History of Essex County, Massachusetts* (2 vols., Philadelphia, 1888), 1:709; 2:709; Samuel Roads, Jr., *The History and Traditions of Marblehead* (Boston, 1880), 730–731; Fannie S. Chase, *Wiscasset in Pownalborough* (Wiscasset, Maine, 1941), 495; sketches of James Bowdoin and James Bowdoin, Jr., by William A. Robinson, of John

Nathaniel Gorham (Charlestown)   William Pearson (Gloucester)
David Thatcher (Yarmouth)   John Dunlap (Brunswick, Me.)
Thomas Davis (Plymouth)   David Silvester (Pownalborough)
Francis Cabot (Salem)   James Bowdoin (Boston)
George Cabot (Beverly)   James Bowdoin, Jr. (Dorchester)
Israel Thorndike (Beverly)   John Hancock (Boston)
William Gray, Jr. (Salem)   William Phillips (Boston)
John Glover (Marblehead)   Ebenezer Wales (Dorchester)
Jonathan Glover (Marblehead)   John Coffin Jones (Boston)
Daniel Rogers (Gloucester)   Thomas Russell (Boston)

Three of the delegates who voted for ratification were tradesmen (retail shopkeepers): [92]

Bailey Bartlett (Haverhill)
Elijah Dwight (Great Barrington)
Joseph M'Lellan (Portland)

Two were tavern- and innkeepers, who were customarily licensed liquor dealers that often sold other goods: [93]

Lawson Buckminster (Framingham)
Noah Goodman (South Hadley)

Four were capitalistic manufacturers: [94]

Benjamin Blaney (Malden), owner of a tannery.
Abraham Fuller (Newton), maltster.
Michael Farley (Ipswich), owner of a tannery.
Dummer Sewall (Bath), owner of a lumber mill.

Ten were artisans and mechanics: [95]

Stephen Dana (Cambridge), carpenter.
Joseph Hosmer (Concord), carpenter.

Hancock by James T. Adams, and of William Phillips by Claude M. Fuess in the *Dictionary of American Biography; History of the Town of Dorchester* (published anonymously, Boston, 1851), 584; Justin Windsor, *The Memorial History of Boston* (4 vols., Boston, 1881–1882), 4:212; John Coffin Jones Papers, in the Baker Library, Harvard University.

[92] Hurd, *Essex County*, 2:2009–2010; Charles J. Taylor, *History of Great Barrington (Berkshire) Massachusetts* (Great Barrington, 1928), 260; William Willis, *The History of Portland* (2 vols., Portland, 1883), 2:180.

[93] Josiah H. Temple, *History of Framingham, Mass., 1640–1880* (Framingham, 1887), 491; Sylvester Judd, *History of Hadley* (Springfield, 1905), 299, 385.

[94] Deloraine Pendre Corey, *The History of Malden, Massachusetts, 1633–1785* (Malden, 1889), 360n; Samuel F. Smith, *History of Newton, Mass.* (Boston, 1880), 779–780; Hurd, *Essex County*, 1:619; Henry W. Owen, *History of Bath, Maine* (Bath, 1936), 101, 128.

[95] Lucius R. Paige, *History of Cambridge, Mass., 1630–1877* (Boston, 1877), 528; *The Centennial of the Social Circle in Concord* (published anonymously, Cambridge, 1882), 114–119; Josiah H. Temple and George Sheldon, *A History of the Town of Northfield, Mass.* (Albany, New York, 1875), 319, 356, 475; Hurd, *Essex County*, 2:1471; Charles E. Banks, *The History of Martha's Vineyard, Dukes County, Mass.* (3 vols., Edgartown, Massachusetts, 1911–1925), 3:316; Arthur L. Perry, *Williamstown and Williams College* (n.p., 1899), 161–162; Chase, *Wiscasset in Pownalborough*, 16.

Ebenezer Janes (Northfield), maker of gravestones.
Willis Patten (Amesbury), blacksmith.
William Mayhew (Edgartown), boatbuilder.
Tompson J. Skinner (Williamstown), carpenter.
Moses Davis (Edgecomb), carpenter and boatbuilder.
Shearjashub Browne (Barnstable), precise occupation unknown.
Jonathan Howes (Yarmouth), precise occupation unknown.
Joseph Palmer (Falmouth), precise occupation unknown.

Twenty-one were lawyers: [96]

William Symmes, Jr. (Andover)   Abner Morgan (Brimfield)
Caleb Strong (Northampton)   William Cushing (Scituate)
John Davis (Plymouth)   Joseph Cushing (Hanover)
Nathan Cushing (Scituate)   Tristam Dalton (Newbury)
Rufus King (Newburyport)   Theophilus Parsons (Newburyport)
Edward Pulling (Salem)   Josiah Smith (Plymouth)
Joshua Thomas (Plymouth)   John Sprague (Lancaster)
Theodore Sedgwick (Stockbridge)   David Mitchell (North Yarmouth)
Fisher Ames (Dedham)   Increase Sumner (Roxbury)
Christopher Gore (Boston)   Thomas Dawes, Jr. (Boston)
John Baxter, Jr. (Medfield)

Ten were physicians: [97]

[96] Sarah Loring Bailey, *Historical Sketches of Andover, Mass.* (Boston, 1883), 396–399; Charles M. Hyde, *Historical Celebration of the Town of Brimfield* (Springfield, 1879), 179–180; Duane H. Hurd, *History of Plymouth County, Mass., with Biographical Sketches* (Philadelphia, 1884), 10, 11, 59–60; Jedediah Dwelling and John F. Simmons, *History of the Town of Hanover, Mass.* (Hanover, 1910), 96, Genealogy section, 130; Samuel Deane, *History of Scituate, Mass.* (Boston, 1831), 260; Hurd, *Essex County,* 1:xx, xxiv; James D. Phillips, *Salem and the Indies* (Boston, 1947), 216; Duane H. Hurd, *History of Worcester County, Mass., with Biographical Sketches* (2 vols., Philadelphia, 1889), 1:xxi; William M. Sargent, "The Mitchell Family," in *Old Times of North Yarmouth, Me.,* vol. 2, no. 4 (October 1, 1878); William T. Davis, *Professional and Industrial History of Suffolk County, Mass.,* 1:246 (Boston, 1894); William S. Tilden, ed., *History of the Town of Medfield, Mass., 1650–1886* (Boston, 1887), 318; *Biographical Directory of Congress* (1927 edition), 876, 1024, 1540; Zechariah Chafee's sketch of Increase Sumner and Samuel E. Morison's sketch of Fisher Ames, in the *Dictionary of American Biography;* Sedgwick Papers, in the Historical Society of Massachusetts.

[97] *The Medford Historical Register,* 1:109–116 (published anonymously, Medford, 1898); Charles A. Nelson, *Waltham, Past and Present; and Its Industries* (Cambridge, 1879), 91, 96; Duane H. Hurd, *History of Bristol County, Mass.* (Philadelphia, 1883), 227; *Ship Registers of Dighton–Fall River, Mass.* (Boston, 1939) (see index); John J. Currier, *History of Newbury, Mass., 1635–1902* (Boston, 1902), 667; Cyrus Eaton, *History of Thomaston, Rockland, and South Thomaston, Maine* (2 vols., Hallowell, Maine, 1865), 2:214; Chase, *Wiscasset in Pownalborough,* 606–608; Windsor, *Memorial History of Boston,* 4:212; sketch of Cotton Tufts by Henry R. Viets in the *Dictionary of American Biography.* That certain of the men were physicians is inferred from their titles as printed in the lists of delegates in the Boston *Massachusetts Centinel* of January 16, 1788.

John Brooks (Medford)   Charles Whitman (Stow)
Leonard Williams (Waltham)   William Baylies (Dighton)
Samuel Nyre (Salisbury)   Enoch Sawyer (Newbury)
David Fales (Thomaston)   Thomas Rice (Pownalborough)
Charles Jarvis (Boston)   Cotton Tufts (Weymouth)

Jarvis and Baylies also owned vessels engaged in ocean-borne commerce.

Fifteen were clergymen: [98]

Isaac Backus (Middleborough)   Levi Whitman (Wellfleet)
Samuel West (New Bedford)   Samuel Niles (Abington)
John Carnes (Lynn)   William Shaw (Marshfield)
Moses Hemmenway (Wells)   Joseph Jackson (Brookline)
Samuel Perley (Gray)   Phillips Payson (Chelsea)
Nathaniel Robbins (Milton)   Daniel Shute (Hingham)
Samuel Stillman (Boston)   Thomas Thatcher (Dedham)
Anthony Widbird (Braintree)

Eleven were engaged in miscellaneous unclassified occupations: [99]

Abraham Bigelow (Weston), schoolteacher.
Daniel Noyes (Ipswich), schoolteacher.
Nathaniel Wells (Wells), schoolteacher.
Kimball Clark (Harwich), fisherman.
Hezekiah Hooper (Bridgewater), student at Harvard College.
George Partridge (Duxbury), sheriff of Plymouth County.
Jonathan Titcomb (Newburyport), holder of various remunerative local offices, who in 1789 became the first naval officer for the port of Newburyport.
William Sever (Kingston), judge, not a lawyer.
Charles Turner (Scituate), retired minister.
Samuel Baker (Bolton), judge, not a lawyer.
Samuel Adams (Boston), politician.

Thirteen of the delegates favoring ratification constituted a group that might be described as gentleman-capitalists. They were men of means, large landowners, renters, money-lenders, and investors in various local business ventures.[100]

[98] Thomas Weston, *History of the Town of Middleborough, Mass.* (Cambridge, 1906), 402–405; Everett I. Nye, *History of Wellfleet* (n.p., 1920), 14: Hurd, *Bristol County*, 74; Hurd, *Plymouth County*, 482, 1165; Howard K. Sanderson, *Lynn in the Revolution* (2 vols., Boston, 1909), 2:245; Edward E. Bourne, *The History of Wells and Kennebunk* (Portland, 1875), 723 ff.; W. W. Clayton, *History of Cumberland County, Maine* (Philadelphia, 1880), 301. That Jackson, Payson, Robbins, Shute, Stillman, Thatcher, and Widbird were clergymen is inferred from the title "Rev." preceding their names in the list of delegates published in the *Massachusetts Centinel* of January 16, 1788.

[99] Josiah Paine, *A History of Harwich* (Rutland, Vermont, 1937), 348; Edward C. Mitchell, *History of Bridgewater, Mass.* (Bridgewater, 1897), 195; Hurd, *Plymouth County*, 10, 267, 362; Hurd, *Essex County*, 2:1750; Deane, *Scituate*, 361; Hurd, *Worcester County*, 1:389.

[100] Weston, *Middleborough*, 386–387; Duane H. Hurd, *History of Middlesex County* (2 vols., Philadelphia, 1890), 2:633; Paige, *Cambridge*, 529; Daniel White Wells and Reuben Field Wells, *A History of Hatfield, Mass.* (Spring-

Isaac Thomson (Middleborough)
Francis Dana (Cambridge)
John Ingersoll (Westfield)
Benjamin Greenleaf (Salem)
Nathaniel Barrell (York)
Benjamin Lincoln (Hingham)
William McIntosh (Needham)

Eleazer Brooks (Lincoln)
John Hastings (Hatfield)
William Pynchon (Springfield)
John Low (Gloucester)
William Heath (Roxbury)
Richard Cranch (Braintree)

Thirty-nine were farmers: [101]

Benjamin Browne (Lexington)
Elisha Porter (Hadley)
Elisha May (Attleborough)
Sylvester Richmond (Dighton)
Israel Fearing (Wareham)
John Turner (Pembroke)
Josiah Goddard (Athol)
Jacob Bradbury (Buxton)
Samuel Merrill (North Yarmouth)
William McCobb (Boothbay)
Daniel Howard, Jr. (Bridgewater)
John Pitts (Dunstable)
J. Choate (Ipswich)
Jonathan Cogswell (Ipswich)
Simeon Miller (Manchester)
Edmund Lazell (Cunningham and Plainfield)
William Almy (Westport)
Hezekiah Hooper (Bridgewater)
Ephraim Wilder (Sterling)

D. Taylor (New Marlborough)
Joseph B. Varnum (Dracut)
Benjamin Sheldon (Northampton)
Moses Wilmarth (Attleborough)
Walter Spooner (New Bedford)
John Burnham (Lynn)
Cornelius Dunham (Tisbury)
John Ashley, Jr. (Sheffield)
Isaac Snow (Harpswell)
John Fox (Portland)
Daniel Howard (Bridgewater)
Jabez Fisher (Franklin)
Asahel Wheeler (Sudbury)
Israel Clark (Topsfield)
Jacob Herrick (Wenham)
Daniel Thruston (Branford)
Thompson Maxwell (Buckland)
James Williams (Taunton)
David Wilder (Leominster)
Elisha Carpenter (Becket)

The occupations of thirty-nine of the delegates favoring ratification were not ascertained.

field, 1910), see index; John H. Lockwood, *Westfield and Its Historical Influences, 1669–1919* (2 vols., Springfield, 1922), vol. 1, *passim;* Mason A. Green, *Springfield, 1636–1886: History of Town and City* (Springfield, 1888), *passim;* Hurd, *Essex County,* 2:1753; Currier, *Newbury,* 293; Babson, *Gloucester,* 421; John J. Babson, *Notes and Additions to the History of Gloucester* (Gloucester, 1876), 42–43; Charles E. Banks, *History of York, Maine* (2 vols., Boston, 1935), 2:60–63; William S. Patee, *A History of Old Braintree and Quincy* (Quincy, 1878), 490 ff.; George K. Clark, *History of Needham, Mass., 1711–1911* (Cambridge, 1912), *passim;* biographical sketch of William Heath by Ralph V. Harlow and of Benjamin Lincoln by James T. Adams in the *Dictionary of American Biography.*

[101] Silas Roger Coburn, *History of Dracut, Mass.* (Lowell, 1922), 418–419; Judd, *Hadley,* 382, 386, and Genealogy section, 114; James R. Trumbull, *History of Northampton, Mass.* (Northampton, 1902); John Daggett, *A Sketch of the History of Attleborough* (Boston, 1894), 483 ff., 561, 619; Hurd, *Bristol County,* 171, 226; *Ship Registers of Dighton–Fall River* (see index); Hurd, *Plymouth County,* 223–224, 241; Hurd, *Essex County,* 2:1181–1182; Banks, *Martha's Vineyard,* 1:212; 2:162; Lilley B. Caswell, *Athol, Mass., Past and Present* (Athol, 1899), 239; *History of Berkshire County, Mass.* (2 vols., pub-

OCCUPATIONS OF DELEGATES WHO VOTED AGAINST RATIFICATION

Three of the delegates who opposed ratification were merchants directly engaged in interstate and foreign commerce: [102]

Nathaniel Leonard (Taunton), who also owned vessels and several iron foundries, forges, and slitting and rolling mills.

Samuel Nasson (Sanford), who also owned vessels and practiced law.

William Widgery (New Gloucester), who also owned and built vessels.

Four were tradesmen (retail storekeepers): [103]

Martin Kinsley (Hardwick), who was also a physician.

Isaac Pepper (Ware), who also owned a tavern and four farms.

Aaron Wood (Boxford).

Dr. Joseph Wood (Grafton), who also practiced medicine and operated a tavern.

Ten were keepers of taverns and inns and also sold retail liquor and other goods: [104]

Phaneul Bishop (Rehoboth)	Jonathan Bullard (Oakham)
Moses Hale (Winchendon)	Esias Preble (York)
Daniel Putman (Fitchburg)	Moses Richardson (Medway)
Benjamin Sawin (Marlborough)	Obadiah Sawtell (Shirley)
Moses Severance (Montague)	Ebenezer Tisdale (Easton)

lished anonymously, New York, 1885), 2:550; *A Report of the Proceedings at the Celebration of the First Centennial Anniversary of the Incorporation of the Town of Buxton, Maine* (published anonymously, Portland, 1874), 241–242; Wheeler and Wheeler, *Brunswick*, 853; "Genealogical Notes," in *Old Times of North Yarmouth*, 8:1209 (October 1, 1884); Willis, *Portland*, 2:191 and elsewhere; Francis B. Greene, *History of Boothbay, Southport, and Boothbay Harbor, Maine, 1623–1905* (Portland, 1905), 570 and elsewhere; Records of the Loan of 1790, vol. 287, folio 87, in the National Archives (Howard is there described as a "yeoman"); Mortimer Blake, *A History of the Town of Franklin, Mass.* (Franklin, 1879), 157; Harding, *The Contest in Massachusetts*, 77n; New England Tax Materials, 1658–1850, MS 92, vol. 2, in the Baker Library, Harvard University. A number of the delegates are identified as farmers only by inference: that is to say, when the histories of their towns include lists of all persons in other occupations and they are not listed, or when they are described as living on farms, or when there were no places of employment in their towns at the time except farms. The last sixteen men named are here classified as farmers on this basis. Richmond also had a part interest in a sailing vessel, and Wilmarth was also a part-time bootmaker.

[102] Samuel Hopkins Emery, *History of Taunton, Mass.* (Syracuse, New York, 1893), 613–644; Edwin Emery, *The History of Sanford, Maine, 1661–1900* (Fall River, 1901), 487–488; *Biographical Directory of Congress* (1927 edition), 1698; *The New Gloucester Centennial* (Portland, 1875), 78–81.

[103] Lucius R. Paige, *History of Hardwick, Mass.* (Boston, 1883), 407–408; *Biographical Directory of Congress*, 1187; Arthur Chase, *History of Ware, Mass.* (Cambridge, 1911), 94, 118, 194, 266, 272; Sidney Perley, *The Dwellings of Boxford, Essex County, Mass.* (Salem, 1893), 33–36; Frederick C. Pierce, *History of Grafton, Worcester County, Mass.* (Worcester, 1879), 387–389, 608.

[104] *Biographical Directory of Congress* (1927 edition), 704; Henry P. Wright, *Soldiers of Oakham, Mass. in the Revolutionary War, and War of 1812, and the Civil War* (New Haven, 1914), 57–58; Henry B. Wright and E. D. Har-

Thirteen were capitalistic manufacturers: [105]

Josiah Allis (Whatley), owner of potash works, a broom manufactory, and grist and sawmills.

Artemus Brigham (Northborough), owner of grist and sawmills.

Stephen Maynard (Westborough), proprietor of a tannery.

Nicholas Jenks (Brookfield), proprietor of an ironworks.

John Frye (Royalstown), proprietor of a grist mill.

Amos Singletary (Sutton), proprietor of grist and sawmills.

Israel Hutchinson (Danvers), proprietor of a lumber mill, also a housewright.

Nathaniel Marsh (Haverhill), manufacturer of hats.

Thomas Mighill (Rowley), proprietor of a malthouse.

Valentine Rathbun (Pittsfield), owner of fulling mills.

David Stearns (Milford), owner of a sawmill and of interests in other manufacturing enterprises.

Isaac Soule (Middleborough), owner of a tannery, a brick kiln, two blacksmith shops, and shares in other ventures.

Ephraim Williams (Ashfield), owner of several lumber mills.

Two were artisans and mechanics: [106]

William Jones (Bristol), joiner.

Samuel Reed (Littleton), cooper.

vey, *The Settlement and Story of Oakham, Mass.* (New Haven, 1947), 284–286; Abijah P. Marvin, *History of the Town of Winchendon* (Winchendon, 1868), 431; Banks, *History of York*, 2:325; Frederick A. Currier, "Tavern Days and the Old Taverns of Fitchburg," in the *Proceedings of the Fitchburg Historical Society*, 2:85–126 (Fitchburg, 1897); James F. D. Garfield, "Fitchburg Soldiers of the Revolution," *ibid.*, 4:208 (1908); Ephraim O. Jameson, *The History of Medway, Mass., 1713 to 1885* (n.p., n.d.), 515; Ella M. Bigelow, *Historical Reminiscences of the Early Times in Marlborough, Mass.* (Marlborough, 1910), 182–183; Seth Chandler, *History of Montague: A Typical Puritan Town* (Montague, 1910), 141 and elsewhere; William L. Chaffin, *History of the Town of Easton, Mass.* (Cambridge, 1886), 189, 440.

[105] James M. Grafts, *History of the Town of Whatley, Mass.* (Orange, Massachusetts, 1899), 252–260, 358; Josiah C. Kent, *Northborough History* (Newton, Massachusetts, 1921), *passim;* Heman DeForest and Edward C. Bates, *The History of Westborough, Mass.* (Westborough, 1891), 190–191; Josiah H. Temple, *History of North Brookfield, Mass.* (Boston, 1887), 12; Lilley B. Caswell, *History of the Town of Royalstown, Mass.* (Royalstown, 1917), 185–187; William A. Benedict and Hiram A. Tracy, *History of the Town of Sutton, Mass., 1704–1876* (Worcester, 1878), 726–728; Harriet Tapley, *Chronicle of Danvers (Old Salem Village), Mass., 1632–1923* (Danvers, 1923), 81–83; George W. Chase, *The History of Haverhill, Mass.* (Haverhill, 1861), 433, 539; Amos E. Jewett and Emily Mabel Adams Jewett, *Rowley, Mass., "Mr. Ezechi Rogers Plantation," 1639–1850* (Rowley, 1946), 255 and index; Joseph E. A. Smith, *The History of Pittsfield, Mass.* (2d edition, 2 vols., Springfield, 1876), 1:37, 136, 165; Adam Ballou, *History of the Town of Milford* (Boston, 1882), 1030; Weston, *Middleborough*, 350–351; Frederick G. Howes, *History of the Town of Ashfield* (Ashfield, 1910), 220–221.

[106] John Johnston, *A History of the Towns of Bristol and Bremen in the State of Maine* (Albany, New York, 1873), 379–382; *Proceedings of the Littleton Historical Society, 1894–1895* (Littleton, 1896), 21.

Six were lawyers: [107]

William Bodman (Williamsburg)   John Jennings (Ludlow)
Samuel Field (Deerfield), who also   David Murray (Newcastle)
owned a store.   Benjamin Adams (Ashby)
Jonathan Grout (Petersham)

Seven were physicians: [108]

Thomas Kittredge (Andover)   Benjamin Morse (Groton)
John Taylor (Douglas)   Nathaniel Low (Berwick)
Thomas Smith (Sandwich)   Marshall Spring (Watertown)
Samuel Willard (Uxbridge)

One of the delegates opposed to ratification, Noah Alden (Bellingham), was a Baptist minister.[109]

Five were engaged in miscellaneous unclassifiable occupations: [110]

Timothy Blair (Blanford), surveyor.

Joseph Davis (Holden), retired minister, now engaged in pursuit of science and petty business activities.

Timothy Fuller (Princeton), minister who had been removed from his position for loyalism, now teaching school and dabbling in business.

John Webber (Bedford), retired sea captain.

Abraham White (Norton), retired taverner, now a politician.

Fifteen were gentleman-capitalists—that is, men of means, large land-owners, renters, money-lenders, and investors in various local ventures: [111]

[107] Phyllis B. Deming, *A History of Williamsburg in Massachusetts* (North-ampton, 1946), 24, 25, 28; George Sheldon, *A History of Deerfield* (2 vols., Deerfield, 1896), vol. 2, part 2, p. 159; *Biographical Directory of Congress* (1927 edition), 623, 1039; Alfred Noon, *The History of Ludlow, Mass.* (Spring-field, 1912), 291–292; David Q. Cushman, *The History of Ancient Sheepscot and Newcastle* (Bath, Maine, 1882), 157.

[108] Bailey, *Historical Sketches of Andover*, 157–159, 359; Samuel A. Green, *Groton Historical Series*, 2:116 (Groton, 1890); William A. Emerson, *History of the Town of Douglas* (Boston, 1879), 231. That Low, Smith, Spring, and Willard were physicians is inferred from the titles accompanying their names in the list of delegates published in the *Massachusetts Centinel* of January 16, 1788.

[109] George F. Partridge, *History of the Town of Bellingham, Mass., 1719–1919* (Bellingham, 1919), 107, 113.

[110] Sumner Gilbert Wood, *The Taverns & Turnpikes of Blanford, 1733–1833* (n.p., 1908), 272; David F. Estes, *The History of Holden, Mass., 1684–1894* (Worcester, 1894), 254–255; Francis E. Blake, *History of the Town of Princeton* (2 vols., Princeton, 1915), 1:146–157; Abram E. Brown, *History of the Town of Bedford, Mass.* (Bedford, 1891), section 2, p. 42; George F. Clark, *A History of the Town of Norton* (Boston, 1859), 303, 515, and elsewhere.

[111] Ithamar B. Sawtelle, *History of the Town of Townshend, 1676–1878* (Fitchburg, 1878), 237, 431, 433; John S. Barrows, *Fryeburg, Maine: An His-torical Sketch* (Fryeburg, 1938), 53, 70, 195, 242; Francis M. Thompson, *History of Greenfield* (2 vols., Greenfield, 1904), 1:424–425, 2:667, 687, 894; Charles S. Pease, ed., *History of Conway, 1767–1917* (Springfield, 1917), 71, 248–249, 312; Emory Washburn, *Historical Sketches of the Town of Leicester, Mass.* (Boston, 1860), 183–184; Judd, *Hadley*, 403; Benedict and Tracy, *Sutton*, 233, 340; George F. Daniels, *History of the Town of Palmer, Mass.* (Palmer,

Daniel Adams (Townshend)	Moses Ames (Fryeburg)
Consider Arms (Conway)	Malachi Maynard (Conway)
Moses Bascom (Greenfield)	Samuel Denny (Leicester)
Benjamin Eastman (Granby)	David Harwood (Sutton)
Jeremiah Learned (Oxford)	Aaron Merrick (Palmer)
John Minot (Chelmsford)	Timothy Parker (Sturbridge)
Benjamin Thomas (Middleborough)	William Thompson (Billerica)
Timothy Winn (Woburn)	

Thirteen were farmers: [112]

Joshua Bean (Winthrop)	Stephen Holden (Westminster)
Jesse Bradley (Lee)	Stephen Longfellow, Jr. (Gorham)
Zaccheus Crocker (Sunderland)	Joseph Sheple (Groton)
Daniel Forbes (Brookfield)	John Pratt (Mansfield)
John Goldsbury (Warwick and Orange)	Jacob Willard (Ashburnham)
	Richard F. Cutts (Berwick)
Jonathan Green (Stoneham)	Peter Osgood (Andover)

The occupations of eighty-nine delegates opposing ratification were not ascertained because of the lack of local histories and town records.

PUBLIC SECURITY HOLDINGS OF DELEGATES
VOTING FOR RATIFICATION

The following fifty-eight delegates who voted for ratification were owners of the amounts of public securities indicated: [113]

1889), 213–214, 219, and elsewhere; Wilson Waters, *History of Chelmsford, Mass.* (Lowell, 1917), 395; Estes, *Holden*, 301–302; Weston, *Middleborough*, 329; Henry A. Hazen, *History of Billerica, Mass.* (Boston, 1883), 149, 247; Samuel Sewall, *The History of Woburn* (Boston, 1868), 650–651.

[112] Everett S. Stackpole, *History of Winthrop, Maine* (Auburn, Maine, 1925), 39, 85–86; Charles M. Hyde and Alexander Hyde, *Lee, Mass.* (Springfield, 1878), *passim;* John M. Smith, *History of the Town of Sunderland, Mass.* (Greenfield, 1899), 164, 310; Temple, *North Brookfield*, 265n, 590; Jonathan Blake, *History of the Town of Warwick* (Boston, 1873), 70 and elsewhere; William B. Stevens, *History of Stoneham, Mass.* (Stoneham, 1891), 65; William S. Heywood, *History of Westminster, Mass., 1728–1893* (Lowell, 1893), 208, 703–704; Hugh D. McLellan, *History of Gorham, Maine* (Portland, 1903), 640–641; Green, *Groton Historical Series*, 2:120; Ezra S. Stearns, *History of Ashburnham, Mass.* (Ashburnham, 1887), 480–481, 980. Classification of some of the men as farmers has been arrived at through the process of elimination described in note 101 above. Pratt, Cutts, and Osgood are described as "yeomen" in their public security accounts, to be cited below.

[113] Records of the Loan of 1790, vol. 266 (Register of Specie Certificates), folios 47–48; vol. 279 (Subscription Register, Assumed Debt), accounts 26, 48, 92, 122, 161, 186, 189, 201, 211, 212, 241, 265, 274, 281, 310, 372, 379, 390, 428, 441, 443, 457, 458, 551; vol. 280 (Subscription Register, Assumed Debt), accounts 733, 735, 778, 782, 783, 854, 879, 1011, 1060, 1068, 1070, 1116, 1118, 1162, 1163, 1185, 1268, 1274, 1284, 1313, 1323; vol. 282 (Register of Certificates for Debts due by the U.S. in the State of Massachusetts, 1783–1786), accounts 226, 231, 232, 233, 240, 609, 961, 1023, 1278, 1323, 1368, 1416, 1945; vol. 283 (Register of Interest Certificates, 1786), folios 3, 10, 14; vol. 284 (Account of Certificates for Liquidated Debt), folio 108; vol. 286 (Subscription Register, Domestic Debt),

Increase Sumner ($407)
John Glover ($1,921)
Daniel Howard ($199)
John Fox ($6,092)
Moses Hemmenway ($507)
William Heath ($2,527)
Thomas Davis ($2,340)
Nathan Cushing ($3,067)
John Burnham ($1,010)
Samuel Adams ($12,478)
Francis Dana ($11,809)
Jonathan Glover ($13,970)
George Partridge ($2,195)
Thomas Dawes, Jr. ($30)
Charles Jarvis ($25,872)
William Pynchon ($641)
John Dunlop ($1,283)
Richard Manning ($7,217)
Christopher Gore ($32,882)
Theophilus Parsons ($6,827)
Isaac Backus ($397)
William Phillips ($71,073)
Anthony Widbird ($3,632)
Thomas Russell ($61,943)
William Shaw ($64)
William McIntosh ($396)
Walter Spooner ($730)
Charles Whitman ($580)
John Coffin Jones ($47,357)

William Pearson ($1,793)
Thomas Jones ($500)
Cotton Tufts ($3,603)
William Cushing ($303)
David Mitchell ($293)
Thomas Cutts ($10,396)
William Gray, Jr. ($4,633)
Nathaniel Wells ($240)
Joseph Jackson ($6)
Stephen Dana ($5)
Ebenezer Warren ($533)
Tristram Dalton ($12)
Joseph Palmer ($211)
Israel Thorndike ($17,943)
Theodore Sedgwick ($1,680)
John Davis ($1,147)
James Bowdoin ($10,956)
Azor Orne ($880)
Bailey Bartlett ($800)
Richard Cranch ($1,240)
John Low ($717)
Caleb Davis ($1,040)
Benjamin Lincoln ($13,087)
Caleb Strong ($10,903)
Benjamin Greenleaf ($2,354)
Seth Newton ($10)
Benjamin Sheldon ($52)
John Sprague ($5)
Fisher Ames ($35)

PUBLIC SECURITY HOLDINGS OF DELEGATES
VOTING AGAINST RATIFICATION [114]

John Pratt ($244)
Comstock Betts ($35)
Joseph Stone ($5)
John Wood ($236)
Edward Pierce ($6)
Aaron Wood ($13)
Timothy Winn ($1,078)
Amos Singletary ($92)
John Minot ($302)

William Thompson ($19,487)
Amos Fisk ($22)
John Chamberlain ($49)
Samuel Willard ($66)
Hezekiah Broad ($385)
Thomas Mighill ($294)
David Bigelow ($499)
Richard Cutts ($379)
Peter Osgood ($1,381)

entry dated December 28, 1790; vol. 287 (Subscription Register, Domestic Debt), folios 16, 45, 87, 114, 119, 172, 173, 177, 183, 198, 215, 225, 229; vol. 288 (Subscription Register, Domestic Debt), accounts 1188, 1191; all in the National Archives.

[114] *Ibid.*, vol. 266, folios 25, 41, 63, 113; vol. 279, account 65; vol. 280, account 959; vol. 282, accounts 37, 404, 950, 1132, 1292, 1375, 1421, 1796, 1871, 1995; vol.

It is clear from these figures that three times as many security holders voted for the Constitution as voted against it, and that nearly a third of those who voted for the Constitution held securities, whereas only a tenth of those voting against ratification held securities. As indicated earlier, then, the ownership or non-ownership of public securities apparently was an element influencing ratification.

The occupational data presented above may be summarized as follows:

Commercial.—Delegates identifiable as merchants favored the Constitution, their vote for ratification being 20 to 3 (87 per cent for). Retail commercial groups opposed the Constitution by a vote of 14 to 5 (74 per cent opposed). Considered together, these commercial classes favored the Constitution by a vote of 25 to 17 (60 per cent for).

Manufacturing.—Capitalistic manufacturers opposed the Constitution by a vote of 13 to 4 (76 per cent against). Artisans and mechanics voted 10 to 2 in favor of ratification (83 per cent for). Manufacturing interests as a whole opposed the Constitution, 15 to 14 (52 per cent against).

Professional.—Professional groups favored the Constitution, their total vote being 46 to 14 in support of ratification (77 per cent for). The vote of the lawyers was 21 to 6 (78 per cent for), that of the physicians 10 to 7 (59 per cent for), and that of the ministers 15 to 1 (94 per cent for).

Gentleman-Capitalists.—Gentleman-capitalists opposed the Constitution, 15 to 13 (54 per cent against).

Miscellaneous.—Delegates whose occupations are identifiable but not classifiable favored the Constitution, 11 to 5 (69 per cent for).

Farmers.—Delegates identifiable as farmers favored the Constitution, 40 to 13 (75 per cent for).

Unknown.—Of the delegates whose occupations were not

283, folios 8, 10; vol. 287, folios 71, 113, 116, 132, 133, 263, 264, 287. Eight other holders among the opponents of the Constitution had received certificates in exchange for depreciated continental money, but they are not listed here because the amounts cannot be ascertained and because it appears probable that all of them disposed of their securities prior to 1788.

ascertained, 38 (29.9 per cent) favored the Constitution and 89
(70.1 per cent) opposed it.

Second, the data may be summarized to show the occupational makeup of the two sides, the advocates and the opponents
of ratification:

	RATIFICATIONISTS	ANTI-RATIFICATIONISTS
OCCUPATIONAL GROUP	Per Cent	Per Cent
Commercial	13.4	11.2
Manufacturing	7.6	8.9
Professional	24.6	8.4
Miscellaneous	5.8	3.0
Gentleman-capitalists	6.9	8.9
Farmers	21.4	7.7
Unknown	20.3	52.9
Total	100.0	100.0

Within the limitations imposed by the lack of data, it is possible to make a general evaluation of Beard's interpretation of
the contest in Massachusetts. Beard is apparently on sound
ground in asserting that public security holders and shippers
constituted a considerable part of the dynamic element in the
movement for ratification, for, together with lawyers and
clergymen, these groups furnished the leaders of the Federalists.
But he is wrong in his appraisal of the opposition. The leadership of the opposition was furnished by retail storekeepers,
manufacturers, gentlemen-capitalists, and even a number of
public security holders—personalty groups that Beard assumes
were virtually unanimous in support of ratification. The
Federalists were far more successful in winning support among
farmers, artisans, and mechanics—the very economic groups
Beard assumes they were fighting—and by virtue of this support
they were able to carry the convention's vote in favor of ratification.

SOUTH CAROLINA

SOUTH CAROLINA brought the Federalists within one state of
their immediate goal by becoming the eighth state to ratify

when, on May 23, 1788, its convention approved the Constitution by the comfortable margin of 149 votes to 73.

The campaign and the contest over ratification in South Carolina were, in view of the confusion and noise that had attended the state's political activity since the peace, remarkably quiet and orderly. The Constitution was first published in the state on October 4. Immediately thereafter, in the pattern followed in several other states, rival "news" releases began to appear from the northward—Federalist propaganda from Philadelphia and anti-Federalist propaganda from New York. In December locally written articles, arguing both the pros and the cons, began appearing in local newspapers. Most of this local material was highly philosophical in tone, making only occasional reference to any practical effects the Constitution might have on South Carolina.[115]

The legislature began a brief debate on the question of calling a ratifying convention shortly after it convened in regular session in mid-January, 1788. Ex-governor Rawling Lowndes (who owned almost $60,000 in public securities, and whose brother owned another $25,000 in securities) led a futile attempt to prevent the calling of a convention. The legislators, however, though many of them expressed reservations about the Constitution, apparently felt that the issue was one that should be decided by the voters and a convention. Elections were called for April 11 and 12, and a convention for the first week in May. Returns of the elections are available only for St. Philip's and St. Michael's Parish (Charleston), which elected 32 delegates. Of the 1,900 heads of families in that place, 424 went to the polls, and by an overwhelming margin elected a slate unanimously favorable to ratification.[116]

---

[115] *Charleston Morning Post and Daily Advertiser,* Charleston *Evening Gazette,* Charleston *State Gazette of South Carolina,* and *Columbian Herald, or the Independent Courier of North America* (Charleston), October–December, 1787.

[116] Debates in the legislature are recorded in Elliott's *Debates,* 2:253–317. For a summary of the events between the time of the legislative debates and the elections, see the *State Gazette* and the *Columbian Herald,* January–April, 1788. Election returns are printed in the *Columbian Herald* of April 17, 1788. Lowndes' securities are recorded in vol. 1258, folio 256, of the Old Loan Records of the Loan of 1790, in the National Archives; those of Edward Lowndes are recorded in volume 1258, folio 253.

The convention met on May 6. The preliminary activities it engaged in were little more than those of a debating society, for the sentiments of the members on the question of ratification were a foregone conclusion. The two weeks occupied in discussion gave pretentious planters ample opportunity to display their knowledge and forensic talents. After passing a resolution declaring it to be South Carolina's understanding that powers not expressly conferred on the general government by the Constitution were reserved to the several "sovereign" states, the convention ratified the Constitution by a majority of more than two to one.[117]

In view of South Carolina's great wealth and strength, the relative ease with which ratification was accomplished is somewhat surprising, and the movement deserves careful study. For Beard South Carolina offered no challenge to his thesis; in his opinion, it "presents the economic elements in the ratification with the utmost simplicity."[118] Close examination, however, reveals that in actual fact South Carolina presented the economic elements in the ratification with paradoxical complexity. For one thing, the private debtor element in South Carolina was largely identical in personnel with the largest holders of the public debt. For another, the very persons who in 1785–1786 had caused the passage of stay laws, tender laws, and paper-money legislation led the movement for ratification in 1788, and those who led the opposition to the Constitution in 1788 had also fought the debtor-relief laws of 1785–1786.

Three basic sets of factors, each growing out of the war, may be cited as the most important practical considerations influencing South Carolina's acceptance of the Constitution: the war experience itself, the financial condition of the state resulting from the war, and the economic effects of the war and their political consequences.[119]

---

[117] Elliott's *Debates*, 2:318–341.

[118] Beard, *Economic Interpretation*, 288.

[119] The first two elements in the ratification cited here correspond to those given by Charles G. Singer in his *South Carolina in the Confederation* (Philadelphia, 1941), 163. Singer also concluded, however (p. 164), that the "most important cause of the strength of federalism in South Carolina lay in the desire of the Charleston merchants for Congress to have enough control over

One of these elements was the military lesson the war had taught. The state had learned that its geographical position made it vulnerable to attacks by Indians on the frontier and by foreign powers on both land and sea. Against such attacks the state was virtually helpless, and only a strong general government could furnish the military and naval strength needed for security.

The second element, the state's postwar financial condition, must be considered from the point of view of the state as a whole as well as from that of individual holders of securities. The state had financed its war expenses almost entirely without help from Congress, with the result that it had accumulated a domestic debt of about $4,720,000 and a foreign debt of about $680,000. By 1789 the domestic debt had been reduced to about $2,800,000 through the collection of a part of the state's taxes in securities. In addition the state had sold large quantities of confiscated British and loyalist property, and at the end of 1787 its citizens owed it approximately $2,200,000 for such property. Its net domestic indebtedness had thus been reduced by more than 85 per cent, to about $600,000. And it was clear that when the auditing of South Carolina's accounts with Congress was completed, there would be balances due from the United States in excess of the total state debt. The actual balance due upon completion of the audit proved to be almost $1,500,000.[120]

These figures and facts suggest one powerful motive for ratification. When the general government funded its debts and

commerce to be able to regulate it for the good of the whole." I cannot accept this statement for a number of reasons, most of which will be apparent from my analysis of the attitudes of the merchants which follows.

[120] Tax, General, Received, 1783–89, and Accounts, Commissioners of Treasury, Cash Received and Paid, 1783–1789, both in the State Finance Manuscripts File, in the South Carolina Archives, Columbia; Charleston, Port of, Accounts and Statements, 1783–1786, in Legislative System Manuscripts File, in the South Carolina Archives; *Acts, Ordinances, and Resolves of the General Assembly of the State of South Carolina* 1783, 1784 (Charleston, 1784, 1785), acts of March 12, 1783, and March 26, 1784. Beginning in 1784 a careful system of property evaluations was established, on which all future taxes were based, with the result that the tax burden was more equitably distributed and the tax load was not oppressive. Figures in the above documents are converted here from pounds to dollars at the contemporary rate of exchange in South Carolina, 4s. 8d. = $1.00.

assumed state obligations South Carolina would be relieved of a debt of $2,800,000. True, this gain was only a nominal one, for as an importer of some $2,000,000 worth of foreign goods annually South Carolina would pay a sizeable portion of the duties levied by the new Congress for the support of the debts. A second gain was a real one, however: South Carolina's credit of $1,500,000 would yield an income from the United States of about $75,000 a year, a sum adequate to pay the state's civil expenses with thousands of dollars to spare, and no state taxes would be necessary for years. Furthermore, the state was collecting large sums in United States securities in payment for the confiscated property it had sold, and by the time the Loan of 1790 went into effect South Carolina owned almost $2,000,000 worth of these securities.[121]

The third major set of factors that disposed South Carolina toward ratification grew out of its postwar economic and political experience. Postwar difficulties stemmed from the British occupation in 1780, when by three military edicts issued in rapid succession all the property of the twenty leading Whig families of the state was confiscated, almost all the property of twenty-five more leading citizens was confiscated, and twenty-six other leading citizens were seized and put aboard prison ships, causing them immense property losses and severe personal hardships. The ravages of war were particularly great in the South Carolina low country, the seat of its plantation aristocracy. The entire low country was devastated and seventy-one of the leading families of the aristocracy were virtually crushed. When the invaders departed, they completed the spoliation by taking thousands of slaves with them. Meantime the middle and up country, where the lesser planters and farmers dwelled, suffered very little material damage from the war.[122]

---

[121] In 1794 South Carolina became the owner of virtually all the United States securities in the state when it created a loan at six per cent interest and permitted holders of United States securities to exchange them for new South Carolina securities, par for par. Inasmuch as the United States securities bore an average of less than five per cent interest, the state thereby passed on a part of its interest-income surplus to the individual public creditors in the state. The records of this loan are preserved in the South Carolina Archives.

[122] For the two confiscation edicts and the imprisonment edict see the Charleston *Royal South Carolina Gazette*, November 27, 1780, and the Philadelphia *Pennsylvania Packet*, January 2, 30, 1781.

When, at the end of 1782, the occupation ended and planters returned to their despoiled plantations there still remained in Charleston a large number of British merchants with about £500,000 worth of goods, slaves, and provisions. Before the troops were evacuated these merchants petitioned to be allowed to stay in Charleston long enough to dispose of their wares. The returning planters were in a squeeze. Little in the way of goods could be expected in the spring importations of 1783, for the war was still in progress. Yet it was imperative that they acquire sufficient goods in time to get crops planted if they were not to be deprived of crops and income until the harvests of November-December, 1784, two full years away. In the absence of the legislature South Carolina's Governor John Matthews and the Privy Council authorized the merchants to remain for six months. The merchants themselves were in a desperate plight; not only were they on a tenuous footing but they had suffered substantial losses at the hands of the departing British soldiers, who left them without paying their debts. The merchants naturally charged all the traffic would bear, and it would bear plenty. They sold their stocks to the returning planters at prices and interest rates that were little short of fantastic.[123]

Confident in the potentially enormous output of their plantations, the planters restocked by plunging deeply into debt. They remained confident through the widespread failures of rice and indigo crops in 1783, shrugging off these failures as the result of plantation maladjustments following the evacuation. The extent of importations in the spring of 1784 demonstrated their optimism: they purchased about $3,000,000 in ordinary imports and more than 4,000 slaves, costing over $750,000. Then a rare bit of misfortune overtook them. In 1784 and again in 1785 the rice and indigo crops were extremely poor. It was

[123] John Lewis Gervais to Leonard DeNeufville, April 13, 1786, in Gervais and Owen Personal Miscellaneous File, in the Manuscripts Division of the Library of Congress. Gervais claimed that the British merchants sold these goods for no less than a million pounds. See also the "Diary of Timothy Ford," in the *South Carolina Historical and Genealogical Magazine,* 12:193 (1912); Governor Matthews' address to the legislature, published in the *Pennsylvania Packet* of April 3, 1783; and South Carolina news reports in the issues of January 13 and June 19, 1783.

the first time within anyone's memory that three successive crops had failed. The fact that the law of averages had been violated was little consolation, however, and at the end of 1785 the planters staggered under a tremendous burden of debt. They owed about $6,000,000, the equivalent of the gross production of the entire state for about two and a half normal years. With few exceptions the planters who had been named in the confiscation and imprisonment edicts were at the head of the long list of debtors at the beginning of 1786.[124]

Meantime, in 1783–1784, South Carolina merchants got off to a bad start in their attempt to re-establish commercial relations and to recoup their wartime losses. The British merchants who had goods on hand took virtually all the lucrative business during the first half of 1783. The resentment of the local merchants against the British and Loyalists was intense, and they began to enlist the aid of the Charleston artisans and mechanics and organize mobs and terroristic activities against the foreigners. When the British departed in mid-1783 they were replaced both in a business capacity and as objects of the local merchants' hostility by agents for British merchants, the resident South Carolina factors. Intense bitterness between merchants and factors ensued, and throughout 1783 and 1784 Charleston was the scene of mob violence directed by the two groups against each other.[125]

[124] A summary table of the economic plight of the planters, as revealed by imports and exports, was compiled by "R" and printed in the *Charleston Morning Post* of February 28, 1787. These figures correspond to those I arrived at after tabulating and studying entries in the manuscript Book of Manifests and Entries and in Charleston, Port of, Account of Exports, 1782–1786, in the Legislative System File, both in the South Carolina Archives. Other contemporary estimates of importations of slaves are close to those given by "R"—for example, John Rutledge's in his speech on the floor of the House of Representatives, published in the *Charleston Evening Gazette* of September 28, 1785, and the report in the *Evening Gazette* of September 14, 1785. Further data on exports are contained in John Drayton, *A View of South Carolina, As Respects Her Natural and Civil Concerns* (Charleston, 1802), 173.

[125] These activities have been traced in the various Charleston newspapers through 1783 and 1784. Alexander Gillon emerged as the principal leader of the radical merchant element, and Christopher Gadsden was the leading factor in the disputes. See the articles written by Gadsden under the pseudonym "A Steady and Open Republican," in the Charleston *Gazette of the State of South Carolina*, May 13, July 17, July 22, August 5, 1784, and the articles written in answer to Gadsden.

The planter aristocracy, which had no particular love for either merchants or factors, nonetheless tended to side with the factors because they blamed the merchants for the original wave of mob violence. In mid-1784 the planters were definitely drawn into the dispute as an anti-merchant faction by a complicated series of personal incidents.[126]

Meanwhile the smaller planters and farmers of the interior were experiencing rapid growth and unprecedented prosperity as a result of the spread of tobacco culture to the farms above and near the fall line. The expansion of tobacco planting in the area may be seen in the statistics for rice and tobacco production over a quarter of a century. In 1760 the South Carolina tobacco crop was only 0.04 per cent as valuable as the rice crop; by 1769 it was 0.5 per cent as valuable; by 1783, 8 per cent; by 1785, 11 per cent; and by 1787 no less than 28 per cent, despite an increased rice crop in that year. South Carolina tobacco was of good quality and brought as high prices in world markets as the tobacco of Virginia and Maryland. In addition to the gains they derived from increased tobacco culture, the back-country farmers made further profits from increases in the production and selling prices of lumber, skins, and provisions. South Carolina merchants won most of the trade of the middle and up country during the 1780's by giving them favorable marketing terms. One result was that the back-country folk, already unsympathetic with the difficulties of the low-country planters, could, when they took a political stand at all, be counted on to side with the merchants.[127]

The basic alignments of interest groups in South Carolina politics in 1782–1785 were roughly as follows. The merchants,

[126] For example, see the account of the incident involving William Thompson and John Rutledge, in the *Gazette of the State of South Carolina*, April 29, 1784, and of the incident involving Henry Peronneau and Daniel Horry, *ibid.*, July 15, August 9, 12, 1784.

[127] These statistics are derived from the sources cited in note 124 above, for the postwar period, and from the *South Carolina & American General Gazette* (Charleston), which published annual reports of exports in November of each year from 1760 to 1769. The location of most of the tobacco planting in the state is manifest from the sites named for tobacco warehouses in the act of March 25, 1785. Three were located in Charleston, one in each of the other two ports, and twelve on or above the fall line.

with regular support from the artisans and mechanics of
Charleston and occasional support from a large part of the back
country and a few of the low-country planters, formed the
"radical" element. The planters and factors formed the core
of the opposition conservative element. The latter coalition was
able to retain control of the state government by virtue of the
constitutional apportionment of representation in the legislature, which gave the 6,700 families of the low country 126 representatives and the 19,400 families of the middle and up country only 76 representatives.[128]

The economic troubles of the planters were increasing all
the while, however, and when the activities preliminary to har-
vesting in the late summer of 1785 demonstrated that a third
poor rice and indigo crop was in the offing, their difficulties
assumed the aspect of an emergency. There began to be widespread executions for debts and forced sales of property, and
it appeared that the aristocracy's very survival was endangered
by economic losses. Accordingly a "Special Session to Consider
the State of the Republic" was called for the last week in September. The political shoe was on the other foot now, and it
was the planters' turn to be the "radicals" and the merchants'
turn to be "conservatives." [129]

About a hundred members of the legislature, almost all of
whom were from the low country, convened on September 27,
1785, barely forming a quorum. Under the leadership of the
Rutledges, the Pinckneys, Ralph Izard, Pierce Butler, David
Ramsay, and others high in the aristocracy, a radical program
for the relief of debtors was enacted. There were two main
pieces of legislation, an issue of £100,000 ($428,571) in paper
money to be lent on real estate mortgages of three times the

[128] The standard source on the distribution of representation is William
Schaper's "Sectionalism and Representation in South Carolina," in the *Annual
Report of the American Historical Association*, 1900, pp. 5 ff. Control of the
legislature meant control of local government as well, since local officials were
appointed by the legislature.

[129] *Gazette of the State of South Carolina*, and *Charleston Evening Gazette*,
September, 1785. In 1783 and 1784 the merchants' faction had styled itself "Republicans" and had called its planter-factor opposition "Nabobs." During the
crisis of 1785–1786 this nomenclature was dropped.

sum borrowed, and the famous "Pine Barren Act." The latter act permitted debtors the privilege of tendering worthless land in payment of debts and, since it allowed creditors to refuse the lands by relinquishing the right to sue during the life of the act, worked in effect as a stay law. Two other principal bills were considered by the special session. One was a measure prohibiting importation of slaves for three years, which was killed when John Rutledge pointed out that the slaves imported since the peace, about seven thousand in number, had constituted only a small part of the postwar imports and the ensuing indebtedness. A bill giving Congress power to regulate trade was indefinitely postponed.[130]

The attitudes of the merchants and the back country toward these acts are significant.[131] Some of the merchants, being debtors themselves, supported the legislation. Most of them, however, followed the lead of merchant-legislator Alexander Gillon, who met with the merchants at the end of each day's sessions to discuss the activities of the House. These merchants resigned themselves to the fact that the planters could not be stopped from carrying out their program. Gillon introduced amendments to the paper bill which would have made merchants, as the leading public creditors, the principal beneficiaries of the issue, but when this was rejected he contented himself with efforts to keep the legislation within bounds. The merchants supported the paper when it was issued, and when the planters, after balking at first, agreed to co-operate, the paper

[130] Debates in the legislature during this session are reported in the *Charleston Evening Gazette*, beginning with the issue of September 28, 1785. The leaders of the aristocracy were at times in dispute about the details of the paper act; some wanted as much as £400,000 to be issued, others as little as £83,000. The acts are contained in the *Statutes at Large of South Carolina*, edited by Thomas Cooper and Daniel McCord (10 vols., Columbia, 1836–1840), 4:710–716. That the Pine Barren Act actually operated as a stay law has not been generally recognized by historians, but that it did so operate is apparent from a careful reading of the act itself. For contemporary recognition of its nature, see the speech of Alexander Gillon in the *Charleston Evening Gazette* of March 23, 1786. Gillon warned that when the act expired it would "be in the power of the merchants to sue almost the whole of the country."

[131] This summary of the attitudes of groups has been derived from the debates and by correlating recorded individual attitudes with the economic and geographical backgrounds of the delegates.

was accepted at or near its face value as long as it was in circulation.[132]

The back country was represented in the special session by only a handful of men. One, Judge Henry Pendleton, led a movement to cut down the amount of the paper issue, and he unequivocally opposed the Pine Barren Act. The principal up-country leader present was Patrick Calhoun, who led his fellow back-countrymen in a futile attempt to kill both bills by indefinite postponement. Outside the legislature the most ardent spokesman against the measures was Aedanus Burke, who is considered by most historians to have been a "radical." [133]

The emergency legislation proved successful as stop-gap measures. The crops of 1786–1787, while not yet of bumper proportions, exceeded spring imports for the first time since 1775, and conditions were generally improved. The next year the crops broke previous records for total production, and by the time the ratifying convention met in May, 1788, almost everyone had recovered or was well on the road to recovery.

Debtor-relief laws no longer being necessary, the planters could consider the Constitution calmly and intelligently and on its merits. Had it appeared two years or even one year earlier, or had there been another crop failure in 1787–1788, their attitudes might have been considerably different. As it was, the planters approved the Constitution for a multitude of lesser reasons as well as the two major reasons cited earlier.

Though the decision on ratification was one which, because of the unequal representation, was to be made by the planters alone, the merchants and factors were not without influence in shaping this decision, and their attitudes are of significance. Many of them could and did support ratification for the same reasons as did the low-country planters: the consciousness of military vulnerability, the gains that might be expected from the funding of the war debts by the United States, and intelligent consideration of the merits of the Constitution. Further, many

[132] *Charleston Morning Post, Charleston Evening Gazette,* and *Gazette of the State of South Carolina,* August, 1786; Jensen, *The New Nation,* 319; Ramsay, *History of South Carolina,* 2:185.

[133] See Burke's presentment to the Grand Jury at Beaufort, in the *Gazette of the State of South Carolina,* November 17, 1785.

who were creditors could appreciate the protection against further debtor-relief laws that the Constitution promised. This consideration was perhaps minimized by the fact that the danger of such laws had now passed for the time being and that in the event of a recurrence of the difficulties of 1785 the planters would doubtless be sufficiently intelligent to devise legislation of this sort that did not violate the Constitution.

Another consideration, however, namely that exclusive power to regulate commerce was to reside in the new government, affected the commercial classes in several ways. Since the New England states and perhaps others could be counted on to attempt to exercise this regulatory power by enacting commercial restrictions against Britain, the factors could see in this clause sufficient economic grounds for harboring strong reservations about the Constitution. The attitudes of merchants, on the other hand, were shaped by more complex considerations. Virtually all the trading based on rice and indigo was carried on by means of a single round-trip voyage each year; that is, these crops were shipped to Europe between November and March in vessels which returned with European goods in the spring. It was impossible to make the round trip twice in the season from November to March, and consequently it was not economically feasible for local merchants to build and own enough vessels to carry all their own exports.

Locally owned vessels carried about 25 per cent of the rice and indigo exported annually. Before the war the merchants owning such vessels had employed them during the off-season in trade in provisions with the British West Indies. After 1783, the ports of these islands having been closed to American shipping, they were forced to trade with the less desirable markets of the non-British islands in the West Indies. In their capacity as *shippers*, such merchants supported any proposed commercial restrictions designed to force the British to reopen these ports.[134]

[134] For an example of clear contemporary thinking on the nature of South Carolina's trade and the effects that could be expected from congressional regulation of it, see the debates over the granting of such power which took place in the House in February, 1786, as recorded in the *Charleston Morning Post*.

On the other hand, the merchants in their capacity as *traders* feared such legislation. About 40 per cent of South Carolina's trade was carried in vessels belonging to other states and about 35 per cent in British and other foreign bottoms. This healthy competition obviously meant higher profits for local merchants, because it kept freight rates low. Should the British be shut out of this carrying trade, freight rates would skyrocket, and since there were usually limits to what planters would pay for goods, only part of the increased cost could be passed on to consumers and the rest would come out of the merchants' profits.[135]

Still another consideration caused different merchants to re-act differently to the commerce clause. Those whose principal trade was with the back country usually owned enough vessels to carry all their exports, which consisted of tobacco, skins, and lumber, commodities that were produced and exported at different seasons of the year. Suffering nothing from being shut out of the British West Indies, and neither desiring nor fearing competition, these merchant-shippers had nothing to gain from the talked-of restrictions against the British. But while they had little to lose, the possibility that unnecessary tinkering with the natural course of trade might harm the commercial community in one way or another sufficed to cause many of them to oppose the Constitution. Furthermore, those who traded with the Indians had reason to fear the loss of lucrative trade in skins if the new national government should force the Indians deeper into the interior in order to clear the way for settlers.[136]

The various groups of merchants and the factors were thus forced to weigh conflicting interests. The great majority of them were security owners, and they stood to gain by the ap-

[135] It was this line of reasoning which had brought George Mason, James McHenry, and other southerners in the Philadelphia Convention to demand that no commercial regulations should be passed without the concurrence of the representatives of two-thirds of the states in the new Congress.

[136] This might partially explain the opposition to the Constitution on the part of John L. Gervais, holder of a large amount of securities, powerful merchant, and president of the Charleston Chamber of Commerce, who conducted an extensive trade in skins with the Indians. See Gervais to Leonard DeNeufville, April 13, 1786, in Gervais and Owen Miscellaneous File, in the Manuscripts Division of the Library of Congress.

preciation of their securities. But the factors had to weigh this advantage and the advantage of precluding further debtor-relief legislation against the possibility that Congress might adopt a commercial policy inimical to their primary interests. Rice and indigo merchants had to weigh these advantages and their prospective gains as shippers against the possibility of losses in their trading activities. Finally, merchant-shippers who traded with the back country had to weigh the prospective advantages against their reluctance to permit governmental tampering with their business. In the end these conflicts of interest probably induced more merchants and factors to support than to oppose the Constitution. At the same time merchants were the principal leaders of the opposition in the ratifying convention.

The opposition, aside from that furnished by merchants, came from three major sources. Nearly half of it, judging from votes in the ratifying convention, came from low-country planters.[137] A handful of these were planters in a desperate economic plight who desired further debtor legislation, but the great majority were men who had been unaffected by postwar economic difficulties. This latter group was an extremely conservative—that is, provincial—one, and though the individuals who comprised it had nothing to lose from ratification and, indeed, many of them were public security holders, they opposed the essentially radical step of creating a national government and surrendering South Carolina's quasi-sovereignty to it. Some considered South Carolina sufficiently well endowed to prosper as an independent republic, and their personal prosperity strengthened this conviction. Others preferred the creation of a multiplicity of confederations, one of which would consist of the Carolinas and Georgia.[138]

Another substantial part of the opposition came from tobacco-planting farmers in the middle and up country. A measure of

[137] Only about fifteen of the votes against ratification in the convention were cast by planters who both lived in and represented the low country. As many more, however, were low-country planters who were elected to the convention as representatives from places in the interior.

[138] For one serious and elaborate proposal of this kind see the *Charleston Morning Post*, March 15, 29, April 3, May 19, 1787.

their opposition may be attributed to the same considerations as governed the conservative low-country planters and another portion to their long-standing habit of opposing almost everything favored by the low-country planters, opposition that stemmed from a variety of political, social, economic, and geographical differences.

Finally, there was considerable opposition high in the up country of the District of 96, born of the widespread loyalism in that area. Some places, where there had been violent hostility between Tories and Whigs, and where Whigs were now in a majority, apparently opposed the Constitution on the ground that it provided safe refuge for the Tories. Libby believed that, by the same token, the Federalism of two up-country districts stemmed from the fact that Tories were in a majority there. On the other hand, some places had opposed the Revolution because of their essential conservatism and their habit of opposing, as Scotch-Irish Presbyterian frontiersmen, anything favored by the Anglican and Huguenot aristocrats of the low country, and they now opposed the Constitution for the very same reason.[139]

The occupations and property holdings of the delegates in the ratifying convention substantiate the above analysis of alignments. These economic interests are tabulated below.[140]

[139] The questions arising from loyalism in the up country have never been satisfactorily studied. Libby, in his *Geographical Distribution of the Vote*, page 44, makes the above observation without benefit of any primary research. Singer devotes a chapter of his *South Carolina in the Confederation* to "Treatment of Loyalists," but this leaves much to be desired with respect to the up country. Robert W. Barnwell's "Migration of Loyalists from South Carolina," in *Proceedings of the South Carolina Historical Society*, 1937 (Columbia, 1938), Claude W. Van Tyne's *The Loyalists in the American Revolution* (New York, 1902), and Allen Nevins' *The American States during and after the Revolution, 1775–1789* (New York, 1924) all touch on the subject. The source materials I have explored are sufficient to indicate that the problems are complex ones which will require much further study before they can be understood.

[140] The data on security holdings are from the Records of the Loan of 1790, in the National Archives, as follows: vol. 1258 (Journal of the Assumed Debt, S.C.); vol. 1259 (Journal of the Public [continental] Debt, S.C.); and vol. 1262 (Ledger of the Domestic Debt); and also from Alexander S. Salley, ed., *Stub Entries to Indents Issued in Payment of Claims against South Carolina Growing out of the Revolution, Books L–N* (Columbia, 1910), *Book X*, part 1 (Columbia, 1925), and *Books Y–Z* (Columbia, 1927). The funding records

Economic Interests of Delegates Voting
for Ratification

Six of the delegates were merchants engaged in foreign trade:

Josiah Smith (Charleston), amount of land, if any, unknown, 13 slaves, $94,829 in securities as a member of the firm of Smith and Darrell, and $5,226 in his own name.[141]

Edward Darrell (Charleston), amount of land unknown, 9 slaves, the securities of the above-mentioned firm as a partner, and $27,843 in his own name.[142]

John Edwards (Charleston), 19 slaves, $108,859 in securities.[143]

Lewis Lesterjette (Orange), back-country merchant and planter, 24 slaves.[144]

Joseph Manigault (Christ Church), 2 slaves, $43,446 in securities.[145]

Nathaniel Russel (Charleston), 16 slaves, $45,397 in securities.[146]

Five of the delegates were factors for British merchants:

Edward Blake (Charleston), land and buildings in Charleston valued at $1,671, 14 slaves in the city and 56 slaves on a plantation in St. Andrew's, $14,500 in securities. Blake had borrowed paper money from the state.[147]

Daniel DeSaussure (Charleston), erstwhile partner of Smith and Darrell, now a factor, 394 acres valued at $4,285, 16 slaves, $4,922 in securities, $2,037 of which was co-owned with Smith and Darrell. DeSaussure was

cover a period beginning three years after the convention, and the *Stub Entries to Indents* used here cover the two and a half years before the convention. I have assumed that it is just as likely that delegates who held securities shortly before the convention continued to hold them during the convention as it is that delegates who funded securities after the convention had held those securities at the time of the convention. In the many instances in which securities were held both before and after the convention, they are counted only once, of course.

[141] *Census of 1790, Heads of Families, South Carolina,* 39 (hereafter cited as *Census of 1790, S.C.*); Records of the Loan of 1790, vol. 1258, folios 43, 99, 198; vol. 1259, folio 17. The delegates who represented St. Philip's and St. Michael's Parish, Charleston, are here designated only as representing Charleston.

[142] *Census of 1790, S.C.,* 38; Records of the Loan of 1790, vol. 1258, folio 195; vol. 1259, folio 9; vol. 1262, folio 18; Book of Manifests and Entries, 98, in the South Carolina Archives.

[143] *Census of 1790, S.C.,* 39; Records of the Loan of 1790, vol. 1258, folio 19.

[144] *Census of 1790, S.C.,* 61; Book of Manifests and Entries, 143, in the South Carolina Archives.

[145] *Census of 1790, S.C.,* 36; Records of the Loan of 1790, vol. 1258, folio 57.

[146] *Census of 1790, S.C.,* 38; Records of the Loan of 1790, vol. 1258, folio 16; vol. 1259, folio 4; Book of Manifests and Entries, 215, in the South Carolina Archives.

[147] *Census of 1790, S.C.,* 34; Records of the Loan of 1790, vol. 1258, folio 45; vol. 1259, folio 22; Loan Office Manuscripts: Appraisals and Certificates, May 30, 1785, in the South Carolina Archives.

one of the persons who had been imprisoned during the war, and in 1786 he borrowed paper money from the state.[148]

Christopher Gadsden (Charleston), 128 slaves. Gadsden had been listed in the first confiscation edict and he suffered an additional loss, amounting to more than $4,000, when his uninsured wharves were burned during the riots of 1783.[149]

Thomas Gadsden (Charleston), son and partner of the former, 13 slaves.[150]

Richard Lushington (Charleston), $989 in securities.[151]

Seven of the delegates were artisans and mechanics or were engaged in miscellaneous occupations in Charleston. Charleston "mechanics" were often actually the heads of large construction organizations using crews of slaves.

Daniel Cannon (Charleston), a carpenter, 31 slaves, $271 in securities.[152]

William Johnson (Charleston), a blacksmith, 12 slaves, $5,212 in securities.[153]

Michael Kalteisen (Charleston), a mariner, $2,767 in securities.[154]

Thomas Sommersall (Charleston), whose property holdings were not ascertained.

Anthony Toomer (Charleston), a bricklayer, 12 slaves, $543 in securities.[155]

John Joyner (St. Helena's), a mariner and part-time planter, 730 acres valued at $1,473, a town lot valued at $130, 59 slaves, $14,640 in securities.[156]

Daniel Stevens (Charleston), sheriff, 386 acres valued at $3,376, 6 slaves. Stevens had borrowed paper money from the state.[157]

Sixteen of the delegates were lawyers. The principal wealth of most lawyers, as of members of other groups, was in land and slaves.

[148] Loan Office Manuscripts: Appraisals, Certificates, and Plats, April 7, 1786, in the South Carolina Archives; *Census of 1790, S.C.,* 40; Records of the Loan of 1790, vol. 1258, folio 30; vol. 1259, folios 10, 83; Book of Manifests and Entries, 250; Charleston *South Carolina Gazette and General Advertiser Extraordinary,* May 10, 1783.

[149] *Census of 1790, S.C.,* 38, 51; Philadelphia *Pennsylvania Packet,* October 23, 1783; Charleston *South Carolina Gazette,* October, 1783.

[150] *Census of 1790, S.C.,* 38; Book of Manifests and Entries, 157, 291.

[151] Book of Manifests and Entries, 175; Salley, *Stub Entries to Indents, Books Y–Z,* 131.

[152] *Census of 1790, S.C.,* 42; Records of the Loan of 1790, vol. 1259, folio 10.

[153] *Census of 1790, S.C.,* 43; Records of the Loan of 1790, vol. 1258, folio 151; vol. 1259, folio 21.

[154] *Census of 1790, S.C.,* 34; Salley, *Stub Entries to Indents, Books Y–Z,* 124.

[155] Records of the Loan of 1790, vol. 1258, folio 163; Book C, 1793–1800, vol. 27, p. 758, of the Will Book Collections, in the Charleston Free Library.

[156] Tax Returns, St. Helena's Parish, 1798, in the South Carolina Archives; Salley, *Stub Entries to Indents, Books Y–Z,* 264.

[157] *Census of 1790, S.C.,* 44; Loan Office Manuscripts: Appraisals, Certificates, and Plats, April 31, 1786.

John F. Grimke (Charleston), 6 slaves, $14,437 in securities.[158]

Hugh Rutledge (Charleston), 6 slaves.[159]

William Smith (St. James's, Goose Creek), $11,910 in securities.[160]

John Parker, Jr. (St. James's, Goose Creek), 146 acres valued at $3,214, $3,038 in securities. Parker had borrowed paper money from the state.[161]

Charles Pinckney (Christ Church), whose interests were described earlier, pages 80–81.

Charles C. Pinckney (Charleston), interests described earlier, page 80.

John Matthews (Charleston), 12 slaves in the city and 229 slaves on two plantations outside the city, $130 in securities. Matthews had lost his property under the second confiscation edict.[162]

John Rutledge (Christ Church), interests described earlier, pages 79–80.

Edward Rutledge (Charleston), 16 slaves, $1,331 in securities.[163]

Thomas Bee (Charleston), 19 slaves in the city and 165 slaves on his plantation.[164]

John J. Pringle (Charleston), attorney-general of South Carolina, lot in Charleston valued at $3,214 exclusive of buildings, 22 slaves. Pringle had borrowed paper money from the state.[165]

Jacob Read (Christ Church), 11 slaves, $492 in securities.[166]

Henry Pendleton (Saxe-Gotha), no securities, slaves not ascertainable because he died before the Census of 1790 was taken.[167]

[158] *Census of 1790, S.C.*, 42; Records of the Loan of 1790, vol. 1258, folio 66; vol. 1259, folio 16; O'Neall, *Bench and Bar of South Carolina*, 2:597. An additional $14,000 in securities is recorded for Grimke in the account in vol. 1258, folio 66, but this entry represents securities acquired in 1792 and 1795.

[159] *Census of 1790, S.C.*, 42; O'Neall, *Bench and Bar*, 2:597.

[160] Records of the Loan of 1790, vol. 1258, folio 45; O'Neall, *Bench and Bar*, 2:603.

[161] Records of the Loan of 1790, vol. 1258, folio 43; Loan Office Manuscripts: Appraisals, Certificates, and Plats, April 28, 1786; O'Neall, *Bench and Bar*, 2:602.

[162] *Census of 1790, S.C.*, 38, 51, 33; Records of the Loan of 1790, vol. 1258, folio 202; O'Neall, *Bench and Bar*, 1:213 ff.

[163] *Census of 1790, S.C.*, 42; Records of the Loan of 1790, vol. 1258, folio 38. An additional $531 in securities, acquired by Rutledge in 1792, is also recorded in this entry.

[164] *Census of 1790, S.C.*, 37, 39; O'Neall, *Bench and Bar*, 2:597.

[165] *Census of 1790, S.C.*, 42; Loan Office Manuscripts: Appraisals, Certificates, and Plats, April 20, 1786. An entry in volume 1258, folio 257, of the Records of the Loan of 1790 refers to securities acquired by Pringle in 1796. Beard (page 289) mistakenly lists Pringle as a security holder at the time of the convention.

[166] *Census of 1790, S.C.*, 38; Records of the Loan of 1790, vol. 1258, folio 160; vol. 1259, folios 86, 95; Levinus Clarkson Letters and Documents, in the Manuscripts Division of the Library of Congress.

[167] O'Neall, *Bench and Bar*, 1:31 ff.

Thomas Waties (Prince George's, Winyah), a lot in Georgetown valued at $3,214 exclusive of buildings, 50 slaves. Waties had borrowed paper money from the state.[168]

Thomas Heyward, Jr. (Charleston), 5 slaves. [169]

Richard Hutson (St. Andrew's), 264 acres valued at $3,214, 17 slaves, $115 in securities. Hutson had lost his property under the second confiscation edict, and had borrowed paper money from the state.[170]

Five of the delegates were physicians:

John Budd (Charleston), 1,000 acres valued at $2,143, 4 slaves, $641 in securities. Budd had borrowed paper money from the state.[171]

David Ramsay (Charleston), lots in Charleston valued at $10,286 exclusive of buildings, 6 slaves, $4,605 in securities. Ramsay had borrowed paper money from the state in 1786, and in 1789 he was heavily indebted to various persons.[172]

William Read (Christ Church), 9 slaves, $6,287 in securities.[173]

John Harris (District of 96), 100 acres valued at $107, one slave, $9 in securities.[174]

James Stuart (St. Helena's), two tracts valued at $5,507, 83 slaves. Stuart had borrowed paper money from the state.[175]

Two of the delegates were clergymen:

Francis Cummins (New Acquisition), 2 slaves.[176]

Henry Holcom (St. Peter's), no known property holdings.

Eighty-seven of the delegates were large planters:

Thomas Allston (All Saints'), 203 slaves.[177]

[168] *Census of 1790, S.C.*, 56; Loan Office Manuscripts: Appraisals, Certificates, and Plats, March 24, 1786; O'Neall, *Bench and Bar*, 1:43 ff.

[169] *Census of 1790, S.C.*, 34; O'Neall, *Bench and Bar*, 2:597.

[170] *Census of 1790, S.C.*, 34; Records of the Loan of 1790, vol. 1259, folio 84; Loan Office Manuscripts: Appraisals, Certificates, and Plats, May 1, 1786; O'Neall, *Bench and Bar*, 1:211 ff.

[171] *Census of 1790, S.C.*, 39; Salley, *Stub Entries to Indents, Books Y–Z*, 3; Loan Office Manuscripts: Appraisals, Certificates, and Plats, May 12, 1786.

[172] *Census of 1790, S.C.*, 42; Records of the Loan of 1790, vol. 1258, folio 16 (recorded in this same entry is also $5,820 in securities acquired in 1792; another $3,521 in securities which was acquired in 1794 is recorded in vol. 1258, folio 236); Loan Office Manuscripts: Appraisals, Certificates, and Plats, April 3, 1789; Jacob Read to Ann Van Horne, March 14, 1789, in the Levinus Clarkson Letters and Documents, in the Manuscripts Division of the Library of Congress.

[173] *Census of 1790, S.C.*, 39; Records of the Loan of 1790, vol. 1259, folio 29.

[174] Tax Return, District of Ninety-Six, 1787, in the South Carolina Archives; Salley, *Stub Entries to Indents, Books Y–Z*, 67.

[175] *Census of 1790, S.C.*, 10; Loan Office Manuscripts: Appraisals, Certificates, and Plats, May 4, 1786.

[176] *Census of 1790, S.C.*, 57.

[177] *Ibid.*, 50. An entry in vol. 1258, folio 236, of the Records of the Loan of 1790 records the acquisition of securities in 1795.

William Allston, Jr. (Prince George's), land valued at "upwards of six thousand guineas" ($27,000). Allston's father's estate, which the son was to inherit, consisted of 26,590 acres valued at $44,228, nine town lots valued at $2,610, and 60 slaves. Allston had borrowed paper money from the state.[178]

John Barnwell (St. Helena's), 560 acres valued at $9,514, town lots valued at $700, 83 slaves. He had borrowed paper money from the state.[179]

Robert Barnwell (St. Helena's), 1,708 acres, 48 slaves, $342 in securities.[180]

Lemuel Benton (St. David's), 1,050 acres valued at $6,964, 45 slaves. Benton had borrowed paper money from the state.[181]

John Blake (Charleston), Charleston lots valued at $3,214 exclusive of buildings (other landholdings unknown), 38 slaves. Blake had borrowed paper money from the state.[182]

John Chesnut (District East of the Wateree), 9,509 acres valued at $4,946, town lots valued at $6,428, 126 slaves, $7,430 in securities. Chesnut had borrowed paper money from the state.[183]

John A. Cuthbert (Prince William's), 3,968 acres in 1798, 53 slaves in 1790. Cuthbert had borrowed paper money from the state.[184]

John Crosskeys (St. Bartholomew's), 1,175 acres valued at $3,000, $241 in securities.[185]

John Dawson (St. George's, Dorchester), 13 slaves, $14,434 in securities.[186]

John Deas, Jr. (St. James's, Goose Creek), 631 acres valued at $8,751 "and upwards" exclusive of buildings, 170 slaves, $1,517 in securities. Deas had borrowed paper money from the state.[187]

[178] Tax Returns, Prince George Parish, 1786; Loan Office Manuscripts: Appraisals, Certificates, and Plats, May 6, 1786; both in the South Carolina Archives.

[179] *Census of 1790*, S.C., 13; Tax Returns, St. Helena's Parish, 1798; Loan Office Manuscripts: Appraisals, Certificates, and Plats, May 8, 1786; both manuscripts in the South Carolina Archives.

[180] *Census of 1790*, S.C., 10; Tax Returns, St. Helena's Parish, 1798; Records of the Loan of 1790, vol. 1258, folio 226.

[181] *Census of 1790*, S.C., 45; Loan Office Manuscripts: Appraisals, Certificates, and Plats, July 28, 1786.

[182] *Census of 1790*, S.C., 37, 38, 40; Loan Office Manuscripts: Appraisals, Certificates, and Plats, April 28, 1786.

[183] Tax Returns, District East of the Wateree, 1787; Loan Office: Appraisals, Certificates, and Plats, March 22, 1786; Records of the Loan of 1790, vol. 1258, folio 74. This entry records an additional $512 which was acquired later.

[184] *Census of 1790*, S.C., 10; Tax Returns, Prince William's Parish, 1798; Loan Office Manuscripts: Appraisals, Certificates, and Plats, June 26, 1786.

[185] Tax Returns, St. Bartholomew's Parish, 1786; Salley, *Stub Entries to Indents, Books Y–Z*, 88.

[186] *Census of 1790*, S.C., 38; Records of the Loan of 1790, vol. 1258, folio 142. Another John Dawson, a merchant, lived in Charleston at this time. The delegate John Dawson is identified in most documents as a "planter."

[187] *Census of 1790*, S.C., 36; Salley, *Stub Entries to Indents, Books Y–Z*, 89, 112, 207; Loan Office Manuscripts: Appraisals, Certificates, and Plats, April 29, 1786.

Stephan Devaux (Prince William's), 1,350 acres valued at $6,291, $49 in securities. Devaux had borrowed paper money from the state.[188]

William Dewitt (St. David's), 2,240 acres valued at $3,428, 55 slaves, $33 in securities. Dewitt had borrowed paper money from the state.[189]

Charles Drayton (St. Andrew's), 10,361½ acres valued at $4,761, 158 slaves.[190]

Glen Drayton (St. Andrew's), 4,920 acres valued at $8,901, 135 slaves, $114 in securities. Drayton had borrowed paper money from the state.[191]

Isaac Dubose (St. James's, Santee), lot in Charleston valued at $4,268 exclusive of buildings (other landholdings unknown), 6 slaves in Charleston and 103 slaves on his plantation, $678 in securities. Dubose had borrowed paper money from the state.[192]

Samuel Dubose (St. Stephen's), one tract of 250 acres valued at $5,240, other landholdings and slaveholdings unknown. Dubose had borrowed paper money from the state.[193]

William Dunbar (District between Savannah River and North Fork of the Edisto), 1,340 acres valued at $4,050 in his own name and 2,600 acres valued at $11,143 held as a tenant in common with Robert Lark, 17 slaves. Dunbar had borrowed paper money from the state.[194]

William Elliott (St. Helena's), 830 acres and 47 slaves in 1798 (earlier holdings unknown), $4,126 in securities.[195]

John Fenwick (St. Peter's), 766 acres valued at $4,103, 40 slaves. Fenwick had borrowed paper money from the state.[196]

William Frierson (Prince Frederick's), 26 slaves.[197]

Thomas Fuller (St. Andrew's), 4,982 acres and Charleston lots valued at $3,428, 110 slaves.[198]

John Glaze (St. George's, Dorchester), 67 slaves.[199]

[188] Salley, *Stub Entries to Indents, Books Y–Z*, 163; Loan Office Manuscripts: Appraisals, Certificates, and Plats, May 8, 1786.

[189] *Census of 1790, S.C.*, 47; Salley, *Stub Entries to Indents, Books Y–Z*, 15; Loan Office Manuscripts: Appraisals, Certificates, and Plats, July 12, 1786.

[190] Tax Returns, St. Andrew's Parish, 1787.

[191] *Census of 1790, S.C.*, 34; Tax Returns, St. Andrew's Parish, 1787; Records of the Loan of 1790, vol. 1259, folio 73; Loan Office Manuscripts: Appraisals, Certificates, and Plats, May 8, 1786.

[192] *Census of 1790, S.C.*, 25, 33; Salley, *Stub Entries to Indents, Books Y–Z*, 76, 113; Loan Office Manuscripts: Appraisals, Certificates, and Plats, March 31, 1786.

[193] Loan Office Manuscripts: Appraisals, Certificates, and Plats, May 1, 1786.

[194] *Census of 1790, S.C.*, 99; Loan Office Manuscripts: Appraisals, Certificates, and Plats, May 16, 1786.

[195] Tax Returns, St. Helena's Parish, 1798; Records of the Loan of 1790, vol. 1258, folio 93.

[196] *Census of 1790, S.C.*, 32; Loan Office Manuscripts: Appraisals, Certificates, and Plats, May 5, 1786.

[197] *Census of 1790, S.C.*, 19, 51.

[198] *Ibid.*, 34, 42; Tax Returns, St. Andrew's Parish, 1787.

[199] *Census of 1790, S.C.*, 37, 40.

George Haig (St. Paul's), 8,327 acres and 195 slaves in 1786 in St. Paul's Parish, and 81 on other plantations. By 1790 he had acquired 75 more slaves in St. Paul's Parish.[200]

Paul Hamilton (St. Paul's), 1,602 acres, 38 slaves.[201]

Isaac Harlestone (St. Thomas and St. Dennis), 117 slaves, $11,347 in securities. Harlestone's property was confiscated under the first confiscation edict.[202]

Matthias Hutchinson (St. George's, Dorchester), $19 in securities; other property holdings unknown.[203]

Hezekiah Mahams (St. Stephen's), $1,193 in securities; other property holdings unknown.[204]

Joachim Hartshorne (St. Peter's), 47 slaves, $314 in securities.[205]

Thomas Horry (St. James's, Santee), 256 slaves.[206]

Benjamin Hicks, Jr. (St. David's), 269 acres valued at $3,315, 48 slaves. Hicks had borrowed paper money from the state.[207]

John Huger (St. Thomas and St. Dennis), 1,721 acres valued at $17,644, 223 slaves, $3,933 in securities. Huger had borrowed paper money from the state.[208]

Thomas Hutson (Prince William's), 831 acres valued at $7,286. Hutson had borrowed paper money from the state.[209]

Ralph Izard (St. James's, Goose Creek), 602 slaves, $20,865 in securities. Izard's property had been confiscated under the first confiscation edict.[210]

Ralph Izard, Jr. (St. Andrew's), 14 slaves.[211]

Daniel Jenkins (St. John's, Colleton), 106 slaves.[212]

Isaac Jenkins (St. John's, Colleton), 45 slaves.[213]

Francis Kinloch (Charleston), land valued at $4,500, 244 slaves. Kinloch had borrowed paper money from the state.[214]

[200] *Ibid.*, 37, 96, 98; Tax Returns, St. Paul's Parish, 1786.

[201] Tax Returns, St. Paul's Parish, 1788.

[202] *Census of 1790, S.C.*, 44; Records of the Loan of 1790, vol. 1258, folio 26; vol. 1262, folio 56.

[203] Salley, *Stub Entries to Indents, Books Y–Z*, 128.

[204] *Ibid.*, 8.

[205] *Census of 1790, S.C.*, 12; Salley, *Stub Entries to Indents, Books Y–Z*, 199.

[206] *Census of 1790, S.C.*, 34, 37, 39.

[207] *Ibid.*, 46, 98; Loan Office Manuscripts: Appraisals, Certificates, and Plats, July 27, 1786.

[208] *Census of 1790, S.C.*, 42, 45; Records of the Loan of 1790, vol. 1262, folio 62; Loan Office Manuscripts: Appraisals, Certificates, and Plats, May 1, 1786.

[209] Loan Office Manuscripts: Appraisals, Certificates, and Plats, April 15, 1786.

[210] *Census of 1790, S.C.*, 33, 34, 37, 44; Records of the Loan of 1790, vol. 1258, folio 27; vol. 1259, folio 8.

[211] *Census of 1790, S.C.*, 42.

[212] *Ibid.*, 32.

[213] *Ibid.*, 32.

[214] *Ibid.*, 42, 55; Loan Office Manuscripts: Appraisals, Certificates, and Plats, May 11, 1786.

Cleland Kinloch (Prince George's, Winyah), 300 slaves.[215]

Thomas Jones (Charleston), 12 slaves, $3,422 in securities.[216]

John Kean (St. Helena's), 2,320 acres and $1,100 in town lots in 1798 (earlier landholdings unknown), 50 slaves, $93 in securities.[217]

Thomas Karwon (St. Thomas and St. Dennis), 53 slaves, $86 in securities.[218]

James Ladson (St. Andrew's), 1,717 acres valued at $10,384, 142 slaves.[219]

Henry Laurens (St. John's, Berkley), 2,961 acres valued at $8,134, town lots valued at $22,071, 298 slaves, $12,717 in securities in his own name and $7,836 with Keating Simons. Laurens suffered doubly during the war, having been captured on the high seas while en route to Holland to become United States minister to that country. He was imprisoned in the Tower of London and later exchanged for no less a person than Lord Cornwallis. Meanwhile his property had been seized under the first confiscation edict.[220]

Henry Laurens, Jr. (St. John's, Berkley), property held independently of his father unknown.

Edward Lightwood (Charleston), 1,164 acres valued at $7,998, a Charleston lot valued at $3,214 exclusive of buildings, 73 slaves, $1,808 in securities. Lightwood had borrowed paper money from the state.[221]

John Lightwood (Prince William's), 1,000 acres valued at $3,428, 27 slaves, $69 in securities. Lightwood had borrowed paper money from the state.[222]

John Lloyd (St. Bartholomew's), 108 slaves, *probably* no securities.[223]

Thomas Legare (St. John's, Colleton), 51 slaves.[224]

John McPherson (Prince William's), 564 acres valued at $4,286, 107 slaves, $70 in securities. McPherson had borrowed paper money from the state.[225]

---

[215] *Census of 1790, S.C.*, 56.

[216] *Ibid.*, 43; Records of the Loan of 1790, vol. 1258, folio 31.

[217] *Census of 1790, S.C.*, 11; Tax Returns, St. Helena's Parish, 1798; Salley, *Stub Entries to Indents, Books Y–Z*, 22.

[218] *Census of 1790, S.C.*, 44; Salley, *Stub Entries to Indents, Books Y–Z*, 302.

[219] *Census of 1790, S.C.*, 34, 40, 55; Tax Returns, St. Andrew's Parish, 1787.

[220] *Census of 1790, S.C.*, 31; Tax Returns, St. John's Parish (Berkley), 1793; Records of the Loan of 1790, vol. 1258, folios 34 and 230; vol. 1259, folio 7; vol. 1262, folio 14. In these and other entries Laurens is listed for other sums, all representing later acquisitions and transfers of securities.

[221] *Census of 1790, S.C.*, 34, 39; vol. 1258, folio 78; vol. 1259, folio 73; Loan Office Manuscripts: Appraisals, Certificates, and Plats, April 28, 1786.

[222] *Census of 1790, S.C.*, 12; Loan Office Manuscripts: Appraisals, Certificates, and Plats, April 26, 1786.

[223] *Census of 1790, S.C.*, 34, 36. Another John Lloyd, a Charleston merchant, was active at this time. Securities recorded in Records of the Loan of 1790, vol. 1258, folio 83, totaling $47,283 in various transactions between 1793 and 1795, are apparently those of the merchant.

[224] *Census of 1790, S.C.*, 32, 42.

[225] *Ibid.*, 12, 42; *Stub Entries of Indents, Books Y–Z*, 70; Loan Office Manuscripts: Appraisals, Certificates, and Plats, April 15, 1786.

William Robinson (District between Savannah River and North Fork of the Edisto), 21 slaves.[226]

Jacob Rumph (Orange), 23 slaves.[227]

James Maine (Prince William's), 3,823 acres valued at $2,043 in 1798 (earlier holdings unknown), 48 slaves in 1798 (earlier holdings unknown).[228]

Gabriel Manigault (St. James's, Goose Creek), 255 slaves.[229]

Lewis Miles (St. James's, Santee), 31 slaves.[230]

Lewis Morris (Charleston), 18 slaves. In 1786 Morris purchased confiscated lots in New York City for £308.[231]

John Mayrant (St. James's, Santee), 60 slaves.[232]

Ephraim Mikel (St. John's, Colleton), 80 slaves.[233]

Isaac Motte (Charleston), 1,267 acres valued at $8,145, 40 slaves, $12,787 in securities. Motte's property had been seized under the first confiscation edict, and in 1786 he borrowed paper money from the state.[234]

William Moultrie (St. John's, Berkley), 800 acres valued at $5,143, 352 slaves. Moultrie's property had been seized under the first confiscation edict, and in 1786 he borrowed paper money from the state.[235]

Richard Muncreef, Jr. (St. John's, Colleton), 53 slaves.[236]

John Palmer (St. Stephen's), 100 slaves.[237]

Isaac Parker (St. Thomas and St. Dennis), 101 slaves.[238]

John Peyre (St. Stephen's), 56 slaves.[239]

James Postell (St. George's, Dorchester), 69½ acres valued at $2,143 (on one plantation, probably more on others), 42 slaves. Postell had borrowed paper money from the state.[240]

---

[226] *Census of 1790, S.C.*, 35, 98.
[227] *Ibid.*, 98.
[228] Tax Returns, Prince William's Parish, 1798.
[229] *Census of 1790, S.C.*, 36, 38, 44, 45.
[230] *Ibid.*, 37.
[231] *Ibid.*, 39; Harry B. Yoshpe, *The Disposition of Loyalist Estates in the Southern District of the State of New York* (New York, 1939), 128. Beard (page 289) lists Morris as a security holder, but I found his name in none of the records.
[232] *Census of 1790, S.C.*, 18.
[233] *Ibid.*, 32.
[234] *Ibid.*, 12, 28; Records of the Loan of 1790, vol. 1258, folio 44 (a small additional sum is recorded in this entry, a later acquisition); Loan Office Manuscripts: Appraisals, Certificates, and Plats, March 30, 1786.
[235] *Census of 1790, S.C.*, 31, 40, 96; Loan Office Manuscripts: Appraisals, Certificates, and Plats, March 30, 1786.
[236] *Census of 1790, S.C.*, 32, 43.
[237] *Ibid.*, 44.
[238] *Ibid.*, 42, 45.
[239] *Ibid.*, 44.
[240] *Ibid.*, 12; Loan Office Manuscripts: Appraisals, Certificates, and Plats, June 7, 1786.

William Postell (St. George's, Dorchester), 6,600 acres valued at $17,267, 155 slaves.[241]

Roger Parker Saunders (St. Paul's), 88 slaves.[242]

William Scott (St. Andrew's), lot in Charleston valued at $2,143, plantation lands of unknown extent, 70 slaves. Scott had borrowed paper money from the state.[243]

Thomas Screven (St. Thomas and St. Dennis), 60 slaves.[244]

John Simmons (Prince William's), 113 slaves.[245]

Joseph Slann (St. Paul's), 1,080 acres, 63 slaves.[246]

William Smelie (St. John's, Colleton), 105 slaves.[247]

Samuel Smith (Prince George's, Winyah), 71 slaves.[248]

Peter Smith (St. James's, Goose Creek), 64 slaves, $571 in securities.[249]

Calvin Spencer (St. David's), 23 slaves, $245 in securities.[250]

Seth Stafford (St. Peter's), 18 slaves.[251]

Samuel Taylor (St. David's), 76 slaves, $3,108 in securities.[252]

Joshua Toomer (Christ Church), 940 acres valued at $3,514, 60 slaves.[253]

William Thompson (St. Matthew's), 802 acres valued at $12,857, 154 slaves, $239 in securities. Thompson had borrowed paper money from the state.[254]

Alexander Tweed (Prince Frederick's), 19 slaves, $324 in securities.[255]

Arnoldus Vanderhorst (Christ Church), Charleston lot valued at $4,286 exclusive of improvements, plantation lands of unknown extent, 180 slaves. Vanderhorst's property was seized under the second confiscation edict, and in 1786 he borrowed paper money from the state.[256]

Samuel Warren (St. James's, Santee), 82 slaves, $3,196 in securities.[257]

[241] *Census of 1790*, S. C., 35, 37; Tax Returns, St. Paul's Parish, 1789.
[242] Tax Returns, St. Paul's Parish, 1786.
[243] *Census of 1790*, S.C., 34; Loan Office Manuscripts: Appraisals, Certificates, and Plats, August 1, 1786. Scott should not be confused with a Charleston merchant and several back-country farmers of the same name.
[244] *Census of 1790*, S.C., 39, 45.
[245] *Ibid.*, 11.
[246] Tax Returns, St. Paul's Parish, 1788.
[247] *Census of 1970*, S.C., 32.
[248] *Ibid.*, 56. It is difficult to distinguish the delegate from a Georgetown merchant of the same name. One of them borrowed paper money in 1786.
[249] *Ibid.*, 36; Records of the Loan of 1790, vol. 1262, folio 68.
[250] *Census of 1790*, S.C., 48; Records of the Loan of 1790, vol. 1259, folio 79.
[251] *Census of 1790*, S.C., 13.
[252] *Ibid.*, 48; Salley, *Stub Entries of Indents, Books Y–Z*, 236.
[253] Tax Returns, Christ Church Parish, 1786.
[254] *Census of 1790*, S.C., 96; Salley, *Stub Entries of Indents, Books Y–Z*, 144, 266; Loan Office Manuscripts: Appraisals, Certificates, and Plats, May 8, 1786.
[255] *Census of 1790*, S.C., 42; Records of the Loan of 1790, vol. 1258, folio 137.
[256] *Census of 1790*, S.C., 32, 34, 11; Loan Office Manuscripts: Appraisals, Certificates, and Plats, February 7, 1786.
[257] *Census of 1790*, S.C., 37; Records of the Loan of 1790, vol. 1258, folio 139.

Morton Waring (St. George's, Dorchester), 28 slaves.[258]

Thomas Waring (St. George's, Dorchester), 27 slaves, $118 in securities.[259]

William Washington (St. Paul's), 12,650 acres valued at $28,856, Charleston lots valued at $8,574, 363 slaves, $11,044 in securities. Washington was deeply in debt in 1786 and sought a loan in Holland through anti-Federalist John L. Gervais.[260]

William H. Wigg (St. Helena's), 590 acres valued at $4,172, 103 slaves. Wigg had borrowed paper money from the state.[261]

Hugh Wilson (St. John's, Colleton), 84 slaves.[262]

William Wilson (Prince Frederick's), 1,150 acres valued at $375 in Prince Frederick's and 14 slaves in the same place, apparently 46 more slaves in Prince George's Parish.[263]

Paul Worley (St. Matthew's), 52 slaves.[264]

Fifteen of the delegates were smaller planters and farmers:

Donald Bruce (Orange), 11 slaves.[265]

Robert Brownfield (St. David's), co-owner of 12 slaves.[266]

Richard Withers (St. James's, Santee), co-owner of 15 slaves. Withers' property was confiscated under the second confiscation edict.[267]

Samuel Earle (North Side of Saluda), 12 slaves.[268]

William McCaleb (South Side of Saluda), 8 slaves.[269]

John Miller (South Side of Saluda), no slaves, $83 in securities.[270]

Jonathan Clark (District between Savannah River and North Fork of the Edisto), 2 slaves.[271]

John Collins (District between Savannah River and North Fork of the Edisto), 16 slaves.[272]

Stephen Smith (St. James's, Goose Creek), 10 slaves, $75 in securities.[273]

[258] *Census of 1790*, S.C., 33.

[259] *Ibid.*, 32; Salley, *Stub Entries of Indents, Books Y–Z*, 99.

[260] Tax Returns, St. Paul's Parish, 1786; Records of the Loan of 1790, vol. 1259, folio 4; Gervais to DeNeufville, April 13, 1786, in the Gervais and Owen Personal Miscellaneous File, in the Manuscripts Division of the Library of Congress.

[261] *Census of 1790*, S.C., 11; Loan Office Manuscripts: Appraisals, Certificates, and Plats, May 2, 1786.

[262] *Census of 1790*, S.C., 32.

[263] *Ibid.*, 53, 56; Tax Returns, Prince Frederick's Parish, 1786. The identity of the holder of the forty-six slaves is not certain.

[264] *Census of 1790*, S.C., 96.

[265] *Ibid.*, 98.

[266] *Ibid.*, 53.

[267] *Ibid.*, 54.

[268] *Ibid.*, 68, 70.

[269] *Ibid.*, 81.

[270] *Ibid.*, 82, 85; Salley, *Stub Entries of Indents, Books Y–Z*, 181.

[271] *Census of 1790*, S.C., 83.

[272] *Ibid.*, 101.

[273] *Ibid.*, 63; Salley, *Stub Entries of Indents, Books Y–Z*, 32.

James Pettigrew (Prince Frederick's), no slaves, $23 in securities.[274]
John Thomas, Jr. (North Side of Saluda), one slave, $27 in securities.[275]
John Hunter (Little River), 7 slaves.[276]
Lewis Fogartie (St. Thomas and St. Dennis), 10 slaves.[277]
Joseph Vince (District between Savannah River and North Fork of the Edisto), 550 acres valued at $2,143, 9 slaves. Vince had borrowed paper money from the state.[278]
Thomas Wadsworth (Little River), 6 slaves.[279]
Benjamin Smith (St. James's, Goose Creek), 10 slaves.[280]

ECONOMIC INTERESTS OF DELEGATES VOTING
AGAINST RATIFICATION

Four of the delegates were merchants engaged directly in interstate and foreign trade:
John L. Gervais (District of 96), lot in Charleston valued at $3,428 exclusive of improvements, 57 slaves, $22,500 in securities. Gervais, who lived in Charleston (though he represented the District of 96 in the convention), was president of the Charleston Chamber of Commerce, fiscal agent for the state's foreign debt, and a leader in the erstwhile merchant's faction. His property had been confiscated under the first confiscation edict, and in 1786 he borrowed paper money from the state.[281]
John Bowman (St. James's, Santee), slave trader, 293 slaves on his own plantations, $50 in securities.[282]
William Kennedy (Upper or Spartan District), back-country merchant, one slave, $305 in securities.[283]

[274] *Census of 1790*, S.C., 60; Salley, *Stub Entries of Indents, Books Y–Z*, 137.
[275] *Census of 1790*, S.C., 69; Salley, *Stub Entries of Indents, Books Y–Z*, 165.
[276] *Census of 1790*, S.C., 73.
[277] *Ibid.*, 45.
[278] *Ibid.*, 99; Loan Office Manuscripts: Appraisals, Certificates, and Plats, May 15, 1786.
[279] *Census of 1790*, S.C., 75.
[280] *Ibid.*, 43.
[281] *Ibid.*, 31, 42; Records of the Loan of 1790, vol. 1258, folios 213, 215; vol. 1259, folio 83; Loan Office Manuscripts: Appraisals, Certificates, and Plats, April 22, 1786; Gervais and Owen Papers, *passim*, in the Manuscripts Division of the Library of Congress. Gervais had also been issued $877.34 in state securities, which was probably included in the securities he funded; Salley, *Stub Entries of Indents, Books Y–Z*, 150.
[282] *Census of 1790*, S.C., 37; Salley, *Stub Entries of Indents, Book X*, part 1, p. 141; Book of Manifests and Entries, 278.
[283] *Census of 1790*, S.C., 91; Salley, *Stub Entries of Indents, Book X*, part 1, p. 131; *Books Y–Z*, 296; Book of Manifests and Entries, 135. The importation recorded there is of goods costing almost $15,000, and it is one of many entries, which indicates that Kennedy's volume of business was not small.

Keating Simons (St. John's, Berkley), 1,000 acres valued at $3,214, 78 slaves, $7,836 in securities co-owned with Henry Laurens. Simons was a charter member and director of the Bank of South Carolina, founded in 1788. He had borrowed paper money from the state.[284]

One of the delegates, Benjamin Cudworth (District East of the Wateree), was a factor. He owned 7 slaves; his property had been seized under the first confiscation edict.[285]

Three of the delegates were lawyers:

Aedanus Burke (Lower District between Broad and Saluda Rivers), one slave, $5,252 in securities.[286]

James G. Hunt (New Acquisition), no slaves, $22 in securities.[287]

Samuel Lowry (New Acquisition), 5 slaves.[288]

One of the delegates, Peter Fayssoux (St. John's, Berkley), was a physician. He held 81 slaves.[289]

Thirty-one of the delegates were large planters:

Edmond Bellinger (St. Bartholomew's), at least 13,000 acres (2,397 acres in one district of St. Bartholomew's alone valued at $7,723), 85 slaves on that plantation, 59 on another, perhaps more, $924 in securities.[290]

John Lewis Bourjin (St. Peter's), 750 acres valued at $24,643, $34 in securities. Bourjin had borrowed paper money from the state.[291]

John Bowie (District of 96), 7,108 acres, 15 town lots, 121 slaves, $6,056 in securities.[292]

J. Burgess, Jr. (Prince Frederick's), 28 slaves.[293]

[284] *Census of 1790, S.C.,* 31; Records of the Loan of 1790, vol. 1258, folio 230; Book of Manifests and Entries, 97, 153; State Finance File: Banks, in the South Carolina Archives; Loan Office Manuscripts: Appraisals, Certificates, and Plats, April 24, 1786.

[285] *Census of 1790, S.C.,* 23. For identification of Cudworth as a factor, see the advertisements of Cudworth and Waller in the various Charleston newspapers of the period.

[286] *Census of 1790, S.C.,* 42; Salley, *Stub Entries of Indents, Books Y–Z,* 106, 125; O'Neall, *Bench and Bar,* 1:35 ff.

[287] O'Neall, *Bench and Bar,* 2:601; Salley, *Stub Entries of Indents, Books L–N,* 323.

[288] *Census of 1790, S.C.,* 13, 15; O'Neall, *Bench and Bar,* 2:602.

[289] *Census of 1790, S.C.,* 31, 39.

[290] *Ibid.,* 34; Tax Returns, St. Bartholomew's Parish, Districts of Combahee and Cheraw, 1786; Salley, *Stub Entries of Indents, Books L–N,* 5; and see the John A. Cuthbert file in Loan Office Manuscripts: Appraisals, Certificates, and Plats, June 2, 1786. Bellinger was the son of Landgrave Edmund Bellinger, who was given a landgrave patent for 48,000 acres, 13,000 acres of which he had surveyed before his death and passed to his son.

[291] Salley, *Stub Entries of Indents, Books Y–Z,* 162; Loan Office Manuscripts: Appraisals, Certificates, and Plats, May 2, 1786.

[292] Tax Returns, District of Ninety-Six, 1787; Records of the Loan of 1790, vol. 1258, folio 192.

[293] *Census of 1790, S.C.,* 19.

John Cook (Fairfield County), 33 slaves, $66 in securities.[294]

Joseph Culpeper (Saxe-Gotha), 22 slaves, $626 in securities.[295]

Patrick Dollard (Prince Frederick's), 500 acres, 27 slaves.[296]

William Fitzpatrick (Saxe-Gotha), 25 slaves.[297]

Melcher Garner (St. Paul's), 4,904 acres valued at $11,143, 81 slaves in 1786, 91 slaves in 1787, 87 slaves in 1790.[298]

John Gray (District of 96), 410 acres, 18 slaves, $1,403 in securities.[299]

Richard Hampton (Saxe-Gotha), 950 acres valued at $4,273, two tracts and a ferry owned with brother Wade valued at $10,346 "and upward," 30 slaves, $5,825 in securities owned with brother Wade. Hampton had borrowed paper money from the state.[300]

Wade Hampton (Saxe-Gotha), 1,311 acres valued at $12,731 "and upward," a lot in Charleston valued at $2,700 exclusive of buildings, the above-mentioned tracts held with brother Richard valued at $10,346, another plot of 18,150 acres which he leased, 86 slaves, $10,046 in securities, part of which he owned with Richard as stated above. Hampton also held vast tracts of western lands running perhaps into hundreds of thousands of acres. He had borrowed paper money from the state, apparently for use in land speculation.[301]

William Hill (New Acquisition), 84 slaves, $175 in securities.[302]

Thomas Howell (District between Broad and Catawba Rivers), 33 slaves.[303]

Adam Crain Jones (District of 96), 1,581 acres, 22 slaves, $266 in securities.[304]

[294] *Ibid.*, 20; Salley, *Stub Entries of Indents*, Book X, part 1, 64; *Books Y–Z*, 206.

[295] *Census of 1790, S.C.*, 94; Salley, *Stub Entries of Indents, Books L–N*, 122.

[296] *Census of 1790, S.C.*, 50; Tax Returns, Prince Frederick's Parish, 1786.

[297] *Census of 1790, S.C.*, 94.

[298] *Ibid.*, 37; Tax Returns, St. Paul's Parish, 1786, 1789.

[299] Tax Returns, District of Ninety-Six, 1787; Salley, *Stub Entries of Indents, Books L–N*, 14.

[300] *Census of 1790, S.C.*, 34, 62, 97; Salley, *Stub Entries of Indents, Books Y–Z*, 172; Loan Office Manuscripts: Appraisals, Certificates, and Plats, May 28, 1786, and also the Miscellaneous File in this collection.

[301] *Census of 1790, S.C.*, 27; Salley, *Stub Entries of Indents, Books L–N*, 15, 146; *Books Y–Z*, 172, 177; Loan Office Manuscripts: Appraisals, Certificates, and Plats, May 13, 17, 19, 1786, and also the Miscellaneous File in this collection; South Carolina Miscellaneous File in the Manuscripts Division of the Library of Congress. The sketch in the 1927 edition of the *Biographical Directory of Congress*, page 1055, states that Hampton was the wealthiest planter in the south and the owner of 3,000 slaves when he died. Both his own fortune and that of his brother Richard were built on land speculations. It is probable that they borrowed paper money with which to invest in lands.

[302] *Census of 1790, S.C.*, 28; Salley, *Stub Entries of Indents*, Book X, part 1, p. 204; *Books Y–Z*, 256.

[303] *Census of 1790, S.C.*, 31.

[304] Tax Returns, District of Ninety-Six, 1787; Salley, *Stub Entries of Indents, Books Y–Z*, 274.

James Knox (Chester District), 29 slaves, $263 in securities.[305]

James Martin (New Acquisition), 2,516 acres valued at $8,060, 24 slaves, $1,168 in securities. Martin had borrowed paper money from the state.[306]

James Lincoln (District of 96), 33 slaves.[307]

William Meyer (District between Broad and Catawba Rivers), 19 slaves.[308]

William Miles (St. Andrew's), 525 acres valued at $2,550, 19 slaves, $1,024 in securities.[309]

Benjamin Postell (St. Bartholomew's), 1,000 acres valued at $2,475, 97 slaves. Postell had been seized and imprisoned aboard a prison ship during the war.[310]

William Read (Prince Frederick's), 72 slaves, $417 in securities.[311]

William Clay Snipes (St. Bartholomew's), 87 slaves, $650 in securities. Snipes's property had been confiscated under the first confiscation edict.[312]

Charles Sims (Upper or Spartan District), 22 slaves, $1,215 in securities.[313]

O'Brien Smith (St. Bartholomew's), 55 acres valued at $3,428 on one plantation (other landholdings unknown), 146 slaves.[314]

Thomas Sumter (District East of the Wateree), 114,820 acres, number of slaves unknown, $1,625 in securities.[315]

Thomas Taylor (District between Broad and Catawba Rivers), 300 acres valued at $10,286 on his "upper plantation" and 1,250 acres valued at "upwards of" $14,915 on his lower plantation, 70 slaves, $1,030 in securities. Taylor had borrowed paper money from the state.[316]

John Threewits (Saxe-Gotha), 18 slaves, $567 in securities.[317]

[305] *Census of 1790*, S.C., 15; Salley, *Stub Entries of Indents, Books Y–Z*, 123.

[306] *Census of 1790*, S.C., 17; Salley, *Stub Entries of Indents, Books L–N*, 19, 43; *Book X*, part 1, p. 8; *Books Y–Z*, 155, 211; Loan Office Manuscripts: Appraisals, Certificates, and Plats, April 22, 1786.

[307] *Census of 1790*, S.C., 59.

[308] *Ibid.*, 26.

[309] Tax Returns, St. Andrew's Parish, 1787; Salley, *Stub Entries of Indents, Books L–N*, 338; *Book X*, part 1, p. 80; *Books Y–Z*, 282.

[310] *Census of 1790*, S.C., 35; Tax Returns, St. Bartholomew's Parish, 1786. Postell may have owned more land; he was the tax collector for his parish, and he recorded for taxation only forty-three of his ninety-seven slaves.

[311] *Census of 1790*, S.C., 31, 52; Salley, *Stub Entries of Indents, Books L–N*, 169.

[312] *Census of 1790*, S.C., 35; Salley, *Stub Entries of Indents, Books L–N*, 214; *Books Y–Z*, 169.

[313] *Census of 1790*, S.C., 90; Salley, *Stub Entries of Indents, Book X*, part 1, pp. 106, 136; *Books Y–Z*, 97.

[314] *Census of 1790*, S.C., 34; Tax Returns, Charleston Neck, 1786.

[315] Salley, *Stub Entries of Indents, Books L–N*, 307; *Book X*, part 1, p. 51; Anne King Gregorie, *Thomas Sumter* (Columbia, 1931), 216.

[316] *Census of 1790*, S.C., 27; Records of the Loan of 1790, vol. 1259, folios 71, 76; Loan Office Manuscripts: Appraisals, Certificates, and Plats, May 9, 13, 30, 1786.

[317] *Census of 1790*, S.C., 94; Salley, *Stub Entries of Indents, Book X*, part 1, p. 35.

Llewellen Threewits (Saxe-Gotha), 17 slaves, $408 in securities.[318]

Paul Walter (St. Bartholomew's), 2,936 acres valued at $2,910, 45 slaves.[319]

John Wilson (St. Paul's), 904 acres in St. Paul's and 288 acres in Cheraw, the latter valued at $3,215, 84 slaves, $361 in securities. Wilson had borrowed paper money from the state.[320]

Twenty-seven of the delegates were lesser planters and farmers:

Joseph Brown (Chester District), 400 acres, 7 slaves, $154 in securities.[321]

Thomas Brandon (Upper or Spartan District), 11 slaves, $154 in securities.[322]

James Craig (Fairfield County), 7 slaves, $83 in securities.[323]

Zachariah Bullock (Upper or Spartan District), 11 slaves, $1,332 in securities.[324]

William Butler (District of 96), 6 slaves.[325]

Joseph Calhoun (District of 96), 3 slaves.[326]

John Chisholm (St. Peter's), 6 slaves, $20 in securities.[327]

Samuel Dunlap (District East of the Wateree), 8 slaves, $323 in securities.[328]

Thomas Dunlap (District East of the Wateree), one slave, $63 in securities.[329]

Andrew Hamilton (District of 96), 4 slaves.[330]

John Hampton (Lower District between Broad and Saluda Rivers), 12 slaves, $1,453 in securities. Brother of Richard and Wade Hampton.[331]

John Lowry (District East of the Wateree), 225 acres, 2 slaves, $96 in securities.[332]

[318] *Census of 1790*, S.C., 94; Salley, *Stub Entries of Indents, Book X*, part 1, p. 36.

[319] *Census of 1790*, S.C., 34; Tax Returns, St. Bartholomew's Parish, 1786. Like Postell, Walter was a tax collector for St. Bartholomew's Parish in 1786, and like Postell listed himself as the holder of fewer slaves than he actually owned, twenty-eight instead of forty-five.

[320] *Census of 1790*, S.C., 37; Tax Returns, St. Paul's Parish, 1786; Salley, *Stub Entries of Indents, Books L–N*, 37; *Books Y–Z*, 146; Loan Office Manuscripts: Appraisals, Certificates, and Plats, June 10, 1786.

[321] Tax Returns, District of Ninety-Six, 1787; Salley, *Stub Entries of Indents, Book X*, part 1, p. 206.

[322] *Census of 1790*, S.C., 90; Salley, *Stub Entries of Indents, Books Y–Z*, 196.

[323] *Census of 1790*, S.C., 20; Salley, *Stub Entries of Indents, Books Y–Z*, 265.

[324] *Census of 1790*, S.C., 93; Salley, *Stub Entries of Indents, Book X*, part 1, pp. 63, 144, 222; *Books Y–Z*, 162.

[325] *Census of 1790*, S.C., 65.

[326] *Ibid.*, 57.

[327] *Ibid.*, 13; Salley, *Stub Entries of Indents, Books Y–Z*, 15.

[328] *Census of 1790*, S.C., 23; Salley, *Stub Entries of Indents, Books Y–Z*, 50.

[329] *Census of 1790*, S.C., 23; Salley, *Stub Entries of Indents, Books Y–Z*, 300.

[330] *Census of 1790*, S.C., 59.

[331] *Ibid.*, 98; Salley, *Stub Entries of Indents, Books Y–Z*, 158, 272, 280.

[332] Tax Returns, District East of the Wateree, 1787; Salley, *Stub Entries of Indents, Books Y–Z*, 300.

James Jordan (Upper or Spartan District), 13 slaves, $2,280 in securities.[333]

Edward Lacy (Chester District), 2 slaves.[334]

Andrew Love (New Acquisition), 3 slaves.[335]

John McCaw (New Acquisition), 3 slaves, $525 in securities.[336]

Edmund Martin (District of 96), 7 slaves.[337]

William Massey (District East of the Wateree), 11 slaves, $12 in securities.[338]

Adam Meek (New Acquisition), 5 slaves, $235 in securities.[339]

John Montgomery (District East of the Wateree), one slave, $1,759 in securities.[340]

Robert Patton (New Acquisition), 15 slaves, $347 in securities.[341]

Robert Rutherford (Lower District between the Broad and Saluda Rivers), 14 slaves.[342]

Samuel Watson (New Acquisition), no slaves, $82 in securities.[343]

Joshua Saxon (Little River District), 5 slaves, $307 in securities.[344]

Samuel Saxon (Little River District), 3 slaves.[345]

Abraham Smith (New Acquisition), 10 slaves, $69 in securities.[346]

Philemon Waters (Lower District between the Broad and Saluda Rivers), 12 slaves, $2,346 in securities.[347]

Four of the delegates whose other interests are not known were holders of public securities:

Andrew Baskins (District East of the Wateree), $212.[348]

Jacob Brown (Fairfield County), $155.[349]

---

[333] *Census of 1790, S.C.*, 90; Salley, *Stub Entries of Indents, Books Y–Z*, 269.

[334] *Census of 1790, S.C.*, 13.

[335] *Ibid.*, 29.

[336] *Ibid.*, 30; Salley, *Stub Entries of Indents, Books L–N*, 45.

[337] *Census of 1790, S.C.*, 67.

[338] *Ibid.*, 24; Salley, *Stub Entries of Indents, Books Y–Z*, 302.

[339] *Census of 1790, S.C.*, 29; Salley, *Stub Entries of Indents, Books L–N*, 39.

[340] *Census of 1790, S.C.*, 24; Salley, *Stub Entries of Indents, Book X, part 1*, pp. 170, 214; *Books Y–Z*, 288.

[341] *Census of 1790, S.C.*, 29; Salley, *Stub Entries of Indents, Book X, part 1*, p. 192; *Books Y–Z*, 156.

[342] *Census of 1790, S.C.*, 78.

[343] Salley, *Stub Entries of Indents, Book X, part 1*, p. 108.

[344] *Census of 1790, S.C.*, 73; Salley, *Stub Entries of Indents, Books L–N*, 308; *Books Y–Z*, 311.

[345] *Census of 1790, S.C.*, 73.

[346] *Ibid.*, 30; Salley, *Stub Entries of Indents, Books L–N*, 203; *Book X, part 1*, p. 191; *Books Y–Z*, 166.

[347] *Census of 1790, S.C.*, 77; Salley, *Stub Entries of Indents, Books L–N*, 203; *Book X, part 1*, p. 191; *Books Y–Z*, 166.

[348] *Ibid., Books L–N*, 5; *Books Y–Z*, 211. Baskins is described as a "Planter" in vol. 1258, folio 105, of the Records of the Loan of 1790.

[349] Salley, *Stub Entries of Indents, Book X, part 1*, p. 62.

John Lindsay (Lower District between the Broad and Saluda Rivers), $1,551.[350]

Hugh White (District East of the Wateree), $521.[351]

On two of the delegates no information was found.

These diverse data may be brought to a focus in the following generalizations about the economic interests of the friends and enemies of the Constitution in South Carolina. The majorities by which merchants, factors, lawyers, planters, and farmers favored ratification was for each group about the same as the overall majority in the convention—about two to one. To put it another way, the basic economic interests of the two sides, apart from immediate circumstances, were virtually the same. The Federalists and the anti-Federalists were both largely men of wealth and they had, proportionately, about the same amounts of the same kinds of property, the most important of which were land and slaves.

Professor Beard focused his attention on two economic elements in the ratification: public securities, which he assumed was the dynamic element in the ratification, and a complex of elements associated with private indebtedness, paper money, and other "debtor legislation," which he assumed was the principal motivating element in the opposition. Each of these economic elements may be weighed in turn, as they applied to South Carolina.

Public Securities.—Sixty-two (41.6 per cent), or two of every five, of the delegates who voted for ratification held public securities. Fifty (68.5 per cent), or two of every three, of the delegates who voted against ratification held securities. Members of both sides held securities in widely varying amounts. Perhaps the most important fact about the security holdings of the members, however, is not that large numbers of delegates held them, but that the amounts, with the exception of the holdings of some Charleston merchants and a few planters on each side, were small as compared with the other property holdings of the delegates. Only a handful of delegates held more than

[350] *Ibid.*, pp. 75, 166, 200, 214.
[351] *Ibid.*, *Books L–N*, 247, 317; *Books Y–Z*, 157.

$5,000 in securities, which was less than the value of the average, the mean, and the median slaveholdings of members on either side.

Private Indebtedness and Paper Money.—The Federalist group was clearly the group that had favored paper money. Forty (26.8 per cent) of them borrowed paper of the issue of 1786, and if those members whose names were on one of the three wartime edicts are added as probable debtors (not including those on the lists who borrowed paper money), the total is fifty Federalist delegates, or more than one in three. The anti-ratificationists, on the other hand, included only eight borrowers of paper (10.9 per cent), and the delegates named in the edicts who did not borrow paper bring the total to only eleven (15.1 per cent).

The conclusion seems inescapable that Beard was not only wrong on both counts, but that the actual situation was precisely the reverse of what he assumed it to be. That is to say, the conflict over ratification was not one in which holders of public securities were aligned in favor of the Constitution and advocates of paper money and other debtors were against it, but one in which the latter favored the Constitution and most holders of public securities opposed it.

These facts make it seem likely that Beard's elements may have been of some influence, but in a way quite different from what he supposed. It may have been that the Federalists, being a group of desperate debtors, sorely needed the cash they would receive as a result of the funding of the public war debts, despite their great wealth in land and slaves. Their opponents, being largely free of personal debts, were not pressed for cash and consequently could afford to disregard their public security holdings as a consideration in making a decision.

New Hampshire

New Hampshire's ratifying convention met twice before it came to a decision with respect to the Constitution. It met first in February, 1788, at which time a clear majority of its delegates were opposed to ratification. After ten days of debate some members seemed to be wavering, and the Federalists, not yet daring to risk a vote, succeeded in obtaining an adjournment of the convention for four months. In the interim a high-pressure campaign was launched in those anti-Federalist areas that gave most promise of a change of sentiment. When the convention reconvened in June the alignments were still dangerously close, but after four days of debate the vote was put and the Constitution was approved by a majority of only ten of the 104 voting delegates. New Hampshire thus became the ninth state to ratify, the Constitution had at last been brought into legal existence, and the Federalists could now proceed to organize the new national government.[352]

From start to finish the task of the friends of ratification in New Hampshire was to overcome the general apathy with which the people of the state greeted the Constitution. Beginning at the end of September a powerful propaganda campaign, all on behalf of ratification, was conducted in the Portsmouth newspapers, but this medium reached only a handful of towns in the area immediately adjacent to Portsmouth, and other means had to be employed.[353]

State President John Sullivan, a staunch friend of the Constitution, called a special session of the legislature in December, 1787, for the purpose of calling a ratifying convention, though the regular session was scheduled to meet only a month later. Unless this was a maneuver designed to circumvent expected opposition from the country members, however, it was unsuccessful, for less than forty of the hundred-odd members appeared for the special session. Lacking a quorum, the legislature hesitated a few days, then proceeded to do business without a quorum.

Since many of the more lethargic towns in the interior often

[352] Joseph B. Walker, *A History of the New Hampshire Convention for the Investigation, Discussion, and Decision of the Federal Constitution* (Boston, 1888), *passim.*

[353] Portsmouth *New Hampshire Spy*, September 29, 1787, and succeeding issues.

refused even to send representatives to the legislature, and the more remote towns usually combined in groups of two to five to send representatives, it was feared that not enough towns would be represented in the proposed convention to permit it to do business. In a clever maneuver a handful of Federalist legislators attempted to put through a motion that the ratifying convention should consist of two delegates from each town. If they succeeded, it was expected that the convention would have a disproportionate number of delegates from towns around Portsmouth in Rockingham County. The move was rejected, however, by a vote of 14 to 24, largely because only eight representatives from Rockingham County and none from Portsmouth itself were in attendance in the special session.

The quorumless legislature then resorted to another stratagem to overcome the apathy of the voters. A principal reason for the failure of towns to send representatives to the legislature was the cost, which was borne by the individual towns. To make it easier for the towns to send delegates, it was decided that the convention should meet at Exeter, where the legislature would also meet, in mid-February, when the regular session of the legislature would adjourn. With a plea to the towns to take advantage of this bargain package and to hold special town meetings to elect delegates, the special session adjourned.[354]

The strategy was successful, for about a fifth of the towns named their legislative representatives as delegates to the convention. Meantime enthusiastic friends and enemies of the Constitution sent riders to remote communities to enlist support for their respective sides. As a result, when the convention met on February 18, it was the most nearly complete representation of the towns the state had ever witnessed. Exclusive of the four-

---

[354] "Journals of the House of Representatives," in *Early State Papers of New Hampshire*, edited by Albert S. Batchellor, vol. 21 (Manchester, 1891). Since the convention was called by a session of the legislature in which there was no quorum, neither was actually a legal body and thus, technically speaking, New Hampshire has never yet ratified the Constitution and entered the Union. The frugal Yankees had adopted the joint method earlier in sending delegates to the Philadelphia Convention: New Hampshire authorized any two of its delegates in Congress to double as delegates in the convention.

teen delegates from the towns on the northern frontier, most of whom were committed to opposing the Constitution, the convention was divided almost equally.[355]

When the convention got under way the Federalists argued the merits of the Constitution clause by clause, while the anti-Federalists, under the able leadership of Joshua Atherton, a brilliant ex-Tory country lawyer, focused their attack on the fact that the Constitution sanctioned slavery. The Federalists appealed to reason, their opponents to religious sympathies, and religion was considerably the stronger in New Hampshire. During the course of the debates, however, Judge Samuel Livermore, a Princeton-educated lawyer who had moved to the northern frontier before the war to begin a long and successful career, and a man of great influence among his neighbors, privately persuaded several delegates from his neighborhood to support ratification. A number of the converts approached John Langdon, the leader of the Federalist forces on the floor of the convention, and told him they were bound by their instructions to vote against ratification but would seek new instructions if the convention should temporarily adjourn. Considering a postponement better than an absolute rejection, Langdon exerted his influence on the convention and it adjourned, to reconvene in Concord on June 18.[356]

In the intervening four months the ratificationists, while continuing their written appeals in the Portsmouth newspapers, concentrated on winning the northern towns and the towns on the Connecticut River. The Connecticut River towns in the state of Connecticut assisted this effort by printing newspaper appeals and sending them up the river to former citizens of

[355] Portsmouth *New Hampshire Spy*, January and February, 1788. The Journals of the House indicate that the largest previous attendance was 85, in February, 1786, whereas there were 112 men in the ratifying convention. Walker, *New Hampshire Convention*, 7–21. The Boston *Massachusetts Centinel* of March 1 contains a report on the electioneering of the opponents of the Constitution, and there is evidence of such activities on the part of the Federalists in various town meeting records.

[356] Walker, *New Hampshire Convention*, 22–30. Langdon's action is explained in his letter to Rufus King, February 23, 1788, quoted by Walker (page 29n).

Connecticut now residing in New Hampshire. The argument most consistently presented was that in the event of invasion from Canada—a real danger, it was alleged—New Hampshire's northern frontier would be highly exposed.[357]

The campaign was a success. The northern delegates came to the second session prepared to support ratification, 11 to 3, and after only four days of further discussion the vote was taken and the Constitution was ratified, 57 to 47.[358]

Economic factors seem to have had very little weight with most voters in New Hampshire, except perhaps as ultimate causes of symptomatic conditions, as the fundamental characteristics and the immediate postwar history of the state attest.

A large portion of the New Hampshire population was characterized by an uninformed lethargy combined with an intense and narrow localism. The hard work that attends rural life in a cold, mountainous country, the closed-in environment, and the absence of social or economic stimuli made the majority of the citizenry almost unbelievably apathetic toward all political matters except those immediately concerning the towns in which they lived or their neighboring communities. A case in point is the history of the state's efforts to draw up a state constitution between 1781 and 1784. It was an almost impossible task. Many towns refused to send delegates, with the result that the convention usually lacked a quorum, the delegates who did meet knew little of what they were about, half the towns refused to vote on various questions put to them, and the other half were divided in several ways. The convention finally completed its labors by copying, for the most part, from the Massachusetts constitution. The finished document was never actually ratified, but the convention, anticipating that most towns would take no

[357] See the Portsmouth *New Hampshire Spy* of April 15, 1788, and the Hartford *Connecticut Courant* of March 3, 1788, for examples of propaganda on the subject of "our proximity to Canada, Nova Scotia, &c., the very great danger we are in of being attacked on either quarter."

[358] Walker, in his *New Hampshire Convention*, 43n, tells of a "well-authenticated tradition" that a prominent Concord Federalist gave a dinner on the last day of the convention, to which he invited a number of anti-Federalist delegates. He reportedly succeeded in keeping them at his house with a bountiful repast of food and drink until after the votes were cast.

action, had submitted it to them with the notification that failure to vote on it would be construed as approval of the document. It was by this procedure that the state constitution had been brought into existence.[359]

In view of this characteristic apathy and provincialism it is a great deal more difficult to understand the votes for ratification in New Hampshire than the votes against it. A long step in the direction of such an understanding may be taken by making a careful analysis of the patterns and nature of localism in the state.

New Hampshire had three major river systems, the Piscataqua and its tributaries in the southeast corner of the state, which emptied into the Atlantic at Portsmouth; the Merrimac and its tributaries, which flowed down the center of the state into Massachusetts and thence eastward into the sea at Newburyport; and the Connecticut, which flowed southward and formed the state's western border. Each of these river systems was an avenue of communication, and the towns along their banks formed the three discrete subprovinces of the state. Between these river systems were mountains, which separated the three areas and isolated the mountain towns from one another.

The Piscataqua area had the most regular communication with the outside world, and it was the most advanced, best informed part of the state. The economic interests of the area, in addition to shipping, are disclosed by its exports: about half its income was derived from lumber and lumber products, a fifth from fishing, a fifth from shipbuilding, and a tenth from farm products. The Merrimac area was considerably less advanced and more provincial, though it communicated and traded regularly with the outside world through Newburyport. Its principal exports were lumber and lumber products, farm

[359] This characterization is based upon study of countless local histories and the manuscript records of virtually every town in the state. The account of the state constitution is based on both town records and the reports of the activities of the convention published in the Portsmouth *New Hampshire Gazette* from 1781 to 1784, particularly the issues of February 3 and June 28, 1783, in which the convention published a summary of its activities. A secondary account is the chapter on "The Evolution of State Government" in Richard F. Upton's *Revolutionary New Hampshire* (Hanover, 1936).

products, and manufactures processed from farm products. The Connecticut valley area, which had been settled principally by migrants from Connecticut, communicated only irregularly with the communities to the south. Its interests were almost exclusively agrarian; only about half the towns in the valley even had gristmills and less than half had stores or even villages in which stores could locate. The towns above Hanover on and near the Connecticut River, comprising the newly settled northern frontier, were made up almost entirely of farmers, as were the mountain and hill towns between the rivers. Both the northern frontier towns and the mountain towns were virtually isolated, even from one another.[360]

The voting habits of the people and their representatives followed areal patterns more clearly than those of perhaps any other state.[361] The Piscataqua area, with the interesting exception of Portsmouth, almost invariably voted as a unit. In popular elections in the 1780's it voted for General John Sullivan of Dover for state president, and in the legislature its representatives voted for the vigorous promotional program he represented. The Merrimac area likewise voted as a unit, and almost invariably on the opposite side from the Piscataqua area. For president it regularly supported John Langdon of Portsmouth, and in the legislature it was usually opposed to any action de-

[360] Jeremy Belknap, *The History of New Hampshire* (3 vols., Boston, 1792), vol. 3; James E. Defebaugh, *History of the Lumber Industry of North America* (2 vols., Chicago, 1906, 1907), vol. 2; William G. Saltonstall, *Ports of Piscataqua* (Cambridge, 1941); miscellaneous data from various newspapers, especially the *New Hampshire Gazette*, the *New Hampshire Mercury*, and the *New Hampshire Spy* (all published in Portsmouth) and numerous town histories. Three criteria have been used in estimating the relative isolation of the individual towns: (1) analysis of the topography of the state, with due allowance for the fact that topography changes; (2) whether the town had a store; and (3) whether it annually elected town inspectors of lumber prior to the passage of the state inspection act in 1785. Almost all towns that had intercourse with the outside world elected such inspectors, and the more advanced towns elected inspectors of other marketable commodities. These data have been derived from the Microfilm Collection of Town Records in the New Hampshire State Library, a virtually complete set of records up to about 1800.

[361] I have worked out the patterns of voting in presidential elections from documents in the Microfilm Collection of Town Records, and of voting in the legislature by tabulating and charting all the votes recorded in the journals of the House of Representatives, 1776–1789.

signed to interfere with the status quo. Portsmouth joined the Merrimac area in supporting Langdon but voted with its neighbors in the legislature. The isolated mountain and hill towns, when they participated in state politics at all, joined the Merrimac area both in voting for Langdon and in supporting a conservative program in the legislature. The ex-Connecticut men of the Connecticut valley, who usually had more political sophistication than the locally born citizenry, were markedly independent in their attitudes and actions. In presidential elections they voted for third and fourth candidates. In the legislature, when they sent representatives, their representatives took a third position, submitting sets of counter-proposals for each piece of proposed legislation.[362] The northern frontier towns rarely participated in state politics; when they did, most of them ordinarily voted for Samuel Livermore for president and followed Livermore's lead in matters of state policy.

Of the economic factors that must be reviewed as possible influences impelling a majority of the towns to vote for ratification, two may be rejected as unimportant. The protection of creditors promised by the Constitution may be ignored on two counts. First, the restrictions against stay laws were virtually meaningless in most of New Hampshire outside the Piscataqua area, for in at least two-thirds of the towns of the interior there were no attorneys available to prosecute executions for debt. Secondly, a comparison of the votes in the referendum of 1786 on a proposed issue of paper money with the votes on ratification in 1788 shows that there was almost no correlation. Of the seventy-six towns whose votes on both issues are known, twenty-eight that had voted for paper money also voted against the Constitution, and fifteen that had voted against paper money voted for the Constitution. On the other hand, twenty towns voted for both paper money and the Constitution, and thirteen voted against both. Thus the votes of forty-three towns support Beard's and Libby's premise that there was a connection

[362] The independent attitude of the Connecticut valley towns was demonstrated most clearly in 1782 when fourteen of them voted to secede from New Hampshire to join the new "outlaw" state of Vermont. This failing, they agitated for some time to set up another independent state.

between paper money and the Constitution, whereas the votes of thirty-three towns do not.[363]

Private ownership of public securities was likewise of little weight in the contest, for there were very few large security holders in the state. Of the total state debt of $282,000, about $150,000 was owned by thirty-two citizens of Massachusetts, two citizens of Britain, and two newcomers to New Hampshire. The state debt owned in the state had a par value of only about $120,000, which appreciated about $50,000 as a result of the funding of the debt. By far the greater share of this amount was owned by the fifty-odd merchants of Portsmouth, which means that the remaining 141,000 inhabitants of the state were devoid of this "considerable dynamic." Ownership of the $482,000 of continental debt in the state was distributed in much the same way as ownership of the state securities, with the important exception that the state government owned $137,000, more than a fourth of the total. In a word, then, the public debt was important in only two respects in bringing about ratification in New Hampshire: John Langdon, who held $26,000 in continental securities, and some of his fellow merchants were doubtless influenced by their holdings to vote for the Constitution, and their potent political influence was thus cast in its favor. Secondly, the state government's ownership of securities may also have induced some of the better informed citizens, who really needed little inducement, to support ratification.[364]

The proposed regulation of commerce by the general government was of considerable moment to two segments of the population in the Piscataqua area: that engaged in shipbuilding and that occupied in fishing. The shipbuilders had a strong motive for supporting ratification, inasmuch as the prosperity of

[363] The observation regarding the absence of lawyers is based on a study of local histories, almost all of which contain sections listing men of the towns who have been engaged in various occupations. The votes on paper money were tabulated from documents in the Microfilm Collection of Town Records.

[364] The figures are compiled from the following volumes of the Records of the Loan of 1790, in the National Archives: vol. 242, Journal of the Domestic Debt, 1791–96, and vol. 249, Subscription Register, Assumed Debt of New Hampshire. The figure for the total amount of continental securities funded in the state is from Summary Volume 174A, Treasury Department, in the same collection.

their industry depended in large measure upon the prosperity of the Massachusetts shipowners, who bought most of the vessels built in New Hampshire, and who were suffering great losses from British commercial restrictions. The fishermen, who suffered from the erratic policy of the French crown with respect to the importation of American fish into the French West Indies, likewise stood to benefit from regulation of commerce by the general government.

The other major interests of the Piscataqua area, the lumbering, farming, and shipping interests, as well as those of the interior areas, had less to gain from general commercial regulation. None of them was dependent upon Britain or the British West Indies for its prosperity, and the other ports of the world were open to their vessels and their wares.

The influence of economic factors in effecting ratification was thus confined largely to the Piscataqua area, five-eighths of whose delegates voted for ratification. Economic factors could account for a maximum of perhaps a third of the votes there, but it is worth repeating that in the contest the political influence of leading men of the area extended into other areas. Two other important influences, one external and the other internal, induced the area to support ratification. First, it was exposed, to a far greater extent than the other parts of the state, to information from the outside world. It is significant, too, that most of its contacts with other American ports were with Boston and with the Robert Morris mercantile element in Philadelphia, perhaps the two leading centers of nationalism on the continent.[365] Secondly, ratification of the Constitution would release the Piscataqua area from dependence on the ultraconservative interior for positive legislation—economic or otherwise—for such legislation could now come from Congress.[366]

[365] These commercial patterns were noted as I tabulated entrances and clearances of vessels, as recorded in Portsmouth newspapers. The business connections between John Langdon and Robert Morris are described in the sketch of Langdon's interests, page 39, above.

[366] The Piscataqua area got most of the economic legislation it desired during the 1780's but found the interior immovable on political questions and on such matters as the organization of the state militia. The economic legislation of 1784–1789, as recorded in volume 4 of *Laws of New Hampshire, Including*

With respect to the Connecticut valley area, where about five-sixths of the towns voted for ratification, Beard follows Libby in the rather absurd assertion that the towns there were "commercial" by virtue of their location on the river and that it was as commercial communities that they supported ratification. How the Constitution was to benefit the farmers and the dozen or so storekeepers and millers in this area by enabling Congress to regulate commerce is left unexplained, as is the fact that the towns immediately down the river in Massachusetts (closer to the sea and thus, by Beard's reasoning, more "commercial") voted against ratification.[367]

In point of fact the geographical position of these towns did help to shape their attitudes toward the Constitution, but not in the way set forth by Beard. There were three principal factors. In the first place the region had some communication with the outside world and thus tended to be less provincial than isolated interior towns. The significance of this factor must not be overrated, however, for the Merrimac region, which opposed the Constitution, had easier, quicker, and more frequent contact with the world outside New Hampshire than did the Connecticut valley. Secondly, the great majority of the settlers in the region had come up the river from Connecticut. This acted as a Federalizing influence in several ways, principally in that the citizens of the area were subject to the influence of the river towns in Connecticut, every one of which voted enthusiastically for ratification. In the third place, ratification of the Constitution was considered by many to be a prerequisite to the recognition of the statehood of Vermont, which was contested by New York. Since a strong element on the New Hampshire side of the Connecticut River desired to be attached to Vermont, this factor doubtless influenced some voters of the region.

The considerations that influenced the Connecticut River area to vote for ratification also helped to some extent to shape the

Public Acts and Resolves with an Appendix Embracing the Journal of the Committee of Safety (5 vols., Bristol, New Hampshire, 1916), is a classic mercantilistic system adapted to New Hampshire.

[367] Beard, *Economic Interpretation*, 255; Libby, *Geographical Distribution of the Vote*, 11.

attitudes of the northern frontier area. As stated earlier, however, the most important element there was the personal influence of one man, Judge Samuel Livermore of Holderness.

The remaining towns of the state, lacking the stimuli that influenced these other regions, acted in their customary lethargic fashion and opposed the Constitution. There were no immediate reasons for this opposition except the fundamental apathy of the people, their supreme localism, and their unwillingness to submit to any change.

Study of the economic backgrounds of the personnel of the ratifying convention leads to the conclusion that economic considerations could have had little weight in determining the decision of most members of the convention. The known economic interests of the delegates were as follows.

Economic Interests of Delegates Voting for Ratification

Seven of the delegates were merchants:

John Langdon, whose interests have been described earlier, pages 38–39.

Christopher Toppan (Hampton), who had shipbuilding and fishing interests and who owned $12,118 in continental and state securities.[368]

Nathaniel Rogers (Newmarket), who was also engaged in shipbuilding.[369]

Henry Prescutt (New Castle), who owned a house and wharf valued at about $467 and stock in trade worth about $783.[370]

Pierse Long (Portsmouth), who also owned sailing vessels.[371]

Ezra Green (Dover), a physician turned merchant, who was actually a storekeeper who bought his wares at wholesale from Portsmouth merchants.[372]

John Taylor Gilman (Exeter), whose mercantile ventures were sporadic. Gilman's principal property consisted of a 61-acre farm, Maine lands valued at about $1,767, and $18,676 in state and continental securities.[373]

---

[368] Batchellor, ed., *State Papers of New Hampshire*, 22:855 (Concord, 1893); Records of the Loan of 1790, vol. 242, folios 6, 48; vol. 249, folios 19, 20.

[369] Batchellor, ed., *State Papers of New Hampshire*, 22:843–844.

[370] Microfilm Collection of Town Records: Newcastle, Book VII, pp. 99–100.

[371] *Biographical Directory of Congress* (1927 edition), 1237.

[372] Chandler E. Potter, *The Military History of the State of New Hampshire* (Concord, 1866), 269n.

[373] Microfilm Collection of Town Records: Exeter, Book II, p. 526; Records of the Loan of 1790, vol. 242, folios 5, 45; vol. 249, folios 20, 21.

Seven of the delegates operated mills:

Elisha Whitcomb (Swanzey), who owned a sawmill, a grist mill, and a large farm.[374]

John Sullivan (Durham), owner of twenty clothing mills. Most of his mills had been destroyed by fire, however, in October, 1787.[375]

James Gray (Epsom, Northwood, and Allentown), who was taxed for a 14-acre farm and a small mill in 1793, as well as 337 acres of unimproved land.[376]

Nathan Goss (Rye), owner of a grist mill.[377]

Amos Dakin (Mason and Raby), who was the "sole owner, of the mills and water power and farm, at the village." [378]

Jonathan Chase (Cornish and Grantham), owner of a combination grist mill and sawmill, who also kept a store, farmed, and operated a ferry across the Connecticut River.[379]

Joseph Blanchard (Chester), owner of a fulling mill.[380]

Four of the delegates were lawyers:

Samuel Livermore (Holderness, Campton, and Thornton), chief justice of the state supreme court.[381]

John Pickering (Portsmouth), the town attorney of Portsmouth.[382]

Elisha Payne (Lebanon), who also owned a grist mill and a sawmill.[383]

Benjamin West (Charleston).[384]

Four of the delegates were physicians:

Ichabod Weeks (Greenland), who also owned a 77-acre farm and mills.[385]

[374] Benjamin Read, *History of Swanzey, New Hampshire* (Salem, 1892), 223–235, 565.

[375] Durham Tax Inventories, 1788, in Town Records Collection, in the Historical Society of New Hampshire; Portsmouth *New Hampshire Spy*, October 13, 1787. On February 29, 1788, Sullivan announced through an advertisement in the *Spy* that the desperate state of his affairs made it necessary for him to call in the debts due him.

[376] Microfilm Collection of Town Records: Epsom, Book I, p. 326.

[377] Langdon B. Parsons, *History of the Town of Rye, New Hampshire* (Concord, 1905), 219.

[378] John B. Hill, *History of the Town of Mason, New Hampshire* (Boston, 1858), 274–275.

[379] William H. Child, *History of the Town of Cornish, New Hampshire, 1763–1910* (Concord, 1911).

[380] Benjamin Chase, *History of Old Chester from 1719 to 1869* (Auburn, New Hampshire, 1869), 473.

[381] Sketch of Samuel Livermore by E. V. Moffett in the *Dictionary of American Biography; Biographical Directory of Congress* (1927 edition), 1231; Walker, *New Hampshire Convention*, 19n.

[382] Walker, *New Hampshire Convention*, 8n.

[383] *State Papers of New Hampshire*, 22:848–849; Charles A. Downs, *History of Lebanon, New Hampshire, 1761–1887* (Concord, 1908), 144.

[384] *State Papers of New Hampshire*, 22:847–848.

[385] Greenland Town Records, vol. 3, in Town Records Collection, in the Historical Society of New Hampshire.

Josiah Bartlett (Kingston), who also owned $1,421 in continental and state securities.[386]

Thomas Stow Ranney (Brentwood).

Edmund Chadwick (Deerfield).[387]

Five of the delegates were clergymen: [388]

Aaron Hall (Keene).

Samuel Langdon (Hampton Falls).

Benjamin Thurston (North Hampton).

Jeremiah Fogg (Kensington).

Amos Moody (Pelham), who owned $128 in continental securities.

Fifteen of the delegates were farmers:

Frances Worcester (Plymouth and Rumney).[389]

Robert B. Wilkins (Henniker and Hillsborough).[390]

Ebenezer Smith (Meredith).[391]

Benjamin Bellows (Walpole).[392]

John Calfe (Hampstead).[393]

Oliver Shepherd (Alstead).[394]

John Weeks (Lancaster, Northumberland, Stratford, Dartmouth, Piercy, Cockburn, and Coleburn). The land which Weeks held in Effington as a nonresident was sold for taxes in 1785.[395]

Joshua Morss (Hopkinson), owner of 43½ acres of wild land valued at about $367.[396]

Samuel Hale (Barrington), owner of 44½ acres, 12 acres of which was wild land.[397]

---

[386] *State Papers of New Hampshire*, 22:824 ff. (Concord, 1893); Records of the Loan of 1790, vol. 242, folio 6; vol. 249, folio 15.

[387] That Ranney and Chadwick were physicians is inferred from their titles in the list of delegates published in Walker's *New Hampshire Convention*, 10, 11.

[388] Simon G. Griffin, *A History of the Town of Keene* (Keene, 1904), 231–232, 605; Walker, *New Hampshire Convention*, 9 and 9n; Records of the Loan of 1790, vol. 242, folio 21; Roland D. Sawyer, *The History of Kensington, New Hampshire, 1663–1945* (Farmington, Massachusetts, 1946), 153–154. The Jeremiah Fogg who is recorded as having funded continental securities in New Hampshire in 1791 was not the delegate, the latter having died in 1789.

[389] Ezra S. Stearns, *History of Plymouth, New Hampshire* (2 vols., Cambridge, 1906) 1:412 ff.

[390] Potter, *Military History of New Hampshire*, 363.

[391] *State Papers of New Hampshire*, 22:852.

[392] *Ibid.*, 21:782–783.

[393] *Ibid.*, 21:786 ff.

[394] Microfilm Collection of Town Records: Alstead, Book II, p. 351.

[395] A. N. Somers, *History of Lancaster, New Hampshire* (Concord, 1899), 372, 414; Portsmouth *New Hampshire Gazette*, January 21, 1785.

[396] Microfilm Collection of Town Records: Hopkinson, Book V, p. 109.

[397] Microfilm Collection of Town Records: Barrington, Book II, p. 350.

Samuel Griffin (Dublin and Packersfield), owner of 11¾ acres of farmland and 75 acres of wild land valued at 50 cents.[398]

Charles Glidden (Northfield).[399]

Joseph Gerrish (Boscawen).[400]

Jonathan Freeman (Hanover).[401]

Jonathan Chesley (Barnstead).[402]

James Betton (Windham).[403]

Thomas Bartlett (Nottingham), owner of 54 acres of farmland and 200 acres of vacant land valued at $500.[404]

One of the delegates, Daniel Beede (Sandwich), had $381 in continental securities, but his occupation and other interests are unknown.[405]

The occupations and property holdings of fourteen of the delegates who voted for ratification were not ascertained.

ECONOMIC INTERESTS OF DELEGATES VOTING AGAINST RATIFICATION

Two of the delegates were storekeepers:

Timothy Taylor (Merrimac), who also owned a 17½-acre farm.[406]

Jonathan Dow (Weare).[407]

One of the delegates, Stephen Dole (Bedford), was a ship's carpenter.[408]

Four of the delegates were lawyers:

Joshua Atherton (Amherst).[409]

Nicholas Austin (Middletown, Wakefield, and Effingham), who was also engaged in sizeable real estate deals.[410]

[398] Microfilm Collection of Town Records: Nelson (formerly Packersfield), Book I, p. 650.

[399] Lucy R. H. Cross, *History of Northfield, New Hampshire, 1780–1905* (Concord, 1905), part 2, pp. 136–138.

[400] Charles C. Coffin, *The History of Boscawen and Webster from 1733 to 1878* (Concord, 1878), *passim.*

[401] *Biographical Directory of Congress* (1927 edition), 989.

[402] Robert B. Caverly, *History of Barnstead from Its First Settlement in 1727 to 1872* (Lowell, 1872), 118 and elsewhere.

[403] Leonard A. Morrison, *The History of Windham in New Hampshire, 1719–1883* (Boston, 1883), 337–344.

[404] Microfilm Collection of Town Records: Nottingham, Book I, p. 398.

[405] Records of the Loan of 1790, vol. 242, folio 18.

[406] Microfilm Collection of Town Records: Merrimack, Book III, p. 151.

[407] William Little, *The History of Weare, New Hampshire, 1735–1888* (Lowell, 1888), 627.

[408] Peter B. Woodbury, Thomas Savage, and William Patten, eds., *History of Bedford, New Hampshire* (Boston, 1851), *passim.*

[409] Walker, *New Hampshire Convention,* 15n.

[410] Advertisements in *Fowle's New Hampshire Gazette* (Portsmouth), February 4, 1785.

Daniel Grout (Acworth, Lempster, and Marlow).[411]

William Harper (Sanbornton).[412]

Six of the delegates were owners of manufactories:

Joseph Hutchins (Haverhill, Piermont, Warren, and Coventry), owner of a grist mill.[413]

Jonathan Gaskill (Richmond), owner of a tannery and a farm.[414]

Charles Barrett (New Ipswich), owner of "extensive mills," pearl and potash works, a glasshouse, several farms, and lands in Maine. Barrett designed and paid for the construction of a system of canals which made George's River (a tributary of the Merrimac) navigable, thus connecting his town with Newburyport.[415]

Nathaniel Bean (Warner), owner of "mills." [416]

Stephen Fifield (Candia), owner of a sawmill.[417]

Jeremiah Clough (Canterbury), owner of a sawmill and a 114-acre farm, who had £100 ($333.33) of money loaned at interest.[418]

Two of the delegates were physicians:[419]

Solomon Harvey (Chesterfield).

Benjamin Jones (Lydenborough).

Two of the delegates were clergymen: [420]

Jonathan Remele (Newport).

William Hooper (Medbury).

Two of the delegates were petty village capitalists:

Benjamin Emery (Concord).[421]

---

[411] Microfilm Collection of Town Records: Acworth, Book I, pp. 78, 294–299.

[412] Moses T. Runnels, *History of Sanbornton* (2 vols., Boston, 1882), 2:326–327.

[413] William F. Whitcher, *History of the Town of Haverhill, New Hampshire* (Haverhill, 1919), 551.

[414] William Bassett, *History of the Town of Richmond, New Hampshire* (Boston, 1884), 173.

[415] *The History of the Town of New Ipswich* (Boston, 1852), 221–223, 330–333.

[416] Walter Harriman, *The History of Warner, New Hampshire* (Concord, 1879), 235.

[417] J. Bailey Moore, *History of the Town of Candia* (Manchester, 1893), 252.

[418] James O. Lyford, *History of the Town of Canterbury, New Hampshire, 1727–1912* (Concord, 1912), 192–196; Microfilm Collection of Town Records: Canterbury, Book II, p. 124.

[419] That Harvey and Jones were physicians is inferred from their titles, as listed in Walker, *New Hampshire Convention*, 16, 18.

[420] Edmund Wheeler, *The History of the Town of Newport, New Hampshire, from 1766 to 1876* (Concord, 1879), 515; Walker, *New Hampshire Convention*, 14n.

[421] Walker, *New Hampshire Convention*, 108.

Joseph Badger (Gilmantown), who owned $1,932 in continental and state securities.[422]

Nine of the delegates were farmers:

Thomas Penniman (Washington and Stoddard), who was sufficiently prosperous to loan the town £100 ($333.33).[423]

Thomas Bixby (Francestown), who owned 14 acres of farmland and 56 acres of unoccupied land.[424]

Ebenezer Cummings (Nottingham and West).[425]

William Page (Goffstown), who owned 5 acres of farmland and 60 acres of unimproved land.[426]

Abel Parker (Jaffrey).[427]

Matthias Stone (Claremont).[428]

Jedidiah Tainter (Marlborough).[429]

Othniel Thomas (Rindge).[430]

Caleb Winch (Fitzwilliam).[431]

The occupations and property holdings of nineteen of the delegates were not ascertained.

Thus only thirty of the 104 delegates who voted on the question of ratification are known to have held any kind of personalty whatever, even when the term is stretched to include country grist mills. Of these, nineteen voted in favor of ratification (one ratificationist in three held such interests) and eleven voted against ratification (one anti-Federalist in four held such interests). Only six (10.5 per cent) of the delegates favoring ratification and only one of the delegates opposing ratification held securities.

[422] *State Papers of New Hampshire*, 21:781–782; Records of the Loan of 1790, vol. 242, folio 20; vol. 249, folio 5.

[423] George N. Gage and others, *History of Washington, New Hampshire* (Claremont, 1886), 25, 563.

[424] Microfilm Collection of Town Records: Francestown Selectmen's Book, vol. 4, Tax Inventory, 1790.

[425] Kimball Webster, *History of Hudson, New Hampshire* (edited by George W. Browne, Manchester, 1913), 302.

[426] Microfilm Collection of Town Records: Goffstown, vol. F, p. 8a.

[427] Walker, *New Hampshire Convention*, 18n.

[428] Otis F. R. Waite, *History of the Town of Claremont* (Manchester, 1895), 468.

[429] Microfilm Collection of Town Records: Marlborough, Book I, p. 225.

[430] Ezra S. Stearns, *History of the Town of Rindge, New Hampshire* (Boston, 1875), 727–728.

[431] John F. Norton, *The History of Fitzwilliam, New Hampshire, from 1752 to 1887* (New York, 1888), 131.

The general conclusions that may be drawn about the nature of the contests over ratification in Pennsylvania, Massachusetts, South Carolina, and New Hampshire are these:

Each of these states, after struggles of varying intensity, ratified the Constitution over the opposition of a considerable number of its inhabitants.

In a very general way the geographical areas that were predominantly Federalist were, more often than not, areas in which ideas were disseminated with relative ease, and the areas that were predominantly anti-Federalist were, more often than not, areas in which ideas were less readily disseminated. In other respects, however, the roots of Federalism and anti-Federalism were different in the four states.

In Massachusetts the contest over ratification was essentially the outgrowth of a struggle between coalitions of economic-interest groups that had developed since 1780, if not earlier. The issue was complicated, however, by a large number of considerations that were fundamentally noneconomic.

In New Hampshire the contest over ratification was basically a contest between two small groups whose economic interests were similar except that the Federalist group had a slightly larger number of the "dynamic" personalty interests. These two groups vied with each other to win the support of the lethargic, semi-isolated farmers who constituted a majority of the state's population. At first the anti-Federalists were able to win a majority of the voters to their side by playing on their lack of information and appealing to religious sentiment. Ultimately, by combining an appeal to reason with the personal influences of their leaders, the Federalists were able to win the support of a majority of these farmers and carry the ratification.

In Pennsylvania the struggle was a continuation of a long-standing contest between highly developed political parties. The factors dividing the two parties were a complex of philosophical, geographical, religious, ethnic, social, economic, and purely political elements. The success of the Federalists can be attributed largely to the speed and precision with which they executed a well-planned campaign for ratification.

In South Carolina the advocates of ratification were wealthy planter-aristocrats who had enacted paper-money and other debtor legislation; they were supported by a majority of the merchants, factors, lesser planters, and farmers. The opponents of ratification were wealthy planter-aristocrats who had opposed these debtor-relief laws; they were supported by a minority of the merchants and lesser planters and farmers. Most of the issues on which the two groups differed were social, geographical, economic, and political differences of long standing, but a large part of the motivations both for support of and for opposition to ratification had roots in the war and the immediate postwar history of the state.

Professor Beard explains these struggles largely in terms of economic classes, stating that the leadership and much of the rank and file of the Federalists was comprised of men of wealth, and that the opponents to the Constitution were principally small farmers and propertyless urban groups. He asserts that among the wealthy Federalists were found virtually all the holders of public securities and men having commercial and other personalty interests, and that the poor farmers who made up most of the opposition to ratification were virtually identical with the groups that had supported paper money and "other schemes for the relief of debtors" in 1785–1787.

None of Beard's propositions holds for these states. In all four of them wealth was about equally distributed between the two sides.

More specifically, the role of the paper-money issue in the contest over ratification can be clearly traced in three of the four states. In Pennsylvania the paper-money party was by and large identical with the anti-Federalist party, but the nexus was with holders of public securities, not with private debtors. In New Hampshire the advocates and the opponents of paper money were about equally divided on the question of ratification. In South Carolina the personnel of the paper-money party was in general identical with that of the Federalist party.

Beard's division of the contestants into public security holders and other personalty interests on the one hand and small farmers and propertyless urban groups on the other can be tested for all four states. In one state, Massachusetts, public security holders and certain other suffering personalty groups—not all personalty groups—clearly constituted a large part of the dynamic elements in ratification, but ratification was achieved not because the opposition of farmers and the lower urban classes was overcome but because the ratificationists had the support of these groups. In another state, New Hampshire, a large majority of the delegates on both sides were small farmers and others having no personalty interests of any sort. In two states, Pennsylvania and South Carolina, the distribution of occupations and the holdings of most forms of property were about the same on both sides, but public security holders constituted a much larger proportion of the opponents of ratification than of the Federalists.

The conclusion seems inescapable, then, that Beard's economic interpretation of ratification in these four states is fundamentally without factual foundation.

VII

Ratification in States Generally Opposed to the Constitution

THE Constitution having been ratified by the requisite nine states, these states could now proceed to organize the government of the United States. The five weakest of them had ratified by large margins, as had been expected. The four stronger ones which the Federalists had believed could also, with sufficient effort, be brought to ratify had likewise fulfilled expectations. There now remained four strong states in which obviously there were large numbers of persons who were satisfied with the way their problems were being met under the Articles of Confederation.

These states were Virginia, New York, North Carolina, and Rhode Island. In each of them it was expected that ratification, if it was achieved at all, would be attended by considerable difficulty. The Federalists had the upper hand now because they had a nine-state Union, but the possibility that one or even all of these remaining states might refuse to ratify was not at all remote. Their ratification was essential to the success of the Union, if only because their exclusion would divide the nation's territory into three non-contiguous parts.

Virginia

Virginia's ratification was almost as important to the Federalists as that of the first nine states. Without those nine states the Constitution could not be put into operation. Without Virginia, George Washington, the man whose unrivalled prestige made him the obvious choice for the office, could not be elected president. After a brilliant contest between powerful strategists Virginia ratified the Constitution on June 25, 1788. The victory of the Federalists was now all but complete.

Because of the refusal of George Mason and Edmund Randolph to sign the Constitution at the close of the Philadelphia Convention, even those who had little knowledge of the state's internal affairs expected ratification in Virginia to be difficult. It was feared that a ratifying convention might not even be called. But this obstacle did not materialize. The Virginia legislature issued a call for a convention immediately after it convened in October, 1787, before the serious debate on the issue began. Despite the fact that of the members of the legislature who were later to serve as delegates to the convention, exactly half were to vote against ratification, the call for a convention was issued unanimously. There was some dispute over details. A bill originating in the House called for elections in March and the opening of the convention in May; the Senate proposed amendments providing that the election dates should coincide with the state's traditional April elections, and that the meeting of the convention be advanced to June. These amendments the House accepted. The battle for ratification was now about to begin.[1]

A full seven months was occupied in campaigning for the elections to the convention. The opponents of the Constitution clearly had an edge in the published propaganda. Mason's lengthy and solemn statement of his objections, Randolph's letter to the legislature explaining why he had refused to sign

[1] *Journal of the House of Delegates of the State of Virginia* (Richmond, 1828), October 25, 1787. The bill formally became law on December 12, 1787. Exactly why the opponents of ratification offered no opposition to the calling of a convention is not clear. There were thirty-two delegates in the House who later voted against ratification and the same number who later voted for ratification. Patrick Henry, the leader of the opposition to the Constitution in Virginia, was probably caught off guard before he could organize his forces and estimate his strength in the House. Rather than risk defeat there, he doubtless felt that it was better to put the decision to a convention; furthermore, victory in the House would only be temporary, whereas victory in a convention would be more nearly final. And in a showdown fight in a convention Henry, with his almost hypnotic oratory, excelled. Also, he thought he could count on Edmund Randolph's support in a convention, and Randolph was not a member of the House.

the document, and Richard Henry Lee's masterful letter to the governor and the arguments he presented in newspapers and pamphlets were widely spread. Neither the barrage of newspaper propaganda from the northward, the anonymous writings on behalf of ratification in the newspapers of Norfolk, Richmond, Fredericksburg, and Alexandria, nor even the classic Federalist Papers, imported from New York and circulated in Virginia in quantity, could match the influence of these open declarations of Mason, Randolph, and Lee.[2]

The printed word reached only a limited audience in the vast spaces of Virginia, however, and forty-six of the delegates to the convention were to come from counties west of the Blue Ridge, where there was almost no circulation of printed matter.[3] More important were oral discussions, the focusing of campaigns on particular areas, and the careful selection of candidates, and in these matters the friends of ratification were perhaps shrewder than their opponents. One technique which they used with signal success was to induce retired military heroes, whom they assumed would be under the great Federalist influence of George Washington, to become candidates for seats that would otherwise be likely to go to men who were regularly elected to the legislature and who it was assumed would be under the influence of the great anti-Federalist Patrick Henry.[4]

When the vigorous campaign was over and election returns were in, the Federalists had apparently won a clear victory. A careful Federalist survey made shortly after the elections showed that eighty-five candidates, exactly half of the total, had

[2] The printed campaign may be traced in the Richmond *Virginia Independent Chronicle*, the *Norfolk and Portsmouth Journal*, the *Virginia Herald, and the Fredericksburg Advertiser*, the *Virginia Journal and Alexandria Advertiser*, and other Virginia newspapers. Arguments for and against the Constitution appeared in virtually every issue of these newspapers from October, 1787, to June, 1788.

[3] Hugh Blair Grigsby, *The History of the Virginia Federal Convention of 1788, with Some Account of the Eminent Virginians of That Era Who Were Members of the Body*, edited by R. A. Brock (2 vols., Richmond, 1890, 1891), 1:31n, records that Humphrey Marshall, a Kentucky delegate, had traveled far into the densely populated parts of Virginia, on his way to attend the convention, before he saw his first number of the *Federalist*.

[4] *Ibid.*, 1:32. Data on the military backgrounds of the elected delegates are given below, pages 262–263.

been elected as Federalists. Sixty-six had been elected as anti-Federalists and three were considered "doubtful." With respect to sixteen delegates, twelve from Kentucky and four from the Trans-Alleghany area, it was not known what instructions they had received nor what their attitudes were. The task of the ratificationists appeared to be simply to hold their own and win one of the sixteen westerners. By the time the convention met, their position was stronger and victory seemed assured, for Edmund Randolph, who had been counted as an opponent, had changed his mind and announced his support of ratification.[5]

No one in the Federalist camp was overconfident, however, for it was impossible to ignore the almost magical power of Patrick Henry. With his prestige, his inspiring oratory, and his genius for creating and capitalizing on a dramatic moment, Henry was a formidable opponent. He was supported by William Grayson, a lawyer of prestige who had great personal influence with the half dozen men in the convention who had served in his regiment during the war. Colonels Benjamin Temple and Robert Lawson, both heroes of the war, and Theodorick Bland, vice-president of the Virginia Society of the Cincinnati, were expected to help Grayson break the military phalanx in the Federalist ranks. Finally, there was George Mason, renowned as the framer of the Virginia Bill of Rights, a man with enormous personal prestige. The strongest assets of the anti-ratificationists were age, prestige, and Patrick Henry.

The Federalist leaders devised their strategy with painstaking

---

[5] David Henley to Samuel Henley, April 18, 1788, in Personal Miscellaneous File in the Manuscripts Division of the Library of Congress. There has long been speculation as to the decision of the voters in Virginia, and it has often been assumed that the anti-Federalists had an elected majority. This contemporary document would seem to end the speculation. David Henley, a Federalist tobacco buyer in the employ of partners of Robert Morris, constructed and enclosed in this letter a table which gives all the above information. This remarkable document contains a few errors of detail—for example, Henley lists John Stringer of Northampton as John "Stratton," but there are only two significant errors of fact. He lists two Federalists, George and Roger Thompson, as the elected delegates from Lincoln County, whereas these two men were actually defeated by anti-Federalists John Logan and Henry Pawling. It is significant that Henley lists James Monroe as a Federalist and Edmund Randolph as an anti-Federalist, indicating that immediately after the elections the Federalists were mistaken about the positions of these two important men.

thoroughness. Realizing that no one man was a match for Henry, they worked as a team. As his equal in prestige they could offer Edmund Pendleton, his foe since the celebrated legislative battles of the 1760's, and George Wythe, beloved mentor of a half dozen lawyers in the convention. To deal with Henry's logic they employed Madison and Marshall. When Henry shifted his ground and talked of Virginia affairs, they countered with George Nicholas. For the dirty work, the infighting, they employed one of the few men who dared battle Henry in that area, Edmund Randolph.

Despite the careful plans, the keen strategy, and the persuasive oratory of the Federalists, Henry and the other anti-ratificationists managed to convert three of the elected Federalists and enlist ten of the twelve Kentucky delegates. The conversion of the three Federalists Henry apparently achieved with one brilliant speech portraying the destruction of liberties that would ensue from ratification, a portrayal so vivid that one witness "involuntarily felt his wrists to assure himself that the fetters were not already pressing his flesh." The support of the Kentuckians was won by a dramatic introduction of the question of the proposed Jay-Gardoqui Treaty, providing for the surrender of navigation of the Mississippi to Spain. The Federalists managed to enlist the four Trans-Alleghany delegates, one of the three "undecided" delegates, and two of the Kentucky delegates. When the final vote was taken on June 25, the Constitution was ratified by a slim margin, the vote being 89 votes to 79.[6]

It is evident even from a reading of the debates in the convention that there is no simple explanation of the movement for ratification in Virginia. To explain the votes in full would be to write the history of Virginia from 1758 to 1788. Much light can be shed on the question, however, by an analysis of

[6] *Ibid.* The analysis of the shifting of votes is based on a comparison of Henley's pre-convention summary with the final vote, allowance being made for the four cases in which Henley was in error. The first volume of Grigsby's *Virginia Convention* is an excellent description of the maneuverings in the convention, despite the fact that Grigsby wrote with a strong anti-Federalist bias.

the origins and development of the principal issues upon which Virginia's vote turned.

These must be considered in the light of Virginians' attitude toward their state. Virginia has been called the Prussia of the American Confederation. To Virginians it was even more than that. So strongly imbued were they with state consciousness and pride that many of them applied the term "my country" only to Virginia, using various other terms to signify the United States.[7] This state particularism, of long standing, had been augmented after the war when the state, now free from the commercial and political shackles that had bound it under the crown, enjoyed an unprecedented wave of prosperity; everyone except the planters on the depleted tobacco lands of the tidewater was inspired with a confidence Virginians had never known before.[8]

The task of the advocates of ratification was to overcome this state particularism. The problem of their opponents was to preserve and augment it.

[7] It is a striking fact, not without significance in the contest, that except for a handful of men who had opposed Henry politically for two decades, the leadership and the ranks of the delegates elected as Federalists were composed largely of young men in their twenties and thirties. The leaders on the anti-Federalist side and many of their followers were men between the ages of forty-five and seventy. The younger men had come of age when talk of the "Union" and "hang together or hang separately" was in vogue; the older men were of a generation that talked more of "rights" than of Union and thought of Virginia as a unique province under the British crown.

[8] The port of Norfolk had been burned and deserted during the war, but it had since been rebuilt and by 1788 rivaled Boston, New York, Philadelphia, and Charleston. The tonnage destined for foreign places clearing Virginia ports was greater than that of any other state, and though Virginia did not own a half dozen seaworthy vessels in 1782, by 1788 fully a third of its foreign trade was being carried in Virginia bottoms. Virginia vessels were favored by special legislation, and there was stiff competition among French, British, and other American vessels to get a share of the Virginia trade. Freight rates were only slightly above prewar levels, whereas the price of tobacco had nearly doubled. Data on shipping have been taken from Naval Officer Returns, in the Virginia State Library at Richmond, from which I have tabulated all pertinent information regarding ocean-borne commerce for the period 1782–1789. Prices and freight rates for the 1760's and 1770's are quoted in the Williamsburg *Virginia Gazette*, postwar prices and freight rates in the Alexandria *Virginia Journal*, the Richmond *Independent Chronicle*, the Richmond *Weekly Advertiser*, the Richmond *American Advertiser*, the *Fredericksburg Advertiser*, the Philadelphia *Evening Herald*, and the New York *Daily Advertiser*, 1783–1789.

Seven basic sets of factors may be profitably examined as possible determinants of the votes in the convention: the backgrounds of the delegates, the war experiences of various sections of the state, personal influences, military connections, the effects of the treaty of peace, Robert Morris, and the Mississippi River question.

Several of the delegates were not native Virginians. Four of them had been born and had grown up abroad, a fifth came from Pennsylvania, and a sixth had been taken to England by his loyalist parents as a young man and had returned after the peace. None of these men had the passionate provincial feelings of the other delegates, and all six were unwavering friends of ratification.

A second factor was the lesson the war had taught respecting military defense. Those places that had suffered damages from the war at first hand were acutely conscious of their military vulnerability, and their provincialism withered in the face of the realization that only a strong union could provide military security. The greatest wartime losses had been suffered by the counties of York, James City, Warwick, Elizabeth City, and Gloucester, which had been the battlegrounds preceding and during Yorktown, and the borough of Norfolk, which had been the victim of naval warfare. Almost every plantation in these counties had been burned to the ground. These areas sent eleven delegates to the convention, ten of whom voted for ratification.[9]

A third factor was the personal influence of some of the delegates. A complex network of lesser influences pervaded the convention: Randolph, Madison, Nicholas, Pendleton, and Wythe on one side and Grayson, Benjamin Harrison, and Mason on the other had personal followings of varying sizes. In the main, however, the contest was one between the rival influences of two giants, George Washington and Patrick Henry. Throughout the continent as a whole Washington enjoyed a prestige with which no other man's could compare. In

[9] The Richmond *Virginia Gazette or the American Advertiser*, January 26, 1782, describes the war losses by counties.

Virginia, however, Henry's influence, except among the military, was probably greater than Washington's. At least two dozen of the delegates were men who had, over the past six years or more, consistently followed Henry's lead on virtually every issue in the legislature, and Henry's prestige extended his influence far beyond his immediate political following. Except among the few men with whom he regularly corresponded, Washington's influence outside the military is difficult to measure.

Military service also played a role in the contest over ratification. The Federalists, as has been said, had selected as many military men as possible as candidates for the convention. Forty-six of the eighty-nine Federalist delegates had been officers in the Revolutionary armies, and twenty-three more had been militia officers, about half of whom had seen combat. Henry Lee summarized Federalist logic in the choice of military candidates in a speech attacking Henry's appeal to provincialism. One would think, Lee said, "that the love of an *American* was in some degree criminal, as being incompatible with a proper degree of affection for a Virginian. The people of America, sir, are one people. I love the people of the North, not because they have adopted the Constitution, but because I fought with them as countrymen, and because I consider them as such." [10]

Despite the fact that three-fourths of the delegates who favored ratification had seen military service, however, it is possible to overestimate this factor. The anti-ratificationists countered with the influence of Grayson and other distinguished veterans, and with Henry's eloquent championing of the superiority of the civil authority over that of the military. The presence of so many military men in the Federalist ranks actually frightened some delegates and made them receptive to Henry's vivid prognostication of armed hordes marching under the banner of the new government to subvert Virginia liberties.

---

[10] Tabulations from John H. Gwathmey, *Historical Register of Virginia in the Revolution: Soldiers, Sailors, Marines, 1775-1783* (Richmond, 1938). Lee's speech is quoted in Grigsby's *Virginia Convention*, 1:160. Grigsby attributed the success of the Federalists almost exclusively to the influence of the ex-officers.

As a result of these counter-influences, thirty-five men who had served as officers in the Revolutionary armies voted against ratification.[11]

The fifth set of factors, the issues relating to the treaty of peace, was the most complex of all. Two sections of the treaty, one providing for the evacuation of the British military outposts in the Northwest Territory and the other for the restoration of property to legitimate owners on both sides, were of immense significance to Virginia. These provisions affected Virginians for four reasons: 1) The Northwest posts were an obstacle to the westward migration of Virginians, and were therefore inimical to the interests of residents of the Valley and Trans-Alleghany regions, and to those of the land speculators who held titles to vast tracts in the Territory. 2) Virginia had lost some thirty thousand slaves, more than a tenth of the total number in the state, through confiscation by the British army. 3) Virginia had confiscated large quantities of British and loyalist property, principally the vast Fairfax estate in the Northern Neck, around Alexandria. 4) Virginia planters owed British merchants more than two million pounds sterling (nearly ten million dollars) for prewar purchases. The treaty affected Virginians favorably with respect to the first two matters, unfavorably with respect to the other two.[12]

During the 1780's the treaty had been disregarded on all four matters. The British had refused to evacuate the posts and to restore or make restitution for the slaves, the Virginians had made no effort to restore the property they had confiscated and had passed legislation prohibiting the collection of the debts. During the war they had gone so far as to permit debtors to

---

[11] It is significant that militiamen voted against ratification, 24 to 23, whereas soldiers of the continental line voted for ratification, 46 to 35. If the latter figures are a valid measure of influences, however, they would seem to indicate that Washington's influence even among the veterans was very little stronger than Henry's.

[12] On the confiscation of slaves see Lewis C. Gray, *History of Agriculture in the Southern United States to 1860* (2 vols., Washington, 1933), 2:595-596. Estimates of the size of the debt vary. The £2,000,000 figure is Jefferson's estimate and the one most often quoted. On all matters regarding the treaty, and particularly on economic matters, see Isaac S. Harrell, *Loyalism in Virginia* (Philadelphia, 1926).

write off their obligations by paying nominally equivalent sums of depreciated paper money into the state treasury and twice, in 1784 and 1787, they had expressly refused to open their courts to suits by British creditors.

The Constitution promised an end to the treaty holiday. In theory, it made treaties the supreme law of the land; in practice, it established a government which could require the British to abide by the treaty and which would open its own courts to suits by British subjects seeking restoration of their property.[13]

One of these four issues, that concerning the Northwest posts, was a relatively simple one. Few of the delegates from the Valley and Trans-Alleghany regions were debtors to British merchants, and all of them resented the presence of the British across the Ohio River in the Northwest Territory. These areas sent twenty-eight delegates to the convention, twenty-seven of whom voted for ratification.[14]

The other issues arising from the treaty were extremely complex. The areas that had suffered most from British depredations were, in the main, the very same areas in which debts to British merchants were most heavily concentrated. The area that had the most to lose from a restoration of sequestered property, the Northern Neck, was the area where Washington lived and exerted his greatest influence. Attitudes with respect to the treaty varied with individual attitudes toward the British and

[13] The British watched the contest in Virginia with keen interest. A British factor who witnessed the convention wrote home two days after the convention adjourned that the "recovery of the British debts can no longer be postponed." Francis N. Mason, ed., *John Norton & Sons, Merchants of London and Virginia* (Richmond, 1937), 460.

[14] The counties in these areas were Augusta, Berkeley, Botetourt, Frederick, Greenbriar, Hampshire, Hardy, Harrison, Monongalia, Ohio, Randolph, Rockbridge, Rockingham, and Shenandoah. It should not be inferred that this was the only motive for ratification in these places, though it was one of the strongest. All the other conditions favorable to ratification were also present here to a lesser or greater degree. For example, ten of the fourteen delegates from the Valley were veterans of the continental line. Again, the great majority of the population in the two areas consisted of relatively recent immigrants from the north, mostly Scotch-Irish and Germans, none of whom had the deep-seated Virginia provincialism. Furthermore, the inhabitants from west of the mountains welcomed the prospect of an energetic general government which could pave the way for expansion into territory then occupied by Indians.

the loyalists, which in turn were born of the amount of personal suffering endured at the hands of the British as well as a number of other factors.

In general, there were four shades of opinion regarding the treaty. One small group favored unconditional obedience to its terms on the part of the United States, either because they considered it a matter of national honor or, more often, because they were pro-British. A second group, which included a large number of the inhabitants of the western regions, favored making strong concessions to the British as a show of good faith, in the hope that the British would respond by abiding by the treaty themselves. A third and larger group would refuse to abide by the treaty until Britain made overtures indicating a clear intention to abide by all its terms. This group was subdivided into two factions: one wanted to work actively through Congress for British compliance and the other wanted merely to wait. The fourth group was unconditionally opposed to complying with the disputed parts of the treaty then or at any time in the future.[15]

While there existed these four shades of opinion and the lines separating them were not clearly drawn, in the ratifying convention the delegates could vote only one of two ways, yes or no. This being the case, it was obvious that the influence of the treaty in shaping attitudes toward ratification would depend largely upon the ability of partisan leaders to convince the delegates of the safety or insecurity of their interests. On the question of the property confiscated by Virginia, the Federalists, under the leadership of John Marshall—who was himself deeply interested financially in the sequestered Fairfax estate—obviously were the more convincing. All the delegates from the Northern Neck, with the lone exception of George Mason, voted for ratification.

The question of the British debts was not settled with such unanimity. Leaders on both sides had taken advantage of the

---

[15] These various shades of opinion are derived from a study of Virginia newspapers and the journal of the House of Delegates. Particularly revealing are the voluminous debates and the instructions to delegates that were printed in the newspapers from October, 1783, to the summer of 1784.

wartime act to write off old debts by paying depreciated paper to the state. Federalists such as Pendleton, Lee, Fleming, Alexander White, Zachariah Johnston, Paul Carrington, Marshall, Thomas Walke, and Robert Breckenridge had made such payments, as had Harrison, Henry, and Joseph Jones of the opposition.[16]

During the 1780's seven votes were taken in the House of Delegates on the various issues concerning the treaty. On only three of these was the issue clear-cut. On November 17, 1787, a proposal was made that all legal obstacles to the collection of the debts be removed, provided this could be done equitably and with some order. A comparison of the votes on this question with the vote on ratification seven months later is of considerable interest.[17]

The delegates who were later to vote for ratification opposed this proposal, twenty-two votes to six. The delegates who later voted against the Constitution voted, despite the opposition of both Henry and Mason, in favor of the resolution, sixteen votes to ten.

The counties east of the Blue Ridge which were to favor ratification cast fourteen votes in favor of the proposal and twenty-one against it. The counties east of the Blue Ridge which were to oppose the Constitution voted for the proposal, twenty-three to fourteen. From the four counties which were to be divided on ratification, three legislators later attended the convention, two of whom voted for the proposal. In the state as a whole, the counties that were to favor ratification opposed the proposal forty-four to twenty, and the counties that were to oppose ratification favored the proposal, twenty-eight to twenty-one.

On the same day, November 17, a vote was taken on a resolution that Virginia refuse to comply with the treaty until every other state passed a blanket law repealing all acts contrary to

[16] Harrell, *Loyalism in Virginia*, 27–28, 81–84, 171; Grigsby, *Virginia Convention*, 2:96.

[17] All the following votes are taken from the *Journal of the House of Delegates*, October Session, 1787, pp. 51–52. One of the other votes on the treaty during the period was taken on December 3, 1787, and the three others had been taken in 1784.

the treaty. This was virtually impossible of attainment, so in effect the proposal was to refuse to abide by the treaty at all, under any circumstances. The delegates who later voted for the Constitution supported this resolution, twenty-three to five, and the delegates who were to oppose ratification voted against the resolution, twenty to four. Later in the day the proto-Federalists voted, four to twenty-three, against a proposal that Virginia comply with the treaty if Britain indicated its intention of doing so. The anti-Federalist delegates-to-be supported this measure, twenty to six.

A great majority of the proto-Federalists, then, were opposed to the collection of the debts on any terms. On the other hand, sixteen of the twenty-six delegates who later opposed the Constitution favored collection of the debts without qualification, and four more favored collection if Britain could be induced to abide by the treaty.

It is clear, then, though it may be paradoxical, that if there was a debtors' faction in Virginia politics, it was largely identical in personnel with the pro-ratificationist group.[18]

The sixth major element influencing the movement for ratification was the connection of the Virginia movement with Robert Morris of Philadelphia. That gentleman had been suspect in Virginia since his reign as superintendant of finance in 1781–1783, and Virginians were inclined to be hostile to any movement in which he had a part. Perhaps a more important cause of their antipathy was born of Morris' contract with the corrupt French Farmers-General, giving him a monopoly of the French tobacco trade. Though shrewd Scotch-Virginian traders ultimately found ways to circumvent the monopoly and to trade on a large scale directly with France, Morris was tempo-

[18] There were many debtors among the Federalists besides those indebted to British merchants. For example, virtually all the fourteen delegates from the Valley, who voted unanimously for ratification, were debtors, and most of them were in the courts being sued for debts at one time or another during the 1780's. There were thousands of suits for the recovery of debts in the Valley during the decade. Freeman H. Hart, *The Valley of Virginia in the American Revolution, 1763–1789* (Chapel Hill, 1942), 123, 124n, 132. Half the Federalists in the convention, at the very least, were heavily in debt. A number of their opponents were doubtless debtors too, but the Federalists were debtors who had enacted debtor legislation, and the anti-Federalists had opposed such laws.

rarily able to force the price of tobacco in Virginia down from forty shillings to twenty-two shillings a hundredweight, and the experience won him the hostility of most Virginians. His signature on the Constitution did nothing to make the document more palatable to them.[19]

The seventh and final major element was the question of the navigation of the Mississippi, which has been previously mentioned and is discussed more fully on pages 366–367.[20]

From the foregoing it would appear that only one economic consideration (navigation of the Mississippi) had a decisive influence on the final votes in the ratifying convention. The votes cut across all other economic issues in no meaningful pattern whatever; the decision did not turn on such questions. Furthermore, study of the occupations and property holdings of the members of the convention demonstrates that there was no line of division on the basis of individual property holdings. As the following tabulation shows, the property holdings of ratificationists and anti-ratificationists were virtually identical except that more small farmers from the interior supported ratification than opposed it.[21]

[19] See page 55 above.

[20] Two minor issues, paper money and religious freedom, may be dismissed as unimportant in the contest. There was not the remotest possibility of a paper issue in Virginia. A petition in favor of paper money had been rejected in 1786 by 85 votes to 17, and only two members of the House who later voted for ratification and four who voted against ratification voted for paper. *Journal of the House of Delegates*, October Session, 1786, November 1, 1786. The Virginia Baptist Association resolved unanimously in March, 1788, that the Constitution failed to provide adequate safeguards to religious liberty. The Baptists in Virginia were concentrated in the Southside (lower piedmont), which voted 28 to 2 against ratification. Large majorities of the delegates on both sides had been champions of religious liberty, however, and a survey of the religious affiliations of the delegates reveals no patterns of division along religious lines.

[21] All property holdings cited, unless otherwise documented, are taken from the tax roll books in the Virginia State Library. These consist of two kinds of books, one listing land, the other personalty. The books are arranged chronologically by counties, and are unpaged. The mere listing of the property held by the delegates constitutes a citation to the proper books. All references and property holdings are for 1788 unless otherwise indicated. Thus the landholdings of Levin Powell, for example, are from the Loudon County Land Book, 1788, and his personalty, except securities, is from the Loudon County Personalty Book, 1787. The land values are expressed in Virginia currency: 6 shillings = $1; £1 = $3.33 1/3.

ECONOMIC INTERESTS OF DELEGATES VOTING
FOR RATIFICATION

One delegate voting for ratification, Levin Powell (Loudon), was a merchant. The amount of his stock in trade was not ascertained, but one sloop belonging to him appears regularly in the manuscript Naval Officer Returns—that is, the customs office records of Virginia—for the period. He also owned 1,836 acres of land in five parcels, valued at £464. His personalty consisted of 22 slaves above the age of twelve, 18 horses, 24 cattle, and a two-wheeled chair (1787). He held $321 in continental securities.[22]

Seventeen were lawyers. Their property holdings were as follows.

John Blair (York), whose interests have previously been sketched in connection with his attendance at the Philadelphia Convention (page 74, above).

James Innes (Williamsburg), 200 acres valued at £92 10s. in York County (1786), no city property; 15 adult slaves (that is, slaves above the age of twelve) in Williamsburg, a cow, 3 horses, and a two-wheeled carriage (1786).

George Jackson (Harrison), amount of land unknown; 3 adult slaves, 8 horses. Jackson owned continental securities on which he received $59.40 interest payments in 1788.[23]

James Johnson (Isle of Wight), 300 acres valued at £88 15s.; 5 adult slaves, 4 horses.[24]

Gabriel Jones (Rockingham), 1,102 acres in Augusta County, 1,004 acres in Rockingham County, and 650 acres in Spotsylvania, having a total value of £996 17s. 10d.; 16 adult slaves, 6 horses, and a two-wheeled carriage. Jones owned $399.97 in continental securities.[25]

James Madison, Jr. (Orange), whose interests are described on pages 72–73.

Humphrey Marshall (Fayette), 4 slaves, 10 horses. The land books for Fayette County (Kentucky) are missing; in all likelihood Marshall's total

[22] Data on Virginia-owned securities cited in this chapter are from the Records of the Loan of 1790, vols. 1112–1115 (Virginia Loan Office, Register of Assumed Debt); vol. 1116 (Register of Interest Payments, Liquidated Debt, 1786–87 [certificates of indebtedness issued]); vol. 1118 (Virginia Loan Office, Register of Public Debt); vols. 1078–1079 (Registers of Loan Office Certificates, 1785–1786); vol. 1081 (Register of Certificates of Interest, 1786–88), all in the National Archives. Powell's securities are from vol. 1118, account dated April 30, 1791 (no page reference).

[23] Records of the Loan of 1790, vol. 1081, January 7, 1788; identified as an attorney in the 1927 edition of the *Biographical Directory of Congress*, 1142.

[24] *Biographical Directory of Congress* (1927 edition), 1153.

[25] Records of the Loan of 1790, vol. 1118, July 21, 1791; Grigsby, *Virginia Convention*, 2:16–19.

landholding was the 4,000-acre bounty he had been granted for war service.[26]

John Marshall (Henrico), no taxable personal property. The land books for his county are no longer extant, but Marshall owned 4,000 acres of Kentucky land that had been granted to him as a bounty for war service. He owned $6,205 in state securities.[27]

Andrew Moore (Rockbridge), 610 acres valued at £154; 5 adult slaves.[28]

George Nicholas (Albemarle), 3¼ town lots with annual rentals totaling £90 and 1,122 acres valued at £282 3s.; 22 adult slaves, 15 horses.[29]

George Parker (Accomac), 470 acres valued at £137 19s.; no slaves or other personalty.[30]

Edmund Pendleton (Caroline), 3,875 acres valued at £975 6s.; 44 adult slaves, 21 horses, one chariot; listed in 1787 as the owner of 105 head of cattle.

Edmund Randolph (Henrico), whose interests are listed on pages 74–75.

Charles Simms (Fairfax), 11 acres valued at £11 11s.; no slaves, 2 horses. Simms owned $1,816 in state securities and was speculating in western lands, having acquired at least 16,000 acres in military bounties from various individuals.[31]

Archibald Stuart (Augusta), 440 acres valued at £82 5s.; one slave, 2 horses. Stuart owned continental securities on which he was paid $77.30 interest in 1788.[32]

Alexander White (Frederick), 664 acres valued at £597 12s.; 9 adult slaves, 9 horses, a four-wheeled phaeton. White owned $1,619 in state securities.[33]

George Wythe (York), whose interests are sketched on pages 73–74.

Five were physicians:

William Fleming (Botetourt), 2,398 acres in Botetourt and 400 acres in Buckingham, with a total value of £386 19s.; 7 adult slaves, 11 horses.[34]

[26] *Biographical Directory of Congress*, 1289; Gwathmey, *Virginians in the Revolution*, 501.

[27] Gwathmey, *Virginians in the Revolution*, 502; Records of the Loan of 1790, vol. 1113, folio 175.

[28] *Biographical Directory of Congress*, 1326–1327.

[29] Nicholas' legal career is sketched in Grigsby's *Virginia Convention*, 2:281 ff.

[30] *Ibid.*, 2:376.

[31] Records of the Loan of 1790, vol. 1113, folio 72; Charles Simms Papers, in the Manuscripts Division of the Library of Congress.

[32] Records of the Loan of 1790, vol. 1081, January 14, 1788; Grigsby, *Virginia Convention*, 2:9–15.

[33] Records of the Loan of 1790, vol. 1113, folio 43; *Biographical Directory of Congress*, 1688.

[34] Grigsby, in his *Virginia Convention*, 2:40 ff., states that Fleming ceased to practice before the war; but he is listed as having been taxed as a "practicing physician" in 1787.

Walter Jones (Northumberland), 636 acres valued at £182 17s.; 25 adult slaves, 8 horses, a four-wheeled phaeton; $485 in continental securities.[35]

Miles King (Elizabeth City), half of a town lot with annual rent of £26 10s. and 604 acres in five parcels, having a total valuation of £356 18s.[36]

David Stuart (Fairfax), 1,665 acres valued at £723 13s.; 14 adult slaves, 4 horses; $2,024 in continental securities.[37]

James Taylor (Norfolk County), 165 acres valued at £120 6s.; 4 adult slaves, 3 horses; $1,443 in continental and state securities.[38]

Two were ministers:

Robert Andrews (James City), who owned neither land nor slaves in James City County, but who owned two town lots in Williamsburg with a yearly rent of £16 10s. He also owned $13,030 in various forms of securities, most of them state securities.[39]

Anthony Walke (Princess Anne), who owned 3,881½ acres in three parcels in Princess Anne and 50 acres in Norfolk County, having a total value of £1,689 15s., and 12 town lots of unknown value; 48 adult slaves, 23 horses, a four-wheeled phaeton.[40]

Sixty-four were planters and lesser farmers:

John Allen (Surry), 2,000 acres in James City County and 200 acres in Surry, having a total value of £2,004 3s.; owned no slaves in his own name. In 1787 Allen had owned continental securities on which he received $554.70 interest, but by 1791 the total face value of his securities was only $105.[41]

Burdet Ashton (King George), 350 acres valued at £110 16s.; 34 adult slaves, 13 horses.

Burwell Bassett (Newkent), 5,880 acres in four parcels, having a total value of £3,729 9s.; 81 adult slaves, 23 horses, a coach, a phaeton, and a chair.

[35] *Biographical Directory of Congress*, 1164. Jones was also taxed as a practicing physician.

[36] I am not certain that King was a physician. Gwathmey's *Virginians in the Revolution* states that King was a surgeon's mate during the war. The Elizabeth City County personal property books are missing for the years 1782–1806, and it is thus impossible to ascertain whether King paid a physician's tax.

[37] Records of the Loan of 1790, vol. 1118, September 7, 1791; Grigsby, *Virginia Convention*, 2:373.

[38] Taylor is called "Doctor" in his securities accounts, vol. 1113, folio 163, and vol. 1118, September 20, 1791, of the Records of the Loan of 1790, and in the Norfolk County Tax Records, but he paid no physician's tax.

[39] Records of the Loan of 1790, vol. 1113, folios 35, 121; vol. 1115, folio 26; vol. 1118, May 9, September 10, 1791; Grigsby, *Virginia Convention*, 2:377.

[40] Grigsby, *Virginia Convention*, 2:129n, 381.

[41] Records of the Loan of 1790, vol. 1081, March 22, 1787; vol. 1116, folio 76. Allen's name is listed in the Surry County personalty books under that of his father, William Allen, the head of the family. William Allen owned 54 adult slaves, 18 horses, and a four-wheeled chariot.

Benjamin Blount (Southampton), 1,450 acres valued at £1,026 13s.; 19 adult slaves, 12 horses, and a two-wheeled chair.[42]

Robert Breckenridge (Jefferson), whose landholdings consisted of the 3,110-acre bounty he had received for war service.[43]

Humphrey Brooke (Fauquier), 400 acres valued at £257 18s.; no slaves or other personalty.

Rice Bullock (Jefferson), whose land consisted of his 2,666-acre military bounty.[44]

Nathaniel Burwell (James City), 5,608 acres in Frederick County, 1,800 acres in York County, and 1,288 acres in James City County, having a total value of £7,886 3s., and a 5,400-acre tract in Kentucky received as a military bounty; 21 adult slaves and 19 horses on the Frederick County plantation and 34 slaves, 10 horses, a chariot, and a two-wheeled carriage on the James City County plantation; $307 in state securities.[45]

William Overton Callis (Louisa), 660 acres valued at £343 15s., and a 4,000-acre tract in Kentucky received as a military bounty; 10 adult slaves, 3 horses.[46]

Paul Carrington (Charlotte), 1,815 acres valued at £1,817 17s.; 33 adult slaves, 21 horses, and a two-wheeled chariot; $891 in state securities.[47]

William Clayton (Newkent), 1,808 acres valued at £1,055 8s.; 23 adult slaves, 16 horses, one chair.

George Clindinnen (Greenbriar), five parcels totaling 3,140 acres, valued at £628 17s. (1789); 2 adult slaves, 9 horses.

John Hartwell Cocke (Surry), 1,377 acres valued at £987 18s.; 22 adult slaves, 6 horses, a four-wheeled chaise; two continental certificates, one having a face value of $454 and the other of $298. On the latter Cocke received $54 for three years' back interest in 1786.[48]

Francis Corbin (Middlesex), 200 acres valued at £196 13s.; 14 adult slaves, 5 horses.

William Darke (Berkeley), 4 adult slaves, 15 horses. The records of landholdings in his county are no longer extant, but it is known that Darke had received 8,660 acres in bounties for military service. He also owned $4,078 in state securities.[49]

Cole Digges (Warwick), 3,013 acres in Warwick and 560 acres in James City County, total value £1,837 18s., and 2,666 acres of Kentucky land

---

[42] Blount's landholdings are taken from the 1784 land books, which contain additions recorded in 1785 and 1786, making the proper total for 1788.

[43] Gwathmey, *Virginians in the Revolution*, 90.

[44] *Ibid.*, 114.

[45] *Ibid.*, 115; Records of the Loan of 1790, vol. 1113, folio 78.

[46] Gwathmey, *Virginians in the Revolution*, 122.

[47] Records of the Loan of 1790, vol. 1113, folio 72.

[48] Records of the Loan of 1790, vol. 1078, January 18, 1786; vol. 1079, October 26, 1786; vol. 1081, October 26, 1786.

[49] *Ibid.*, vol. 1114, March, 1793; Gwathmey, *Virginians in the Revolution*, 207.

received as a bounty for military service; 34 adult slaves, 20 horses, a two-wheeled chair.[50]

Littleton Eyre (Northampton), 1,504 acres valued at £752; 48 adult slaves, 23 horses.

Daniel Fisher (Greensville), 752 acres valued at £419 13s.; 43 adult slaves, 37 cattle, 14 horses, and a two-wheeled chair, all owned jointly with three other men; $442 in continental securities.[51]

William Fleet (King and Queen), 296¼ acres valued at £307 7s.; 7 adult slaves, 6 horses.

Thomas Gaskins (Northumberland), 700 acres valued at £575 8s. and 8,832 acres of Kentucky land received as a bounty for military service; 21 adult slaves, 9 horses, and a four-wheeled phaeton; $358 in continental securities, on which he received $60 for three years' interest in 1787.[52]

James Gordon (Lancaster), 686 acres valued at £359 14s.; 35 adult slaves, 10 horses, a four-wheeled post chaise, and a chair.

James Gordon (Orange), 36 adult slaves, 14 horses; no land is listed in Gordon's name in the Orange County Land Books. One of the two James Gordons owned continental securities on which he received $162 interest in 1787.[53]

Ralph Humphreys (Hampshire), landholdings unknown; no slaves, one stud valued at £1 5s. for a season's coverage.

Zachariah Johnston (Augusta), 697 acres in Augusta valued at £211 15s. and 440 acres in Botetourt valued at £594; 3 adult slaves, 16 horses; continental securities on which he received $30 interest in 1787.[54]

Samuel Kello (Southampton), 700 acres valued at £317 18s.; 13 adult slaves, 6 horses, and a post chaise.

Henry Lee (Westmoreland), 955 acres in Fairfax and 1,645 acres in Westmoreland having a combined value of £1,161 13s., one town lot with £5 yearly rent, and 8,239 acres in military bounty lands; 50 adult slaves, 6 horses, 50 cattle, and a four-wheeled chariot (1787).[55]

Thomas Lewis (Rockingham), 1,960 acres valued at £645; no slaves or other taxable personalty.

Warner Lewis (Gloucester), 3,024 acres valued at £3,729 (1787); 153 adult slaves, 45 horses, 224 cattle, one post chaise, and one chair; $4,672 in continental securities.[56]

William McClerry (Monongalia), one slave, one horse; the land books for his county are no longer extant.[57]

[50] *Ibid.*, 225.
[51] Records of the Loan of 1790, vol. 1118, August 17, 1791.
[52] *Ibid.*, vol. 1078, April 9, 1785; vol. 1079, January 4, 1787; vol. 1116, folio 27; Gwathmey, *Virginians in the Revolution*, 299.
[53] Records of the Loan of 1790, vol. 1081, January 4, 1787.
[54] *Ibid.*, vol. 1081, January 4, 1787.
[55] Gwathmey, *Virginians in the Revolution*, 465.
[56] Records of the Loan of 1790, vol. 1112, folio 103; vol. 1118, June 11, 1791.
[57] No search for records was made in West Virginia, where Monongalia County is now located. The current spelling is Monongahela.

Martin McFerran (Botetourt), 319 acres valued at £526; no slaves or other taxable personalty; continental securities on which he was paid $41.50 interest in 1787.[58]

William McKee (Rockbridge), 134 acres valued at £5; 4 slaves, 6 horses.

William Mason (Greensville), 828 acres valued at £565; no slaves, 2 horses.

Thomas Matthews (Norfolk Borough). No tax returns for the borough as distinct from the county exist for these early years, and Matthews' name does not appear on the county listings. He owned $524 in continental securities.[59]

Wilson Cary Nicholas (Albemarle), no landholdings recorded; 41 adult slaves, 21 horses, and a phaeton.

David Patteson (Chesterfield), 810 acres valued at £435 7s. (1789), 28 town lots with a yearly rent of £58 14s.; 14 adult slaves (1789), 9 horses, a phaeton, and one stud horse; continental securities on which he received $20 interest in 1786. Patteson was opposed to ratification and he voted with the anti-Federalist minority for a proposal to ratify conditionally. This failing, he voted for ratification.[60]

William Peachey (Richmond), 500 acres valued at £631 5s.; 39 adult slaves, 8 horses, 42 cattle (1786); $805 in continental securities.[61]

Martin Pickett (Fauquier), 1,063 acres valued at £403 8s.; 17 adult slaves, 13 horses.

John Prunty (Harrison), size of landholdings unknown; no slaves, 5 horses.

Willis Riddick (Nansemond), 500 acres valued at £395 16s. and 4,000 acres of western land received as a bounty for war service.[62]

Jacob Rinker (Shenandoah), 478 acres valued at £111 10s.; no slaves, 34 cattle, 10 horses (1787).[63]

William Ronald (Powhatan), 3,074 acres in Powhatan and 1,370 acres in Goochland, total value £2,218 17s.; 48 adult slaves, 28 horses, a phaeton in Powhatan, and 2 slaves in Goochland.

Abel Seymour (Hardy), landholdings unknown; 2 adult slaves, 9 horses.

Solomon Shepherd (Nansemond), 529 acres valued at £698 14s.; taxable personalty unknown; $1,017 in continental securities.[64]

Thomas Smith (Gloucester), 630 acres valued at £345; 31 adult slaves, 10 horses, and a phaeton; $268 in continental securities.[65]

[58] Records of the Loan of 1790, vol. 1081, October 22, 1787.

[59] *Ibid.*, vol. 1116, folio 51 and an unnumbered folio.

[60] *Ibid.*, vol. 1081, June 6, 1786.

[61] *Ibid.*, vol. 1079, April 15, 1787.

[62] Gwathmey, *Virginians in the Revolution*, 664.

[63] Jacob Rinker, Sr., and Jacob Rinker, Jr., are listed separately in the Shenandoah Records. I have assumed that the elder Rinker was the delegate. The property owned by the son included land valued at £131 and personalty consisting of 7 horses and 21 cattle. He owned no slaves.

[64] Records of the Loan of 1790, vol. 1118, May 6, 1791.

[65] *Ibid.*, vol. 1078, December 23, 1785. Thomas Smith, Jr., is also listed in the land books for Gloucester County as the owner of 43 acres valued at £26, 10 shillings.

Adam Stephen (Berkeley), data on landholdings unavailable; 29 adult slaves, 40 horses; continental securities on which he was paid $614 interest in 1787.[66]

John Stringer (Northampton), 400 acres valued at £200; 11 adult slaves, 5 horses; $704 in continental securities.[67]

John Stuart (Greenbriar), 2,100 acres valued at £300; 6 adult slaves, 16 horses; $16 in continental securities.[68]

James Taylor (Caroline), 2,070 acres valued at £2,105; 40 adult slaves, 12 horses, 48 cattle, and one phaeton (1787). An unidentified James Taylor funded $419 in continental securities. Whether it was this delegate, or Dr. James Taylor of Norfolk, or some other James Taylor cannot be ascertained.[69]

William Thornton (King George), 400 acres valued at £426 14s.; 15 adult slaves, 13 horses; $1,224 in continental securities.[70]

Walker Tomlin (Richmond), 274 acres valued at £124 8s.; 60 adult slaves, 7 horses, 80 cattle (1786); $499 in continental securities.[71]

Henry Towles (Lancaster), 485 acres in Lancaster and 1,230 acres in Culpeper, total value £396 7s.; 12 adult slaves, 5 horses, and a carriage.

Isaac Vanmeter (Hardy), landholdings unknown; 9 slaves and 10 horses co-owned with Jacob Vanmeter; $2,385 in continental securities.[72]

Thomas Walke (Princess Anne), 1,000 acres valued at £425; 18 adult slaves, 15 horses, a two-wheeled carriage, and a stud horse worth £1 10s. for seasonal covering. Walke's slaves had been confiscated by Lord Carleton during the war, and he had paid off prewar debts by payments into the state treasury.[73]

Bushrod Washington (Westmoreland), land valued at £1,300; 19 adult slaves, 12 horses, a six-wheeled phaeton, a chair, and a stud horse worth 12 shillings for a season's covering.

James Webb (Norfolk County), 878 acres valued at £256 1s. (1787); 21 adult slaves, 6 horses, and a two-wheeled carriage.

Worlich Westwood (Elizabeth City), 1¾ town lots with annual rental of £20 and 498 acres valued at £262 6s.; personal property unknown.

John Williams (Shenandoah), one town lot with a £5 yearly rental and 61 acres valued at £28 4s.; 5 adult slaves, 5 horses. Williams was the clerk of the Shenandoah County Court in 1788–1789.

Benjamin Wilson (Randolph), size of estate unknown.

John Wilson (Randolph), size of estate unknown.

[66] Records of the Loan of 1790, vol. 1116, folios 176–177.
[67] *Ibid.*, vol. 1113, folio 77.
[68] *Ibid.*, vol. 1118, September 21, 1791.
[69] *Ibid.*, vol. 1118, April 19, 1791.
[70] *Ibid.*, vol. 1079, October 30, 1786.
[71] *Ibid.*, vol. 1079, March 24, 1787.
[72] *Ibid.*, vol. 1118, December 7, 1790, October 8, 1792.
[73] Grigsby, *Virginia Convention*, 2:96.

John S. Woodcock (Frederick), 500 acres valued at £236 13*s*.; 7 adult slaves, 11 horses, and a four-wheeled stage coach.

Andrew Woodrow (Hampshire), landholdings unknown; 2 adult slaves, 4 horses; continental securities on which he received $416 interest in 1786.[74]

Archibald Woods (Ohio), 400 acres valued at £33 6*s*.; personalty unknown; $519 in state securities.[75]

ECONOMIC INTERESTS OF DELEGATES VOTING
AGAINST RATIFICATION

Four of the anti-Federalist delegates were merchants:

Isaac Coles (Halifax), brother-in-law of Elbridge Gerry, having, like Gerry, married one of the daughters of the New York City merchant James Tompson. Coles owned, in addition to his mercantile property, 1,640 acres of land valued at £792 13*s*., 13 adult slaves, and 13 horses.[76]

Stephen Pankey (Chesterfield), who owned, in Chesterfield, a store, a town lot with yearly rental of £160, 1,587 acres of land valued at £706 16*s*., 6 adult slaves, and 3 horses, and in Powhatan 573 acres valued at £180 4*s*. Pankey also owned $111 in continental securities.[77]

Parke Goodall (Hanover), who owned a retail store, an unknown amount of land, 16 adult slaves, 8 horses, and $186 in continental securities.[78]

Henry Dickenson (Russell), who owned a country store, 150 acres valued at £26 17*s*., one slave, and 7 horses.

Twelve were lawyers:

Cuthbert Bullitt (Prince William), 527 acres in Prince William and 2,200 acres in Botetourt, total value £398 9*s*.; 5 adult slaves, 5 horses, and a four-wheeled chair.[79]

John Dawson (Spotsylvania), 588 acres valued at £271 19*s*.; 23 adult slaves, 6 horses, and 10 cattle (1787). Dawson and anti-Federalist James Monroe shared a house in Fredericksburg which they rented from anti-Federalist Joseph Jones.

William Grayson (Prince William), 2 town lots, 685 acres valued at £475 4*s*., and 7,592 acres of western land received as bounties for military service.[80]

Patrick Henry (Prince Edward), 8,534 acres in Henry County and 70 acres in Prince Edward County, total value £3,757 19*s*.; 40 adult slaves, 29 horses, and a two-wheeled coach.

[74] Records of the Loan of 1790, vol. 1081, June 13, 1786.

[75] *Ibid.*, vol. 1115, folio 25.

[76] Grigsby, *Virginia Convention*, 2:374–375.

[77] Records of the Loan of 1790, vol. 1079, January 25, 1789; vol. 1081, May 31, 1786.

[78] *Ibid.*, vol. 1118, April 5, 1791.

[79] Grigsby, *Virginia Convention*, 2:380.

[80] Gwathmey, *Virginians in the Revolution*, 323; *Biographical Directory of Congress* (1927 edition), 1030.

Samuel Hopkins (Mecklenburg), 875 acres valued at £295 6s. and 7,833 acres of Kentucky land received as military bounties; 21 adult slaves, 16 horses, and a chair; $5,133 in continental securities.[81]

Joseph Jones (Dinwiddie), 2,503 acres valued at £2,189 14s.; 19 adult slaves, 19 horses, and a four-wheeled chariot; $32 in state securities.[82]

Henry Lee (Bourbon), whose holdings of land and slaves are not ascertainable.[83]

Stephens Thomson Mason (Loudon), 1,000 acres valued at £758 6s.; 71 slaves, 28 horses, 76 cattle, a four-wheeled chaise, and a stud valued at 18 shillings for a season's covering (1787); continental securities on which he drew $32 interest in 1788.[84]

James Monroe (Spotsylvania), no listing of either land or slaves in the county other than the house he rented with Dawson. He owned 5,333 acres of Kentucky land which had been granted to him for military service.[85]

Abraham Trigg (Montgomery), 155 acres valued at £100; 5 adult slaves, 7 horses.[86]

John Tyler (Charles City), 569 acres valued at £344 6s.; slaveholdings not ascertainable.[87]

Edmund Winston (Campbell), 500 acres valued at £220; 17 adult slaves, 15 horses.[88]

One of the anti-ratificationist delegates, Theodorick Bland (Prince George), was a physician. Bland owned 1,339 acres valued at £880 14s. and 6,666 acres of Kentucky land received as a bounty for military service; 19 adult slaves, 10 horses, and a four-wheeled carriage; more than $5,000 in state and continental securities.[89]

One of the anti-ratificationist delegates, Charles Clay (Bedford), was a minister.[90]

Sixty of the delegates who voted against ratification were planters and farmers:

Robert Alexander (Campbell), 1,742 acres valued at £545 13s.; 10 adult slaves, 21 cattle, and a two-wheeled carriage (1787).

[81] Gwathmey, *Virginians in the Revolution*, 391; Records of the Loan of 1790, vol. 1118, November 22, 1790.

[82] *Biographical Directory of Congress*, 1163; Records of the Loan of 1790, vol. 1115, folio 55.

[83] Lee's career is sketched in Grigsby's *Virginia Convention*, 2:368.

[84] Records of the Loan of 1790, vol. 1081, January 7, 1788. Mason's legal career is traced in Grigsby's *Virginia Convention*, 2:225 ff., and in the 1927 edition of the *Biographical Directory of Congress*, 1297.

[85] Gwathmey, *Virginians in the Revolution*, 557.

[86] Identified as a lawyer in the 1927 edition of the *Biographical Directory of Congress*, 1627.

[87] Sketched briefly in Grigsby's *Virginia Convention*, 1:251.

[88] Identified as a lawyer, *ibid.*, 2:369.

[89] Records of the Loan of 1790, vols. 1114, 1115, 1116; Gwathmey, *Virginians in the Revolution*, 69.

[90] Grigsby, *Virginia Convention*, 1:255.

Thomas Allen (Mercer), the size of whose estate is not ascertainable.

Thomas Arthurs (Franklin), 717 acres valued at £337 18s.; 6 adult slaves, 8 horses.

David Bell (Buckingham), 426 acres in Buckingham valued at £111 16s. and 501 acres in Lunenburg valued at £204 14s.; slaveholdings unknown.

Edmund Booker (Amelia), 568 acres valued at £305; 16 adult slaves, 5 horses.

John H. Briggs (Sussex), 3,025 acres valued at £995; 4 adult slaves, 5 horses.

Andrew Buchanan (Stafford), one town lot with £50 annual rental, 364 acres in Stafford and 600 acres in Washington, having a total value of £298 19s.; 9 adult slaves, 6 horses, and a four-wheeled carriage.

Samuel Jordan Cabell (Amherst), 1,444 acres in Amherst and 4,400 acres in Buckingham having a total value of £1,597 13s. and 7,833 acres of Kentucky land received as a military bounty; 21 adult slaves, 11 horses, and a four-wheeled phaeton; $4,529 in continental securities.[91]

William Cabell (Amherst), 17,837 acres valued at £6,596 11s.; 54 adult slaves, 22 horses, a four-wheeled carriage, and two chairs; $209 in continental securities.[92]

George Carrington (Halifax), 1,974 acres valued at £1,077 6s.; 12 adult slaves, 7 horses; $2,837 in continental and $112 in state securities.[93]

Thomas Carter (Russell), 400 acres valued at £38 6s.; one slave, 11 horses.

Richard Cary (Warwick), 350 acres valued at £186 13s.; 24 adult slaves, 12 horses, a two-wheeled chair, and one stud valued at £1 for a season's covering.

Green Clay (Bedford), 690 acres valued at £311 5s.; 6 adult slaves, 6 horses.[94]

Thomas Cooper (Henry), 1,163 acres valued at £702 12s.; 7 adult slaves, 11 horses.

Walter Crockett (Montgomery), 478 acres valued at £140; 3 adult slaves, 9 horses.

Edmund Custis (Accomac), 534 acres valued at £255 18s.; 18 adult slaves, 11 horses; $1,837 in continental securities.[95]

Thomas H. Drew (Cumberland), 90 acres valued at £46 10s. and 4,000 acres of Kentucky land received as a bounty for military service; no slaves; $466 in continental securities.[96]

Joel Early (Culpeper), 881 acres valued at £474 1s.; 31 adult slaves, 9 horses.

John Early (Franklin), 615 acres valued at £184 2s.; 7 adult slaves, 3 horses; continental securities on which he received $45.80 interest in 1786.[97]

[91] Records of the Loan of 1790, vol. 1116, folios 3, 28, 187 (unnumbered, my count); Gwathmey, *Virginians in the Revolution,* 119.

[92] Records of the Loan of 1790, vol. 1118, February 28, 1791.

[93] *Ibid.,* vol. 1078, April 9, 1785; vol. 1118, March 15, 1791.

[94] Grigsby, *Virginia Convention,* 2:378.

[95] Records of the Loan of 1790, vol. 1079, October 24, 1786; vol. 1078, April 25, 28, 29, May 23, 26, October 17, 26, December 26, 1785, January 7, 1786.

[96] *Ibid.,* vol. 1116, folio 130; Gwathmey, *Virginians in the Revolution,* 236.

[97] Records of the Loan of 1790, vol. 1081, November 13, 1786.

Samuel Edmiston (Washington), 400 acres valued at £98 6s. (1786); 17 adult slaves, 16 horses, and 36 cattle (1785).

Thomas Edmunds (Sussex), 3,804 acres valued at £1,541 8s. and 4,000 acres received as a bounty for military service; 34 adult slaves, 14 horses, and a four-wheeled carriage; $9,190 in state and $50 in continental securities.[98]

John Evans (Monongalia), landholdings unknown; 2 adult slaves, 6 horses; continental securities on which he received $371 interest in 1787.[99]

John Fowler (Fayette), landholdings unknown; 10 adult slaves, 2 horses, and 8 cattle (1787); $1,679 in state and $102 in continental securities.[100]

John Guerrant (Goochland), 636 acres valued at £334 2s. (1789); 15 adult slaves, 12 horses, and a two-wheeled carriage.

Joseph Haden (Fluvanna), 899 acres valued at £294 8s.; 7 adult slaves, 4 horses.

Benjamin Harrison (Charles City), size of estate not ascertained.

Binns Jones (Brunswick), 400 acres valued at £171 13s.; 27 adult slaves, 7 horses, and 22 cattle (1787).

John Jones (Brunswick), 901 acres valued at £412 9s.; 45 adult slaves, 18 horses, 44 cattle, a phaeton, and a chair (1787); $1,136 in continental securities.[101]

Richard Kennon (Mecklenburg), 1,094 acres valued at £1,120 7s. and 5,416 acres received as a bounty for military service; 38 adult slaves, 20 horses, a four-wheeled phaeton, and one stud.[102]

Robert Lawson (Prince Edward), 894 acres valued at £283 2s. and 10,000 acres received as a military bounty; 11 adult slaves, 9 horses, and a coach.[103]

John Carter Littlepage (Hanover); landholdings not ascertained; 9 adult slaves, 13 horses; $10 in continental securities.[104]

John Logan (Lincoln), size of estate not ascertained.

John Marr (Henry), 1,034 acres valued at £458; 7 adult slaves, 16 horses, and a four-wheeled carriage.

George Mason (Stafford), whose enormous estate is described on page 72, above.

Joseph Michaux (Cumberland), 995 acres valued at £555 10s.; 26 adult slaves, 8 horses, and 35 cattle (1787).

John Miller (Madison), size of estate not ascertained.

James Montgomery (Washington), 400 acres valued at £98 6s. (1786); 3 adult slaves, 10 horses, and 16 cattle (1785).

Charles Patteson (Buckingham), 1,984 acres valued at £528 2s.; 31 slaves (1790).

[98] *Ibid.*, vol. 1113, folios 2, 160; vol. 1118, December 23, 1790.
[99] *Ibid.*, vol. 1116, folios 11, 121, 129 (121 and 129 are unnumbered).
[100] *Ibid.*, vol. 1113, folio 105; vol. 1078, April 9, 1785.
[101] *Ibid.*, vol. 1078, April 12, 1785.
[102] Gwathmey, *Virginians in the Revolution*, 441.
[103] *Ibid.*, 462.
[104] Records of the Loan of 1790, vol. 1116, folio 6.

Jonathan Patteson (Lunenburg), 300 acres valued at £138 14s.; 5 adult slaves, 4 horses.

Henry Pawling (Lincoln), size of estate not ascertained.

John Pride (Amelia), 440 acres valued at £236 10s.; 23 adult slaves, 10 horses.

Thomas Read (Charlotte), 2,143 acres valued at £1,581 4s.; 29 adult slaves, 16 horses, and a four-wheeled phaeton; $554 in continental securities.[105]

Samuel Richardson (Fluvanna), 963 acres in Fluvanna and 546½ acres in Goochland, total value £577; 13 adult slaves and 10 horses in Fluvanna and 9 adult slaves and 7 horses in Goochland; $2,413 in continental and $435 in state securities.[106]

Holt Richeson (King William), 1,615 acres valued at £759 7s. (1785 tax return plus additions recorded in returns for 1786 and 1787) and 6,000 acres received as a bounty for military service; 23 adult slaves, 7 horses.[107]

Thomas Roane (King and Queen), 3,968½ acres in King and Queen and 516 acres in Middlesex, total value £3,676 4s.; 29 adult slaves, 13 horses, a six-wheeled phaeton and a chair.

Alexander Robertson (Mercer), size of estate not ascertained.

Christopher Robertson (Lunenburg), 600 acres valued at £487; 9 adult slaves, 3 horses, and a two-wheeled carriage.

Edmund Ruffin, Jr. (Prince George), 1,582 acres and 4 town lots, total value £1,541 17s.; 24 adult slaves, 14 horses.

William Sampson (Goochland), 375 acres valued at £137 12s.; 10 adult slaves, 6 horses.

Meriwether Smith (Essex), 2½ town lots with an annual rent of £18, 800 acres valued at £1,077 6s.; 61 adult slaves, 8 horses, 60 cattle, and a two-wheeled carriage (1786).

John Steel (Nelson), 3,055 acres awarded as a bounty for military service; $3,905 in continental securities.[108]

French Strother (Culpeper), 1,110 acres valued at £877 19s. (1789); 23 adult slaves, 18 horses (1790); $191 in continental securities.[109]

Benjamin Temple (King William), 2,285 acres valued at £1,434 (1785 tax return plus additions as recorded in 1787 tax returns) and 7,555 acres received as a bounty for military service; 36 adult slaves, 11 horses, a phaeton, and a chair.[110]

John Trigg (Bedford), 363 acres valued at £272; 8 adult slaves, 6 horses, and a two-wheeled carriage.

[105] *Ibid.*, vol. 1118, December 3, 1790. Read is the only anti-Federalist mentioned by Beard (page 287) of whom he says specifically that he was not a security holder.

[106] Records of the Loan of 1790, vol. 1115, folio 19; vol. 1118, March 14, 1791.

[107] Gwathmey, *Virginians in the Revolution*, 662.

[108] *Ibid.*, 737; Records of the Loan of 1790, vol. 1112, folio 133; vol. 1118, November 30, 1790, September 30, 1791.

[109] *Ibid.*, vol. 1118, October 22, 1790.

[110] Gwathmey, *Virginians in the Revolution*, 763.

Thomas Turpin, Jr. (Powhatan), 866 acres valued at £342 15s.; 18 adult slaves, 15 horses, a four-wheeled chaise, and a chair; continental securities on which he received $429.30 interest payments in 1788.[111]

James Upshaw (Essex), 220 acres in Essex and 2,119 acres in Caroline County, total value £570 1s.; 21 adult slaves, 5 horses, and 20 cattle (1786); $128 in continental securities.[112]

Matthew Walton (Nelson), the size of whose estate was not ascertained. Walton owned continental securities on which he received $213 interest payments in 1786.[113]

William Watkins (Dinwiddie), 1,929 acres valued at £1,063 19s.; 24 adult slaves, 8 horses, and a two-wheeled chair; continental securities on which he received $7 interest in 1786.[114]

William White (Louisa), 795 acres valued at £289 18s.; 7 adult slaves, 7 horses; $1,828 in state and $1,695 in continental securities.[115]

Robert Williams (Pittsylvania), 3,866 acres valued at £1,240 6s.; 36 adult slaves, 17 horses; continental securities on which he received $7.56 interest payments in 1786.[116]

John Wilson (Pittsylvania), 4,891 acres valued at £2,237 11s.; 27 adult slaves, 14 horses, and a four-wheeled stage wagon.

To bring all these sketches to a focus, the following general observations may be made. First, the occupations and security holdings of the delegates may be summarized as follows:

| | VOTING AYE | | VOTING NAY | |
OCCUPATIONS	No.	Per Cent	No.	Per Cent
Merchants	1	1.1	4	5.0
Lawyers	17	19.1	12	15.2
Physicians	5	5.6	1	1.3
Ministers	2	2.2	1	1.3
Miscellaneous	—	—	1	1.3
Planters and farmers . .	64	72.0	60	75.9
SECURITY HOLDINGS				
Continental securities . .	28	31.4	20	25.3
State securities	7	7.9	1	1.3
Both kinds of securities	1	1.1	6	7.6
Total holders	36	40.5	27	34.2

[111] Records of the Loan of 1790, vol. 1081, October 5, 1786, January 7, 1788.
[112] *Ibid.*, vol. 1078, April 29, October 21, November 23, 1785, January 1, 1786.
[113] *Ibid.*, vol. 1081, June 1, 1786.
[114] *Ibid.*, vol. 1081, May 30, 1786.
[115] *Ibid.*, vol. 1113, folio 160; vol. 1118, March 2, September 20, 1791, June 8, August 2, 1792.
[116] *Ibid.*, vol. 1116, unnumbered page 171.

It is clear that with respect to occupations there were no important differences between the delegates who voted for ratification and those who voted against it. The group that favored ratification included a larger number of security holders, it is true, but the margin of difference is not significant.

The foregoing sketches reveal that the forms of property most frequently held in significant quantities by delegates, irrespective of occupations or vote on ratifiication, were land and slaves. The figures for values of lands for tax purposes may or not represent their true value, but for comparative purposes they are valid, since they were arrived at by a uniform system. The values of the landholdings of the delegates voting for and against ratification may be summarized as follows:

	Holdings Unknown		£0–£150 ($0–$500)		£150–£300 ($500–$1000)		£300–£600 ($1000–$2000)		£600–£1500 ($2000–$5000)		£1500+ ($5000+)	
	No.	Per Cent	No.	Per Cent	No.	Per Cent	No.	Per Cent	No.	Per Cent	No.	Per Cent
Ayes	23	25.9	12	13.5	12	13.5	17	19.1	16	17.9	9	10.1
Nays	14	17.7	9	11.4	12	15.2	18	22.8	15	19.0	11	13.9

It should be pointed out that the great majority of the delegates for whom data on property holdings are unavailable were from areas across the mountains, where land values were low. When this is taken into account, it appears that approximately the same proportions of delegates on the two sides held large and moderate amounts of land, but that the number of small landholders who supported ratification was considerably in excess of the number who opposed it.

The slaveholdings of the delegates may be summarized as follows:

	Holdings Unknown		None		1–9		10–19		20–49		50+	
	No.	Per Cent	No.	Per Cent	No.	Per Cent	No.	Per Cent	No.	Per Cent	No.	Per Cent
Ayes	14	15.8	11	12.4	21	23.6	16	17.9	22	24.7	5	5.6
Nays	14	18.2	1	1.3	23	29.1	15	19.0	22	27.8	4	5.0

Significantly, most of the Federalists whose slaveholdings are unknown are those from areas west of the mountains, where slaveholdings were generally small, whereas most of the anti-Federalists whose slaveholdings are unknown were from areas of large plantations.

From the foregoing tables it would appear that planters who had large or moderately large slaveholdings were divided almost equally on the question of ratification, but that the great majority of the small farmers who owned no slaves or very few slaves voted for the Constitution.

Professor Beard interpreted the contest in Virginia on the basis of the geographical distribution of the votes. Largely disregarding the fact that more than a fourth of the delegates were frontier farmers from areas west of the Blue Ridge, he focused his attention primarily on the eastern part of the state. There he found that a substantial majority of the tidewater counties voted for ratification and a sizeable majority of the piedmont counties against it. He ascribed to these areas economic characteristics which close examination would have revealed they did not have, and concluded that most of the support for the Constitution came from wealthy planters and security holders, and most of the opposition from small, slaveless farmers and debtors.

The precise opposite is nearer the truth. Public security holders were almost equally divided and the majority of the small farmers supported ratification. The wealthy planters were almost equally divided on the question of ratification, but planter-debtors, and particularly the planters who had brought about the passage of laws preventing the collection of British debts, favored ratification by a substantial margin.

New York

THE people of the state of New York were overwhelmingly opposed to the Constitution, and the delegates they elected to the state's ratifying convention were anti-ratificationists by a majority of more than two to one. Only after the convention learned that New Hampshire and Virginia had ratified was their resistance broken. In the face of this news the anti-Federalist delegates decided, at a caucus held on the evening of July 25, 1788, that certain of their number should vote for the Constitution, and on July 26 the document was ratified by a vote of 30 to 27.

New York's opposition, headed by Governor George Clinton, had begun long before the Philadelphia Convention of 1787 completed its labors. Its delegation to that body voted at the outset against the creation of a general government, and on July 7 they left the Convention. Before the end of July there was in wide circulation a report—originating with Clinton's political enemy Hamilton but nonetheless valid—that Governor Clinton was busily organizing opposition to any product that might issue from the Convention. In September there began in the Clintonian press a series of attacks on some of the delegates, and repeated newspaper articles gratuitously defending Clinton's right to oppose the Convention confirmed the talk of Clinton's opposition.[117]

A series of articles in opposition to the Constitution was written by Clinton before it was in existence, and on September 27, concurrently with the publication of the document in New York, the first of them, published over the pseudonym "Cato," made its appearance. A host of wordy arguments on both sides of the issue then began to appear in pamphlets and newspapers. The most celebrated were those appearing in the *Independent Journal* over the signature "Publius," later republished as the Federalist Papers. Brilliant though they were, they were smothered by the deluge of anti-Federalist propaganda and were of virtually no influence in deciding votes except in the immediate vicinity of the City.[118]

[117] New York *Daily Advertiser*, July 21, 1787; *New York Journal and Weekly Register*, September 6, 13, 20, 1787; Henry Cabot Lodge, ed., *The Works of Alexander Hamilton* (10 vols., New York, 1904), 8:180.

[118] *New York Journal*, September 27, 1787. The *Journal* was the principal Clintonian newspaper. Additional propaganda may be seen in the *New York Packet & American Advertiser*, the New York *Independent Journal*, the New York *Daily Advertiser*, the *Country Journal and Poughkeepsie Advertiser*, and other newspapers from October, 1787, to July, 1788. There are numerous editions of the *Federalist*. It was common with Hamilton to make a brilliant

New York anti-ratificationists organized powerful machinery not only to work against the Constitution in New York but also to unite anti-Federalists everywhere in a concentrated effort to prevent ratification. For the state campaign clubs named "Federal Republican" or sometimes simply "Republican" were organized in each county; committees of correspondence were appointed and regular meetings held. The central organization had headquarters at the customs house in New York City. It directed the state campaign, served as a clearinghouse for the writing of anti-ratificationist propaganda and for the selection and distribution of the best of it throughout the United States, and corresponded with such anti-Federalist leaders as Grayson, Mason, Richard Henry Lee, and Henry of Virginia, Atherton of New Hampshire, Samuel Chase of Maryland, Rawling Lowndes of South Carolina, Gerry of Massachusetts, Timothy Bloodworth of North Carolina, and others.[119]

Clinton ignored requests that he call a special session of the legislature in the fall of 1787, and by the time the New York legislature met and got around to calling a convention five states had already ratified. At the end of January, 1788, the House resolved to call a convention after defeating by two votes a proposal to attach to the resolution a preamble censuring the Philadelphia Convention for exceeding its powers. On the same day the Senate concurred in the resolution, also by a two-vote majority. The resolution provided that the convention be held

argument that was of little effect in influencing votes. One of the most powerful and profound speeches he ever made was that which he delivered in the Assembly in February, 1787, on the question of granting the Congress power to levy imposts. The day-long speech excited the admiration of all who heard it and left Hamilton doubled up in pain from physical exertion, but the proposal he had advocated was rejected by a substantial vote. *Daily Advertiser,* February 27, 1787. After Hamilton had made a five-hour speech in the Philadelphia Convention William Samuel Johnson of Connecticut wrote that "the gentleman from New York . . . has been praised by everybody, he has been supported by none." The most profound of Hamilton's reports as secretary of the treasury, that on manufactures, was in large part not acted upon by Congress.

[119] Ernest W. Spaulding, *New York in the Critical Period, 1783–1789* (New York, 1932), 221. The influence of the propaganda emanating from this center I have traced in newspapers in every state. This machinery in New York was the national center of anti-Federalist organization, as the Robert Morris headquarters in Philadelphia was the center for Federalist activities.

in Poughkeepsie in June and the election of delegates in the
third week of April. For these special elections all property
qualifications were dropped, and all free adult male citizens
were given the right to vote for delegates.[120]

The elections resulted in a smashing defeat for the Federalists.
Anti-ratificationist candidates received more than 14,000 of the
known votes as against only 6,500 for the Federalists. Federalists
carried only the City and County of New York and three other
counties with a total of nineteen delegates; their opponents
carried nine counties with a total of forty-six delegates. The
popular mandate was clear. It remained to be seen what the
politicians would do with it.[121]

When the convention met on June 17 there was not much,
for the moment, that the politicians could do. The Federalists
unleashed a brilliant array of debaters, led by Hamilton, Robert
R. Livingston, and John Jay. The Clintonians occasionally answered through Melancton Smith, Lansing, and Clinton himself, but more often they followed their customary parliamentary practice of sitting quietly, confident of their voting

[120] *Votes and Proceedings of the Assembly of the State of New York*, 11th
Session, 1st Meeting (New York, 1788), January 31, 1788, pp. 47–48; *Votes
and Proceedings of the Senate of the State of New York*, 11th Session, 1st
Meeting (New York, 1788), January 31, 1788, pp. 20–21. No explanation for
the special expansion of the franchise was given, and it seems impossible to
determine which party was responsible for it. As there was no call for votes
on the issue in either house, it may have passed unanimously.

[121] A summary of election returns for five counties appears in the *New
York Journal* of June 5, 1788; for Orange County see the *Daily Advertiser*,
June 14, 1788; for Queens County (incorrectly called Suffolk therein), *ibid.*,
June 7, 1788; for Dutchess County the Poughkeepsie *Country Journal*, June 3,
1788; and for Westchester County the *Daily Advertiser*, June 3, 1788. The
two counties for which the votes are unknown (Washington and Suffolk) and
which sent anti-Federalist delegates had 32,000 inhabitants in 1790, and in
Washington County the majority for the winning candidates was reported to
have been "two to one." The two Federalist counties for which votes are
unknown (Kings and Richmond) had only 8,300 inhabitants in 1790. Though
these were four of the five least populous counties in the state, these facts
would seem to indicate that the total vote gave the anti-Federalists an even
greater majority of the popular vote, probably about 16,000 as against 7,000
for the Federalists. Beard (*Economic Interpretation*, 244–245) mistakenly places
Queens as a Federalist county and errs in the addition of the total delegates.
Spaulding's *New York in the Critical Period*, 200–203, contains an analysis of
the votes. Spaulding repeats Beard's erroneous figure for the total number
of delegates.

strength.[122] On the present occasion, however, they were uneasy. They were hesitant to reject the Constitution outright, perhaps because they were mindful of the vituperation that had been heaped upon them when they killed the proposed congressional impost early in 1787. They preferred to wait and let some other state be the first to do so.

Eight states had ratified when the New York convention met. The New Hampshire and Virginia conventions were in session at the time, and it appeared likely that one or both of those states might reject the Constitution. When the news of New Hampshire's ratification reached Poughkeepsie on June 24, the Clintonians were depressed, and when news of Virginia's ratification came on July 2, their spirit was broken. As late as July 15, however, only five of their number had joined the Federalists.[123]

The convention approached a stalemate. The Clintonians were divided; one group wanted to reject the Constitution despite the approval of ten states, the other was ready to ratify conditionally, the condition being that New York would automatically retract its ratification unless a second federal convention, to revise the work of the first, were called within a stated period. Hamilton and his allies took advantage of this temporary indecision to employ perhaps the only device that could have succeeded. They solemnly declared that if the convention rejected the Constitution the City and County of New York would secede from the state and join the Union by itself. The announcement was not made on the convention floor, but in repeated private conversations with individual Clintonians. Whether the City would actually have carried out its threat is beside the point; what is important is that the Clintonians became convinced that it would do so. Rumors were printed in

[122] See "Leo" in the *Daily Advertiser* of February 27, 1787, for a complaint against this practice. This writer said that the Clintonians were willing to debate endlessly on petty matters, but that when vital issues were under consideration they became silent and voted as a bloc.

[123] Elliott's *Debates*, vol. 2 (vote recorded on July 15); Spaulding, *New York in the Critical Period*, 257, 261. Clarence E. Miner's *Ratification of the Federal Constitution by the State of New York* (New York, 1921) contains a narrative of the proceedings of the convention.

the City newspapers that the secession movement was already being organized, and Clintonian delegates were privately pressured at every opportunity.[124]

The secession rumor having taken effect, the Federalists clearly had the upper hand. The Clintonians made a last vain effort to secure a conditional ratification, but when the Federalists assured them that the new government would not accept such a ratification, they gave up. On July 25 they held the caucus mentioned earlier and decided that some of their number should vote for ratification.[125] Apparently the plan was to make the decision rest on a one-vote margin, but one of the Clintonians failed to show up for the vote and Clinton himself, as president of the convention, abstained from voting, so that the final vote was 30 to 27.[126]

The steps by which both the opposition to and the support for ratification had developed in New York stand out distinctly in the history of the state during and after the Revolution. Before these steps can be traced, however, two sets of facts about the state's war experience must be understood as the factors that conditioned the atmosphere in New York during the period.

The first is that New York City was occupied by the British

[124] Jay, in a letter to Washington, May 29, 1788, stated the Federalists' intention to use this tactic. Henry P. Johnson, ed., *Correspondence and Public Papers of John Jay* (4 vols., New York, 1890), 2:334. Rumors of the City's threatened secession were published in the *New York Packet* in May and several times in the Philadelphia *Pennsylvania Gazette* in June and July. Paul Leicester Ford, in the introduction to his edition of *The Federalist* (New York, 1898), page 38, declares that only the threat of secession forced New York to ratify. I agree with this view.

[125] The delegates who changed sides were, in my opinion, selected by design from the counties around the City. Beard (page 245) implies that the delegates who changed sides did so because they held securities; but, as will be shown, the changes of votes resulted in a higher percentage of security holders among the opponents of ratification than there had been before. The deliberate selection of delegates from southern counties to make the change would have had a reasonable basis. Several of the governor's closest friends and ablest henchmen, such as Samuel Jones and Melancton Smith, were from these counties, and in the event of a rising tide of Federalism in their areas their political careers would be protected by votes for the Constitution.

[126] The story of the caucus is derived from William Dunlap's *History of the New Netherlands, Province of New York, and State of New York, to the Adoption of the Federal Constitution* (2 vols., New York, 1840), 2:281n. Dunlap reported that he had received the information from an eye-witness.

from 1776 to 1783. During this long occupation the Whigs in New York came to hate the British and Loyalists with an intensity perhaps unmatched in any other state. The second conditioning factor stemmed from the first. Loyalists in New York were numerous and many of them were wealthy, and the Revolutionary government ordered the confiscation and sale of their estates. The quantity of these sales was enormous, amounting in the Southern District alone (the City and environs) to more than a half million pounds, New York currency ($1,250,000). The opportunities to purchase large parts of these estates for later resale in small tracts set off a wave of speculation that lasted well into the 1790's. The speculative mania was intensified by an act of 1780 which gave holders of soldiers' depreciation certificates special purchase rights and made other securities as well as specie legal tender as payment for the confiscated property. Large-scale speculations and manipulations in these securities as well as in land resulted. An atmosphere charged with speculative frenzy conditioned all economic and political activity during the decade following the peace.[127]

The first step in the development of attitudes toward the Constitution was the rise to power of George Clinton. The prewar struggle between the DeLancey family and allied clans and the Livingston family and its allies culminated with the Declaration of Independence and the framing of a state constitution by the triumphant Livingstonians in 1776–1777. By means of campaign maneuvers among the soldiers Clinton was elected first governor of the state in 1777 in a surprise victory over Philip Schuyler, a higher ranking member of the Whig faction of the

---

[127] For an excellent description of speculation in forfeited estates see Harry B. Yoshpe, *The Disposition of Loyalist Estates in the Southern District of the State of New York* (New York, 1939), 59–60, 63–78, 114–115, and elsewhere. This work is an invaluable contribution to the history of the period. It is to be regretted that the author never fulfilled his ambition to complete a study of the subject for the entire state. All the evidence would seem to indicate that the speculative mania pervaded the entire state. Many prominent upstate Clintonians were speculating in confiscated property and securities. For evidence of such speculation around Albany see the sketch of Robert Yates appended to the 1821 edition of Yates's notes on the Philadelphia Convention. The speculative wave abated somewhat in 1786, for reasons which will be pointed out below.

colonial aristocracy. Clinton solidified his hold on the government, won the support of much of the aristocracy by his conservative administration, and was re-elected for a succession of three-year terms covering fifteen years. Until the Constitution was ratified Clinton held virtually unchallenged power in the politics of the state.[128]

At the beginning, and as long as New York City was occupied, Clinton and his followers were strongly pro-Union. The next steps in the shaping of attitudes on the issue of 1788 were those that led New York to a break with its sister states. The first and most important was the termination of the war; when the pressing military need for co-operation ended, New York's devotion to the Union declined considerably.

The next clear steps were a series of events that engendered distrust and even disgust with the Confederation Congress. The first was the handling of the Vermont question. The Vermont area was claimed by both New York and New Hampshire, and after much wrangling the Congress indicated in mid-1783 that it was disposed to recognize the grants New Hampshire had made in Vermont but that apart from this it was unwilling to take any decisive action on either state's claims.[129]

The second and third issues that bred hostility toward Congress were related to the treaty of peace. The Tory-hating, speculating New Yorkers considered that the treaty gave unnecessary benefits to Loyalists, and its ratification aroused in the minds of some New Yorkers the suspicion that Congress was soft on Tories. More important was the weakness shown by Congress in failing to force Britain to abide by the treaty with respect to garrisons inside the United States. Five of the frontier outposts which the British continued to occupy in violation of the treaty were inside the limits of New York. Not only was the maintenance of the posts an insult to New York,

[128] Carl L. Becker, *History of the Political Parties in the Province of New York, 1760 to 1776* (Madison, 1909); Ernest W. Spaulding, *His Excellency George Clinton, Critic of the Constitution* (New York, 1938); Spaulding, *New York in the Critical Period*, 95–100.
[129] In Edmund C. Burnett's *The Continental Congress* (New York, 1941), pages 540–546, is a good brief summary of the Vermont dispute.

but it cut New Yorkers off from a share in the lucrative western fur trade.

In the face of this demonstration of the weakness of Congress, New Yorkers could do one of two things: they could seek a stronger union or they could decide to go it alone. A strong faction in the legislature, consisting almost exclusively of followers of Clinton, was ready by 1784 to pursue the latter course. The complaints with respect to the treaty came to a climax in March, 1784, when both houses resolved to lay an ultimatum before Congress. First declaring that New York was "disposed to preserve the Union" and that it had "an inviolable Respect for Congress," the legislature gave Congress two months "after nine States shall be represented in Congress, subsequent to this State being represented there" in which to take decisive action regarding New York's complaints. If Congress failed to respond, the resolution continued, "this State, with whatever deep Regret, will be compelled to consider herself as left to pursue her own Councils, destitute of the Protection of the United States." [130]

Clinton himself was not yet ready to adopt such extreme measures. He acted as an apologist for Congress and sought to discourage the adoption of the resolution. Seven months later, after Congress had resolved in June to do what it could about the British posts, Clinton urged the legislature to accept that as compliance with New York's ultimatum.[131] But when two more elements had entered the picture, Clinton was ready to join his political allies in moving toward a complete break with the Union.

At some time toward the end of 1785 or the beginning of 1786 Clinton began to realize the enormous potential New York had in her natural advantages: a central location, excellent soil, a thrifty and energetic people, a superb system of inland waterways, and a great natural port serving three states, among others. Somewhere along the line, as the City recovered

---

[130] *Votes and Proceedings of the Senate,* 7th Session, 1st Meeting, March 2, 1784. The Assembly concurred on April 22.

[131] *Votes and Proceedings of the Assembly,* 7th Session, 1st Meeting, March 2, 1784, 8th Session, 1st Meeting, October 18, 1784.

from the war with almost incredible speed, as the entire state underwent an economic boom and tremendous expansion, and as the state collected handsome sums in the form of duties on imports for the tri-state area, George Clinton came to visualize clearly a plan for fulfilling New York's destiny as the Empire State.

One more step was necessary. Despite his re-election in 1780 and 1783, Clinton was not sure of his political strength. His previous victories had been scored during the war, and the lower counties and the City had not yet had an opportunity to vote in a gubernatorial election. When, in the elections of April, 1786, no candidate could be found to run against him and the legislative candidates he was backing were elected by great majorities, assuring complete control of both houses, this last reservation vanished. The Clintonians were now prepared to "secede" from the Union.[132]

Two features of the Clintonian program, enacted in 1786–1788, were of primary importance in determining the state's relations with the Union. One was the state's rejection of the proposed amendment to the Articles of Confederation which would have given Congress power to levy import duties with which to fund its debts. New York approved the amendment only conditionally in 1786, after the other twelve states had ratified it; and when Congress declared that acceptance of this conditional ratification would invalidate the ratification of several other states, New York rejected the impost plan outright. This action has been described as the "death knell" of the Confederation Congress.[133]

[132] Election returns for 1786 are scanty. Some of the returns, with a general summary of the results, were published in the *New York Packet* of April 17, May 1, and June 5, 1786. The efforts to find someone willing to challenge Clinton at the polls may be traced in the correspondence between Jay and Philip Schuyler. See Johnston, ed., *Correspondence of Jay*, 3:151–187.

[133] The program is contained in the *Laws of the State of New York Passed at the Sessions of the Legislature* (3 vols., Albany, 1886–1888), vol. 2, covering the sessions from 1785 through 1788. A curious feature of these statutes is the number of basic programs that were to mature or expire in 1800 (a "14-year Plan"), which suggests that the Clintonians set that year as a sort of target date. The struggle over approval of the impost may be traced in New York newspapers; the best accounts are those published in January and February,

Of equal importance was the state's financial program of 1786. Since 1784 there had been agitation in some quarters for an issue of paper money, complaints being rife that the drainage of gold and silver in payment for British manufactures during the last months of the occupation had produced a shortage of specie. The House of Assembly had passed a paper-money measure in 1784 and another in 1785, both of which had been rejected in the Senate. In 1786 the Clinton organization backed the paper issue and combined special features with it to produce an ingenious fiscal scheme.

The plan, all incorporated into a single act, was extremely complex. For present purposes, however, its features may be simplified. Paper money amounting to £200,000, New York currency ($500,000), was to be issued. Of this sum £150,000 was to be lent to individual borrowers, against mortgages on otherwise debt-free real or personal property amounting to two or three times the amount of the loan. The remainder was to be reserved for funding purposes. The entire state debt was funded and two portions of the national debt were assumed: the continental loan office certificates and the so-called Barber's notes, certificates issued by the United States for supplies furnished the continental army. Holders of these continental securities were given the right to exchange them, on loan, for state securities of equal par amounts, bearing interest at the same rate. The remaining £50,000 of the paper-money issue was appropriated for immediate interest payments equal to one-fifth of the back interest due from the United States on these securities.[134]

Continental debts amounting to £557,000 (about $1,395,-

1787, in the *Daily Advertiser*, which printed accounts of the debates of the Assembly on the subject. A secondary account is Thomas Cochran's *New York in the Confederation: An Economic Study* (Philadelphia, 1932).

[134] The act is Chapter 40 of the Acts of 1786, in *Session Laws*, 2:253 ff. The first two dozen sections of the act are identical, except for punctuation and such word changes as the substitution of "State" for "Colony," to the act of 1771 by which the colonial aristocracy emitted paper. The act of 1771, in turn, was virtually identical to an act of 1738. The two colonial acts are in *The Colonial Laws of New York, from the Year 1664 to the Revolution* (5 vols., Albany, 1884), 2:1015 ff. and 5:149 ff. The funding and assumption features of the act of 1786 are in its Article 54.

ooo) were assumed under this act. The state thus shouldered a heavy burden, but it was relieved of obligation to contribute to any further continental requisitions, for the annual interest now due the state government from Congress amounted to more than New York's share of the interest on continental debts. The act also furthered the break with Congress in a more subtle way. The continental debt was considered by many in New York to be the strongest, if not indeed the sole remaining bond with the Union. The reason that loan office certificates and Barber's notes had been chosen for assumption was not, as some charged, that the "honorable members" of the legislature owned only these kinds of debt, but that ownership of these securities was widely spread among at least five thousand holders, a large portion of the voting population. It was, indeed, as one critic charged, "a studied design to divide the interests of the public creditors," to make their welfare contingent on the state's welfare instead of the nation's.[135]

The program met with opposition only in the City, and it was opposed there not primarily by creditors who feared the money would depreciate—the Pennsylvania paper issue was circulating at or near par, and the South Carolina issue and that of New York were to do likewise—but rather by two special groups for two special reasons.[136] In the first place, its anti-

[135] Reports of the operations of the act may be seen in the Report of the Committee on the Treasury to the House of Assembly, January 16, 1788, published in the *New York Journal* of January 31, 1788. A brilliant analysis of the implications of the paper-funding-assumption act is the contribution of "Gustavus," in the *New York Packet* of April 13, 1786. I have been unable to ascertain who "Gustavus" was; judging from the style and the reasoning, I should guess either Hamilton or Schuyler.

[136] Attempts were made to defeat the measure through appeals to numerous motives, one of which was of course the creditor's fear of depreciation. To charge that persons who advocate a particular piece of legislation are tainted with fraudulent motives is a technique as old as the art of politics. The most powerful piece against paper was Thomas Paine's "Dissertation on Government; the Affairs of the Bank; and Paper Money," which was printed both as a newspaper article and as a pamphlet. Paine was employed by Robert Morris to write this article during the campaign to defeat Pennsylvania's paper-funding-assumption act, and it was reprinted and circulated in great quantity wherever a proposed issue of paper threatened to dissolve the continental debt as a bond of union.

Union implications ran counter to the hopes of the advocates of a stronger union, the great majority of whom were in the City. Secondly, the funding-assumption program affected adversely the interests of speculators in confiscated estates. Purchasers of such property had contracted to buy in the expectation that they would be able to pay their obligations in depreciated public securities. The sudden appreciation of security prices as a result of the funding scheme caught many "bears" in a "bull" market, forcing them to pay from thirty to fifty per cent more for their purchases than they had counted on paying. A little panic of 1786 ensued, causing commodity price gyrations and no small number of bankruptcies—an exact precursor of the larger panic of 1792.[137]

Except for the side effects of the appreciation of securities, however, the program was a complete success. The state government was able to meet its obligations until the United States Loan of 1790 was enacted, and thereafter it literally had more money, in the form of income from the securities it owned, than it knew what to do with. As the state retired its own obligations with the receipts from the sale of confiscated property and public lands and from its impost, more and more of the continental securities "loaned" to the state in 1786 came into its outright ownership. In March, 1790, the state returned the continental securities still outstanding to the original owners, yet

[137] The appreciation of securities, as indicated by quotations in the various New York newspapers, began about three months before the passage of the funding act, in anticipation of the effects of the act. Of the speculators whom Yoshpe lists in his appendixes as operating in confiscated property on an extensive scale, several, including Isaac Gouverneur, John Lawrence, Cornelius Ray, and others, filed bankruptcy petitions in 1786–1787. Their petitions are among those included in the *Votes and Proceedings of the Assembly* for 1786–87. Indications are that timely loans from the Bank of New York saved many more speculators—for example, Comfort and Joshua Sands. See Yoshpe, *op. cit.*, 156. Many historians—for example, Spaulding in his *New York in the Critical Period*—have mistakenly assumed that the bankruptcies and the complaints of the scarcity of money in 1786 and 1787 were manifestations of a commercial depression. Instead, what commercial depression there was resulted from the bankruptcies. When merchants selling securities short for confiscated estates were obliged, because of the appreciation, to dump large quantities of imported goods on the market in order to raise cash quickly, bad effects were felt throughout the commercial community.

Gerard Bancker, as treasurer of the state, was able to fund continental securities amounting to $1,424,041.71 under the Loan of
1790.[138]

The state was equally successful in other respects. Despite
the setbacks caused by the panic of 1786, commercial recovery
was rapid. By 1788 New York City, which at the end of the
occupation in 1783 had been a broken port virtually without
a vessel, was importing and exporting at least three times as
much as it had in its best prewar years, and two-thirds of its
trade was carried in New York bottoms. Despite the outbreak
of Shays' Rebellion in neighboring Massachusetts, no disorders
occurred in New York. Despite the ravages of the Hessian fly,
wheat production on New York farms was greater than it had
ever been, and prices were at far higher levels than before the
war. The Clintonian legislative and administrative program included something for virtually everyone; almost every economic interest and social group was the beneficiary of special
legislation. In short, New York's experiment in independence
was eminently successful. The state had little reason to adopt
any plan for a general government, for it was prosperous and
contented with the government it had.[139]

[138] Records of the Loan of 1790, vol. 548 (Subscription Register of the
Funded Debt), folios 74 to 118, 124 to 126, 134 to 148, and vol. 549, folios 1
to 32, 32 to 78, 81, and 73(2). The state used this surplus in the 1790's to issue
another £200,000 on loan to its citizens on exactly the same terms as the
paper issue of 1786; it exchanged interest-bearing six per cent stock to holders
of deferred six per cent stock in the state; it subscribed to 190 shares of the
newly formed Bank of the United States and to 100 shares of the Bank of
New York; and it levied no direct taxes for a decade. Philip Schuyler, writing
in the *Albany Gazette*, attempted to win support for ratification by pointing
out to the voters that the state would profit handsomely from the funding
and assumption of the debts by the United States; see a reprint of one of these
pieces in the Poughkeepsie *Country Journal* of March 10, 1789. Similar articles
appeared in newspapers of the City; for example, see the *Daily Advertiser*,
February 2 and and 5, 1788. The thesis Cochran presents in his *New York in
the Confederation*, that New Yorkers opposed ratification because the surrender of the impost to a new general government would subject landholders
to a heavy burden of direct taxation by the state, would seem to wither in
the face of these facts. Ratification of the Constitution did not mean an increase of direct taxes, it meant their abolition.

[139] Documents on New York's trade during the period are scarce. I have
tabulated entrances and clearances of vessels from the incomplete returns in
the *New York Journal* and the *Daily Advertiser;* these tabulations show a

The opposition to Clinton consisted of three major groups and an assortment of minor ones, the combined totals of which embraced only a small fraction of the population. One of the major opposition groups was a faction of the aristocracy that had opposed Clinton from the outset. The principal chieftain of these malcontents was Philip Schuyler, whom Clinton had defeated for the governorship in 1777. Schuyler, an otherwise brilliant man, had an almost irrational hatred of Clinton thereafter, and until the day he died he never ceased plotting to subvert his enemy. A man of great influence in the aristocracy, he worked constantly to unify it against Clinton. He never quite succeeded; the powerful Livingston and Van Cortlandt families were split, some supporting and some opposing the governor, and many of the families lower in the aristocracy were Clintonians. But Schuyler was able to weld together a powerful, albeit numerically small, coalition against Clinton.[140]

Immediately related to the group gathered around Schuyler for personal reasons was the second major group in the opposition. This was a nationalistic group headed by Schuyler's son-in-law, Alexander Hamilton. By virtue of his marital connection, his persuasive manner, and his financial genius, Hamilton was able to ingratiate himself with various powerful New York merchants and bankers and to unify them in support of his national-

fairly uniform progress toward the great peak reached by 1788. The Newburyport *Essex Journal and New Hampshire Packet* of February 11, 1789, carries a list of the numbers of vessels of the various kinds of riggings which entered New York in 1788. If it is valid to estimate the tonnage of these vessels on the basis of average sizes of vessels of various riggings entering at Philadelphia, a total of about 75,000 tons entered the port during the year. Madison, quoted in Jensen's *The New Nation*, page 215, estimated the total at 85,000 tons, 55,000 tons of which was owned in New York. The average for 1770–1772 was 26,000 tons. *Ibid.* Ship notices and announcements of cargoes in the *London Daily Universal Register* (microfilm file in the University of Pennsylvania Library) indicates that trade with England in 1785 and 1786, a period usually assumed to have been one of depression in New York City (for example, see Spaulding, *New York in the Critical Period*, 22), was at a uniformly high level.

[140] The description of Schuyler's attitude and his activities is based on a study of the Philip Schuyler Papers, Box 38, in the New York Public Library, and of his correspondence in Johnston, ed., *Correspondence of Jay*, particularly volume 3. Some of Schuyler's activities against Clinton are traced in the two works by Spaulding.

ism. Employing his advantages artfully, he managed to split the mercantile clique which had headed the Sons of Liberty. He found ready support among the merchants who were hostile to the Clinton administration because of losses they had suffered as a result of the funding-paper act of 1786. Another group easily brought into the fold were the merchants who owed money to Loyalists, money they had hoped to avoid paying until the Clintonians decreed that such Loyalist credits were the property of the state and that Loyalist debts were obligations of the state. Many merchants and speculators, including John Lamb, Marinus Willett, Melancton Smith, Henry Wyckoff, and the Sands brothers, remained loyal to Clinton. More, however, like Isaac Roosevelt, the Beekmans, the Jays, the Alsops, and the Lows, either drifted into the nationalist camp or were persuaded to come into it by Schuyler or Hamilton.[141]

A third major element that opposed Clinton was the lesser citizenry of the City, parts of Long Island, and Westchester County. Many of these lesser folk had sided with the Tories during the war, from necessity as well as from inclination. As many more were Whigs who had been trapped behind the lines in 1777 and had no choice but to remain there during the occupation. Tories, Tory-sympathizers, and victims of circumstance were all treated alike in the wave of persecution of Loyalists which Clinton headed after the peace, and few of them were ever inclined to forget or to forgive him. Still another group among the lower ranks in and around the City were the former tenants of Loyalists. The former tenants of James De-Lancey, one of the richest of the Tory landlords, were in a particularly unfortunate situation. The leases of many of them had expired during the war, and in 1780 DeLancey had sold most of his holdings to them. After the war the state had refused to recognize these purchases and the hapless tenants had

---

[141] The occupations of the leading Clintonians and anti-Clintonians in the City have been studied principally through newspaper advertisements. Their operations in securities have been studied in the fiscal records in the National Archives, and their speculations in confiscated property in the appendix tables of Yoshpe's *Loyalist Estates*.

been forced either to purchase their property a second time or suffer ejection. Other tenants, scarcely more fortunate, were ejected or forced to pay high prices for the properties they occupied when speculators operating on a large scale purchased the confiscated property from the state.[142]

Hamilton, Schuyler, and their aristocratic and mercantile allies exploited the hostility of these lower classes toward Clinton, and with their backing organized the only important opposition to Clinton's powerful faction. Only in the City and in Westchester, Richmond (Staten Island), and Kings counties did the anti-Clinton coalition achieve any consistent success, though Albany, Schuyler's home county, occasionally sent anti-Clintonians to the legislature. Every other county in the state supported Clinton, his measures, and his legislative candidates with majorities ranging from substantial to overwhelming.[143]

The vote for delegates to the ratifying convention was cast along precisely the lines indicated above. That is, the City and the counties of Kings, Richmond, and Westchester sent Federalist delegates, and every other county anti-Federalist delegates. The majority asked, with Clinton, why should New York throw its great advantages into a common pot? The opposition to the Constitution was based almost entirely upon New Yorkers' faith in Clinton and his concept of the Empire State.

There were, however, other elements in the City's vote for ratification. Most, though not all, of the mechanics who had supported Clinton in the 1786 elections voted for ratification. One factor was the campaign appeals of the Federalists to this

[142] On the problems of the Tories see Alexander C. Flick, *Loyalism in New York during the American Revolution* (New York, 1901). The plight of the ex-tenants is excellently treated in Yoshpe's *Loyalist Estates*, 32–37, 56–58.

[143] Spaulding's *New York in the Critical Period*, pages 121–130, contains an account of the manner in which Hamilton and his allies exploited the hatred of the persecuted groups for Clinton. Spaulding's accounts of political alignments, however, are not always accurate. The most reliable way to trace alignments is to analyze votes cast in the legislature. I have tabulated all votes cast from 1776 to 1789 in both houses of the legislature on all issues, for the purpose of determining on what percentage of the issues each member voted with each other member. All generalizations made here with respect to factional alignments are based largely on these tabulations.

element. Another was the possibility that under the general government protective tariffs and other legislation designed to promote manufactures would be enacted which would expand the "protected" market for local manufactures from the existing three states to thirteen. This possibility had no appeal to the service industries and the manufacturers who needed no protection, but large numbers of those groups were already hostile to Clinton for the reasons mentioned earlier. Another factor in the vote was the fact that New York City was, for obvious reasons, sensitive about its military vulnerability. Still another was the City's fear that it would be hazardous to remain outside the Union once a general government for the other states had been framed. The Federalists argued, with telling effect, that discriminatory legislation would be urged by New Jersey and Connecticut congressmen anxious to retaliate against New York for the duties which their states had been forced to pay into New York's treasury during the 1780's.

In the showdown over ratification neither party to the conflict had a monopoly on economic interests of any kind. Probably a majority of the five thousand small security holders who had benefitted from the funding-assumption plan of 1786 followed Clinton in opposing the Constitution. Probably a majority of the merchants in the City favored ratification and certainly the great majority of the lower classes in the City did so. The ranks of both parties, however, included approximately equal numbers of large and small landholders and speculators in various forms of property.

While information on the property holdings of individual delegates to the ratifying convention in New York is relatively scant, the available data would seem to confirm these generalizations. Because of the unusually large number of vote changes in the New York convention, the delegates have been divided, in the following summaries of their economic interests, into four groups: 1) those elected as Federalists; 2) those elected as anti-Federalists who voted for ratification; 3) those elected as anti-Federalists who abstained from voting; and 4) those elected as anti-Federalists who voted against ratification.

ECONOMIC INTERESTS OF DELEGATES ELECTED AS FEDERALISTS

James Duane (New York) was a lawyer, landlord with a 40,000-acre estate, and mayor of the City. He was a Federalist despite the fact that he had received substantial benefits from the Clintonians. He was regularly appointed mayor and was enabled to collect a total of £1,613 7s. 1½d. ($4,033.38) from the state for debts owed him by former Loyalists because of the Clintonian policy of assuming the debts as well as the assets of the Loyalists. Duane held $288.67 in continental securities.[144]

Alexander Hamilton (New York) was a lawyer. His interests are outlined on pages 48–49, above.

Richard Harrison (New York) was an ex-Tory lawyer. He owned one share in the Bank of New York (par $250) and was a substantial holder of state securities ($2,452) and the holder of a modest amount of continental securities ($91). He had suffered from the policy that had benefitted Duane, for he owed £1,300 in prewar debts due to Loyalists, and he was required to pay principal and accrued interest amounting to £2,486 5s. 6d. ($6,215.65) to the state.[145]

Richard Hatfield (Westchester) was clerk of Westchester County, a lawyer, and owner of a large confiscated farm which he had purchased for £1,050 ($2,625).[146]

John Sloss Hobart (New York) was associate justice of the New York Supreme Court, though he never completed his legal training. He had purchased sixteen confiscated town lots for £672 ($1,680). Like Harrison, he was a debtor to Loyalists and was required to make payments of £1,800 15s. 5d. ($4,502.91) for an old bond of £1,600 and accrued interest.[147]

[144] Sarah H. J. Simpson's sketch of James Duane in the *Dictionary of American Biography;* Spaulding, *New York in the Critical Period,* 244; Yoshpe, *Loyalist Estates,* 166–176; Records of the Loan of 1790, vol. 545, certificate 2551, in the National Archives. Volumes of the Records of the Loan of 1790 consulted for New York security holdings include the following: vols. 22, 25, and 551 (Ledgers of Assumed 6% Stock, 1791–97); vol. 32 (Ledger, New York Assumed Debt); vols. 548 and 549 (Subscription Registers of Funded Debt); vol. 545 (Register of Certificates Issued for Debts due by the United States, 1784–87). When only six per cent volumes are referred to here, the total amount is to be found in three volumes and the amount stated here is derived from a calculation: six per cents were four-ninths of the total amount issued in original funding operations.

Beard (*Economic Interpretation,* 270) mistakenly lists Duane as among the holders of six per cent stock, and he cites the six per cent ledgers. The reference is to vol. 551, folio 153, which entry records an acquisition of securities by Duane in 1791, three years after the ratifying convention.

[145] Records of the Loan of 1790, vol. 22, folio 82; vol. 548, folio 63; Spaulding, *New York in the Critical Period,* 246; Domett, *Bank of New York,* 133; Yoshpe, *Loyalist Estates,* 179.

[146] Yoshpe, *Loyalist Estates,* 60, 87–88, 148.

[147] *Ibid.,* 32, 126, 181; Charles E. Fitch, *Encyclopedia of Biography of New York* (2 vols., New York, 1916), 1:328.

John Jay (New York) was a lawyer, diplomat, and member of a family of merchants. He owned $17,195.48 in state securities, though he engaged in none of the speculations of the decade. He was also a substantial private creditor and a large landowner.[148]

Philip Livingston (Westchester), a landlord and speculator, owned $7,754 in state securities and had purchased forty-eight confiscated city lots and 268 acres of farmland for a total of £5,080 ($12,700). The operations of the confiscation laws required him to pay £268 8s. 3d. ($671) to the state for an old debt of £200 and interest.[149]

Robert R. Livingston (New York), a landlord and lawyer, was "one of the rich men of the state." While secretary for foreign affairs he was able to spend $3,000 a year beyond his salary. His estate was the Livingston Lower Manor, Clermont, and he also owned a town house and had commercial connections. His security holdings were nominal: $144 in continentals.[150]

Nicholas Low (New York), a merchant, was a director of the Bank of New York and owner of eight shares of bank stock ($2,000 par). He was one of the most active speculators in the City. His purchases of confiscated property totaled $8,250 and after the convention he began acquiring vast quantities of securities. His first funding operation under the Loan of 1790 totaled $38,729, and several of his later fundings ran as high as $20,000.[151]

Lewis Morris (Westchester) was owner of the large estate Morrisania Manor, which had been razed—the land devastated and the house burned— during the war. Morris purchased two parcels of confiscated Loyalist property in Westchester County for a total of £1,524 ($3,810).[152] He owned no public securities.

Isaac Roosevelt (New York), merchant, bank president, owner of a sugar refinery, and speculator, owned five bank shares (par $1,250) and $563 in continental securities of an issue not assumed by the act of 1786, and had purchased confiscated lots in New York City for £4,852 ($12,190). He was also a debtor to Loyalists, having been required to pay £1,406 17s. 6d. ($3,517.18) to the state for an old debt of £900 and interest.[153]

[148] Records of the Loan of 1790, vol. 22, folio 24; vol. 32, folio 158; Johnston, ed., *Correspondence of Jay*, vol. 3.

[149] Records of the Loan of 1790, vol. 22, folio 22; Yoshpe, *Loyalist Estates*, 58, 127, 143, 184.

[150] Records of the Loan of 1790, vol. 545, certificate 608; Spaulding, *New York in the Critical Period*, 245.

[151] Records of the Loan of 1790, vol. 22, folio 72; Domett, *Bank of New York*, 132; Yoshpe, *Loyalist Estates*, 133.

[152] Spaulding, *New York in the Critical Period*, 66; Yoshpe, *Loyalist Estates*, 144.

[153] Records of the Loan of 1790, vol. 545, certificate 6717; Domett, *Bank of New York*, 132; Yoshpe, *Loyalist Estates*, 129, 131, 179.

Gozen Ryerss (Richmond), a merchant, was a member of the firm of Ryerss & Riley, interstate traders. The firm owned a small sloop and 1½ bank shares (par $375).[154]

Philip Van Cortlandt (Westchester), a civil engineer, was the son of anti-Federalist Lieutenant Governor Pierre Van Cortlandt. Young Van Cortlandt loaned considerable sums against mortgages to tenants on Philipse Manor, a "lucrative field" for surplus capital. He owned $1,729 in continental securities that were not assumed under the act of 1786, and he was required to pay the state for an old debt of £92 11s. 10d. ($231.45) due a Tory merchant.[155]

Peter Vandervoort (Kings) was a merchant "of moderate means." [156]

Four delegates, Abraham Bancker (Richmond), Thaddeus Crane (Westchester), Peter Lefferts (Kings), and Lott W. Sarles (Westchester) apparently were all farmers and landowners. Lefferts was of a Loyalist family and was the holder of $512 in continental securities. Bancker was a member of the family of Gerard Bancker, the anti-Federalist state treasurer.[157]

It is to be observed that at least eight of the Federalists had investments or obligations that were either damaged by Clintonian policy (confiscated estate speculations, debts due Loyalists) or by-passed in the assumption act of 1786 (certain forms of continental debt). This factor should not be overrated, however, for as was indicated earlier a number of Clintonians in the City also had just such property.[158]

---

[154] Domett, *Bank of New York*, 134. Ryerss' name appears occasionally in the Philadelphia Customs House Papers in the Historical Society of Pennsylvania as the owner of a small sloop. Beard (*Economic Interpretation*, 270) erroneously lists Ryerss as a security holder at the time of the convention. He cites "N.Y. 3%'s." The reference could be either to vol. 28, folio 75, of the Records of the Loan of 1790, which records the acquisition of securities by Ryerss in 1793, or to vol. 31, folio 463, which records acquisitions in January, May, and June of 1793.

[155] Records of the Loan of 1790, vol. 545, certificates 6783–6784; Spaulding, *New York in the Critical Period*, 246–247; Yoshpe, *Loyalist Estates*, 56, 182. Beard erroneously lists Van Cortlandt as owning funded six per cents. *Economic Interpretation*, 270. Beard's reference is to vol. 22, folio 299, which records Van Cortlandt's acquisition of $176 in securities from his father in August, 1792. The delegate Van Cortlandt disposed of his securities before the Loan of 1790 went into operation, and he never funded any securities under that act.

[156] Spaulding, *New York in the Critical Period*, 247.

[157] *Ibid.*, 247; Records of the Loan of 1790, vol. 545, certificate 7194; miscellaneous biographical data scattered through John T. Scharf's *History of Westchester County, New York* (2 vols., Philadelphia, 1886).

[158] It is possible that the Clintonian speculators in the City had advance information as to which securities would be funded in 1786, and were thus able to avoid losses. Indeed, it is quite possible that several of them made substantial speculative profits.

ECONOMIC INTERESTS OF DELEGATES ELECTED AS ANTI-FEDERALISTS
WHO VOTED FOR RATIFICATION

John DeWitt (Dutchess) was a farmer and landowner, proprietor of a grist mill, and owner of a small amount of securities.[159]

Samuel Jones (Queens), an ex-Tory lawyer, was owner of a landed estate on Long Island and holder of $976 in continental and $1,978 in state securities.[160]

Gilbert Livingston (Dutchess), lawyer and politician, was a brother-in-law of Clinton, having, like Clinton, married a Tappen.[161]

Zephaniah Platt (Dutchess), a Poughkeepsie lawyer, was a speculator in confiscated estates and vacant lands. With others he purchased 11,250 acres and with the help of various other Clintonians built the city of Plattsburg. By 1788 the partners had built grist mills and sawmills and were later to erect forges and furnaces. Platt owned $284 in continental securities.[162]

Henry Scudder (Suffolk) was a farmer and "small landowner." [163]

John Smith (Suffolk), a farmer, was a member of "a prominent family that was well endowed with Suffolk lands." He was one of the many speculators in the Clintonian ranks, having purchased £657 5s. ($1,518.12) worth of confiscated property in Westchester and possibly more upstate. He owned $1,461.67 in continental securities.[164]

Melancton Smith (Dutchess), merchant and lawyer of New York City, was a speculator in confiscated property and western lands. His purchases of forfeited estates amounted to £1,470 in the City and to £1,200 in other places (total $6,675). With Clintonian Marinus Willett he acquired 6,000 acres on the Chenango River, and he bought 1,120 acres

[159] Frank Hasbrouck, *The History of Dutchess County, New York* (Poughkeepsie, 1909), 273. The exact amount of DeWitt's security holdings cannot be ascertained. Three John DeWitts are listed in the Records of the Loan of 1790: "John A." (vol. 545, certificate 863), for $15; "John L." (vol. 545, certificate 1227), for $58; and "John" (vol. 545, certificates 4524–4525), for $220. All were from Dutchess County.

[160] Records of the Loan of 1790, vol. 22, folio 216; vol. 548, folio 71; vol. 551, folio 313; Spaulding, *New York in the Critical Period*, 73, 236.

[161] Spaulding, *New York in the Critical Period*, 235.

[162] *Ibid.*, 236; Dwight H. Hurd, *History of Clinton and Franklin Counties, New York* (Philadelphia, 1880), 149 and note; Records of the Loan of 1790, vol. 545, certificate 5399.

[163] Spaulding, *New York in the Critical Period*, 240.

[164] *Ibid.*, 240; Records of the Loan of 1790, vol. 545, certificate 7004; Yoshpe, *Loyalist Estates*, 145. Beard (*Economic Interpretation*, 270) erroneously lists Smith as the owner of six per cent stock, citing "N.Y. 6%'s" (vol. 22, folio 164). This account shows that Smith first acquired such stock in 1799. He did not fund any securities under the Loan of 1790.

in the Plattsburg venture. He owned $1,537 in state securities and $969 in continentals.[165]

Jesse Woodhull (Orange), landlord, speculator, and capitalist, creditor of a Loyalist, for which he received £529 5s. from the state, was owner of $4,887 in continental and $14,960 in state securities.[166]

The occupations and interests of Stephen Carman (Queens), Jonathan N. Havens (Suffolk), Nathaniel Lawrence (Queens), and John Schenck (Queens) cannot be precisely defined. They were probably all farmers and substantial landowners. Carman and Schenck were ex-Tories. Havens had been educated at Yale and was a devout Presbyterian, perhaps even a minister.[167]

ECONOMIC INTERESTS OF DELEGATES ELECTED AS ANTI-FEDERALISTS WHO DID NOT VOTE

Governor George Clinton was a lawyer, capitalist, land speculator, and money-lender. Clinton's favorite forms of investment were mortgages, direct loans, and land speculations. He had advanced about £5,000 from his own funds to help finance various needs of the armies, and upon being repaid these sums at the end of the war had re-invested them in lands. He owned rental property in the City and lands in almost every county. On a single occasion he purchased large quantities of land in twelve townships, and he made numerous purchases elsewhere. He helped his speculator friend Alexander Macomb acquire 3,600,000 acres of state-owned lands for only 8d. an acre. He owned grist mills and sawmills and investments in various businesses. With Washington he purchased 6,071 acres and to enable Washington to pay for that and purchases of Virginia lands he advanced Washington £4,500 (at 7 per cent), a sum which Washington was not able to repay until 1786. Clinton also made numerous loans to Westchester farmers. In 1788 his personalty, exclusive of lands held for speculation, amounted to about £20,000. His security holdings, though substantial, were modest as compared with his land ventures. He owned $1,288 in continental and $2,431 in state securities.[168]

[165] Records of the Loan of 1790, vol. 22, folio 218; vol. 545, certificates 5559 and 5579; Spaulding, *New York in the Critical Period*, 234–235; Hurd, *Clinton and Franklin Counties*, 149n; Yoshpe, *Loyalist Estates*, 132, 137. Beard (*Economic Interpretation*, 270) erroneously states that Smith funded $10,000 in Connecticut securities. The Connecticut account, vol. 495, folio 125, shows that Smith acquired these securities in 1792.

[166] Records of the Loan of 1790, vol. 545, certificates 4852–4855; vol. 551, folio 125; Yoshpe, *Loyalist Estates*, 169.

[167] Spaulding, *New York in the Critical Period*, 236, 240.

[168] Records of the Loan of 1790, vol. 22, folio 12; vol. 545, certificates 6521 and 7112; vol. 549, folio 98(2); Spaulding, *His Excellency George Clinton*, 115–116, 229–236; Yoshpe, *Loyalist Estates*, 56. Clinton may have held much more in securities, for his name appears often in the Card Index to Ledger

Anthony Ten Eyck (Albany), a lawyer and merchant, owned $1,210 in continental and $1,815 in state securities.[169]

Ezra Thompson (Dutchess), a capitalist, had invested in and developed a lead mine, purchased with another man a township of 25,000 acres, and probably was speculating in confiscated estates.[170]

Peter Vrooman (Albany), a lawyer with mercantile connections, was the owner of a nominal amount of securities, $143 in continentals.[171]

Christopher P. Yates (Montgomery), lawyer and landlord, owned $261 in state securities.[172]

The occupations and holdings of two delegates, David Hedges (Suffolk) and Dirck Swart (Albany), were not ascertained.

Economic Interests of Delegates Elected as Anti-Federalists Who Voted against Ratification

Matthew Adgate (Columbia), lawyer and speculator, owned $291 in state securities.[173]

John Bay (Columbia), lawyer, owned $268 in continental securities.[174]

James Clinton (Ulster), farmer and landlord, and speculator in lands with his brother the governor, purchased £3,112 in confiscated property and owned $6,895 in continental and state securities.[175]

Entries, in the Fiscal Section of the National Archives, with references to funding operations with the Treasury Department. These records are unreliable, however, for the first volumes in the series, covering original funding operations, are no longer extant.

[169] Records of the Loan of 1790, vol. 548, folio 36; vol. 551, folio 197; Spaulding, *New York in the Critical Period*, 238.

[170] Hasbrouck, *History of Dutchess County*, 379; Spaulding, *New York in the Critical Period*, 236.

[171] *Ibid.*, 238; Records of the Loan of 1790, vol. 545, certificates 1926 and 2114.

[172] Spaulding, *New York in the Critical Period*, 149; Records of the Loan of 1790, vol. 551, folio 133. Beard (*Economic Interpretation*, 149) describes Yates as a "large operator" in securities.

[173] *History of Columbia County, New York* (Philadelphia, 1878), 77, 321; Records of the Loan of 1790, vol. 22, folio 224.

[174] *History of Columbia County*, 112; Records of the Loan of 1790, vol. 545, certificate 3210.

[175] *Ibid.*, vol. 22, folio 354; vol. 545, certificates 6114, 6115, 7278; vol. 549, folio 88; vol. 551, folio 215; Spaulding, *New York in the Critical Period*, 233; Spaulding, *George Clinton*, 234; Yoshpe, *Loyalist Estates*, 150n. That Clinton purchased confiscated property is not certain; Yoshpe says that he "located" on the property but that the bill of sale was made to another man. My own cursory examination of the records of the sales of confiscated estates (in the New York Historical Society) reveals that speculators often bought in the names of others property they occupied themselves.

John Frey (Montgomery), lawyer, was a member of a wealthy landed family.[176]

John Haring (Orange), lawyer, owed £427 12s. 3d. in prewar debts to a Tory and was required to pay £527 0s. 10d. to the state for principal and interest on this obligation.[177]

Henry Oothoudt (Albany), a landholder and speculator in lands and a relative of a City merchant, owned $72 in continental securities.[178]

Cornelius Schoonmaker (Ulster), surveyor, farmer, landowner, and speculator, owned $315 in continental securities.[179]

Henry Staring (Montgomery), judge of Herkimer County Court, was owner of a mill and proprietor of "large landed estates." Schuyler, in denouncing the appointment of Staring as a judge by the Clintonians, asserted that he could neither read nor write. However that may be, he was able to accumulate property.[180]

Jacobus Swartwout (Dutchess), landowner and speculator, acquired at least three separate parcels of confiscated property in Dutchess and Orange counties, and probably more elsewhere. He owned 200 acres in the Plattsburg venture with Smith and Platt, and he bought up $7,372 in state securities and $283 in continentals.[181]

Thomas Tredwell (Suffolk), a "distinguished Suffolk lawyer," was owner of 1,120 acres in the Plattsburg venture and probably of land elsewhere, and $209 in continental securities. He had owed an old debt to a Loyalist and was required to pay £260 18s. 3d. ($652.27) to the state for its retirement.[182]

Peter Van Ness (Columbia), judge, lawyer, and landowner, was "a man of means." In 1788 he purchased from the state three parcels of land totaling 86,500 acres, for which he paid £10,782. He also bought

[176] Washington Frothingham, ed., *History of Montgomery County* (Syracuse, 1892), 156, 319.

[177] *Biographical Directory of Congress* (1927 edition), 1061; Yoshpe, *Loyalist Estates*, 182.

[178] Records of the Loan of 1790, vol. 545, certificate 3314; Spaulding, *New York in the Critical Period*, 238; *New York Packet*, August 21, 1786.

[179] Records of the Loan of 1790, vol. 545, certificates 815, 1508, 6093; Spaulding, *New York in the Critical Period*, 233; *Biographical Directory of Congress*, (1927 edition), 1499.

[180] Frank H. Willard and George A. Hardin, eds., *History of Herkimer County, New York* (Syracuse, 1893), 83, 351; Philip Schuyler Papers, Box 38, in the New York Public Library.

[181] Records of the Loan of 1790, vol. 22, folio 121; vol. 545, certificates 4420–4421; vol. 551, folios 125, 131; Spaulding, *New York in the Critical Period*, 235n; Hurd, *Clinton and Franklin Counties*, 149; *Votes and Proceedings of the Assembly*, 11th Session, 1st Meeting, March 7, 1788, p. 118.

[182] Records of the Loan of 1790, vol. 545, certificate 6869; Spaulding, *New York in the Critical Period*, 240; Hurd, *Clinton and Franklin Counties*, 139; Yoshpe, *Loyalist Estates*, 182.

confiscated lots in New York City for £260 and probably confiscated estates elsewhere. He owned $2,010 in continental securities.[183]

Volkert Veeder (Montgomery), a landowner who has been described as "the possessor of comparatively little property," owned $746 in continental securities.[184]

John Williams (Washington and Clinton), physician and "lord of vast estates" with many tenants, is said to have been the largest landholder among the Clintonians, which would place his acreage well into six figures. Williams invested in many ventures and was one of the early promoters of a privately financed Erie Canal. His security holdings, $1,399 in state securities, were an insignificant part of his wealth.[185]

Henry Wisner (Orange), capitalist and manufacturer, was owner of grist and powder mills near Goshen, in which he had manufactured powder for the Continental Army. He owned $3,169 in continental securities.[186]

John Wood (Orange), lawyer and landowner, owned $77 in continental and $235 in state securities.[187]

Dirck Wyncoop (Ulster), a landlord and "man of parts and property," had invested in confiscated property (at least £120) and was the owner of $35 in continental securities.[188]

Robert Yates (Albany) was a lawyer and judge; his interests are sketched on pages 49–50.

The occupations and investments of nine men were not ascertained: Jonathan Akins (Dutchess), Albert Baker (Washington and Clinton), Ebenezer Clark (Ulster), William Harper (Montgomery), David Hopkins (Washington and Clinton), Israel Thompson (Albany), John Cantine (Ulster), Ichabod Parker (Washington and Clinton), and John Winn (Montgomery). Most of them were probably country lawyers, farmers, and landowners. Three were holders of continental securities: Cantine ($32), Parker ($114), and Winn ($255).[189]

It is regrettable that no more information is available about the property holdings of the delegates, particularly vacant lands

[183] Records of the Loan of 1790, vol. 545, certificate 3867; Spaulding, *New York in the Critical Period*, 239; Yoshpe, *Loyalist Estates*, 130.

[184] Records of the Loan of 1790, vol. 545, certificates 2597, 3014, 3916; Spaulding, *New York in the Critical Period*, 241.

[185] *Ibid.*, 73, 239; Records of the Loan of 1790, vol. 22, folio 13; vol. 25, folio 239; *Biographical Directory of Congress* (1927 edition), 1705.

[186] Records of the Loan of 1790, vol. 545, certificates 98–102, 472, 473, 492–499, 503, 512, 514; Spaulding, *New York in the Critical Period*, 234.

[187] Records of the Loan of 1790, vol. 22, folio 208; vol. 545, certificates 556, 5358.

[188] *Ibid.*, vol. 545, certificate 855; Spaulding, *New York in the Critical Period*, 233n; Spaulding, *George Clinton*, 31.

[189] Records of the Loan of 1790, vol. 545, certificates 275, 1339, 1510, 3169, 7087.

and confiscated property purchased from the state.[190] The data presented here on purchasers of confiscated property include only purchases in the Southern District, and most of the Clintonian delegates came from other parts of the state. Even so, more of the anti-Federalists than of the Federalists elected—seven to six—had purchased such property around the City, though the amounts bought by the Federalist delegates were generally larger. Were data available on upstate purchases, perhaps considerably larger numbers of Clintonians would appear as purchasers.

Nonetheless a few general remarks may be made in summary. When the convention opened there were twenty-six delegates among the anti-Federalists who held securities and only nine among those who favored ratification. After various delegates changed sides, six of the security holders among the Clintonians voted for ratification, and three of them abstained from voting. But of those who voted against ratification on the final ballot, seventeen (63 per cent) owned securities, and of those who voted for ratification only fifteen (50 per cent) were security holders.[191] The great landlords in the convention were divided about equally, but the supporters of ratification slightly exceeded the opponents. As indicated earlier, Philip Schuyler had never rested in his efforts to persuade the aristocracy to oppose

[190] It will be observed from the footnotes here that data on several of the delegates were derived from Spaulding's *New York in the Critical Period.* Spaulding's handling of data which I have been able to check reflects either careless work or a disposition, conscious or unconscious, to depict a great split between the two groups along property lines. For example, he accepted Beard's quotations of security holdings, errors included, without checking them, and he did not attempt to discover whether Clintonians were security holders. His use of such terms as "large" and "modest" to describe property holdings is quite misleading. For example, the terms "small" and "modest" are used to describe the purchases of confiscated property made by John Lamb and Marinus Willett, Clintonians in New York City, when in actual fact their purchases of £4,281 and £3,097, respectively, made them among the largest speculators in the City. See Yoshpe, *Loyalist Estates,* appendixes.

[191] There were more large holders among the Clintonians as well as more small holders, but the Federalists Low and Jay held considerably more than any Clintonians. On this matter one may recall Beard (page 272n) on securities as the dynamic element in the ratification: "The point, it may be repeated, is not the amount but the practical information derived from holding even one certificate of the nominal value of $10."

Clinton, and his efforts carried weight; but the great Livingston and Van Cortlandt families were divided, and a number of the lesser members of the aristocracy, hardly poor men themselves, were unequivocal supporters of Clinton and opponents of the Constitution.

According to Professor Beard's interpretive system the conflict in New York was a simple one between security holders (Federalists) and advocates of paper money (anti-Federalists). Such a proposition is self-contradictory, for in New York the term "paper-money advocates" was almost synonymous with the term "security holders." The assertion that security holders were the dynamic element in the ratification in New York is clearly incompatible with the facts. In the absence of further data it would appear that the two parties to the conflict included approximately equal numbers of men of wealth in the form of personalty, that the Federalists were supported by most of the artisans, mechanics, and small farmers in and around the City, and that the Clintonians were supported by most of the smaller upstate farmers.

NORTH CAROLINA

NORTH CAROLINA was the first state to reject the Constitution. Eleven states had already ratified when North Carolina's convention met late in July, 1788, but the state's anti-Federalists were undaunted. They were in a clear majority and apparently they had more courage than their New York counterparts, for they voted against ratification by a thumping 184 to 84 margin. Not until more than a year later, when the general government under the Constitution had been in operation for eight months, did a new convention meet in the state. This time North Carolina ratified by a convention vote of 194 delegates to 77.[192]

[192] Ratification in North Carolina has been the subject of a great deal of historical writing, including Louise Irby Trenholme's *The Ratification of the Federal Constitution in North Carolina* (New York, 1932); A. R. Newsome's "North Carolina's Ratification of the Federal Constitution," in the *North Carolina Historical Review*, 17:287–301 (1940); William C. Pool's "An Economic Interpretation of the Ratification of the Federal Constitution in North Carolina," in the *North Carolina Historical Review*, 27:119–141, 289–313, 437–461 (1950); and parts of numerous other works.

The legislature had been in session two days when, on November 21, 1787, two months after the Philadelphia Convention had adjourned, Governor Richard Caswell presented the Constitution to the lawmakers. Ignoring an attempted filibuster by Thomas Persons, Granville County planter and land speculator, the legislature set December 5 for a discussion of the document. Debates took place on that day, and the next day resolutions calling for a ratifying convention were adopted by both houses. Elections were set for the following March. Five delegates were to be elected from each of the fifty-eight counties and one from each of the six borough towns in the state; all taxpayers were declared eligible to vote. The convention was to assemble at Hillsboro on July 21, 1788.[193]

A fierce campaign ensued. Pennsylvania sent pro-ratificationist propaganda to North Carolina, and the Clintonians in New York sent anti-ratificationist materials and exchanged information and advice with North Carolina anti-Federalists. The imported materials were too erudite for most North Carolinians, however; the most telling arguments were concocted inside the state. The campaign of the anti-Federalists was a peculiar one. Some of them tried to keep the arguments on a sane level, deploring the lack of a bill of rights, predicting exploitation of the South by shrewd Yankees, and warning debtors of British merchants that the federal courts would be opened to suits for debts. More common and more effective, however, were such fantasies as that of Baptist minister Burkitt in Hertford County. That divine told his illiterate flock that the clause in the Constitution providing for what was to become the District of Columbia was a provision for a walled city that would house thousands of soldiers who would be privileged to plunder the country. Anti-Federalist leaders based their appeal on ignorance, the Federalists based theirs on reason. The anti-Federalists won by a landslide.[194]

[193] Walter Clark, ed., *State Records of North Carolina* (26 vols., Winston and Goldsboro, 1886–1907), 20:128–129, 133, 196–197, 369–372.
[194] William K. Boyd, ed., "News, Letters, and Documents Concerning North Carolina and the Federal Constitution," in *Trinity College Historical Papers*, vol. 14 (1922); Trenholme, *Ratification in North Carolina*, 107–132; Master-

Enemies of the Constitution in North Carolina recovered from the shock of the rapid succession of ratifications by New Hampshire, Virginia, and New York and were determined to vote against ratification when the convention met in July. Able debates by James Iredell, Archibald Maclaine, and other Federalists in the convention failed to alter this determination and the opposition, after proposing a long list of amendments, voted by a majority of one hundred against ratification. On August 4 the convention adjourned *sine die*.[195]

Refusing to despair, the friends of the Constitution immediately began a well co-ordinated campaign for a second convention. Iredell and William R. Davie financed the printing of the journal of the first convention for circulation in the back country; pamphlets and editions of *The Federalist* were sent to all parts of the state; and petitions for a new convention were circulated in every county. The tide began to turn, and when the legislature convened in November the Senate passed a resolution calling for a second convention. Shrewd anti-Federalists in the House of Commons, however, sensing that the House was inclined to concur with the Senate, introduced their own resolution, setting the elections for the new convention in August, 1789, almost a year away. Efforts of Federalist senators to obtain an earlier date failed, and the second convention was scheduled to be held in Fayetteville in November, 1789.[196]

The nine-month campaign which followed was the most intensive educational campaign in the state's history. In the meantime national elections were held, George Washington became president, and the government of the United States was organized. No federal armies marched to pillage the country. On the

---

son, *William Blount*, 142-144. See Archibald Maclaine's letter to Iredell, January 15, 1788, in Griffith J. McKee, *Life and Correspondence of James Iredell* (2 vols., New York, 1847), 2:216 ff., for a complaint by a North Carolina Federalist that although the authors of the Federalist were "Judicious and ingenious," the essays were "not well calculated for the common people."

[195] Elliott's *Debates*, 4:1-252.

[196] Clark, ed., *State Records*, 20:477 ff. That the anti-Federalists outmaneuvered the Federalists is not surprising. It should not be assumed from this account that the anti-Federalist *leaders* were not intelligent men, for many of them were as well educated as the leaders of either party in any state. It was the rank and file who were uninformed.

contrary, the First Congress passed twelve proposed amendments to the Constitution, ten of which were later ratified as the Bill of Rights. In the face of the educational campaign and the auspicious start made by the new government, most North Carolinians changed their minds. In the August elections the anti-Federalists were defeated as decisively as the Federalists had been in the earlier elections.[197]

Of the delegates to the second convention, which met on November 16, 1789, 102 had been members of the Hillsboro convention. Thirty-nine of these had been and still were Federalists, twenty who had formerly been anti-Federalists had now changed sides, and forty-three who had been opponents had been re-elected as opponents. Of the 169 new delegates, 135 were Federalists. The convention lasted only five days, and on November 21, 1789, by a vote of 194 to 77, North Carolina became the twelfth state to ratify.

Beard's interpretation of ratification has, in a negative sort of a way, some validity when applied to North Carolina. Certain forms of personalty, Beard maintains, were the dynamics in the movement for ratification. North Carolina seems, on the surface, to have lacked these forms of personalty. This, Beard concludes, "must have had a very deadening effect on the spirit of the movement for ratification." [198]

Yet the matter is not quite so simple as that. The state had western lands, public securities, commerce, and manufacturing, some of them in abundance, but each was neutralized as a potential force in ratification by peculiar features of North Carolina life. Some understanding of the complexity of the economic factors in North Carolina's ratification may be derived from brief consideration of each of these forms of personalty.

In the 1780's North Carolina included within its borders all of the present state of Tennessee. Tennessee lands were disposed of by the state in a loose sort of way which for two

---

[197] The campaign is traced in Newsome's "North Carolina's Ratification," in the *North Carolina Historical Review*, 17:296–299, and in Trenholme's *Ratification in North Carolina*, 192 ff. The second volume of Iredell's *Correspondence* gives an intimate picture from the Federalists' point of view.

[198] Beard, *Economic Interpretation*, 287.

decades made possible a wild orgy of land speculation. Furthermore, if the assertions of a recent scholar are well founded,
business morality in North Carolina was almost unbelievably
low; many local land speculators apparently put their economic
interests above all philosophy of government, sometimes even
above common integrity in government.[199]

This band of avaricious speculators, if such they were, were
singularly unskilled in their art, however, and uninformed
about the political factors that affected the value of their lands.
They followed the proceedings of the Virginia ratifying convention carefully, and they knew of Patrick Henry's sensa-
tional exposé of the proposed Jay-Gardoqui "give-away" of
navigation of the Mississippi. Whether because they feared loss
of the Mississippi, because of ignorance, or because they were
not quite so avaricious as they have been depicted, speculators
in Tennessee lands voted against ratification in the first convention by about five to one. In the second convention they
completely reversed themselves and voted for ratification by
a three to one majority.[200]

Even more interesting and paradoxical in view of the supposed speculative mania in North Carolina is the history of
public security operations in the state from 1787 to 1790. Beard
correctly points out that northern speculators bought up large
quantities of the North Carolina state debt. For example, eleven
outsiders, most of them from New York, executed 131 of the
first 174 subscriptions of North Carolina securities to the Loan
of 1790, and these eleven individuals funded $617,185, more
than a third of the entire assumed debt of North Carolina. Yet
at the time of the first ratifying convention the North Carolina

---

[199] Masterson, *William Blount*, 348–352 and elsewhere.

[200] See the analysis of the North Carolina conventions, pages 318–321 below.
Masterson, in his *William Blount*, pages 135 ff., states that Blount, as a speculator in Tennessee lands, favored ratification during the contests for the first
convention. If this is so, it is curious that Stokely Donelson, Blount's friend
and associate and possessor of hundreds of thousands of acres of Tennessee
lands in his own right, was an opponent of ratification in the first convention.
On Donelson's land speculations see Masterson, *William Blount, passim*, and
Pool, "Economic Interpretation of the Ratification," in the *North Carolina
Historical Review*, 27:299, and for his vote against ratification see Elliott's
Debates, 4:251.

war debt was more than $2,000,000, and almost all of it was owned in the state. Thus the potential "dynamic element in the ratification" existed in 1788, but North Carolinians were either ignorant of what was to their economic advantage or were disposed to put other things first. The chances are that some elements of both were involved.[201]

In the field of manufacturing North Carolina was as productive as any other southern state, yet its manufactures were relatively stable and unaffected by politics. The principal manufactures were rum, which was largely consumed at home, lumber and lumber products, for which there was an insatiable market in the French West Indies as well as in the British West Indies, and naval stores, which were welcomed in markets all over Europe and America. Valuable though they were, almost no North Carolina manufactures were of the sort that could benefit in any appreciable measure from protective tariffs or other governmental measures.

North Carolina's commerce was likewise unique as a potential element in the movement for ratification. It was larger than Beard assumes, for the vessels clearing the state in 1788 measured about 47,000 tons, more than two-thirds as much as cleared wealthy South Carolina.[202] But, as has been observed, except in Massachusetts and Connecticut the secondary effects of commercial intercourse were often more important than the economic effects as a catalyst promoting ratification. That is, 1) places reached by sailing vessels naturally had a broader outlook than isolated places because they participated in a regular exchange of news and ideas as well as goods, and 2) many ports had suffered from ravages of war and were acutely conscious

[201] Records of the Loan of 1790, vol. 1243, folios 7–144, and vol. 1244, accounts 79 and 86 (Subscription Registers, Assumed Debt), in the National Archives; Beard, *Economic Interpretation*, 287; Clark, ed., *State Records*, 21:1445. Only $37,059 in continental securities was funded in North Carolina. Summary Volume 174A. In all likelihood much more was bought in the state and funded elsewhere. Several New York anti-Federalists were among the larger raiders of North Carolina securities. For example, Richard Platt, Walter Livingston, and Robert Gilchrist acquired $324,865, face value, between them. Vol. 1243, folios 7–58, 79–101, 116–121, and vol. 1244, account 79.

[202] Christopher C. Crittenden, *The Commerce of North Carolina, 1763–1789* (New Haven, 1936), chapter 10; Jensen, *The New Nation*, 216–217.

of the need for a general government to provide for the common defense.

The secondary effects were minimized in North Carolina, however, by the odd topography of the state. The chain of narrow, ever-shifting barrier beaches extending from Cape Lookout north to the Virginia border fence off most of the North Carolina coast. Wilmington, located south of the barrier beaches, was the only port in the state to be occupied by the British during the war, and while shippers in the other ports suffered occasional damages, most people in the protected parts of the coastal area emerged from the war with the feeling that they were invulnerable to invasion by sea.

More important than considerations of defense, however, was the lack of internal transportation facilities. Two rivers, the Neuse and the Tar-Pamlico, were navigable by small ocean-going craft for sixty to seventy miles into the interior, and the Roanoke was navigable by rafts and river boats for about the same distance. With these exceptions the state was without any internal transportation facilities other than its usually poor and unreliable roads. North Carolina was the only state except New Hampshire in which the great majority of the population lived at places removed from convenient avenues of transportation, communication, and trade.

The resemblance of North Carolina and New Hampshire with respect to elements affecting the decision on ratification was, indeed, marked. In many ways North Carolina in the 1780's can be accurately described as an oversized version of New Hampshire, set in a warmer climate. It resembled the northern state in its rural isolation, difficulty of communication, and lack of information. The essential difference, and the reason why North Carolina rejected the Constitution completely whereas New Hampshire only came close to rejecting it, was that North Carolina was also a giant. It embraced an enormous territory, and it was populous and self-sufficient. All things considered, North Carolina could probably have come closer to surviving indefinitely as an independent republic than any other state, and except for Rhode Island it was perhaps most inclined to do so.

Granted the above conditions, it was a simple task for the energetic anti-Federalist leaders of North Carolina to exploit provincial feelings, lack of information, and state particularism, and direct them against the Constitution.

The minority favoring ratification in the state was elected almost exclusively from the counties and towns on the Neuse and Tar-Pamlico rivers. In view of the fact that the lower coastal area around Wilmington, a much richer part of the state,[203] voted against ratification, it is interesting to compare the patterns of trade in the two areas. Vessels from the Wilmington area traded largely with ports in South Carolina, Georgia, East Florida, and the West Indies. Those from the upper area traded more with northern ports in the United States. It is significant that of the three hundred or so annual voyages from the area to those northern places, about half were to the nationalist center, Philadelphia. Thus, as in New Hampshire, it was not the mere fact of communication with the outside world, but the character of the places with which regular communication was established, that was an important factor in the development of national-mindedness.[204]

The factors that produced ratification in North Carolina's second convention are not difficult to assess. The principal one was the success of the "educational" campaign, to which several external developments contributed. Beard cites three, the first two of which are sound: the election of Washington as president, the proposal of a Bill of Rights, and the threat of commercial pressures against the state by the general government.[205] The latter would seem to have had virtually no influence, for the commercial parts of the state voted the same way in both conventions. One more element may be added: the discomfort of being outside the Union.

[203] Francis G. Morris and Phyllis Mary Morris, "Economic Conditions in North Carolina about 1780," in the *North Carolina Historical Review*, 16:120, 130 (1930), cited by Pool in his "Economic Interpretation of the Ratification," in the *North Carolina Historical Review*, 27:124–125.

[204] Sources for this analysis of the patterns of North Carolina's coasting trade are the port records and newspaper tabulations cited above in connection with the discussions of ratification in Georgia, Pennsylvania, Maryland, South Carolina, Virginia, and New York.

[205] Beard, *Economic Interpretation*, 236.

A thorough study of the economic interests of the delegates in the two North Carolina ratifying conventions has been made by William C. Pool.[206] To that study two additions can be made: data on the public security holdings of the delegates, which Pool did not consider, and an analysis of the occupations and personalty holdings of the delegates, which information Pool furnishes but does not analyze. These data are given below, following which Pool's own summaries are quoted.

In both conventions security holders were almost entirely unrepresented. In the first convention two delegates who voted against ratification held securities, John Brown of Wilkes County ($4,496) and John Campbell of New Hanover County ($595). Two delegates who voted for ratification also held securities, Nathaniel Allen of Chowan County ($905) and Josiah Collins of Tyrrell County ($17,711), who acquired securities as a purchaser for northern speculators. In the second convention Brown and Campbell again voted against ratification and a third anti-Federalist, Thomas Perkins of Orange County, also held securities ($26). Neither of the Federalists in the first convention was returned to the second convention, but four of the 194 Federalists in the second convention held securities: Hugh Williamson of Tyrrell County ($455 in Pennsylvania securities), Hardy Murfree of Hertford County ($15,370), Samuel Smith of Johnston County ($594), and Adlai Osborne of Iredell County ($158).[207]

In both conventions more than 90 per cent of the delegates were planters and farmers. In the first convention three of the

---

[206] See note 192 above. Pool's account, the result of tedious labors, contains a few minor errors that I have observed, but except for his failure to recognize that some land speculators, such as William Blount, acquired much of their land through agents and hence their names do not often appear in the records, it is basically a sound work. Pool also shows a certain reluctance to term purchasers of Tennessee lands "speculators." My assumption is that anyone buying such lands without any apparent intention of occupying them did so because he expected that they would appreciate in value and that they could be sold at a profit. That is speculation, no more, no less.

[207] Records of the Loan of 1790, vol. 1243, folios 75, 150, 151, 155–157, 160, 175, 176; vol. 1244, accounts 114, 119, 156, 186, 196, 225, 226; vol. 1245 (Subscription Receipts, Public Debts), unpaged entry for Hardy Murfree; all in the National Archives.

Federalists were merchants, four were lawyers, and the remaining 77 were planters and farmers; one of the anti-Federalists was a merchant, two were taverners and tradesmen, one was a lawyer, three were physicians, one was a capitalist, and the remaining 176 were planters and farmers. In the second convention four of the delegates favoring ratification were merchants, two were lawyers, one was a physician, one was a capitalist, and 186 were planters and farmers. One of the delegates voting against ratification was a lawyer, two were physicians, and 74 were planters and farmers.

Substantial numbers of the delegates in the two conventions held personalty of various kinds besides slaves. In the first convention four delegates voting for ratification owned mercantile property, two held securities, four had investments in manufacturing, and eight owned western lands; a total of 19 different men (22.3 per cent) were engaged in nonagrarian occupations and/or owned personalty. Of the anti-Federalists in the first convention four owned mercantile property, two owned securities, five owned manufacturing property, and forty owned western lands; a total of 45 different men (24.5 per cent) were engaged in nonagrarian occupations and/or owned personalty besides slaves.

In the second convention six of the Federalist delegates owned mercantile property, four owned securities, three owned manufacturing property, and 37 held western lands; a total of 52 different men (26.8 per cent) were engaged in nonagrarian occupations and/or owned personalty other than slaves. Of the anti-Federalists in the second convention three owned securities, one owned manufacturing property, and twelve owned western lands; a total of 18 different men (23.4 per cent) were engaged in nonagrarian occupations and/or owned personalty other than slaves.

In both conventions, then, the distribution of personalty in the two parties was almost identical.

Pool's summaries of the landholdings and slaveholdings of the delegates, presented below, likewise show that there was no division of the delegates along economic lines. The first tabulation summarizes, in terms of acreage, the landholdings of Federalist and anti-Federalist delegates in the first convention:

	Not Known		Under 100		100–499		500–999		1000–4999		Over 5000	
	No.	Per Cent	No.	Per Cent	No.	Per Cent	No.	Per Cent	No.	Per Cent	No.	Per Cent
Fed.	9	10	4	4	16	19	10	12	34	40	11	14
Anti-Fed.	14	8	0	0	49	27	33	18	69	37	19	10

The distribution of the slaveholdings of the delegates in the first convention was as follows:

	Not Known		None		1–9		10–19		20–49		Over 50	
	No.	Per Cent	No.	Per Cent	No.	Per Cent	No.	Per Cent	No.	Per Cent	No.	Per Cent
Fed.	15	18	2	2	19	23	17	20	24	28	7	8
Anti-Fed.	56	30	12	7	49	27	39	21	25	13	3	2

Below are shown the landholdings of the members of the first convention who were also members of the second convention, divided into three groups: the thirty-nine delegates who voted for the Constitution both times, the twenty delegates who voted against the Constitution in the first convention but voted for ratification in the second convention, and the forty-three delegates who voted against the Constitution in both conventions:

	Not Known		Under 100		100–499		500–999		1000–4999		Over 5000	
	No.	Per Cent	No.	Per Cent	No.	Per Cent	No.	Per Cent	No.	Per Cent	No.	Per Cent
39 Fed.	3	8	1	2	8	21	6	15	15	39	6	15
20 Anti-Fed.	3	15	0	0	4	20	4	20	8	40	1	5
43 Anti-Fed.	2	5	0	0	10	23	7	16	16	37	8	18

The slaveholdings of the delegates who sat in both conventions, divided as in the preceding tabulation, were as follows:

	Not Known		None		1–9		10–19		20–49		Over 50	
	No.	Per Cent	No.	Per Cent	No.	Per Cent	No.	Per Cent	No.	Per Cent	No.	Per Cent
39 Fed.	6	15	1	2	8	21	12	31	8	21	4	10
20 Anti-Fed.	3	15	1	5	6	30	7	35	3	15	0	0
43 Anti-Fed	11	26	4	9	12	28	8	18	7	16	1	2

The next tabulation shows the landholdings of delegates in the second convention, divided into four groups: all 77 anti-Federalists, all 194 Federalists, the 34 anti-Federalists voting for the first time, and the 135 Federalists voting for the first time:

	Not Known		Under 100		100–499		500–999		1000–4999		Over 5000	
	No.	Per Cent	No.	Per Cent	No.	Per Cent	No.	Per Cent	No.	Per Cent	No.	Per Cent
77 Anti-Fed.	8	10	0	0	24	32	13	17	21	27	11	14
194 Fed.	43	22	1	12	37	19	35	18	55	28	23	12
34 Anti-Fed	6	18	0	0	14	40	6	18	5	15	3	9
135 Fed.	37	28	0	0	25	19	25	19	32	24	16	12

Finally, the slaveholdings of delegates in the second convention, divided as in the preceding tabulation, were as follows:

	Not Known		None		1–9		10–19		20–49		Over 50	
	No.	Per Cent	No.	Per Cent	No.	Per Cent	No.	Per Cent	No.	Per Cent	No.	Per Cent
77 Anti-Fed.	23	30	6	7	22	29	13	17	11	14	2	3
194 Fed.	56	29	3	2	38	19	55	28	32	16	10	5
34 Anti-Fed.	12	35	2	6	10	29	5	15	4	12	1	3
135 Fed.	47	35	1	1	24	18	36	27	21	15	6	4

Dr. Pool summarizes these data as follows: [208]

The inescapable conclusion, therefore, is that an analysis of the personal and real property holdings of those who supported and opposed the Constitution shows that there was no line of property division at all; that is, that men owning substantially the same amounts of the same kinds of property were equally divided on the matter of adoption or rejection. In this connection the debtor class was by no means confined to the small farmer group. The line of cleavage for and against the Constitution was not, as the original economic interpretation has implied, between the substantial property interests on one hand and the small farming and debtor class on the other.

RHODE ISLAND

RHODE ISLAND was the last state to ratify. Not until the United States government under the Constitution had been in opera-

---

[208] Pool, "Economic Interpretation of the Ratification," in the *North Carolina Historical Review*, 28:126. The tables are on pages 125, 438–439.

tion for fifteen months, the state legislature had seven times defeated resolutions to call a ratifying convention, and the convention finally called had met on two separate occasions, did the
little state at last adopt the Constitution. Even then, on May 28,
1790, the vote in the convention was only 34 to 32 in favor of
ratification, the margin being the votes of a single town.

The Constitution was first considered by the Rhode Island
legislature in its February, 1788, session. A motion to call a
convention was rejected by a large majority and in its stead was
adopted a resolution authorizing special town meetings at which
citizens should vote directly on the question of ratification.
The popular vote against ratification was 2,708 to 237. The
only towns voting for ratification were Bristol and Little Compton, the former by a vote of 26 to 23 and the latter by a vote of
63 to 57. Providence and Newport protested against the referendum, with the result that only one man (who voted against
ratification) voted in Providence and only eleven (ten of whom
voted against ratification) in Newport.[209]

Immediately after this rejection of the Constitution by the
voters, a second motion to call a convention was defeated in the
March session of the legislature. During the next two years four
such motions were defeated: in October, 1788, by a vote of 40
to 14; in December of that year by a vote of 44 to 12; in March,
1789, by about the same vote; and in June, 1789, by a slightly
smaller majority. By September, however, the legislature showed

[209] The votes by towns are recorded in Papers Relating to the Adoption of
the Federal Constitution, 17–36, and in Acts and Proceedings of the General
Assembly, 13:465; both manuscripts in the Rhode Island Archives. The *New
York Journal* of April 24, 1788, reported that only 2,900 men had voted on the
referendum, whereas 4,170 had voted in the gubernatorial elections in 1787, "by
which it will appear, that upwards of 1200 freeholders in this state have not
voted on the subject of the proposed national constitution." This estimate is a
reasonably accurate one. In the Providence Town Meeting Records (Office of
the City Clerk, City Hall, Providence), an entry for April 18, 1787, records
that there were 521 qualified freemen (voters) in Providence. The *Newport Mercury* reported that 306 votes were cast in that town in the election of
a deputy governor in April, 1787. This would account for 800 abstainers; the
remaining 400 were scattered throughout the other 28 towns in the state. Not
all those who refrained from voting in the referendum were necessarily opposed to ratification, however. For example, 168 of the Providence freemen
were under temporary disfranchisement because of their refusal to sign a state
oath prescribed earlier by a state "Act to Prevent Bribery and Corruption."

signs of weakening. In that month it requested instructions from the towns on the issue, and in October it voted to print and distribute among the towns 150 copies of the twelve amendments to the Constitution recommended by Congress. But when it convened with new instructions two months later it again refused to call a convention, this time by a vote of 39 to 17.[210]

In January, 1790, the Assembly finally voted in favor of a convention, 34 to 29, only to have the Senate reject the resolution, 5 to 4. The next day, however, when one member was absent, the Senate took another vote. The ensuing tie was broken by Governor John Collins, and a convention was set to be held in South Kingston on March 1, 1790.

When the convention met, opponents of the Constitution had a majority of about a dozen delegates. Unwilling to risk a vote on the Constitution with the proposed twelve amendments, the anti-Federalist leaders avoided the issue by a parliamentary stratagem and after five days of debate the delegates voted 41 to 28 to adjourn until May 24 and to reconvene in Newport.[211]

When it reconvened the convention faced an unexpected problem. The town of Providence had seceded from the state and presented an ultimatum: only if the convention ratified the Constitution unconditionally would it rejoin the state. In the face of this action and the threat of similar action by other towns, the opposition to ratification finally weakened. On the third day of the session the vote was taken, and the Constitution was approved by a majority of two votes.[212]

It has generally been assumed that the contest over ratification in Rhode Island was intimately related to the state's paper-money issue of 1786 and that the paper-money question was

[210] The attempts to call a convention have been traced in *Rhode Island Colonial Records*, 10:271–358. For a good summary see the introduction of Robert C. Cotner, ed., *Theodore Foster's Minutes of the Convention Held at South Kingston, Rhode Island, in March, 1790, Which Failed to Adopt the Constitution of the United States* (Providence, 1929), 13–20.

[211] *Ibid.*, 33–90.

[212] The resolutions adopted by the Providence town meeting were published in the *United States Chronicle* (Providence), May 27, 1790. The journal of the second session of the convention is in William R. Staples' *Rhode Island in the Continental Congress* (Providence, 1870).

simply one of private debtor or paper-money forces opposed to ratification versus private creditor or hard-money forces in favor of ratification. It is sometimes implied and sometimes stated outright, as it was by contemporaries in other states, that "Rogue's Island" was teeming with dishonest debtors, and that the demand for paper money and opposition to the Constitution were both manifestations of a movement by these debtors to defraud their creditors.[213]

Whatever may be the justice of describing the Rhode Islanders as a band of pirates, it does great injustice to their imaginations and financial acumen to assume that their paper was no more than a simple scheme of debtors to defraud creditors. It is true that fiscal matters were at the center of Rhode Island political activity from 1781 to 1791, but the fiscal situation was an extremely complex one. Only through an understanding of the intricacies of the state's financial history during the decade can the background of the contest over ratification be comprehended. The following account is a somewhat simplified summary of this financial history.[214]

Rhode Island's peculiar financial course began in 1782 with the state's rejection of a proposed amendment to the Articles of Confederation that would have given Congress power to collect a five per cent duty on imports into all American ports. All the other states signified their approval, but Rhode Island refused to yield, and when Virginia rescinded its ratification of the amendment the proposal was dead.

Two considerations were widely recognized as the reasons for Rhode Island's rejection of the proposed impost. First, the

---

[213] Beard, *Economic Interpretation*, 28, 237; Frank G. Bates, *Rhode Island and the Formation of the Union* (New York, 1898). Newspapers all over the continent carried derisive accounts of affairs in Rhode Island. See in the New York *Daily Advertiser* of April 6, 1787, an account entitled "The Quintessance of Villainy; or, Proceedings of the Legislature of the State of Rhode-Island &c." It was almost invariably assumed by outsiders that the Rhode Island doings were no more than the activities of dishonest debtors run amuck.

[214] The general data on the chronology of events which follows are derived from the following manuscripts in the Rhode Island Archives: Proceedings of the General Assembly; Papers Relating to the Adoption of the Federal Constitution; Reports to the General Assembly, 1778–1788; and Petitions to the General Assembly, vol. 23. Supplementary information is derived from the printed *Rhode Island Colonial Records*, vol. 10. Specific data are documented separately.

state derived most of its income from trade, and it considered a free-trade policy, or a trade policy designed for and by Rhode Island, to be to its best interest. A second and perhaps more important consideration was that the holders of state securities and the taxpayers of the state saw that if the state surrendered import duties to Congress, a main source of the state's revenues would be sacrificed. In that event state creditors would be left on a tenuous footing and, equally undesirable, the burden of direct taxation to support state debts would be substantially increased.[215]

A third reason for Rhode Island's rejection of the impost plan derived from the activities of speculators in Providence. A dozen or so merchants in Providence, including Nicholas and John Brown, Thomas Jenkins, the firm of Clark and Nightingale, Zachariah and Phillip Allen, Joseph and William Russel, and Jabez Bowen, had acquired among them nearly $250,000 in continental loan office certificates.[216] These speculators exploited the situation in various ways, the method employed by Nicholas Brown being the most common.

Brown owned nearly $100,000 worth of these continental securities. After the impost plan of 1781 had been ratified by the other twelve states, it was easy enough for Brown to convince his mercantile correspondents in other cities that Rhode Island, too, would soon give its approval. When this news was spread, the price of continental loan office certificates rose from about two and a half shillings to four shillings on the pound, and the prices of state securities dropped in almost every state. At the critical moment Brown quietly disposed of about thirty thousand dollars of his loan office certificates in exchange for state securities of Massachusetts, New York, and other states. These transactions completed, he then worked for rejection of the im-

[215] The struggle inside Rhode Island over the impost has been traced in the *Providence Gazette* from January, 1782, to February, 1783. These two principal motives were openly expressed in Rhode Island and they were recognized by contemporaries from other states. For example, see Rufus King's speech in the Philadelphia Convention, recorded in Madison's Journal under date of August 18, 1787.

[216] List of Notes Issued for Consolidating the Securities Issued from the General Treasurer's Office, September, 1782, to June, 1784, in the Rhode Island Archives. This document contains a list of all holders of continental loan office certificates in the state.

post plan by Rhode Island and voted in the legislature against it. When the plan was defeated, the prices of state securities rose again and the prices of continental securities dropped. As a result of his manipulations Brown was about thirty thousand dollars richer.[217]

As the war drew near an end Rhode Island, like most of the other states and like Congress, began to put its financial house in order by "scaling" its war debts to compensate for wartime inflation. That is, for example, if a horse worth ten pounds had been sold for a note of a thousand pounds face value, this note was called in and scaled down to ten pounds, the "real" price or value of the animal. When this process was completed and all accounts had been audited, the state of the various forms of certificates in Rhode Island was, in round figures, as follows: [218]

566 six per cent notes issued for money advanced to the state, held by about 250 individuals, amounting to . . .	£ 50,000
2,416 four per cent notes of the same character, held by about 2,300 individuals, amounting to	£ 46,000
Continental loan office certificates, two-thirds of which were owned in Providence and more than half by twelve men in that city, amounting to $524,000, or	£ 157,200
Claims against Congress for war damages on the part of nineteen towns, most of whose inhabitants had few other securities, amounting to	£ 270,000
Claims of the state government for uncompensated expenditures on behalf of Congress	£ 630,000
Claims of individuals against Congress for goods and supplies furnished; widely held in small amounts, totaling	£ 278,000

[217] Brown's activities have been traced in the various records of the public debt housed in the Rhode Island Archives, and in the Old Loan Records in the National Archives, particularly the volumes for New York and Massachusetts. Much more information about Brown's activities is contained in the Brown Family Papers in the John Carter Brown Library in Providence. I am indebted to Professor James B. Hedges of Brown University, who has for many years had the exclusive use of the Brown Papers, for information on Nicholas Brown. Professor Hedges and I worked out the above analysis of Brown's speculations by pooling our information.

[218] Notes Issued for Consolidating Securities . . ., September, 1782–June, 1784; Ledger A, Accounts of Rhode Island against the United States, folios

It is to be observed that more than half the voters in the state owned four per cent notes. If it were possible to identify all the individuals who owned one of the above forms of debt, it would probably appear that upwards of seventy-five per cent of the voters were security holders. Largely because of this wide distribution of security holdings, but also because the ideal of public integrity was still alive at the end of the war, Rhode Island entertained no thought of repudiating any of these debts. On the contrary, as Congress lagged ever further behind in its interest payments, the state took on more and more of the continental burden, until it was attempting to support the interest on all the continental securities owned in the state. Holders of continental loan office certificates were able to get preferential treatment in these interest payments by exerting their economic and political influence.

At first the state's import duties alone were almost adequate to service the debt, but as the interest burden increased, direct taxes on real property rose rapidly. Five thousand pounds, then ten thousand, twenty thousand, and thirty thousand was levied annually in direct taxes on the freeholders. The towns complained, but most of them collected the levies. The financial situation, however, was fast approaching the absurd dilemma that faced Connecticut taxpayers, many of whom, it will be recalled, were losing their realty because of nonpayment of taxes levied on it for the purpose of supporting interest payments on their securities. The case of the town of South Kingston was typical. That town gradually slipped behind in its tax payments: it was £500 in arrears in 1783, £750 in 1784, more than £1,000 in 1785, and £2,000 by May, 1786. Most of these taxes had been levied to support interest payments on continental and state securities. The town tax collectors were being sent to jail for failure to collect these taxes, yet the town government of South Kingston owned nearly two thousand pounds in continental securities and a similar amount of state securities,

200–203, pp. 500–501; Proceedings of the General Assembly, 13:689; all in the Rhode Island Archives.

and residents of the town owned upwards of twenty thousand pounds in various forms of debt.[219]

In the meantime, toward the end of the war, an apparently irrelevant event occurred that was to alter the course of Rhode Island history. Elizabeth Thurston, the widow of a colonial official of Rhode Island, petitioned the Assembly respecting the official affairs of her late husband. Thurston, a Loyalist, had fled with the colony's records to New York City, where he died during the war. A committee of the Assembly was appointed to investigate the petition, and the records were returned from New York.[220]

As it happened, Thurston's office had been that of Keeper of the Grand Committee Office, the agency that supervised the colony's last issue of paper money. When there had been a pressing need for a circulating medium in colonial days, Rhode Island had frequently resorted to issuing paper money on loan, secured by real estate mortgages and bearing interest payable to the colony. By the end of the war, however, there were few people in the state who could remember the last colonial issue of paper (1750). The only paper money that was clearly remembered in postwar Rhode Island was the issue of wartime bills of credit that had emanated from the Continental Congress, bills which had depreciated in two years to a thousand for one, and thereafter became worthless.

One of the members of the General Assembly at the time the Widow Thurston's petition was presented was a keen, somewhat demagogic politician named Jonathan J. Hazard. Hazard, who owned five different kinds of securities, was one of those persons who was in debt for taxes that had been levied to support the interest on his securities, and he thus felt at first hand the hopeless contradictions in the state's fiscal policy. Mrs.

---

[219] Proceedings of the General Assembly, 12:134–136, 137–139, 160–163, 475, 685–686, 13:109–110, 288, 360; Impost Accounts, *passim;* Reports to the General Assembly, 1778–1788, pp. 74, 90, 94; Papers Relating to the Adoption of the Constitution, 105; Ledger A, Accounts of Rhode Island against the United States, 500; Notes Issued for Consolidating Securities, 1782–1784, *passim;* all in the Rhode Island Archives.

[220] Reports to the General Assembly, 1778–1788, pp. 16, 39, 100, 111, 117. These reports are the source of much of what follows.

Thurston's claim was soon settled, but Hazard, together with friends and allies he began to acquire—Joseph Stanton, Job Comstock, Samuel Potter, Benjamin Arnold, and others—continued to study the late Keeper's records for three years more.[221]

In these records Hazard and his friends found, or thought they found, an answer to Rhode Island's financial predicament. The records demonstrated that the colonial paper money had been successful, that in effect the paper had been a means of creating something out of nothing. Money had been needed, so paper was printed and called money. The paper circulated as money and was eventually retired through repayment of mortgages, foreclosures, and taxes, the tax burden being eased by the increased amount of money in circulation. The borrowers of the paper had repaid the colony almost in full and the colony had collected regular interest payments as well.

Conjecturing about the possibility of employing this same expedient in Rhode Island in the 1780's, Hazard reasoned as follows. Paper money, of an amount approximately equal to the state debt, could be lent on good security and be made legal tender for all public obligations and taxes. Real estate would be the most desirable security, for the right to vote was contingent upon the ownership of land. Strict penalties could be enacted to prevent depreciation of the paper. If it did not depreciate, the interest to be collected on it would be equal to the interest owed by the state. If taxes were then continued at existing levels, they would be easier to pay and would be sufficient to retire the state debt at par in about seven years. The paper could then be retired through further taxes. If, on the other hand, the paper did begin to depreciate, it could be supported by increasing taxes fast enough to absorb the depreciation. In that event the state would retire its debts in very short order, perhaps in a year or two. Whether the paper depreciated or not, the state would be transformed from a debtor paying

---

[221] *Ibid.*; Proceedings of the General Assembly, *passim.* Later a writer in the *Newport Herald* of June 19, 1788, claimed that Hazard was only the nominal leader and that an unnamed Providence merchant and speculator was the "brains" of the paper faction. From all accounts, however, Hazard seems to have been perfectly capable of directing the entire affair.

interest of about a hundred thousand pounds to a creditor collecting interest of about the same amount. Funding of the state
debts would tie the interests of the multitude of state security
holders to the fate of the paper and would thus be an additional
force in maintaining its circulation at about par. The plan
seemed foolproof.

As this scheme was being formulated by Hazard and his associates, developments were taking place which prepared the
citizenry for acceptance of the plan. Most of the towns were
beginning to resent having to support the continental loan
office certificates. The people in the "country" towns on the
western shore considered that this expense should be borne
by Congress, to them virtually a foreign government. The inhabitants of the eastern shore and island towns, who owned
almost no loan office certificates, regarded it as unjust that they
should have to pay taxes to support these securities when they
were receiving no money from either the state or Congress for
their claims against Congress for war losses. Concurrently with
the growth of this unwillingness to continue supporting the obligations of the United States, there was in Rhode Island, as in
other states, a rapidly growing lack of respect for Congress.
Increasing numbers began to feel that the Confederation was
withering away, and Rhode Islanders witnessed the dissolution
with little regret.[222]

Hazard and his allies took these developments into account
and decided that the policy which would suit most people in
the state would be a virtual dissolution of all connections with
the Confederation. New York and Pennsylvania had already
adopted financial systems that amounted almost to declarations
of independence, and the Hazard group felt that the time was
ripe for Rhode Island to do likewise. By the end of 1785 they

---

[222] I have traced the development of attitudes regarding the support of loan
office certificates from the Town Meeting Records in the individual town
halls in the state. The distribution of ownership of the various kinds of public
debt has been ascertained from the fiscal records in the Rhode Island Archives,
cited in note 218 above. General attitudes toward the affairs of the Confederation have been traced in the *Providence Gazette*, the *United States Chronicle*
(Providence), and the *Newport Mercury*, 1785-1786.

had worked out the details of their financial scheme, and now they prepared to execute it.

In February, 1786, a "feeler" proposal for an issue of paper money was made in the lower house in response to petitions submitted by Newport and a half dozen other towns.[223] The proposal was rejected, but the real purpose of it was accomplished when the Assembly agreed to request the towns to give their representatives instructions on the issue at the annual town meetings in April. During the next two months the friends of the Hazard scheme traveled throughout the state explaining the system to countless individuals. The decision of the towns was almost unanimous; only Providence, Newport, and Portsmouth instructed their delegates to vote against paper, and in none of these towns was the vote against paper an overwhelming one.[224]

A law passed in May, 1786, authorized the issuance of a hundred thousand pounds of paper money on the terms originally planned by Hazard and his associates. In most quarters it was accepted immediately, by all ranks of the population and all occupational groups. It was not issued to the "country" or to farmers alone. Nearly fifteen per cent of it was issued in Providence and Newport, in which towns about seventy per cent of the loans were made to merchants. In the state as a whole nearly sixty per cent of the total issue was borrowed by merchants and the wealthier landowners. In each town the minimum sum loaned was from £15 to £22; the total of 554 persons who borrowed this basic minimum unit took out a total of just over

[223] The first petition for paper had come from Newport early in 1785 and is mentioned in the *Providence Gazette* of February 26, 1785. It later appeared that a majority of the freemen of Newport opposed paper, however. The other towns petitioning were Gloucester, Smithfield, Tiverton, Foster, Middletown, and Coventry. Papers Relating to the Adoption of the Constitution, 47, 50, 58, 59, 60, 63. See also Petitions to the General Assembly, vol. 25, part I, p. 59.

[224] The votes in most towns are recorded in their Town Meeting Records. Unfortunately the three towns opposed to paper neglected to record their votes on the issue. Judging by the votes there for governor in 1787, however, as recorded in the Town Meeting Records in Providence (City Hall) and Portsmouth (Town Hall) and the election returns published in the *Newport Mercury*, the vote on paper was not extremely lopsided. Governor John Collins, an outspoken champion of the paper scheme, received from a third to 40 per cent of the vote in each of the three towns.

£ 10,000. At the other end of the scale, about 50 of the wealthier men in the state, those paying the heaviest taxes, borrowed about £30,000 of the total £96,608 actually issued. The friends of the issue included not only the mass of the people but a large share of the wealthier men in the state as well.[225]

The law included a number of devices designed to maintain the par value of the paper, but most of them were too severe and defeated their purpose. Three of the more significant of these were the provision making the paper legal tender for all public and private debts, the disfranchisement of any person who refused to accept the paper at par, and the renowned lodge money or "know ye" clause. This last provided that if a private creditor refused to accept the paper for debts, the debtor could cancel his debt by depositing the paper money with certain courts, publishing a public notice of his action in the newspapers, and informing his creditor of the action. The creditor could then pick up the money or leave it, as he saw fit.

Much can be learned about the nature of the paper money and about its users and backers from these published announcements of deposits of lodge money.[226] In the first place, most of the total of about £17,000 so deposited was lodged and taken out of circulation within a year, so that the amount of paper in circulation after 1786 was never more than £79,000. Secondly, since the lodge money represented all private debts cancelled by the tender of paper contrary to the wishes of the creditor, and since hundreds of thousands of dollars of public debt were involved in the plan, it is clear that the cancellation

[225] The foregoing analysis of the distribution of the loans is based on tabulations made from Grand Committee Office, Account Books A and B, 1786–1803, in the Rhode Island Archives.

[226] All the generalizations about the lodge money which follow are derived from my tabulations of all such transactions as published in the *Providence Gazette*, beginning in August, 1786. Every such announcement published in this newspaper was cross-checked against the announcements in the *Newport Mercury* to insure a complete record. The *Gazette* of January 27, 1787, printed an accurate summary of all lodge money deposited up to that time. The notices include the date, the name and usually the occupation of the debtor and his residence, the name and usually the occupation of the creditor and his residence, the nature of the debt (e.g., mortgage, bond, note of hand), and the sum.

of private debts was only a relatively insignificant by-product of the scheme, not its essential purpose. Finally, in view of the widely accepted notion that the debtor faction was the "country" party, made up of farmers, and that the creditors who suffered from the cancellation of debts in depreciated currency were largely merchants, the following tabulations of lodge-money deposits are of interest.

1. As nearly as can be ascertained, 76 different farmers tendered paper money for debts and 62 different farmers received it; 57 non-farmers tendered paper money for payment of debts and 72 received it. Including those whose occupations are not ascertainable, a total of no more than 156 different persons tendered paper money and a total of no more than 158 received it. Making allowance for those who appear as both debtors and creditors, fewer than 300 different individuals, about two per cent of the adult male population, were involved in the lodge-money transactions in any capacity.

2. Persons known to be farmers or identified as such cancelled debts totaling £6,218 13s. 4d. by depositing lodge money. On the other hand, debts totaling £6,525 2s. 9d. due *to* farmers were written off by lodge-money deposits. Farmers so cancelled a total of only £991 7s. 1d. in debts due to a total of only eight persons known to be or identified as merchants, traders, and shopkeepers. On the other hand, merchant-debtors so cancelled £524 1s. 3d. in debts that they owed to farmers.

3. Thirteen different merchants and traders wrote off debts amounting to £2,824 16s. 3d. by depositing lodge money. The debts due to nineteen different merchants were cancelled by lodge-money deposits, the total sum being £3,332 1s. 11d. Of these write-offs of debts £757 2s. 7d. represented sums due from merchants to other merchants.

In short, there is no foundation in fact for the commonly accepted generalization that the paper-money movement in Rhode Island represented the actions of large bands of debtor-farmers who were using depreciated paper currency to pay obligations due to merchant-creditors.

When it was first issued the paper was acceptable in all

quarters except one: among the holders and speculators in continental loan office certificates. Most of the citizens of Providence held some of these securities and, as was observed earlier, a dozen of the most powerful merchants in the town owned about half of the $524,000 in continental loan office certificates held in the state. It was obvious to these merchant-speculators— it was no secret—that the ultimate plan of the leaders in the paper-money movement was to pay off the state debts and to abandon all responsibility for continental obligations.

As it happened, the very individuals who had acquired the largest amounts of continental loan office certificates were being pressed in 1786 for nearly a hundred thousand pounds in debts they owed British merchants for postwar imports. Had these goods been sold in Rhode Island, the primary consideration of the merchants would have been to collect debts owed them by consumers in the state, and any legitimate plan designed for the improvement of the financial condition of such consumers would have worked to the ultimate benefit of the merchants. But most of the goods had been sold outside Rhode Island, and the profits had already been reinvested, much of them in public securities.[227]

The merchants thus had a great deal at stake as regards their speculations in securities. The question facing them in 1786 was whether to support the paper, collect on their state securities, and lose their investments in loan office certificates. The answer was simple arithmetic. For example, Zachariah Allen owned $600 in state six per cent securities, $15,000 in continental loan office certificates; Nicholas Brown owned $11,000 in state six per cents and $62,000 in continental loan office certificates;

---

[227] For a clear picture of the debts of the Providence merchants, and some notion of the relationship of these debts and security holdings to their opposition to the paper money, see Moses Brown to Champion and Dickson, June 26, 1785, Champion and Dickson to Moses Brown, August 19, 1785, and September 6, 1786, in the Moses Brown Papers, vol. 5; John Brown to Moses Brown, November 27, 1786, in the Peck Collection, vol. 8; and Nicholas Brown to David Howell, March 26, 1785, in the Rhode Island Historical Society Manuscripts, vol. 14; all in the Rhode Island Historical Society.

John Brown owned $3,920 in state four per cent notes and $68,000 in continental loan office certificates. This small group of merchants determined to destroy the entire plan of issuing paper money and retiring state debts.[228]

The favorite strategy of the opponents of the paper was to shout "cheat," to denounce the advocates of paper money as a band of dishonest debtors attempting to defraud their creditors. As has been observed, the paper-money plan had little to do with private debts, but the merchants pretended otherwise, and since they exercised substantial control over the principal means of communication, including the local newspapers, the friends of paper money went largely unheard. A second major charge was that, since the paper would not be accepted outside the state, it would destroy Rhode Island's commerce. This cry was as groundless as the first, for the state's interstate and foreign commerce increased every year the paper-money plan was in operation.[229]

But the constant stream of propaganda against paper money and the private manipulations of the merchant-speculators in continental loan office certificates rapidly undermined popular faith in the currency, and it began to depreciate quickly. In thirty months it depreciated, at an approximately steady rate, to about twelve or fifteen for one—that is, until its market value was about eight cents on the dollar. It remained at this level for two years, after which it rose to six for one, at which rate

[228] Security holdings are taken from the debt records in the Rhode Island Archives, cited in note 218. A few of the Providence merchants, even among those holding continental loan office certificates, were prepared at first to support the paper. The powerful mercantile firm of Clark and Nightingale, for example, which owned $13,000 in loan office certificates, borrowed £2,625 in paper money, apparently with a view to supporting it.

For a clear statement of the calculated efforts of this group to destroy the paper-money plan, see the message of Governor John Collins (who had himself been a merchant all his life) to the Assembly in August, 1786, in Petitions to the General Assembly, vol. 23, p. 58.

[229] Commercial data tabulated from Maritime Papers, Outward and Inward Entries, 1776–1787; Bonds, Masters of Vessels, vols. 9 (part 2), 10, 11; Manifests of Export Cargoes, vols. 1–4; Manifests of Import Cargoes, vols. 1–5; Book of Manifests, 1785–1789; "Miscellaneous, 1777–1786"; all in the Rhode Island Archives.

it circulated until all but a fraction of it was fully retired in 1800.[230]

Undaunted by the depreciation of the currency, the leaders of the paper-money faction pressed forward with their plan to retire state debts. In March, 1787, they called for a referendum on the question of paying the debts, and the vote of the towns was overwhelmingly favorable to the plan. A bill for the purpose was drafted and in 1788 the debts were retired in four quarterly installments. By the end of the year the state was free from debt, and for the first time in more than a decade no expenditures were required for interest payments. By 1789 the state's annual expenses were reduced to less than ten thousand pounds, forty per cent of which was collected in interest payments on the paper loaned and the remainder in the form of import duties. The direct tax load had been abolished.[231]

When the program had run its course its advantages and disadvantages could be assessed. On the debit side there were two results. The worst effect of the paper was the great damage it had done to the reputation of Rhode Island among its sister states. The little state's prestige had already been low, and now it had been reduced still further. A second bad effect was that private creditors suffered from the payment of debts in depreciated currency. As has been indicated, however, these losses were of considerably less importance than has generally been supposed.

[230] Price fluctuations have been traced in a wide variety of sources, including official state and town records, merchants' papers, and newspapers. A full account of the subsequent history of the paper is recorded in Grand Committee Office, Account Book A, pp. 61–110, and Account Book B, *passim*. By 1796, £69,252 of the money had been retired. When the accounts were closed in 1809, £2,580 in bonds was still outstanding, though the money itself had all been destroyed.

[231] The steps in the process of paying the debts have been traced in Acts and Proceedings of the General Assembly, in the Rhode Island Archives, and in the Providence and Newport newspapers for 1787 and 1788. The statement of the state's debts and the plan for their retirement which was submitted to the towns are in Reports to the General Assembly, 1778–1788, p. 116. The decisions of most of the towns on the referendum are recorded in Papers Relating to the Adoption of the Constitution, 45, 46, 48, 49, 51–56, 58, 61–63, 65. A record of the payment of the debt is the MS. Record of Notes on which the State has paid a part agreeably to An Act of Assembly passed at the June Session, A.D. 1791.

On the credit side were many important achievements. Almost everybody involved made money. The state government obviously gained, as did the taxpayers. The holders of state securities gained, for the depreciated paper they received was worth more than the depreciated securities they had owned.[232] Speculators, even those who denounced and worked against the paper, doubtless profited from the gyrations of the currency, despite the fact that large numbers of small holders of the state debt were enabled to receive payment for their securities before they could be bought up and concentrated in the hands of a few speculators. The cash received by the multitudes of Rhode Islanders in payment for their securities was, it is true, depreciated paper, but the paper was acceptable for taxes, and it was funds for the payment of taxes that was the principal need of the small security holders.

The great majority of the citizens recognized these benefits and supported the paper-money leaders from start to finish. By the middle of 1788 all the opposition was coming from Providence, from three other towns that supported Providence by large majorities, and from three towns that wavered and tended to oppose the paper plan by small majorities. The principal reason for the opposition in Providence has been analyzed earlier. The towns that joined Providence in unqualified opposition were Newport, Middletown, and Portsmouth. These towns held audited and approved accounts against the United States for war damages amounting to £124,000, £51,000, and £41,000, respectively. As it was clear almost from the outset that the paper-money program meant, in effect, a break with the United States, these towns quickly withdrew the support they had given earlier to the original plan for an issue of paper. The three wavering towns, Jamestown, Bristol, and Warren, also held large claims against the United States. They supported the

[232] For example, a person owning a four per cent state note of £10 face value prior to May, 1786, could have realized only about 18 shillings by selling it on the open market. In 1788 he was paid the full face value of the note plus accrued interest, a total of £11 4s. The paper money in which he was paid was, at an average price of ten for one, worth £1 2s. 6d. His net gain was thus 4s. 6d., or about 25 per cent.

paper, however, until it had depreciated considerably and the pressure from outside the state had become unbearable, and then they reversed their position by small majorities.[233]

The effect of these financial affairs upon the attitudes of Rhode Islanders toward the Constitution is clear. In general, the towns that constituted the bloc opposed to paper money or, more accurately, the particular individuals in those towns who had induced the towns to oppose paper, formed the hard core of the group that reacted favorably to the Constitution.

Virtually all the rest of the state opposed the Constitution from the moment it appeared. Steeped as they were in democratic traditions, Rhode Islanders could muster no enthusiasm for the republican conservatism of the Constitution, and many sincerely feared the political power vested in the proposed general government. Besides this philosophical consideration, there were three major, immediately practical reasons for the opposition. The first was that although the paper-money plan had just begun to operate in September, 1787, Rhode Island was already too deeply involved in the program to back out. The financial chaos that would have resulted from the abandonment of the plan before it had run its course would have made the existing financial situation seem peaceful and orderly by comparison.

This ground for opposition to the Constitution gave rise to another. The abuse heaped upon Rhode Island by other states caused most of its citizenry to band together more closely in bitter opposition to the United States. True, the abuse sometimes brought the opposite reaction; there were those who felt that Rhode Island should attempt to redeem itself in the public eye and that the only way it could do so was to join the Union. In the main, however, outsiders won very few friends in Rhode Island by hurling derisive epithets.

[233] The development of attitudes on paper money has been traced partly from miscellaneous materials in Papers Relating to the Adoption of the Constitution and partly from the following town records: Middletown Town Meeting Book, 1743–1808, in the Town Hall, Middletown; Portsmouth Town Meeting Records, vols. 1 and 2, in the Town Hall, Portsmouth; Bristol Town Meeting Book, 1781–1811, in the Town Hall, Bristol; and Warren Town Meeting Book, no. 1, 1746–1811, in the Town Hall, Warren.

A third reason for the continued opposition was that, despite much talk of the economic losses that would ensue if the state remained outside the Union, the economic possibilities of independent status were enormous. The most important of such potentials was smuggling to circumvent payment of United States import duties. It hardly needs to be said that smuggling was a form of business activity developed to perfection by the Rhode Island merchants before the war.[234]

In view of the weight of the opposition, then, the critical question to be answered is why six towns in the state changed sides in 1790 and finally voted for ratification. The usual answers to this question are two: that the threat of economic coercion on the part of the government of the United States frightened many, and that the state's merchants, creditors, and advocates of sound money united against farmers, debtors, and advocates of paper money to bring about the shift in votes.[235]

As to the former proposition, it is evident that the disadvantages that would have arisen from commercial legislation against Rhode Island by the United States were more than offset by the possibilities of profits from smuggling. The second proposition, that final victory for ratification was the result of the defeat of one economic class by another, requires careful consideration. The proposition cannot be tested with finality, though a superficial study of the interests of the individual voters in the towns indicates that there is little basis for a class interpretation. A reasonably accurate test, however, may be

[234] On the profits expected from smuggling in the event of Rhode Island's continued refusal to ratify the Constitution, see "Charlestoniensis" in the *Newport Herald* of November 20, 1788. If Rhode Island retained its independence, said the writer, "this State would not become an Algiers [i.e., a center for piracy], as some malevolent scribblers in Massachusetts have impudently asserted, but a St. Eustatius." St. Eustatius was the tiny Dutch Island in the West Indies that served as a base for smuggling into the British West Indies. That Massachusetts, Connecticut, and New York were alarmed at the prospect of smuggling activity by Rhode Island is clearly seen in the remarks of the congressmen from those states and their efforts to induce the United States to use force to bring Rhode Island into the Union. See, for example, the remarks of Benson of New York and Ames of Massachusetts in the House of Representatives on June 5, 1789, in *Annals of Congress*, 1:420 ff.

[235] Beard, *Economic Interpretation*, 237; Bates, *Rhode Island and the Union*, *passim*.

made by studying the immediate economic interests of the delegates to the ratifying convention. Such study reveals the following data.

ECONOMIC INTERESTS OF DELEGATES TO THE RATIFYING CONVENTION

MERCHANTS

Five of the delegates who voted for ratification were merchants and owners or part owners of vessels: [236]

Samuel Allen (Barrington), who owned the principal share of a 60-ton sloop.

Sherjashub Bourne (Bristol), who had from a fourth to a half interest in sloops of 22, 25, 50, 60, and 61 tons and a third interest in brigs of 66, 104, and 147 tons.

John I. Clark (Providence), who owned, with his partner Joseph Nightingale, a fleet of about a dozen vessels.

George Champlin (Newport), who had a half interest in a 125-ton brig and a fifth interest in a 204-ton ship.

Peleg Clarke (Newport), who had a fourth interest in a 208-ton ship and was the sole owner of a 95-ton brig.

Six of the delegates who voted against ratification were merchants and owners or part owners of vessels: [237]

Benjamin Arnold (Coventry), who had a third interest in a 40-ton brig.

Elisha Brown (North Providence), who had a half interest in a 45-ton sloop.

Thomas Rice (Warwick), who had a third interest in a 40-ton brig, a half interest in a 147-ton brig, and a third interest in sloops of 24 and 44 tons.

Andrew Waterman (Smithfield), who had a third interest in a 60-ton sloop.

Gideon Arnold (Warwick), who had a half interest in a 35-ton sloop.

Job Wilcox (Exeter), who had a half interest in a 42-ton sloop.

This weight of merchants on the side of the opponents of ratification is somewhat balanced, however, by the fact that one of the Federalist delegates, Isaac Manchester (Tiverton), was a mariner and two Federalist delegates, George Hazard (Newport) and William Ladd (Little Compton) were merchants who did not own vessels.[238]

[236] *Ship Documents of Rhode Island* (6 vols., mimeographed, Providence, 1938–1941): *Providence*, vol. 1 [part 1], pp. 7, 152; vol. 1, part 2, pp. 845, 858; *Newport*, vol. 1, pp. 45, 172, 184, 487, 507, 528, 568, 653. For vessels owned by John I. Clark see the indexes to the volumes for Providence and Newport.

[237] *Ibid.*, Providence, vol. 1 [part 1], pp. 152, 447; vol. 1, part 2, p. 946; *Newport*, vol. 1, pp. 264, 393, 442, 503, 602.

[238] *Ibid.*, *Providence*, vol. 1 [part 1], p. 263; vol. 1, part 2, p. 860; Cotner, ed., *Foster's Minutes*, 35n; *Providence Gazette*, January 27, 1787 (lodge money notices).

FARMERS

Every delegate in the convention owned farmland or other realty of a value of at least forty pounds, such ownership being the qualification for freemen. It is difficult, if not impossible, to generalize further about the occupations of the delegates, for almost all freemen in Rhode Island had a variety of interests—mercantile, manufacturing, and other personalty as well as farming. Only five delegates who voted for ratification were found to have been farmers who owned no mercantile or manufacturing property in addition to their realty: Benjamin Remington (Jamestown), Nicholas Carr (Jamestown), Joshua Barker (Middletown), Elisha Barker (Middletown), and Burrington Anthony (Portsmouth).[239]

The principal occupation of eight more Federalists was farming, and there were five lawyers, a physician, a hatter, the above-mentioned seven merchants and one mariner, one man who carried on a wagon trade with Boston, and five whose occupations were too varied to classify. The occupations of the opponents of ratification were approximately the same, except that only one anti-Federalist delegate, Joseph Reynolds (Exeter), was found to have been engaged in no economic activity other than farming. Neither party in the convention could reasonably be described as an "agrarian" party.[240]

DEBTORS

Private indebtedness is a nebulous condition, invariably difficult to ascertain. Except for the established fact that John I. Clark, George Champlin, and Peleg Clarke, all of whom favored ratification, were heavily indebted to British merchants,[241] the only information on indebtedness that is conveniently available is that revealed in the lodge-money announcements in the newspapers and in local property evaluations. Three Federalist delegates, Benjamin Remington, Nicholas Carr, and Elisha Barker, claimed exemptions for debts in their tax evaluations.[242] No anti-Federalists were found to have made such claims. Only two delegates who voted for ratification, Samuel Allen (Barrington) and William Ladd (Little Compton), wrote off debts in depreciated currency under the

[239] Jamestown Folder, Property Inventory, 1783; Middletown Folder, Rateable Property, 1783; Portsmouth Property Evaluations, 1783; all in the Rhode Island Archives.

[240] Information on the occupations and property holdings of the delegates has been gleaned from a variety of sources, often more than a half dozen per delegate. The most valuable sources are the town records in the various towns, scattered property evaluations in the Rhode Island Archives, newspaper advertisements, sketches in the notes to Cotner, ed., *Foster's Minutes*, and the genealogical and town history collections in the State Historical Society of Wisconsin. Sketches of five of the delegates are contained in the 1927 edition of the *Biographical Directory of Congress*, and as many more are in the *Dictionary of American Biography*. A list of the delegates, with their votes, appears in the *Providence Gazette* of June 5, 1790.

[241] See the sources cited in note 227 above.

[242] See the sources cited in note 239 above.

lodge-money provision. Only one delegate who voted against ratification, Joseph Reynolds, wrote off debts in this manner.[243] The available facts would seem to indicate that neither side was a debtors' faction, although approximately a fourth of the Federalists were debtors.

PUBLIC CREDITORS

Records for holdings of continental and state debts are complete, and they indicate the following distribution of security holdings in the convention.

Seventeen (50 per cent) of the delegates who voted for ratification were public creditors. The amounts of securities they held, exclusive of accrued interest, were as follows:

Six of them held both continental and state securities: [244]

Jabez Bowen (Providence), $15,948 continental, $391 state.
Henry Marchant (Newport), $619 continental, $747 state.
Benjamin Bosworth (Warren), $787 continental, $395 state.
Isaac Manchester (Tiverton), $95 continental, $446 state.
John I. Clark (Providence), $13,805 continental, $192 state.
John Brown (Hopkinton), $319 continental, $192 state.

Two held only continental securities: [245]

William Barton (Providence), $400.
Benjamin Arnold, Jr. (Warwick), $23.

Nine held only state securities: [246]

Sherjashub Bourne (Bristol), $505.
William Bradford (Bristol), $2,095.
Christopher Greene, Jr. (Warwick), $1,534.
Thomas Allen (Barrington), $50.
John S. Dexter (Cumberland), $623.
Benjamin Remington (Jamestown), $285.
Peleg Clarke (Newport), $13.
Benjamin Bourn (Providence), $452.

Fifteen (47 per cent) of the delegates who voted against ratification were public creditors, as follows:

Five held both continental and state securities: [247]

[243] Lodge money notices in the *Providence Gazette*, January 27, 1787 (summary of notices), and May 26, 1787.
[244] List of Notes Issued for Consolidating the Securities Issued from the General Treasurer's Office, 1, 2, 4, 8, 9, 10, 12, 13, 15; Ledger A, Accounts of Rhode Island against the United States, 497, 499, 500; Record of Notes on which the State Has Paid a Part, 75, 99. Some of the figures in the records are expressed in pounds, others in dollars. All figures are here converted into dollars, at the rate of 3 1/3 dollars per pound.
[245] List of Notes Issued for Consolidating the Securities Issued from the General Treasurer's Office, 2, 10.
[246] *Ibid.*, 1, 3, 9, 11; Record of Notes on which the State Has Paid a Part, 5, 14, 15, 16, 19, 25, 32, 48, 98, 103.
[247] List of Notes Issued for Consolidating the Securities Issued from the General Treasurer's Office, 4, 7, 9, 12; Accounts of Rhode Island against the

Elisha Brown (North Providence), $637 continental, $232 state.
Thomas Rice (Warwick), $569 continental, $720 state.
J. J. Hazard (South Kingston), $8 continental, $291 state.
Andrew Waterman (Smithfield), $240 continental, $2 state.
Joseph Stanton, Jr. (Charlestown), $271 continental, $22 state.

Three held only continental securities: [248]

James Aldrich (Scituate), $5.
Samuel Potter (South Kingston), $15.
Giles Slocum (Portsmouth), $28,253.

Seven held only state securities: [249]

Benjamin Arnold (Coventry), $1,435.
William B. King (Johnston), $9.
Joseph Reynolds (Exeter), $236.
Job Greene (Coventry), $72.
John Williams (Foster), $43.
James Sheldon (Richmond), $3.
John Sayles (Smithfield), $28.

The delegates voting for and the delegates voting against the Constitution, then, held approximately the same amounts of the same kinds of securities, and it would appear that there was no line of cleavage between public creditors and non-creditors. One fact of importance about security holdings, however, will be pointed out later.

PAPER MONEY

The pertinence of all the above data might be questionable if it developed that almost all the friends of paper money were against the Constitution. Such was not the fact, however. Twenty-one of the delegates who voted for ratification (62 per cent) had borrowed paper money in 1786: [250]

Samuel Allen (£60).
Thomas Allen (£54).
Burrington Anthony (£18).
Abraham Barker (£80 10s. 11½d.).
Levi Ballou (£28 14s.).
Joshua Barker (£18 6s.).
William Barton (£12 2s.).
Benjamin Bosworth (£16 16s.).
Benjamin Bourn (£303 6s. 8d.).
Sherjashub Bourne (£461).
Jabez Bowen (£30 9s.).

Nicholas Carr (£37 2s. 3d.).
John I. Clark (£2,625).
Christopher Greene (£21 5s.).
William Ladd (£100 4s.).
Isaac Manchester (£96 2s. 9d.).
Jesse Maxson (£208).
Samuel Pearce (£24 4s. 1½d.).
George Stillman (£21 19s. 5d.).
George Sears (£18).
William Tripp (£18).

United States, 497, 499; Record of Notes on which the State Has Paid a Part, 9, 12, 21, 25, 82, 105, 124.

[248] Accounts of Rhode Island against the United States, 497, 499; Portsmouth Town Meeting Records, vol. 1, entry immediately preceding page numbered 1.

[249] List of Notes Issued for Consolidating the Securities Issued from the General Treasurer's Office, 3, 5, 6; Record of Notes on which the State Has Paid a Part, 8, 19, 27, 51, 93, 134, 140, 149.

[250] Grand Committee Office, Book A, pp. 1, 2, 5, 7, 9, 10, 11, 16, 23, 33, 44, 47, 49, 52, 54, in the Rhode Island Archives.

A slightly smaller number on the other side were borrowers of paper. Twenty delegates who voted against ratification (63 per cent) borrowed paper: [251]

Benjamin Arnold (£170).

Gideon Arnold (£113 15*s*.).

Elisha Brown (£25).

Bowen Card (£17 11*s*.).

Job Comstock (£78).

Eseck Esten (£15).

Job Greene (£140 9*s*.).

J. J. Hazard (£278 10*s*.).

William Matthewson (£22).

Noah Matthewson (£33 6*s*.).

William Nichols (£43 8*s*.).

Pardon Mawney (£14).

Samuel J. Potter (£228 4*s*. 8*d*.).

Joseph Reynolds (£42).

Thomas Rice (£21 5*s*.).

James Sheldon (£90).

Giles Slocum (£36).

Andrew Waterman (£300).

Job Wilcox (£180).

John Williams (£370 18*s*.).

These data may be summarized as follows:

	FEDERALISTS		ANTI-FEDERALISTS	
	No.	Per Cent	No.	Per Cent
Owners of mercantile interests . . .	8	23.5	6	18.7
Owners of continental securities . . .	8	23.5	8	25.0
Owners of state securities	15	44.1	12	37.5
Public debtors (borrowed paper)	21	61.7	20	62.5
Private debtors	8	23.5	1	3.1

It is clear, then, that there is no basis in fact for the traditional explanation of the vote in Rhode Island. To understand that vote it is necessary to turn back to the original alignment on ratification, as it appeared in 1787, an alignment that had grown out of the financial history of the state during the period. Towns having a total of twenty-two delegates were favorable to the Constitution at the outset. The number of delegates finally voting for ratification was thirty-four. This means that twelve delegates, representing six towns, changed sides.

There were two principal economic reasons for the shift.[252]

[251] *Ibid.*, pp. 3, 18, 28, 29, 31, 36, 38, 40, 41, 46, 53, 54, 56–59.

[252] Another issue that doubtless had some influence in shaping opposition to the Constitution was a strong hostility toward slavery, particularly among the Quakers. In December, 1783, Quakers presented a petition for the abolition of slavery (Petitions to the General Assembly, 29:102), which resulted in February, 1784, in "An Act for the gradual abolition of slavery" (*Rhode Island Records*, 12:578–579). In June, 1787, Quakers again petitioned the Assembly

The first was the secession of Providence and the threatened secession of other Federalist towns, including Newport. Most citizens of the state felt that Rhode Island could go it alone, but if the state was to be rent to pieces by secessions and partial ratifications, the advocates of state sovereignty would have a hopeless situation on their hands.

The second reason was the promise of greater profits on public securities. By the time the ratifying convention met for its second session in May, 1790, it had become clear that Congress planned to assume the debts of the states. Rhode Island had paid its debts, after a fashion, but it could enact a law setting up a scale of depreciation on its paper money, declare that because of the depreciation only a part of the debt had been paid, and return the certificates to the original holders.[253]

It will be recalled that the great majority of the backers of paper money had been creditors of the state. Many of them now desired to capitalize on this opportunity to receive payment for their securities a second time. It is further to be observed that six of the twelve delegates who shifted sides between the two sessions of the ratifying convention (Thomas Allen, Samuel Allen, Isaac Manchester, John Brown, Christopher Greene, and John S. Dexter) were holders of state securities.

Most of the anti-Federalists were adamant in their opposition,

for abolition of the slave trade (Petitions to the General Assembly, 23:127), and in October of that year an act abolishing the slave trade was passed. The charter of the Rhode Island Abolition Society was granted in June, 1790 (Petitions to the General Assembly, 25:37); the petition which resulted in the passage of this act stated that the Society had existed for fifteen months. Eight of the 114 charter members of the Society were members of the ratifying convention: Daniel Owen, Joseph Stanton, Jr., James Sheldon, Job Comstock, John Sayles, John Williams, John S. Dexter, and Levi Ballou, only the last two of whom voted for ratification. The slavery question engendered more debate in the South Kingston convention than any other subject; Cotner, ed., *Foster's Minutes*.

[253] See William Ellery to Benjamin Huntington, June 15, 1789, and February 2, 1790, in the Ellery-Huntington Papers, in the Rhode Island Archives. In 1789 Ellery interviewed several anti-Federalist leaders in the state, who told him they planned to ratify later, but changed the subject when Ellery asked them why. In 1790 Ellery got his answer: they were holding out until it was clear that Congress planned to assume the state debts. Other evidence, in petitions preserved in the Rhode Island Archives, for example, suggests that a considerable number of persons were aware of these plans.

but enough of them joined with Federalists to secure passage of a bill in the legislature declaring that only a part of the debt had been paid, as outlined above.[254] That arrangement completed, they were ready to vote for ratification.

The other states that had paid part of their war debts received no credit for their efforts under Hamilton's assumption plan. Under that plan the debts that had been retired were considered retired once and for all. Rhode Island alone, by this last of the series of intricate financial maneuvers it had executed during the decade, was able to pay off its creditors and make it possible for those creditors to receive a second payment, this time from the government of the United States. Thus, even in the act of ratifying the Constitution, Rhode Island paid its disrespects to the Union one last time.

[254] The details of the plan are in Records and Proceedings of the General Assembly, vol. 14. The volume entitled Record of Notes on which the State Has Paid a Part is a record of the second funding of the state debt. Under the plan security holders were debited for the supposed "specie value" of the payments they had received in paper money, and securities for the balance were reissued to them.

PART FOUR: SIGNIFICANCE OF THE DATA

VIII

A Revaluation of the Beard Thesis
of the Making of the Constitution

PROFESSOR Beard interpreted the making of the Constitution as a simple, clear-cut series of events. When all the groups that became Federalists are brought together and analyzed, he asserted, and all the anti-Federalists are brought together and analyzed, the events can be seen as mere manifestations of a fundamentally simple economic conflict. His analysis led him to formulate three basic propositions, one regarding the Philadelphia Convention and two regarding the contest over ratification. In the light of the data in the foregoing chapters, we may now focus our attention upon these three key propositions of Beard's economic interpretation of the Constitution.

THE PHILADELPHIA CONVENTION

FROM his analysis of the Philadelphia Convention, Beard concluded that the Constitution was essentially "an economic document drawn with superb skill" by a "consolidated economic group . . . whose property interests were immediately at stake"; that these interests "knew no state boundaries but were truly national in their scope."

From a thorough reconsideration of the Philadelphia Convention, however, the following facts emerge. Fully a fourth of the delegates in the convention had voted in their state legislatures for paper-money and/or debtor-relief laws. These were the very kinds of laws which, according to Beard's thesis, the delegates had convened to prevent. Another fourth of the delegates had important economic interests that were adversely

349

affected, directly and immediately, by the Constitution they helped write. The most common and by far the most important property holdings of the delegates were not, as Beard has asserted, mercantile, manufacturing, and public security investments, but agricultural property. Finally, it is abundantly evident that the delegates, once inside the Convention, behaved as anything but a consolidated economic group.

In the light of these and other facts presented in the foregoing chapters, it is impossible to justify Beard's interpretation of the Constitution as "an economic document" drawn by a "consolidated economic group whose property interests were immediately at stake."

The Contest over Ratification, First Proposition

Beard asserted that the ultimate test of the validity of an economic interpretation of the Constitution would rest upon a comparative analysis of the economic interests of all the persons voting for and all the persons voting against ratification. He made an analysis of the economic interests of some of the leaders in the movement for ratification and concluded that "in the ratification, it became manifest that the line of cleavage for and against the Constitution was between substantial personalty interests on the one hand and the small farming and debtor interests on the other."

For the purpose of analyzing this proposition it is necessary to employ Beard's own definitions of interest groups. In the paragraphs that follow, as in the foregoing chapters, the term "men of personalty interests" is used to mean those groups which Beard himself had in mind when he used the term, namely money, public securities, manufacturing and shipping, and western lands held for speculation.

From a thorough reconsideration of the contests over ratification the following facts emerge.

1. In three states (Delaware, New Jersey, and Georgia) the decisions of the ratifying conventions were unanimous, and it is therefore impossibile to compare the interests of contending

parties. The following analyses of the conventions in these three states may be made, however.

In Delaware almost 77 per cent of the delegates were farmers, more than two-thirds of them small farmers with incomes ranging from 75 cents to $5.00 a week. Slightly more than 23 per cent of the delegates were professional men—doctors, judges, and lawyers. None of the delegates was a merchant, manufacturer, banker, or speculator in western lands.

In New Jersey 64.1 per cent of the delegates were farmers, 23.1 per cent were professional men (physicians, lawyers, and college presidents), and only 12.8 per cent were men having personalty interests (one merchant, three iron manufacturers, and one capitalist with diversified investments).

In Georgia 50 per cent of the delegates were farmers (38.5 per cent slave-owning planters and 11.5 per cent small farmers), 11.5 per cent were frontiersmen whose economic interests were primarily agrarian, 19.2 per cent were professional men (lawyers, physicians, and professional officeholders), and only 11.5 per cent had personalty interests (all merchants). The interests of 7.7 per cent of the delegates were not ascertained.

Beard assumed that ratification in these states was pushed through by personalty interest groups before agrarian and paper-money groups could organize their forces. The opposite is true. In each of these three states agrarian interests dominated the conventions. In each state there were approximately equal numbers of delegates who had voted earlier for and against paper money.

2. In two states in which the decision was contested (Virginia and North Carolina) the great majority of the delegates on both sides of the question were farmers. In both states the delegates who voted for and the delegates who voted against ratification had substantially the same amounts of the same kinds of property, most commonly land and slaves. A large number of the delegates in the Virginia convention had voted on the question of repudiation of debts due British merchants, and the majority of the delegates who had favored such repudiation voted for ratification of the Constitution. Large numbers

of delegates in both North Carolina conventions were speculating in western lands. In the first convention a great majority of these land speculators opposed the Constitution; in the second a substantial majority of them favored ratification.

Beard assumed that ratification in these states represented the victory of wealthy planters, especially those who were rich in personalty other than slaves, over the small slaveless farmers and debtors. The opposite is true. In both states the wealthy planters—those with personalty interests as well as those without personalty interests—were divided approximately equally on the issue of ratification. In North Carolina small farmers and debtors were likewise equally divided, and in Virginia the great mass of the small farmers and a large majority of the debtors favored ratification.

3. In four states (Connecticut, Maryland, South Carolina, and New Hampshire) agrarian interests were dominant, but large minorities of delegates had personalty interests.

In Connecticut 57.8 per cent of the delegates who favored ratification and 67.5 per cent of those who opposed ratification were farmers. Ratification was approved by 76.2 per cent of all the delegates, by 81.8 per cent of the delegates having personalty interests, and by 73.3 per cent of the farmers in the convention. Here, then, four delegates out of five having substantial personalty interests favored the Constitution. On the other hand, three of every four farmers also favored the Constitution.

In Maryland 85.8 per cent of the delegates who voted for ratification were farmers, almost all of them wealthy slave-owning planters; 27.3 per cent of the opponents of ratification were farmers, all of them substantial slave-owning planters. The opponents of ratification included from three to six times as large a proportion of merchants, lawyers, and investors in shipping, confiscated estates, and manufacturing as did the delegates who favored ratification. It is to be observed, however, that because the vote in the Maryland ratifying convention was almost unanimous (63 to 11), statistics on the attitudes of the various interest groups would show that every major interest group except manufacturers favored the Constitution. A majority of the areas and of the delegates that had advocated paper money also favored the Constitution.

In South Carolina 59 per cent of the delegates who voted for ratification were large slave-owning planters and 10.7 per cent were lesser planters and farmers. Of the delegates who voted against ratification, 41.7 per cent were large slave-owning planters and 34.2 per cent were lesser planters and farmers. Merchants, factors, and mariners favored ratification, 70 per cent to 30 per cent, a margin almost identical to the vote of the entire convention—67 per cent for, 33 per cent against—and manufacturers, artisans, and mechanics were unanimous in support of the Constitution. On the other hand, 35.7 per cent of the delegates who favored ratification were debtors who were in a desperate plight or had borrowed paper money from the state. Only 15.1 per cent of those who voted against ratification were debtors or had borrowed paper money from the state. No fewer than 82 per cent of the debtors and borrowers of paper money in the convention voted for ratification.

As respects New Hampshire, comparisons are difficult because of the lack of adequate information concerning 28.2 per cent of the delegates. Of the delegates whose interests are known, 36.9 per cent of those favoring the Constitution and 25 per cent of those opposing it were farmers; of the known farmers in the convention 68.7 per cent favored ratification. If it is assumed, however, that all the delegates whose interests are not ascertainable were farmers (as in all likelihood most of them were), then 49.1 per cent of the delegates favoring ratification were farmers, 54.3 per cent of those opposing ratification were farmers, and 52.8 per cent of the farmers in the convention voted for ratification. Delegates whose interests were primarily in personalty (merchants, tradesmen, manufacturers, and shipbuilders) voted in favor of ratification, 60.9 per cent to 39.1 per cent. Delegates from the towns which had voted for and against paper money divided almost equally on the question of ratification: 42 per cent of the towns that had voted for paper money and 54 per cent of those that had voted against paper sent delegates who voted for the Constitution.

Beard assumed that in these states ratification was the outcome of class struggles between commercial and other personalty groups (Federalists) on the one hand and farmers and advocates of paper money (anti-Federalists) on the other. This generalization is groundless. In each of these states a majority of the men having personalty interests favored ratification, but in each of them a similar majority of the farmers also favored ratification. In one of these states there was no great demand for paper money, in another a large majority of the friends of paper money favored ratification, and in the other two the advocates of paper money were divided almost equally on the question of ratification.

4. In four states (Massachusetts, Pennsylvania, New York, and Rhode Island) men having personalty interests were in a majority in the ratifying conventions.

In Massachusetts, in the popular vote (excluding that of Maine) men whose interests were primarily non-agrarian favored the Constitution by about three to two, and men whose interests were primarily agrarian opposed the Constitution by about 55 per cent to 45 per cent. In the ratifying convention 80 per cent of the merchants and shippers engaged in water-borne commerce, 77 per cent of the artisans and mechanics, and 64 per cent of the farmers favored ratification. About 83 per cent of the retail storekeepers, 85 per cent of the manufacturers, and 64 per cent of the miscellaneous capitalists opposed ratification. One-fourth of those favoring and one-sixth of those opposing the Constitution were farmers. Of the personalty groups combined, 57.5 per cent opposed and 42.5 per cent favored ratification. The realty groups combined, including artisans and mechanics, favored ratification by 67 per cent to 33 per cent.

In Pennsylvania only 34.8 per cent of the delegates favoring ratification were farmers, and only 26.1 per cent of the opponents were farmers. Almost three-fourths—72.7 per cent—of the farmers in the convention favored ratification. The great majority of the delegates on both sides, however, 84.7 per cent of those favoring and 91.3 per cent of those opposing the Constitution, had substantial investments in one or more of Professor Beard's four forms of personalty.

New York delegates are difficult to classify as farmers because almost all farmers in the convention were also landlords with tenants. Delegates to the state's convention may be classified as elected Federalists, converts from anti-Federalism, delegates who abstained from voting, and anti-Federalists. Of the delegates about whom there is sufficient data on which to generalize, fewer than 20 per cent of each group consisted of farmers who had no tenants and who owned none of Beard's four forms of personalty.

Rhode Island delegates do not lend themselves to occupational classification because almost everyone in the state normally combined in his own economic activities several kinds of functions. Only 11.8 per cent of the delegates favoring ratification and only one of the delegates opposing ratification were found to have no interests except farming. The early opponents of paper money formed the original core of those favoring ratification, yet in the final vote 62 per cent of the delegates voting for ratification and 63 per cent of those opposing ratification were men who had borrowed paper money from the state.

Beard's thesis—that the line of cleavage as regards the Constitution was between substantial personalty interests on the one hand and small farming and debtor interests on the other—is entirely incompatible with the facts.

The Contest over Ratification, Second Proposition

BEARD was less certain of the foregoing point, however, than he was of this next one:

> Inasmuch as so many leaders in the movement for ratification were large security holders, and inasmuch as securities constituted such a large proportion of personalty, this economic interest must have formed a very considerable dynamic element, if not the preponderating element, in bringing about the adoption of the new system. . . . Some holders of public securities are found among the opponents of the Constitution, but they are not numerous.

This proposition may be analyzed in the same manner that Beard's more general personalty-agrarian conclusion was analyzed. To repeat, Beard asserted that public securities were the dynamic element within the dynamic element in the ratification. This assertion is incompatible with the facts. The facts are these:

1. In three states (Delaware, New Jersey, and Georgia) there were no votes against the Constitution in the ratifying conventions, and hence no comparisons can be made. If public securities were the dynamic element in the ratification, however, it would be reasonable to expect that the great majority of the delegates in these states which supported the Constitution so unreservedly should have been security holders. But the fact is that in Delaware only one delegate in six owned securities, in New Jersey 34 per cent of the delegates, and in Georgia only one delegate.

2. In two states (New Hampshire and North Carolina) the numbers of security holders among the delegates were very small. In New Hampshire only 10.5 per cent of those who voted for and only 2.2 per cent of those who voted against ratification held securities. In the first North Carolina convention only 2.4 per cent of the friends and only 1.1 per cent of the opponents of ratification held securities. In the second convention only 2.0 per cent of those favoring and only 3.9 per cent of those opposing the Constitution were security holders. Superficially these facts tend to substantiate Beard's thesis, for these virtually security-less states were slow to ratify the Constitution. It has been shown, however, that actually the reluctance of these states to adopt the Constitution and their vulnerability to raids on their securities by outsiders were both merely surface manifestations of the same underlying conditions—the isolation, the lack of information, and the lethargy of the majority of the inhabitants of North Carolina and New Hampshire.

3. In three states (Rhode Island, Maryland, and Virginia) where there were contests and considerable numbers of security holders, the advocates and the opponents of ratification included approximately the same percentages of security holders: in Rhode Island, 50 per cent of the advocates and 47 per cent of

the opponents; in Virginia, 40.5 per cent of the advocates and 34.2 per cent of the opponents; and in Maryland, 17.4 per cent and 27.3 per cent respectively. The facts relative to these three states clearly contradict Beard's thesis.

4. In two states (Massachusetts and Connecticut) the advocates of ratification included a considerably larger percentage of holders of securities than did the opponents. In Massachusetts 31 per cent of the ratificationists and only 10.1 per cent of the anti-ratificationists were security owners, and in Connecticut 36.7 per cent and 15 per cent respectively. The situations in these two states, and in these two states alone, tend strongly to support Beard's thesis.

5. In three states (Pennsylvania, South Carolina, and New York) a considerably larger percentage of the delegates opposing ratification than of the Federalist delegates held public securities. In Pennsylvania 73.9 per cent of the opponents and 50 per cent of the supporters of ratification were security owners, in South Carolina 71 and 43 per cent respectively, and in New York 63 and 50 per cent respectively. The facts pertaining to these states not only fail to harmonize with Beard's thesis but indicate that there the precise opposite of his thesis is true.

In the light of the foregoing facts it is abundantly evident that there are no more grounds for considering the holding of public securities the dynamic element in the ratification than for considering this economic interest the dynamic element in the opposition. There were, indeed, some holders of public securities among the opponents of the Constitution and, contrary to Beard's assertion, they were as numerous as the security holders among the supporters of the Constitution.

On all counts, then, Beard's thesis is entirely incompatible with the facts. Beard's essential error was in attempting to formulate a single set of generalizations that would apply to all the states. Any such effort is necessarily futile, for the various interest groups operated under different conditions in the several states, and their attitudes toward the Constitution varied with the internal conditions in their states.

IX

Economic Interests and Their Relation
to the Constitution

THE foregoing chapters were designed to test the validity of Beard's interpretation and were necessarily cast, in so far as it was possible to do so, in terms of the broad framework Beard constructed. In these terms conclusions drawn from the data presented were essentially negative. At the same time, however, it appeared that economic factors were by no means without influence in the making of the Constitution. On the contrary, in several instances economic elements were obviously of considerable importance. The critical question is whether, by reorganizing the data, it is possible to reduce them to an economic interpretive system or set of systems that will render intelligible the contests over ratification.

To do this it is necessary at the outset to broaden Beard's classifications of the economic interest groups that existed in 1787, to reappraise their statuses under the Articles of Confederation, and to determine what were the effects upon them of the making of the Constitution. Only in this way can it be determined whether it is possible to devise a meaningful interpretive system or systems by using economic classes or interest groups as a cornerstone.

In re-analyzing economic interests and the effects of the Constitution on them, they can be brought into sharper focus if they are considered as activities of men before they are considered as forms of property—that is, first as occupations and professions, the means of making a living or acquiring wealth and the property incidental or necessary to those means, and then as investments of capital.

In the 1780's substantially all free Americans fell into one or more of four broad occupational categories: farmers, nonagrarian producers, commercial groups, and professional men.[1] The following paragraphs analyze these groups by breaking them down into their lowest common denominators.[2]

Farmers, and by this term one here understands all persons who made their living directly from the soil, constituted the great majority of the population—about seventy-five per cent—and they may be divided into at least thirteen distinct groups with basically different statuses and economic interests.[3] This

[1] Eliminated from consideration here are those groups that were politically mute: children, women, and slaves. This leaves only some 600,000 free adult males who were entitled to express themselves on political questions. This figure takes no account of those few who were disfranchised by law.

[2] In addition to the sources cited with the data presented in Chapters 5, 6, and 7, a multitude of sources have contributed to the following analysis. A few of the most important of them may be mentioned here. The most valuable manuscript collections used were tax evaluation lists, particularly those in the Microfilm Collection of Early Town Records in the New Hampshire State Library at Concord; the Evaluation of 1786 in the Massachusetts Archives at Boston; town records of Rhode Island, some of them in the Rhode Island Archives at Providence, but most in the several town halls; the Evaluation of 1786 in the Connecticut Archives at Hartford; Assessment Lists in the Delaware Hall of Records at Dover; the magnificent collection of county property lists in the Virginia State Library at Richmond; assorted local records in the North Carolina Historical Commission at Raleigh; and the County Lists in the Georgia Department of Archives and History at Atlanta. Two major printed sources are of the same nature, the *Pennsylvania Archives* (lists in Series 3) and, for the southern states, the *Census of 1790*. Customs office records for twenty-four of the thirty leading American ports, 1783–1790, were used in the analysis of commercial interests, along with countless collections of merchants' private papers. Newspapers formed an important auxiliary source of information on all interests. Of the more valuable secondary works, the following were especially useful: Victor S. Clark's *History of Manufactures in the United States* (3 vols., New York, 1929); William B. Weeden's *Economic and Social History of New England* (2 vols., Boston, 1891); James Defebaugh's *History of the Lumber Industry of North America* (2 vols., Chicago, 1906, 1907); Lewis C. Gray's *History of Agriculture in the Southern United States to 1860* (2 vols., Washington, 1933); Richard P. McCormick's excellent study of New Jersey, *Experiment in Independence*; D. Huger Bacot's two fine articles on the South Carolina middle country and up country, in the *South Atlantic Quarterly*, vol. 23 (1924), and the *American Historical Review*, vol. 28 (1923), respectively; and Morris and Morris' study of economic conditions in North Carolina in 1780, in the *North Carolina Historical Review*, vol. 16 (1939).

[3] The agrarian population in 1790 is commonly estimated at about 90 per cent. The lower figure used here is only an estimate, but it is based on a count of the known active places of nonagricultural employment, including shipping,

agrarian class was broadly divided into subsistence farmers (two groups) and marketing farmers (eleven groups). The marketing farmers may be further divided into those not using slave labor (eight groups) and those using slave labor (three groups).

The subsistence farmers may be defined as those who produced nothing that was sold directly to consumers in commercial markets; they produced exclusively or almost exclusively for their own use, and their transactions consisted exclusively of barter with other subsistence farmers and sometimes with millers. Economically, each subsistence farmer was an island. There were some such farmers in every state except possibly Rhode Island. They were located in isolated, though not necessarily remote, places, and their problem was essentially one of transportation. Close examination reveals that there were two kinds of subsistence farmers, depending on the topography and location of the areas in which they lived.

The first group included those who were destined to remain subsistence farmers permanently;[4] neither canals nor roads nor dredging of rivers nor treaties with foreign powers could give them an outlet to the outside world. There were sprinklings of such farmers throughout the country, particularly in hilly and mountainous regions, but the greatest concentration of them was along the stony ridges of New England. The farmers in the hill country north of Lake Winnipesaukee and between the three major rivers of New Hampshire, and those in corresponding areas in Massachusetts and Connecticut, comprised the great majority of the "permanent" subsistence farmers.

Their interests were almost identical everywhere, for they were touched by economic and governmental matters in only one way: through taxation.[5] Since the taxes collected in these

and an estimate of the minimum number of persons necessary to activate such places. It is true that almost everyone was directly or indirectly connected with agriculture, but 75 per cent is, in my opinion, a liberal estimate of the number who derived their livelihoods directly from the soil.

[4] That is, "permanently" under the existing technology. Ultimately, with the coming of the railroad, some of them were connected with the outside world; others remained economically isolated until the advent of the automobile.

[5] These farmers joined with other groups in insurrectionary movements in New Hampshire, Massachusetts, and Connecticut in 1786, all as a protest

three states were used primarily for servicing their mammoth war debts, the formation of the government under the Constitution directly and immediately affected these farmers in a favorable way. The fiscal changes brought about by the new government—the funding of state and national debts, and the shifting of the principal burden of taxation to commerce (that is, to consumers of imports)—could be expected to have reduced the taxes of these farmers to almost nothing, and by 1791 they did just that. The action of these isolated farmers on the issue of ratification, however, as on most political questions, was erratic, for they were, by the nature of their situation, among the most poorly informed citizens of the country on current affairs.

The other kind of subsistence farmers was quite different. They were on or near transportation routes that were economically or politically susceptible of development, and their status was thus temporary. They were found along the Mohawk in New York, in the upper Delaware regions of New Jersey and Pennsylvania, along the Susquehanna and its tributaries, above the fall line of the Potomac and of the James, along the Roanoke and near the Great Dismal Swamp in North Carolina, high on the Cooper and Santee rivers in South Carolina, and west of the mountains, particularly on the Ohio, Tennessee, and Mississippi rivers and their tributaries.

In so far as they were farmers who had good prospects, depending for their progress on the development of better transportation facilities, these subsistence farmers had interests in common with one another and in sharp contrast to those of the first group of subsistence farmers. In other respects, however, their interests differed and sometimes even conflicted. Their interests varied with length of settlement, extent of contact with the outside world, indebtedness contracted to purchase land, the legality of land titles, the quality of land, and the proximity and disposition of Indian tribes.

More fundamentally, their interests differed according to the

against the excessive tax burden on real property and polls. In general, however, they often did not bother to participate in political affairs at all, not even to the extent of holding annual town meetings to vote for state officers.

methods that were necessary to develop their transportation facilities. One or both of two general kinds of action was required: political and economic. Among those needing political action, for example, were the farmers whose outlet to the sea was via the Mississippi. Since Spain controlled New Orleans, their entire future depended on the possibility of negotiating a treaty or reaching some other settlement with Spain. On the other hand, the opening of the James River to the Blue Ridge Mountains depended entirely on the raising of private capital and the physical work of dredging and constructing locks around falls. The opening of the Susquehanna required both political and private economic action. Each subsistence farming area of this type required its own specific remedies.

The scrutiny to which the various interest groups from state to state and area to area were subjected in the preceding chapters indicates that some of these farmers felt that they were well off under the Articles of Confederation, some needed and desired the changes instituted by the Constitution, others saw their prospects threatened or temporarily ruined by the Constitution, and still others were unaffected by political change or were conscious of no effects. Beyond repeating that they had an identity of interest in that they shared a single basic problem, it is therefore impossible to generalize as to the way in which the Constitution affected them or the way in which they reacted to it.

Turning now to commercial farmers, those who regularly brought crops to market to exchange for money or goods, the first groups to be considered are those that employed no slave labor.

At the bottom of the scale of marketing farmers using free labor were what might be termed the wood farmers, those who tilled barren land and reached markets only with lumber and occasional garden products. The only real poor-farmer class in America, they resided in the rocky, infertile areas of New England and in the pine barrens and the depleted tobacco lands of the southern tidewater. Miserable and despised, these people were generally regarded as lazy, irresponsible, and drunken.

Often hiring out as lumber-camp workers in the North and as semi-servile laborers in the South, they frequently made no attempt to till their poor soil. In some places they were deprived of the franchise and in others their votes were reputedly bought. Their most spectacular contributions to the politics of their states were noisy demonstrations and violence; in 1786 they enthusiastically supported Shays' Rebellion in Massachusetts.[6] They had little to gain or to lose by political change. Though lumber was cheap, the market for it was stable. The price of their labor was destined forever to be high; whenever they needed cash to buy rum or to pay taxes or to keep out of debtors' prison, they could always work for others, though they exercised this privilege with great reluctance. One thing promised by the establishment of the new government might have disturbed them: more civil order.

The next class of farmers were the stock raisers of New England, who also occupied poor farmland but who were considerably better off economically than the wood farmers. The stock farmers, though often left out of account in discussions of New England's economy, actually produced almost half the total value of exports from the ports of lower New England. About 15 per cent of New Hampshire's exports consisted of beef and livestock, in Boston and Salem they constituted nearly 10 per cent, and in Connecticut livestock was the principal staple. Ten to twelve thousand horses were exported annually from Connecticut to the West Indies, along with an equal number of cattle, sheep, and hogs; animals constituted more than 75 per cent of the total value of the state's exports.[7]

[6] An excellent description of this class in New England is contained in Jeremy Belknap's *History of New Hampshire* (3 vols., Boston, 1792), 3:210 ff., 261. For graphic accounts of the purchase of votes in the South, see the writings of "Aristides," "Observator," and "An obscure Citizen" in the Richmond *Virginia Gazette and American Advertiser*, March 28 to April 25, 1787.

[7] Records of the Port of New Haven, and An Abstract of Exports from Salem Previous to 1792, both in Customs Office Records in the Fiscal Section of the National Archives; Account of the Exports and Clearances of the Port of Boston for the Years 1787 and 1788, in Massachusetts Miscellaneous Manuscripts, in the Manuscripts Division of the Library of Congress; Hartford *Connecticut Courant*, January 16, 1786, January 15, 1787; Middletown *Middlesex Gazette*, January 22, 1787; New London *Connecticut Gazette*, January 11, 1788; *Providence Gazette*, January 9, 1790.

The interests of the horse and stock raisers had been enhanced by independence, which had opened the insatiable markets of the French West Indies, particularly the island of Martinique, to American livestock and American vessels. It was unlikely that the political changes expected under the new Constitution would affect them any further. They were unaffected by the fact that Congress, by obtaining power to regulate commerce, might be able to open the British West Indies to American shipping, for those markets were already open to American goods. In any event, the French markets were far more important to them. The attitudes and decisions of the horse and cattle farmers, as a class, were therefore shaped by considerations other than their economic interests.

An almost forgotten group, the Narragansett planters, made up the third class of farmers using free labor. Their principal product, horses, was the same as that of the Connecticut stock farmers, but there the resemblance ends. Located on Rhode Island's western shore, these northern aristocrats had once greatly resembled the southern planters, having all the trappings of a great landed gentry, including even slave labor. They had declined greatly by 1787; their slaves were almost all gone and their wealth consisted of little more than land. They still exercised a powerful influence on Rhode Island politics, however, and they still produced their famous luxury staple, the Narragansett pacer.[8]

The Narragansett planters were in a peculiar economic-political situation, one that helped produce the spectacularly radical government of Rhode Island during the 1780's. Both political power and the tax structure in Rhode Island rested on the ownership of land, a basis long since obsolete in Rhode Island's highly developed commercial and manufacturing economy. This conflict between economic realities and political forms came to a crisis in the 1780's when the state's immense

---

[8] See William D. Miller, "The Narragansett Planters," in the *Proceedings of the American Antiquarian Society*, New Series, vol. 43, part 1, pp. 49–115; Edward Channing, "The Narragansett Planters, A Study in Causes," in *Johns Hopkins University Studies in History and Political Science*, Series 4, No. 3 (Baltimore, 1886).

war debt necessitated a tax load which the land could not support, and the tax system broke down. The Narragansett planters were among the leaders of the movement for the radical and extremely complex series of fiscal measures enacted by the state. This was elaborated earlier; for present purposes it is sufficient to recall that in 1787 the program hung in the balance and would have been destroyed by a transfer of supremacy in fiscal matters to the United States, as was provided for in the Constitution. The interests of the Narragansett planters, like those of most citizens of Rhode Island, were closely tied to the success or failure of this fiscal program, and a vote for the Constitution would have been, at least for two or three years after 1787, a vote for their economic ruin.[9]

The fourth group of farmers using free labor were the small farmers of Rhode Island and the immediately adjacent areas of Massachusetts who produced no staple. Bred to the sea and forced by the scarcity of good land to live by their wits, almost all of them combined farming with some kind of maritime or commercial activity. The most common method was for a group of small farmers to build or buy a small sailing vessel jointly. When crops were harvested, instead of selling directly to merchants in Providence or Newport, they loaded their vessels and sailed to better markets to the south. By playing off the differences in prices between the several ports and by following seasonal price variations carefully, they pyramided the income from their crops to as much as two or three times their local value. The confused currency systems prevalent under the Articles of Confederation—four different systems were used by various states, and Congress used a fifth—made possible further profits from an early form of arbitrage.

Their interest was in free trade. Indeed, free interstate commerce and free access to the ports of the West Indies were almost a requisite for their survival. A superficial appraisal would thus seem to indicate that their interests would have dictated an enthusiastic reception of the Constitution. Perhaps of more immediate importance to them, however, was the Rhode Island

[9] See the account of ratification in Rhode Island, Chapter 8, above.

fiscal program. Their attitudes as a self-conscious interest group toward ratification would not have been easy to predict. If it could be assumed, however, that they would gamble that American ports would be free and open to their vessels even if they did not join the new Union, it could probably be further assumed that they would be hesitant about joining the Union. But to both groups of Rhode Island farmers, as to many groups elsewhere, their interests as economic classes were overshadowed by their interests as inhabitants of a particular state.

There was a fifth group of farmers in New England: the tobacco and wheat farmers of the Connecticut valley. Blessed with an abundance of rich land and easy access to market, these farmers ordinarily enjoyed success and prosperity. But they were vitally affected by two political considerations.

Prior to the Revolution they had generally exported and imported via Boston, which they reached by sleds during the winter. After 1783, for various reasons, they traded almost exclusively via the Connecticut through New York City. Beginning in 1784, however, New York levied heavy duties on imports, which meant that farmers (and other consumers) in the Connecticut valley who traded through New York City paid duties for the support of the New York state government. They were also subject to heavy direct or excise taxes, borne chiefly by the farmers, for the support of their own state governments, particularly for servicing their huge war debts. In all likelihood the import duties would be continued or even raised under the Constitution, but the income would be used to cover the assumption of war debts. Thus a vote for ratification was a vote against double taxation, a vote for tremendous tax relief.[10]

The other political consideration, considerably more subtle, affected wheat farmers everywhere. In 1781–1782 Spain had opened some of its American possessions, including Havana, to United States shipping. Havana was such a good market for American wheat that many felt it had saved the United States economy during the hardest war years. But after the peace of

[10] See the accounts of ratification in Connecticut, Chapter 5, and Massachusetts, Chapter 6, above.

1783 Spain reconsidered its position, looked with alarm at the ambitious new country it had helped create, and adopted a general anti-American policy. The main features of this policy were two: 1) it closed all its American possessions to the goods and vessels of the United States and 2) fearful that the westward expansion of the United States would encroach upon its possessions, it blocked navigation of the Mississippi through its control of New Orleans. In this situation some kind of treaty with Spain was highly desirable for wheat farmers and absolutely necessary to westerners. Hence it might seem that both interests should have welcomed the Constitution because it put the United States in a stronger treaty-making position.

But it was generally felt that commercial concessions could be extracted from Spain only by guaranteeing that Americans would not encroach on New Orleans and the west. Wheat farmers and merchants were willing to go this far, for the opening of Spanish-American markets could raise wheat prices by 50 to 100 per cent. On the other hand, trans-Alleghany westerners would gladly sacrifice such markets for the opening of the Mississippi. They were not afraid to offend Spain; indeed, many favored a show of force or at least a general encouragement of filibusters or other forms of physical pressure and extra-legal activity. Thus the interests of the wheat farmers and merchants were directly opposed to those of the trans-Alleghany inhabitants and land speculators.

The ratification of the Constitution did not, of itself, preclude either interest group from realizing its ambitions. In general, however, it could be expected that under the Constitution a policy of force would be rejected in favor of a policy of peaceful negotiations for commercial concessions. In addition, the Jay-Gardoqui negotiations of 1786 had made westerners particularly fearful that easterners would surrender claims to the Mississippi at the first opportunity.[11]

[11] The Jay-Gardoqui negotiations are treated at length in Samuel F. Bemis' *Pinckney's Treaty: A Study of America's Advantage from Europe's Distress, 1783–1800* (Baltimore, 1926), and Arthur P. Whitaker's *The Spanish American Frontier, 1783–1795* (Boston, 1927). For an accurate and lively brief account see Jensen's *The New Nation,* 170–174.

Closely akin to the Connecticut valley farmers were the members of the sixth group, the yeomanry of the middle states: New York, Pennsylvania, Delaware, and New Jersey. Owning from 30 to 240 acres of good land, these farmers concentrated on wheat as a staple, and they were generally prosperous throughout the postwar years. Their farms were not often laden with debts, and they usually lived within their means. As wheat farmers they shared an interest with similar farmers on the Connecticut.

On the other hand, the political interests of these farmers were, by and large, unfavorably affected by the changes resulting from the making of the Constitution. Politically they were probably the most vocal and possibly the strongest single interest group in the United States. About a fourth of them were of Dutch, German, and other national stocks; the remainder were the renowned Scotch-Irish Presbyterians. They had ridden to political strength on the crest of the Revolution, and in the 1780's they exercised substantial control of New York and Pennsylvania politics and played important roles in the politics of New Jersey and Delaware. The shifting of sovereignty from the states to the general government threatened their political supremacy by upsetting the state legislative and administrative programs on which it was based.

The seventh group of slaveless farmers, the Hudson valley patricians, was a unique class. As owners of vast estates of rich farmland which was tilled mostly by tenants, they were primarily landlords rather than farmers. Another characteristic that set them apart from most American farmers was their close identification with mercantile interests. There was hardly a family among them that did not pursue, through one or more of its members, commercial activity on a large scale. As men of great wealth, most of them also had large investments in still other ventures and personal property.[12]

It is therefore impossible to make precise generalizations

---

[12] Virginia D. Harrington, "The Place of the Merchant in New York Colonial Life," in *Proceedings of the New York State Historical Association*, 30:366 (1931).

about their interests. Professors Beard and Cochran have assumed that the burden of taxes had an important bearing on their political attitudes, but this viewpoint neglects the vital fact that, according to the terms of carefully drawn contracts, the taxes on their lands were invariably paid by their tenants. As wheat producers, merchants, holders of public securities, and investors in other fields, they were affected in many ways by politics, but since New York seemed willing and able, at least in the short run, to give them everything they needed, there was little economic reason why they should desire the changes brought about by the Constitution.[13]

The final group of non-slaveholding farmers were the tenant farmers of New York. Economically and politically they were hardly distinguishable from the Scotch-Irish landowning farmers of New York; only their special tenure status made them a distinct group. Until the Revolution a *viva voce* system of voting had made them politically subservient to their manor lords, but Clinton's party had established the secret ballot, accomplishing at once the liberation of a strong new force in state politics and a virtual guarantee that that force would support Clinton candidates.

Since the tenant farmers paid a large share of the direct taxes in the state, it might seem that Beard's argument relative to the shifting of the tax burden (that ratification, by depriving New York of her impost, would necessitate the resumption of heavy land taxes to support the state government) would apply to them. But as a matter of fact ratification in New York meant the virtual elimination of all state taxes, as was explained earlier, and it is hardly likely that many in the state were unaware of this fact. Furthermore, the tenant farmers, like other wheat farmers, had an interest in a Spanish treaty. Thus if they were guided solely by their economic interests these farmers would have voted for ratification.

Among those farmers who held slaves, the economic importance and economic value of slavery varied widely with indi-

[13] Beard, *Economic Interpretation*, xv, xvi, 29; Cochran, *New York in the Confederation;* Spaulding, *New York in the Critical Period,* 154.

vidual cases, as even the most casual glance reveals. In general, however, farms employing slave labor fell into three broad categories: 1) those to which slavery was an auxiliary labor supply, 2) those which were based on slavery but to which the real economic value of slavery was questionable, and 3) those to which slavery was both practical and necessary. Each of these three broad classes consisted of two subgroups.

Generally speaking, the farmers who employed slaves as an auxiliary labor force were classifiable into two groups, on the basis of the permanence of their status. The first group included those who, either from physical necessity—by reason of limited area, distance from markets, quality of land, or other such conditions—or from personal choice, would continue to use only a few slaves indefinitely. The greatest concentrations of such farmers were in the Valley of Virginia and in North Carolina. The entire economy of North Carolina was one that employed slavery but was not based on it. The second group consisted of farmers who used few slaves only because they were in areas that were still in early stages of development, and fully intended ultimately to establish great plantations manned by slaves. These were the farmers of Kentucky and Tennessee, of many parts of the Virginia piedmont, and of the back country of Maryland, South Carolina, and Georgia.

The economic interests of the "permanent" small slaveowners were not directly affected by the Constitution; in a very general way they could expect to benefit from the overall economic improvements anticipated under the new government. More important was the fact that their non-dynamic economic status often gave rise to a provincialism that made them immediately suspicious of basic change and reluctant to place their fortunes in the hands of outsiders.[14] The war experience of North Carolina had aggravated rather than mitigated this attitude. In the

---

[14] This statement does not apply to inhabitants of the Virginia Valley and their neighbors in what is now West Virginia, for the obvious reason that these places were newer, vigorous, and extremely dynamic. The Valley had a cosmopolitan complexion by virtue of being the main highway for migration from the north to Kentucky and Tennessee. Even so, few men in these areas contemplated the development of great plantations, and it is this fact that makes them akin to North Carolinians.

view of North Carolinians, Congress had got North Carolina into a war but had been impotent in the face of the invading British, and it had been Carolina troops and money alone that had saved the Carolinas.

The interests of the "temporary" small slaveowners, a great deal more complex, were more vitally affected by the proposed Constitution. Since for many of them future development depended on the improvement of transportation facilities by private capital, the creation of an abundance of such capital by the funding of the war debts under the Constitution worked immediately to their advantage. Again, many such farmers were in areas where Indians were a menace to development, and the promised strength of the new general government could considerably improve their lot in this respect. Against these advantages deriving from the new system the would-be planters across the mountains weighed the overriding fear that navigation of the Mississippi would be bargained away by the new government. In general, therefore, it could perhaps have been expected that the majorities of both groups of small slaveowning farmers would, if the dictates of their economic interests were obeyed, be reluctant to support ratification, but that their attitudes would vary from one area to another.

The great majority of the second group of slaveholders, those on the "uneconomical" plantations, were in Virginia and Maryland. Caught tight in the grip of their own "tobacco complex," these planters had accumulated great estates and multitudes of slaves, but both their land and their slaves were, as often as not, economic burdens rather than assets. Decades of exploitation by merchants and factors had left many of them hopelessly mired in debt, and decades of tobacco planting had burned up the soil and made barren vast stretches of once-rich farmland. Generally speaking, it was the planters of the older, most aristocratic parts of Virginia and Maryland, the tidewater and the Eastern Shore, who had most nearly exhausted their soil and were most completely entrapped in a web of debts. Those in the newer piedmont areas usually had better land and most of them were not so heavily burdened with debts.

The plantation aristocrats of Virginia and Maryland were a tightly knit group, and socially they were a single, cohesive class. Economically, however, their interests varied widely. They raised different crops: wheat and tobacco. The wheat planters in each state were a fairly unified group, having interests in common with the less aristocratic wheat farmers to the north. The tobacco planters, on the other hand, were as heterogeneous an economic group as could be imagined.

In politics the Virginia and Maryland planters rarely acted as a unit except when their interests as a social class were challenged by some outside group. On so broad an issue as ratification of the Constitution, they could be expected to be as individualistic as any class in America, and their conduct as a class was unpredictable.

The third class of slaveholders, the great rice and indigo plantation aristocrats of the South Carolina and Georgia low country, were a quite different sort. There was no doubt that to them slavery was profitable as well as necessary. Furthermore, a continuous supply of new slaves was imperative, for the oppressive heat and the diseases of the swamps took a heavy toll of laborers.

Blessed with a virtual world monopoly of their staples, these lordly souls were rarely concerned with the international commercial problems that beset tobacco and wheat farmers, and in normal times they almost invariably reaped substantial profits from their crops. Normally they required only two things from government, both of which were offered by the Constitution: stability and protection of the slave trade (or, in a broader sense, a large measure of free trade).

But the 1780's were not normal times. The aristocracy had been forced to start from scratch in 1783, for during the war their lands had been neglected, their buildings destroyed, and their slaves confiscated. During the first two years of peace the price of money, goods, and slaves skyrocketed, and planters were plunged deep into debt. One or two good crops would have put them on their feet, but unfavorable weather and other conditions brought one rice and indigo crop failure after another. The additional burden of the taxes necessary to service large state war debts—neither Georgia nor South Carolina had received any substantial financial aid from Congress—forced the planters in both states to resort to radical fiscal legislation in 1786. In that year the full range of debtor-relief legislation, included paper money, laws staying executions, and tender laws, was forced into passage by the wealthy aristocrats of the two states.[15]

Then a bumper crop in 1787, harvested two months after the close of the Philadelphia Convention, suddenly brought prosperity to most planters and eliminated the need for such debtor relief. By the time the South Carolina ratifying convention met, the constitutional prohibition of such legislation, which in 1786 might have made the document unpalatable to these planters, was no longer significant. On the other hand, the new system promised them three important advantages: stability, protection of the slave trade, and tax relief through the payment of war debts by Congress.[16] If, therefore, they were guided by their economic interests, most of them would have voted for ratification.

One aspect of the economic situation of all slaveholders, however, tended to make them reluctant to surrender control over their affairs to any other body. This was a peculiar commercial vulnerability that attended one-crop economies. The economically sound, as well as the traditional way, for south-

[15] The prevailing notion is that the back-country farmers pushed these measures through over the objections of the low-country planters and merchants. Singer, in his *South Carolina in the Confederation,* page 116, says that in South Carolina the measures were produced by a coalition of back-country farmers and some planters. Actually there were no more than a half dozen delegates from the up country among the total of about one hundred delegates present at the session of the South Carolina legislature which passed these laws. The Georgia paper money was issued to finance an expected Indian war, but planters supported it, and they originated the debtor-relief laws. See the accounts of ratification in Georgia and South Carolina, Chapters 5 and 6, above.

[16] Both South Carolina and Georgia were creditor states. That is, Congress owed them large sums of money for expenditures they made on behalf of the United States during the war. If Congress should assume the payment of state debts as well as liquidate its own obligations, these states would suddenly have large treasury surpluses, and state taxes would be unnecessary for years to come.

erners to reach world markets with their staples was to export at harvest time in the late fall and to import on return voyages in the spring. This meant that the large vessels engaged in the tobacco, wheat, rice, and indigo trade could make only one major voyage a year. This in turn meant that it was not economically feasible for any of the southern states to own enough vessels to carry all their shipping. Thus dependent upon outside shipping, their only protection against commercial exploitation was competition in the carrying trade. If the Constitution were ratified, it was certain that northern commercial groups would attempt, perhaps successfully, to obtain legislation that discriminated against foreign shipping. At least one of the reasons the southern states had joined the movement for independence was their desire to escape the monopolistic control of British and Scotch merchants that prevailed under the Crown, and many planters were reluctant to subject themselves to the possibility of a similar monopoly by Yankee shippers. For this reason some southerners in the Philadelphia Convention had insisted, in vain, that a two-thirds majority of both houses of Congress be required for the enactment of commercial legislation. For the same reason, many southern planters could be expected to oppose ratification of the Constitution.

Of the various non-agrarian occupational classes, the largest, though perhaps politically the weakest, was the manufacturers. Manufacturers fell into three broad categories: 1) service industries, 2) producing industries that had long been integral parts of the American economy, and 3) relatively new capitalistic or corporate manufacturing enterprises.

The service industries included a wide range of crafts that were carried on incidentally to other lines of economic endeavor, such as those of blacksmiths, printers, coopers, carpenters, and the like. Some of these crafts were closely related to farming, some to trade, and others to both farming and trade. Generally speaking, the interests of producers of this kind were similar to those of the economic groups they served, and except where friction between debtors and creditors existed they generally tended to side politically with such groups. That is, a country blacksmith ordinarily saw eye-to-eye on political questions with the farmers in his neighborhood, and ship carpenters ordinarily agreed politically with merchants and shipowners. For this reason, as well as because a large number of them were disfranchised by the widespread landed-property qualifications for voting, men engaged in service occupations were of little weight in the contest over ratification.

The industries that manufactured finished goods for sale in America had grown up in the colonies because their products, though essential to the American economy, could not be produced or transported on a sufficiently large scale or economically enough to warrant production in Britain for export to the colonies. These included such establishments as lumber mills, paper mills, commercial flour mills, distilleries, and pearl ash and potash works. Having sprung up because they were relatively immune to competition, most of them were secure and needed no special governmental protection. Except for the general benefits of good government, which were enjoyed in some states and sadly lacking in others, the interests of these manufacturers would be little affected by the proposed new political system. Their economic interests dictated no particular stand on ratification.

The third general type of manufacturing establishment in the United States, capitalistic or corporate manufacturing, was the opposite of the second type. For the traditional proprietor-manager-worker who hired only a small number of workers it substituted absentee ownership and large numbers of employees —the factory system. This kind of manufacturing venture was new, and it sought to break into fields dominated by foreign producers, particularly British. Though it was more a potential field for investment than an existing occupational interest, the number of such places was multiplying rapidly in the last five years of the 1780's. Many of the new firms concentrated on the textile industry. The Hartford (Connecticut) Woolen Mills, a cotton mill in Beverly, Massachusetts, the carding business in Providence and elsewhere in New England, the Connecticut silk mills, and countless fulling and dyeing mills came into being between 1785 and 1790. In Pennsylvania the iron business was growing rapidly, and such iron products as nails and tools were being produced in new establishments in Rhode Island, all the middle states, and North Carolina.[17] This kind of manufacturing obviously needed the promotion and protection a strong government could offer, and on this ground men engaged in it would be disposed to respond favorably to the new Constitution.

But the number of friends the Constitution would win through its promise of the promotion of manufactures was far greater than the number of persons with economic interests directly at stake. Manufacturing was a great new field for investment and, with the large amounts of liquid capital about to be created by the funding of the war debts, a field that was very attractive to public security holders. To the already skilled inhabitants of overcrowded areas in New England, particularly Connecticut, it offered prospective employment. Finally, the promotion of manufacturing had a strong patriotic appeal as a symbol of the completion of independence and the moulding of a powerful nation.

At the pinnacle of the economic order were the mercantile classes. All men in commerce shared certain interests in that they performed similar operations, but it is a mistake to consider them as a single economic class. They dealt in different products and exchanged on different bases; some imported, some exported, some traded only locally; some were vessel-owning shippers, others had no hand in transportation, and so on. In short, different individuals performed different functions in the trading process, and a half dozen such men could be affected in a half dozen ways by a given economic or political situation. Only in so far as the preponderating portions of their interests and functions coincided can they be considered as special interest groups or economic classes.

[17] Weeden, *Economic and Social History of New England*, vol. 2; Clark, *History of Manufactures*; Bining, *Pennsylvania Iron Manufacturing in the Eighteenth Century*; "Industry," vol. 2 in the Connecticut Archives. The most interesting accounts of these new ventures are those in the contemporary newspapers, particularly those of Hartford and Providence.

The various mercantile classes can perhaps be most clearly delineated by reference to their functions in the process of the exchange of goods. There were four general levels of operators, exclusive of ultimate producers and consumers: 1) *tradesmen* or retail storekeepers, who bought imports from merchants and sold them to consumers, and who bought exports from producers and sold them to merchants; 2) *factors*, the agents of foreign merchants, who established a direct link between producers in one country and consumers in another, and who dealt either at wholesale or at retail; 3) *merchants*, who generally bought and sold only at wholesale, and who ordinarily traded only with other commercial people (American or foreign merchants and American tradesmen); and 4) *shippers*, who might be American or foreign merchants who transported their own goods, or third parties, citizens of any nation, who transported the goods of others in the carrying trade.[18]

The general interests of tradesmen or storekeepers everywhere were similar, the chief variable being the economic characteristics of their customers, particularly the goods or crops which their customers produced. Thus, for example, a storekeeper in Exeter, New Hampshire, had much in common with one in, say, Richmond, Virginia, but his practical problems were obviously quite different, both in terms of the volume and basis on which he did business and in terms of the produce he received in exchange for goods and which he in turn was faced with marketing. Another important variable was the financial condition of individual storekeepers; many were heavy debtors or creditors or both, others were relatively unentangled. Finally, while most dealt in general merchandise, some had separate in-

[18] Historians of the period have been disposed to use the terms "merchants" and "tradesmen" interchangeably and to consider them as a single group, and also to use the term "tradesmen" to denote artisans and mechanics. In eighteenth-century parlance the terms "tradesmen" customarily meant retail storekeepers, although sometimes the more descriptive term "traders" was used. Four chief characteristics distinguished merchants from tradesmen: (1) their volume of gross business was larger; (2) they dealt largely at wholesale with storekeepers and other merchants; (3) they had direct sources of imports and direct connections with foreign markets; and (4) they operated exclusively in port cities.

terests by virtue of specialization in particular lines of goods, such as wines, books, or fine clothing.

On the question of ratification of the Constitution, tradesmen fell into three general groups. Those in the larger cities, who had formed organizations and were strongly class-conscious, generally favored ratification; most of them, particularly those in the ports which were in serious economic difficulties, had been enthusiastic supporters of earlier movements for a general government.[19] Country and village storekeepers, on the other hand, had no awareness of class identity whatever. Their attitudes toward ratification, as toward most political questions, normally depended upon the prevailing attitudes of the other groups in their areas. The third group of storekeepers included those who were in unusual debtor or creditor circumstances. Creditors for large sums in states that had passed extreme debtor-relief legislation could be expected to be strong supporters of the Constitution; debtors in a desperate plight who had benefitted or expected to benefit from such legislation could be expected to oppose the Constitution.

Factors were few in number, and the great majority of them were foreigners (almost exclusively British); at the most, perhaps two or three hundred American citizens were engaged in this business. But because of their great economic power in some areas, particularly among southern planters, the influence of the factors far exceeded their numbers, and the effect of the Constitution on their interests, as well as their attitudes toward it, must be considered. The Constitution had two vital economic aspects to these men, who viewed it through British or pro-British eyes. In the first place it created a Congress with power to regulate commerce and levy duties on imports, and this power would probably be exercised to discriminate against for-

[19] In 1786 the tradesmen of Boston, perhaps the most troubled American port in the 1780's, had attempted to establish committees of correspondence with such groups in other ports. The roster of cities from which Boston received answers to its circular letters constituted a list of ports that were in serious economic difficulty, and in which strong storekeeper support of the Constitution could be later expected: Newport, New Haven, New London, Hartford, Baltimore, and Charleston. These activities can be traced in a general way through the newspapers in the cities named.

eign merchants and ships, particularly those of Britain. To offset this disadvantage the Constitution promised the factors an even more important advantage. Debts due British merchants before independence had been sequestered during the war by Virginia and Maryland, depriving those merchants of an estimated two million pounds sterling. The Constitution, by establishing the peace treaty as supreme law and by creating the federal court system, provided a means not only of recovering these losses, but also of facilitating collection of debts in the future.

Merchants were a fairly cohesive class, held together by regular communication and close personal and family connections as well as by common interests and business relations. Even so, one economic factor divided them into two broad camps. Some merchants combined shipping and trading and made profits from transportation as well as from the exchange of goods, whereas others were exclusively buyers and sellers. Though some vessel-owning merchants operated in every port, their greatest concentrations were in New England; elsewhere they were outnumbered by merchants who owned no shipping.[20]

The interests of merchants who did not own vessels, like those of storekeepers, varied with the commodities they dealt in, the volume of their trade, and other factors. Only one group of merchants had a special interest in political action beyond what was needed for the entire mercantile class: the wheat merchants, whose situation has been outlined in the discussion of wheat farmers above. Except for these, all merchants had a vital interest in free trade, and in this respect their interests

[20] The occupational distribution of persons engaged in ocean-borne commerce was, in very rough figures, as follows. In Boston, of every 100 persons in such trade, approximately 20 were shippers engaged exclusively or almost exclusively in transportation—that is, the carrying trade; 65 were merchants who combined transportation and trading; 12 were merchants who had no interest in vessels; and 3 were factors. In Philadelphia, of 100 such persons, 5 were exclusively shippers, 35 were shipper-merchants, 58 were exclusively merchants, and 2 were factors. In Norfolk 25 were shipper-merchants, 25 were exclusively merchants, and 50 were factors. In Charleston 10 were shipper-merchants, 30 were exclusively merchants, and 60 were factors. These estimates are based upon long and careful study of manuscript port records and tax lists and of advertisments in newspapers of the above-named cities, but they do not represent actual tabulations.

conflicted with those of some shippers and the nascent capitalistic manufacturers. At best legislation designed to promote
American shipping at the expense of foreign shipping failed to
help the merchants, and at worst it was clearly inimical to their
interests. Protective tariffs were definitely against the interests
of importing merchants. While duties for revenue could, within
limits, be passed on to consumers, protective duties, by their
very nature, are designed to force prices of imports above a
competitive level, thus depriving importers of commodities and
markets.

Despite their interest in free trade most merchants had reasons for favoring ratification, albeit with less ardor than shippers
and manufacturers. Merchants in some ports, particularly Philadelphia, New York, and Boston, had experienced economic
difficulties in 1786 and 1787, for different reasons and to different extents in each instance. People are more inclined to accept
political change in times of economic difficulty, whether the
change affects them directly or not. Too, there was a general
feeling, energetically stimulated by pro-ratificationist propaganda, that the adoption of the Constitution would somehow
bring an economic boom. Another consideration, often overlooked, which tended to make merchants favor ratification was
their acute consciousness of vulnerability during war. Inland
residents could talk boastfully of state sovereignty in 1787 and
1788, but to inhabitants of such port cities as New York, Newport, Charleston, and Savannah, which had been occupied and
devastated by British troops virtually until the end of the war
in 1783, such talk did not come easy.[21] The force of all these
reasons made it easier for most merchants to favor the protection of their interests inside the framework of the new Constitution rather than under the existing political arrangements.

---

[21] It is interesting in this connection to observe that eighteen of the first
twenty-nine numbers of the Federalist Papers are devoted, in the main, to discussions of the likelihood of future wars and the ability of the proposed general government under the Constitution to provide for defense. In view of the
fact that New York City, for which the Federalist essays were primarily written, had been under occupation longer than any other place during the war—
nearly seven years—this concentration on the military strength promised by
the Constitution is not without significance.

More strongly in need of positive help from government than any other group in the American economy were the shippers and ship-owning merchants. Certain needs were felt by all shippers, others only by special groups.

The more general difficulties which shippers faced were the direct result of the independence of the several states. Without the powerful deterrent of the British flag, American shipping began to fall prey to the piratical raids of Algerian corsairs immediately after the establishment of peace. For a decade after 1784, except for a brief spell in 1787–1788, when an epidemic of the black plague slowed down the Algerians, no American vessel could sail into southern European or north African waters without danger of plunder and capture by pirates. Somewhat related to this problem were the discriminatory insurance rates charged on American shipping in London: 5 per cent on American vessels and only 2 per cent on British or French vessels making identical voyages. The Constitution, by promising a United States navy, could protect American shipping and reduce the need, if any real need existed, for such high insurance rates. Perhaps more important, by creating a surplus of liquid capital through the funding of the war debts the Constitution would enable American shipping to free itself of this London influence by establishing American insurance companies. Another vital concern of all shippers was free interstate commerce, and this was guaranteed by the Constitution. Though tariff wars between states existed only in Federalist propaganda, it was not inconceivable that they could ultimately break out, and certain barriers had already been raised.

On the other hand, restrictions placed against American shipping by foreign powers, while designed to operate against all shippers, bore hardest on certain ones. The two groups hardest hit were both concentrated in New England: those in trade with the British West Indies and operators of fishing vessels.

The closing of the British West Indies to American shipping late in 1783 did not merely deprive Americans of a share in a heavy and lucrative freight business; it almost paralyzed the New England carrying trade. The New Englanders depended on having, for their larger vessels, one annual European voyage with a staple supplemented by two or three trips to the West Indies, either for direct trade in provisions or for freight from the islands. The trade with the newly opened French West Indies was largely a trade in livestock and lumber, which were best carried in specially built smaller craft, and for this reason the new markets could not take the place of the old. Without the British West Indies the larger Yankee vessels could make only the one main voyage with a staple; for the rest of the year they were idle. Their difficulties were aggravated between 1784 and 1787 by Virginia merchants, who built a large fleet and reduced the availability of tobacco cargoes.

The fishing trade had been treated somewhat better in 1783, John Adams having negotiated a clause into the peace treaty which guaranteed free access to the best fishing banks. But the act that closed the British West Indies to American vessels in 1783 was followed two years later by a French *arrêt* that substantially closed the French West Indies to fish from the United States. As a result fishermen suddenly found themselves with an abundance of fish and almost no place to sell them. The whaling industry suffered even more. Whaling fleets were destroyed and activity was suspended during the war, and when whalers resumed business they found that the whales had either been annihilated or had migrated from their traditional haunts. To make the calamity complete, Britain levied a prohibitive import duty on whale oil, thus closing the major market for the principal whale product.

Exactly what the Constitution could do about these things, or whether it could do anything, was open to question. But New Englanders, led by those in Boston, thought the only solution was to fight Britain with tariffs and embargoes. The all-out effort Massachusetts had made in 1786 to fight Britain with state legislation had proved ineffectual, but the Constitution made it possible to conduct such a cold war on the national level, where success seemed more likely. It mattered little to the shippers that they were being brought into head-on conflict with some other economic groups. Almost all shippers, except possibly those in Virginia (who benefitted in the tobacco trade by favorable state legislation), expected to gain from the ratification of the Constitution.

There remains the fourth broad occupational category, the professions. Professional men can be divided into two groups, lawyers and "all others." The "all others" class was very small, consisting mainly of physicians and a sometimes nebulous officeholding class. Physicians were affected by political change only if they had investments in nonmedical ventures that were affected; they had no interests as a class. The other group, the officeholders, is considerably more interesting.

Professional officeholders, in colonial days by far the most powerful single class, still existed in every state, though they were relatively scarce in New England. Concentrated most heavily in the states between the Potomac and the Hudson, they administered and sometimes virtually controlled government in three vital areas: fiscal operations, collection of customs, and dispensation of justice. The most important offices were those of comptrollers and treasurers, collectors of customs and vendue masters, and judges and clerks of courts. Most of these offices were lucrative—officeholders were the only persons in the country assured of an income in specie—and all were powerful.

The support of the officeholding class was important to both friends and enemies of the Constitution, but its attitudes toward ratification varied from state to state and from one individual to another. The offices would continue to exist or even multiply under the new national government, but the vital question to officeholders was who would fill the offices under the new regime. Support or opposition would depend largely on the answer to this question. In general, those who were insecure in their positions would be somewhat inclined to gamble for better things; those with a bird firmly in hand would be reluctant to surrender it for an identical bird in the bush. And in general, where the officeholding class was weakest, it would tend to follow the lead of dominant political groups; where it was bolder and more solidly entrenched, it would tend to fight ratification.

The last major occupational group, the lawyers, comprised the most influential class in America, though their influence was probably weaker in the 1780's than in any decade in the last half of the eighteenth century. In a sense, a key to the history of the period is the breakdown of the noblest ideal of the Revolution, the concept of a government of laws, and its replacement by a resort to government of expediency, government which could exercise unlimited power on behalf of the majority of the people. The Constitution reversed this trend, and in this respect it was philosophically a lawyer's document if ever one was written. It is not unjust to observe that this philosophical appeal had a practical foundation, for supremacy of law is obviously a prerequisite of supremacy of lawyers. The Constitution had a powerful appeal to lawyers everywhere.

A number of factors, however, worked to dilute this appeal. The political careers of many lawyers and the investments of others were jeopardized by the Constitution. Perhaps more important, the economic interests of lawyers were not entirely severable from those of their clients. Economically, lawyers were divided into two broad camps, country lawyers and lawyers in mercantile cities, and there were as many subgroups as there were classes in the American economy. Thus while the majority of the lawyers were friends of the Constitution, many of them would oppose ratification.

*   *   *

These were the principal occupational classes in the United States, the ways in which they were affected by the proposed Constitution, and the stands they would have taken on ratification had they followed the dictates of their personal economic interests. Since a large number of persons and groups were not vitally affected either way by the Constitution, so far as their occupations were concerned, investments of surplus capital outside one's occupational field could have had great weight in shaping individual attitudes. Those whose occupations were affected in one way by the Constitution while their investments were affected in an opposite way—the interests of a large number of commercial people, in particular, were so split—would have to weigh their interests with special care.

Excluding capital incidental to the occupational fields listed above, capital existed in six major forms. These were money, public securities, vacant lands sold or for sale by the governments, confiscated loyalist property, capitalistic manufacturing, and chartered internal improvement companies.

CAPITAL IN THE FORM OF MONEY

BEFORE any discussion of money is possible it is necessary to make clear the various ways by which money was reckoned. All states used the pound-shilling-pence unit system, a pound consisting of twenty shillings and a shilling of twelve pence. The value of the units varied, however. In addition to sterling, four sets of values were in use in the several states. To reconcile these currency differences in interstate and international transactions, the Spanish milled dollar was used as a common measuring standard, and the Congress used dollars exclusively in figuring its accounts.

The currencies used in the various states are depicted in the following table:

SHILLINGS IN ONE DOLLAR	STATES	VALUE OF ONE POUND IN DOLLARS
8s.	New York, North Carolina	$2.50
7s. 6d.	Pennsylvania, Maryland New Jersey, Delaware	$2.67
6s.	Massachusetts, Rhode Island, New Hampshire, Connecticut, Virginia	$3.33
4s. 8d.	South Carolina, Georgia	$4.28
4s. 6d.	(Sterling)	$4.44

Thus familiarity with six basic rates of exchange was required by persons engaged in commercial activity that extended beyond state borders. Eighteenth-century Americans knew these values as well as twentieth-century Americans knew their

own various coins, however, and they knew the exchange
values of various foreign coins almost as well. Though the
multiplicity of exchanges may be somewhat confusing to historians, it occasioned no great difficulty for Americans of the
period, and it was adequate for their transactions. The promise
of the Constitution that a uniform system of values would be
instituted therefore had a strong appeal only to theoreticians.
The ordinary person, businessman or not, was content to continue the use of the basic exchange most familiar to him.

The various articles that served as money constituted as complex a system as did the rates of exchange. Excluding certificates
of public debt, "money" fell into four broad categories: specie,
public bills, quasi-public paper, and private paper.

Specie requires little comment; it was hard money, gold or
silver. Some states had coined money, but the most common
forms of specie in circulation were British, Spanish, French, and
Dutch coins. There was not then, nor was there ever to be
in the continuously expanding American economy, sufficient
specie with which to transact all normal business. Though
specie was often considered to be the only "real" form of
money, Americans of the post-Revolutionary eighteenth century were considerably more sophisticated in their understanding of the need for and the theory and practice of paper transactions than were their descendants a hundred years later.
Consequently the economy was considerably less sensitive to
fluctuations in the supply of available specie than it was to be
during the last half of the nineteenth century.

Public bills were of two general kinds, those of the Congress
and those of the states.

Continental paper consisted exclusively of bills of credit,
which were actually public obligations, issued to pay in "cash"
for war services and supplies; it was backed by nothing more
than a vague pledge to redeem the bills at some future date, and
the faith of the people in the intention and ability of Congress
to carry out this pledge. Unlike the regular public debt certificates, this paper bore no interest. Public faith in the bills proved
to be virtually nonexistent and justifiably so. By about 1780 the

bills, issued early in the war, had depreciated to a thousand for one and most of them were retired by the states through taxation and various other methods. By the end of the war they had virtually ceased to circulate. The Congress never thereafter manifested any serious intention to redeem these bills, and the Constitution contemplated no such redemption. Provision was made for redeeming a few of them under the Loan of 1790, at the rate of a thousand for one. But this form of currency had ceased to have any practical existence after 1783, and with one exception it did not figure as an element in either private exchanges or public policy.

The exception concerned the citizenry of Massachusetts. When the continental paper was depreciating rapidly, many citizens of Massachusetts had continued to accept it, with a stubborn faith that Congress would ultimately redeem it. Shrewd operators in Connecticut and Rhode Island bought up large quantities of the paper and dumped it on the Massachusetts market. When it became clear that the paper would not be redeemed, hapless citizens of Massachusetts were incensed at Congress for having broken its pledges. They were still more incensed when the Constitution appeared and there was high talk of "restoring public faith and credit," for the Constitution and the new government left the holders of continental paper still holding the bag. Consequently many holders of this form of public paper opposed the Constitution. A large number of the opponents of ratification in Massachusetts were holders of continental paper money.[22]

The state paper was of three major forms: bills of credit, state-bank money, and tax anticipation certificates. Almost all the state bills of credit had been issued to help finance the war and they were, with few exceptions, called in and retired at depreciated rates before 1784. Except in the two states which

[22] Ellsworth of Connecticut charged that Gerry of Massachusetts refused to sign the Constitution because he was a large holder of continental paper. He further charged that in the Philadelphia Convention Gerry had introduced a motion to redeem this paper at par. See Beard, *Economic Interpretation*, 98n. Though no such motion by Gerry appears in any of the records of the Convention, it is quite possible that it was introduced, for the feelings in Massachusetts on the subject were strong.

issued postwar bills of credit, only insignificant amounts of such bills were in circulation in 1787. The two states were North Carolina and Georgia. In 1786 North Carolina issued £100,000 ($250,000) of bills of credit for the retirement of various state obligations, mostly accrued interest on war debts. This money quickly depreciated to about half its face value, but thereafter it circulated at that rate as a more or less satisfactory medium of exchange. The Georgia paper money of 1786, amounting to £30,000 ($128,751), was issued to finance an expected Indian war. When the war failed to materialize, most of the money was called in and destroyed, and the remainder circulated approximately on a par with specie.

The state-bank paper, on the other hand, was an important medium of exchange in the five states which had issued it: Rhode Island, £100,000 ($333,333); New York, £200,000 ($500,000); New Jersey, £100,000 ($266,667); Pennsylvania, £150,000 ($400,000); and South Carolina, £100,000 ($428,-571). These were the issues created during the so-called "paper-money movement" of 1785–1786. For the issuance of most of this money the states had gone into the banking business, printing notes and issuing them on loan, the borrowers paying interest and furnishing the state real-estate and other mortgages as security. The notes so loaned were legal tender only in Rhode Island and New Jersey. In Rhode Island the paper money circulated, with some difficulty, at about ten for one; in the other states, it was widely accepted and circulated at 85 to 100 per cent of its face value.

The Constitution prevented the states from issuing any further bills of credit, and from making anything but specie legal tender. Yet, whatever the intention of the members of the Philadelphia Convention may have been, the states were not specifically forbidden to issue paper money on loan. Thus the "paper-money movement" of 1785–1786, the movement which is generally assumed by Beard and most other historians to have been cut off by the Constitution, was not cut off at all! Indeed, the paper of New Jersey and Pennsylvania continued to circulate as a medium of exchange until the early 1790's, and that of New

York, Rhode Island, and South Carolina until well into the nineteenth century. Furthermore, the state of New York issued new paper on loan, on exactly the same basis as the issue of 1786, in 1796 and again twenty-five years later. It is thus doubtful whether the constitutional restrictions against bills of credit and legal tender laws would have influenced many of the friends of paper money to oppose ratification, or many of its enemies to support ratification. The data presented in the preceding chapters indicates, in fact, that such influence was almost nonexistent.

Tax anticipation certificates, the third form of state paper, were issued from time to time by most states. They were just what their name implies, certificates issued to pay current obligations when the treasury was temporarily without adequate resources. The salaries of the civil list were more commonly paid in these certificates than were any other state obligations. The certificates were redeemable in specie as soon as sufficient taxes were collected, usually within three months' time. This form of money was not affected by the Constitution, and the states continued the practice of issuing it occasionally after the inauguration of the government under the Constitution.

Quasi-public bills were the tobacco warehouse notes of the tobacco-growing states, Maryland, Virginia, North Carolina, and South Carolina. After tobacco was prepared for market and before it was actually shipped, it was stored by its owners in publicly owned warehouses. Notes were given as receipts for the individual amounts so stored. The notes were negotiable and, on proper identification and proof of ownership, enabled the bearers to withdraw the stored tobacco from the warehouses. They thus provided a realistic and ideal medium of exchange in the tobacco-growing states, a medium that was to continue in use long after the adoption of the Constitution. The value of the notes was directly dependent upon the prevailing prices of tobacco.

Private credit existed in three general forms: banking, money-lending, and commodity credit. There were three banks in the United States, the Bank of North America at Philadelphia, the Bank of New York at New York City, and the Bank of Massachusetts at Boston, capitalized at $2,000,000, $318,250, and $100,000, respectively. Their notes provided an important medium of exchange for mercantile transactions in the three cities in which they operated, but their scope of operations did not ordinarily extend beyond these narrow limits.

The Constitution did not affect the notes as currency, nor did it affect the relationships between the bank operators and their mercantile clients. It did, however, affect the stockholders in various ways. Should a national bank be established by the new general government, it was conceivable that it would be a competitor of these private institutions. On the other hand, the relatively huge fiscal transactions of the new government might bring large amounts of new business to the existing banks. Special considerations, however, were more important than general factors, and they predisposed the directors and a large number of the stockholders of each bank toward a favorable reception of the Constitution. As a chartered corporation the Bank of North America had been under direct attack by the Pennsylvania legislature, and such attacks were precluded by the contract clause of the Constitution. The Bank of Massachusetts had recently been given a great fright by Shays' Rebellion (and by the wild rumors that were circulated about the alleged aims of the Shaysites), and for all persons connected with the Bank the constitutional provision for use of federal troops to quell domestic insurrections had a warm and immediate appeal. The Bank of New York was operating without a charter, and in view of its identification with Alexander Hamilton, a bitter political enemy of powerful Governor George Clinton, a charter did not appear to be forthcoming at any time in the foreseeable future. The protection of a national government, though not needed at the moment, was thus felt to be desirable insurance for the Bank.

Money-lending by private individuals was widespread, but its private nature makes it difficult to measure its importance. In a very general sort of way the Constitution affected creditors favorably and debtors unfavorably, by prohibiting stay laws and other state legislation interfering with the payment of debts.

But this restrictive clause would not have influenced creditors to support and debtors to oppose the Constitution unless two concrete conditions existed: 1) the passage or immediate threat of passage of such legislation, and 2) the likelihood of dishonesty on the part of debtors.

Including the three states which had issued paper money and had made it legal tender, seven states had enacted or seemed likely to enact laws interfering with the relations between creditors and debtors: Massachusetts, Connecticut, Rhode Island, New Jersey, North Carolina, South Carolina, and Georgia.

The likelihood of dishonesty on the part of debtors varied with the kinds of loans made to them. Three principal kinds of personal, non-bank loans were common: those made by professional money-lenders, those made as investments in real estate mortgages, and those made on a personal basis with little or no security. There were a small number of professional money-lenders in most American port cities. Their total number in the nation did not exceed one hundred, and perhaps no more than forty or fifty in the seven states named above. Hence, however strained may have been their relations with their debtors from time to time, their influence in favor of or in opposition to the Constitution was infinitesimal. The investment of money in real estate mortgages was somewhat more common, though in 1787 the lands being bought were principally state lands available on easy terms in Vermont, Maine, and the west. This factor made relatively unimportant the number and value of private real estate loans in the seven critical states. The personal loan was by far the most common type of loan but its very nature reduced the likelihood of friction between creditor and debtor and the probability of dishonesty among the debtors. All things considered, the features of the Constitution that protected creditors did not weigh heavily in the contest over ratification.

Commodity credit was a considerably more important factor. Between 1783 and the end of 1787 Britain had exported to the United States goods of various kinds whose value exceeded the value of her imports from the United States by about six million pounds sterling.[23] True, when allowance is made for shipping costs and for the fact that the worth of American products is based on prices in America, not on the much higher sales prices in England, this nominal deficit is greatly reduced, perhaps by half. Furthermore, American trade with other countries almost invariably brought favorable balances to the United States. Even so, a conservative estimate of American debts for commodities imported since the war would be about fifteen million dollars. In addition, southern planters, particular those in Virginia and Maryland, owed at least another ten million dollars for prewar purchases.

The pattern of distribution of these debts, and consequently the effect of the Constitution on the relations between debtors and creditors, was an extremely complex one. In one form of trade consumers owed factors who, in turn, owed British merchants; in another, consumers owed storekeepers who owed merchants who owed British merchants and often shippers as well. Ordinarily the largest debtors were also the largest creditors. When debtors were engaged in occupations or had investments that would benefit substantially from ratification, and were thus enabled to meet their obligations, creditors and debtors alike gained from the constitutional change. Otherwise, because the Constitution prohibited further legislative interference with the collection of debts, and because the new federal courts would be open to suits by British creditors, the benefits that creditors would derive from the adoption of the Constitution depended on where in the pyramid of debts they were situated. The general rule was, the higher one's place in the pyramid, the greater the benefits.

In summary, while the fiscal policies inaugurated by the Federalists under the Constitution simplified and systematized the various forms of money and introduced more order into the relations between creditors and debtors, they did not by any means substitute a "hard money" system for the existing paper

[23] Timothy Pitkin, *Statistical View of the Commerce of the United States* (New Haven, 1835). The statistics of Pitkin cited here were drawn primarily from McPherson, *Annals of Commerce.* McPherson made the tabulations from English customs records.

system. The essential change was a concentration of the machinery which controlled the issue and set the face value of the paper. Before 1789 fiscal power was diversified and divided between private and public agencies inside each state. After 1789 it was largely concentrated and lodged in private and public agencies operating on a national level.[24]

CAPITAL IN THE FORM OF PUBLIC DEBT

THE champions of a general government of the sort established by the Constitution had assumed since as early as 1782 that the public debt was potentially the strongest bond of the Union. By 1787 this expectation had become, in very large measure, only wishful thinking.

The subject of the public debts is an extremely complex one. There were not merely two kinds of public debts, those of the states and those of the United States, but there were seven basic kinds of United States securities and in each state from three to ten kinds of certificates of public debts. In 1787 at least seventy-five forms of public securities were in general circulation.

Now it is true that all war debts were to be funded by the new general government and that the gains to security holders from the appreciation in the market value of the sixty million dollars face value of public securities was between twenty and thirty million dollars.[25] But this fact had a different significance to different kinds of security holders, for the status of the several forms of securities varied widely. The holders of low-priced, unfunded securities obviously had a great deal to gain

[24] It is also worth noting that many of the fiscal devices employed by the American states in the 1780's, though denounced by Federalists and future historians alike as quackery, were adopted in the twentieth century by the national government. The principles of the tax anticipation certificates, the land and commodity banks, and the tobacco notes all came to be accepted as orthodox in the twentieth century, and they formed vital parts of the fiscal machinery of the Federal Reserve System.

[25] Beard (page 35) estimated the profits from appreciation of securities at $40,000,000, and he cited Callender, who wrote in 1796, as having estimated the sum at $25,000,000. My own estimate, based on a rough tabulation of the amounts of each kind of securities and the prices quoted in newspapers from 1787 to 1791, is about $21,450,000.

from the creation of a government that would fund all the war debts. On the other hand, those who held securities that were funded on a solid basis and who were receiving prompt interest payments from the states—much of the continental as well as of the state debts had been so funded—merely had nothing to lose by the adoption of the Constitution. In analyzing the effect of the Constitution on their interests, virtually all security holders weighed their occupational interests, their other investments, and their obligations as well as their security holdings.

The holders of public securities were thus a much divided interest group. In a few states their interests clearly dictated support of the Constitution, and in those states many of them were leaders in the movement for ratification. In others they could support or oppose the Constitution without jeopardizing their investments, and in these states the security holders, as such, were virtually without influence as an element in the ratification.

Capital in the Form of Vacant Lands

The size of the public domain in 1787 staggers the imagination. In addition to confiscated British and Loyalist property, which will be considered separately, it included vast acreages in Vermont, Maine, western New York, western Pennsylvania, and Georgia and almost the entire area between the Alleghany Mountains and the Mississippi River. The total amount of good unoccupied lands was many times the amount of lands already settled.

The sale of the public domain was thought to be a means of retiring the public debts. Consequently the states and, after 1789, the national government began to sell the lands to the highest bidders. The possibilities for making profits from the purchase and resale of these lands were enormous, and thousands of Americans invested their surplus capital in land speculations.

Whether the Constitution would affect such investments favorably or unfavorably depended largely upon three factors:

the validity of titles, the location of the lands, and the form of purchase.

If the validity of his titles to lands was unquestionable, the speculator had nothing to fear from the strong court system about to be established under the Constitution. But many titles were cloudy, and owners of such titles were usually better off under state jurisdictions. Others, however, sought national jurisdiction over such matters because their titles had been invalidated by state governments.

Lands located in areas where the Indians were a threat quickly appreciated in value in the face of the promised strength of the new general government. But in Vermont, Maine, western Pennsylvania, and parts of the transmontane region the values of lands were not affected by this possibility, and of the lands whose value was so effected, a large portion were in areas whose transportation route was via the Mississippi. As indicated earlier, the interests of absentee owners of these lands were identical to those of the settlers already established in such areas: that is, their betterment depended on the opening of the Mississippi for navigation, a goal that many felt would be sacrificed in exchange for commercial concessions from Spain.

If the terms of purchase were cash, or if the lands had already been paid for, the purchases were not affected by the Constitution. Since the land-sales programs were usually designed to help retire the war debts, however, the most common form of purchase involved securities as well as cash. Buyers contracted to pay specified sums, usually making a small down payment in specie and agreeing to pay the remainder in public securities at their face value within a specified period of months or years. In modern parlance, they were selling securities "short"—that is, they were agreeing to deliver to the seller of the land securities they did not at the time possess. Like "short" sellers of a later day, they expected to acquire the securities on the open market at a price less than that at which they agreed to deliver them. But whereas the modern "short" sellers obtain their profits from relatively minor fluctuations, these land speculators operated with enormous margins. Normally a land speculator would expect to make his profits by buying land in large quantities and selling it in small parcels to settlers, but under the special conditions that prevailed under the Articles of Confederation he had an additional opportunity for profit. For example, a speculator might contract to buy a hundred thousand acres of public lands for a dollar an acre, to be paid, let us say, in continental commissary certificates. Let us suppose that these securities were selling on the open market at a fourth of their face value. He would then acquire his lands for an actual cash outlay of only twenty-five thousand dollars, and he had to sell his lands at only their nominal cost to realize a profit of three hundred per cent. Because substantial profit on any such venture seemed certain, many speculators, perhaps the majority, tended to extend themselves to the limit of their resources.

But when the Constitution was ratified, the market price of these securities began to rise, both because of the prospective funding of the Continental debts and because land speculators were busily competing with one another to acquire the necessary securities with which to fulfill their contracts. Our hypothetical purchaser would then find that instead of having to pay only twenty-five thousand dollars in hard money for his lands, he would have to pay almost seventy-five thousand. If the amount he had expected to pay was a large fraction of his total financial resources, the appreciation of public security prices under the Constitution would thus bankrupt him. The panic of 1792, in which hundreds of speculators were bankrupted, came about in precisely this fashion, and it was a direct result of the funding of the debts under the Constitution.

CAPITAL IN THE FORM OF CONFISCATED ESTATES

THIS form of investment was similar to investment in public lands. It was, however, affected only adversely by the adoption of the Constitution. Titles to such purchases were invariably jeopardized, for the peace treaty had provided for the restoration of such property, and the Constitution made treaties part of the "supreme law of the land." Furthermore, almost all purchasers of confiscated property bought on terms requiring installment payments in public securities. The appreciation in market prices of securities damaged the interests of purchasers of this property in the same way it damaged those of purchasers of government lands.

CAPITAL IN THE FORM OF MANUFACTURING

THIS form of capital has been treated earlier. Manufacturing stood to benefit considerably by the establishment of the new system, both because of the creation of liquid capital through the appreciation of securities and because of the possibility that protective tariffs would be enacted by the new government. It is important to observe, however, that the interests of manufacturers were in direct conflict with those of land speculators. The manufacturers needed appreciation of securities, the land speculators would suffer from it. The land speculators required governmental support of westward expansion, whereas the manufacturers benefitted from some immobility of the population and the accumulation of large pools of laborers.

CAPITAL IN THE FORM OF STOCK OF INTERNAL IMPROVEMENT COMPANIES

THREE important companies for the development of internal navigation had been chartered and organized during the 1780's: the Potomac River Company and the James River Company in Virginia, and the Cooper-Santee Canal Company in South Carolina. The interests of all three companies would be favorably affected by the expected appreciation of public securities in that it would increase the capital available to them. The interests of the Potomac Company, which required legislation by three states in order to carry out its aims, would be furthered in another way by the establishment of the Constitution, for the new system was to bring interstate waterways under a single jurisdiction. This advantage was only a nominal one, however, for it was still within the power of states to prevent developments they considered undesirable.[26]

SUMMARY

THERE were in the United States in 1787 at least twenty basic occupational groups having distinctly different economic characteristics and needs, and there were six basic forms of capital in addition to capital incidental to occupational activity. Most of the occupational groups and all the forms of capital may be divided into two to seventy-five subdivisions. Of the grand total of major economic interest groups and forms of investment, about 30 per cent were affected by the Constitution directly and immediately in a favorable way, and about 15 per cent were directly and immediately affected in an unfavorable way. The remaining 55 per cent were either not directly affected at all or were affected in indefinite, indecisive, or unpredictable ways.

Among the more important groups that were affected favorably there were numerous conflicts. The interests of manufacturers were opposed to those of importing merchants and of land speculators. The interests of public security holders were divided: the interests of those favorably affected by ratification coincided with those of manufacturers but conflicted with those of land speculators and purchasers of confiscated property. The interests of wheat merchants and wheat farmers also conflicted with those of many land speculators, and so on.

It is therefore not even theoretically possible to devise a single set of alignments on the issue of ratification that would explain the contest as one in which economic self-interest was the principal motivating force.

[26] A good case in point is that of the Susquehanna River. The development of navigation on that river would bring substantial economic advantages to central Pennsylvania, but the principal benefits of the trade resulting from the development would go to Baltimore, the first major port below the mouth of the river. Such development was opposed by Philadelphia, which desired a less logical development, a canal from the Susquehanna to the Delaware. The Pennsylvania legislature, under the influence of Philadelphians, was able to block the development of the Susquehanna for decades.

It may still be possible, however, to explain the contest as fundamentally an economic conflict. The effects of the Constitution on economic interests were born of a number of variables, the most important of which was the state jurisdiction under which interests were pursued. The holders of a particular kind of public securities and the shipowning merchants in New York, for example, were not affected in precisely the same way as were such groups in New Hampshire or Georgia. When allowance is made for this fact the data can be brought into focus and, within the framework of the new system of categories of interest groups presented here, some assessment may be made of the role of economic forces in the contest over the Constitution.

X

Economic Interpretation and the Constitution

AT THE outset four general questions were posed to be answered in the present work: 1) Is Beard's economic interpretation an adequate explanation of the making of the Constitution? 2) If not, can any economic interpretation "explain" the event, partly or wholly? 3) What generalizations, if any, can be drawn from the present study about the usefulness of economic interpretation in historical analysis? 4) If no economic interpretation is adequate, what avenues of exploration seem to promise a better understanding of the making of the Constitution?

THE BEARD INTERPRETATION

CHAPTER eight above, and the earlier chapters of which it is a summary, demonstrated the inadequacy of Beard's interpretation. The facts did not substantiate his assumptions; the details were found to be incompatible with the broad outlines he sketched. Beard asked the wrong questions, questions which, in the way they were phrased, were meaningless. The Philadelphia Convention, as a body, was acting *neither* as "a consolidated economic group" *nor* "merely under the guidance of abstract principles of political science." The contest over ratification was *neither* an economic class struggle *nor* "the product of some abstract causes remote from the chief business of life—gaining a livelihood." By asking invalid questions Beard arrived at an interpretation that obscures rather than illuminates the role of economic forces in the making of the Constitution.

Economic Interpretation of the Constitution

How far, then, can one go in interpreting the making of the Constitution in economic terms? That is to say, to what extent did economic factors in fact condition or determine the outcome? They were obviously of some weight; the critical question is whether it is possible to reduce them to systematic interpretive generalizations. If the preceding chapters establish anything, it is that the interplay of conditioning or determining factors was extremely complex. It is clear that the making of the Constitution cannot be rendered intelligible in terms of any single system of interpretation; that it is only through simultaneous application of several systems that sense can be made of the multitude of pertinent factors. Hence the immediate question becomes, can an adequate pluralistic economic interpretation be devised?

At least four hypotheses in addition to that formulated by Beard, each of which has a measure of applicability, can be induced from the data presented.

First Hypothesis

ONE may begin by attempting to formulate a proposition as closely related to Beard's as possible. It too should be cast in terms of motivations, specifically that men were motivated in the contest over the Constitution by their judgment of what direct and immediate effect it would have on them economically. For such a proposition Beard's simple system of classifications of economic interests must be replaced by the analysis of the potential effects of the Constitution on economic interests which was made in the preceding chapter.

That analysis demonstrated that the interest groups could not have been aligned in such a way as to make the contest over ratification a direct economic conflict involving either a majority of the interest groups or a majority of the inhabitants of the country. The interests of too many of these groups were not directly affected; too many groups had so great a diversity of interests that they were affected both favorably and unfavorably; and there were conflicts of interests between groups, even among those who clearly stood to gain. A rigid system based on economic motivations, then, is not suitable.

A flexible system, however, can be devised and cast into a different and more plausible form. Suppose that this were the nature of the contest: that, at bottom, several or all of the interest groups which could be expected to benefit formed a dynamic inner core in the movement for the Constitution, and/or those affected in an unfavorable way formed a dynamic inner core of the opposition. Each can be thought of as an active minority seeking to win sufficient support from those who were unaffected, or who were affected both favorably and unfavorably, to bring about or to defeat the ratification. Such support could have been solicited through appeals to various noneconomic motivations: political philosophy, ideals, prejudices, fears of one sort and another.

The ideal requirements for testing this hypothesis seem to be four:[1] 1) It would need to be ascertained what interest groups existed, who comprised them, and how they were affected economically, or thought they would be, by the making of the Constitution. 2) It would need to be learned which of the groups directly affected acted according to the dictates of their economic interests. Those who acted thus, if any did so consistently, would form the hypothetical dynamic groups. 3) It would need to be ascertained what means were commonly used in political controversies to persuade voters to act in one way or another, and whether the hypothesized dynamic interest groups had access to and did in fact employ them. 4) It would

---

[1] Several conditions and limitations are implicit in these requirements. It is necessary to assume, for working purposes, that the individuals involved had a conscious image or knowledge and understanding of how their interests were affected, whenever this cannot be established factually. Moreover, it is necessary to assume that to idealize individuals as abstract economic men in this respect is a valid operational procedure. As to the means of persuasion, it must be recognized that except in a few instances where individualized persuasion can be traced through personal correspondence and similar records, one must depend for sources on the grossest of media used for communicating propaganda, ideas, and arguments, such as the press, the pulpit, and oratory and debate in the ratifying conventions. It is thus necessary to assume for working purposes that it is sufficient to examine these media.

need to be demonstrated what degree of correlation existed between the efforts to persuade voters and their actual votes on ratification.

SECOND HYPOTHESIS

SHOULD rigorous analysis of the first proposition demonstrate it to be unworkable, in whole or in part, it would still be possible to construct a different system whereby the issue might be seen as having turned primarily upon considerations of immediate economic self-interest. Suppose the first proposition is precisely reversed. Suppose the struggle over ratification to have been a struggle (or more properly, a number of struggles) for political power, with something other than economic interests as the primary driving force. It would seem axiomatic that any political faction or party seeking to acquire or to retain political power must, whatever its own inner dynamics, strive for the support of various economic groups that are of political weight. The contending political groups can thus be thought of as the dynamic elements in the contests, seeking support from the population at large through appeals to economic self-interest, real or imagined, indigenous or implanted, and actually determining the outcome in this way. The result of the contest would then be seen to have pivoted and turned largely upon the anticipated effects of the Constitution on economic interests.

The requirements for testing this proposition seem to be four: It would need to be determined 1) whether various contending political groups did exist prior to the contest over ratification; 2) whether such groups were primarily economic in character (this might reasonably be inferred from the outcome of the tests to which the first hypothesis was subjected); 3) whether such groups made a concerted effort to persuade voters to support or oppose the Constitution on the basis of their real or supposed economic interests; and 4) whether a very large proportion of the participants in the contest did vote according to the dictates of their economic interests, as these interests were pictured by the dynamic political groups.

THIRD HYPOTHESIS

THE movement for the making of the Constitution can be interpreted in economic terms in still another way. This is an approach that is quite different from the hypothesis that there was a direct connection between votes on ratification and the economic interests or selfish personal motivations of the participants. Suppose the economic and political situations in 1787 to have been intertwined in such a way that any action taken in one area must inevitably have affected the other to approximately the same extent. If, for example, some element in the relationship between government and private economy prevented either from operating effectively—that is, if the needs of the two were incompatible—it would follow that a major change in the governmental system would bring a fundamental change in the economy as well, and any proposed political change would necessarily hinge upon economic factors.

The requirements for testing this proposition can be stated only generally and tentatively. It would be necessary 1) to explore the whole range of the economy in each jurisdiction, to determine in what ways it operated; 2) to explore the whole range of polity in each jurisdiction, for the same purpose; 3) to induce from these data the requirements for the successful functioning of that economy and polity; and 4) to determine whether the needs of either were in any way incompatible with those of the other.

Because the contest over the Constitution was at once *a contest* and *thirteen contests*, it is conceivable that any or all of these first three hypotheses will serve to make the contests in one or more states intelligible and yet be entirely inapplicable in others. A fourth, somewhat broader hypothesis, to be stated in a moment, may possibly be meaningful only when the contest is viewed as a single contest rather than a number of contests. Accordingly it seems proper to pause here to consider whether any of the first three hypotheses will serve as an adequate interpretive framework for the data that have been presented.

Since the hypotheses were induced from the data, satisfaction of the stated requirements for testing them would be no more than repetition and rearrangement of those data. Certain general conclusions about the economic aspects of the contests in the several states were drawn in connection with the accounts of each. Here it is sufficient to re-view those conclusions in the light of the foregoing hypotheses.

For one state, New Hampshire, the first hypothesis—that the dynamic groups for and against the Constitution were selfishly motivated economic groups, appealing for voter support primarily on noneconomic grounds—has some measure of validity, if the hypothesis is qualified to indicate 1) that the dynamic pro-ratification groups, essentially economic groups, were also impelled by noneconomic considerations of varying potency; and 2) that the interests of the leaders of the opposition were so diverse as to suggest that no connection existed between their conduct and those interests.

For three states, Maryland, Pennsylvania, and New York, the second hypothesis—that the dynamic groups favoring and opposing the Constitution were essentially noneconomic groups struggling for political power, who sought and received support primarily through appeals to the economic self-interest of the voters—has a substantial measure of validity. The extent to which appeals were cast in economic terms varied, however. In Maryland and Pennsylvania the economic appeal was more intense and more widespread than in New York, where the appeals were much more diversified. In none of these states was the appeal for support from economic groups on economic grounds entirely successful.

For four states, New Jersey, Connecticut, Rhode Island, and Massachusetts, the third hypothesis—that the needs of government and economy conflicted with each other in such a way that any political change was necessarily an economic event—has a very substantial measure of validity. In New Jersey the contradiction between the needs of the government and the economy accounts for a considerable measure of the state's strong support of the Constitution. In Connecticut this contradiction was even more important in determining the course of the contest over ratification, inasmuch as it affected a greater segment of the citizenry and affected them more deeply. In addition, both of the first two hypotheses are applicable in large measure in Connecticut, the first among the supporters, the second among the opponents of ratification. In Rhode Island the contradiction, while as strong as in New Jersey and Connecticut, had a less direct and less immediate effect. Here it was not the contradictions per se, but the situation resulting from the state's vigorous efforts to solve the problems they posed, that had an immediate influence in the contest over the Constitution. Furthermore, the political alignments born of Rhode Island's efforts to solve local problems locally brought, in the ratification, a division along the lines suggested by the first hypothesis. In Massachusetts the conflict between the needs of economy and government formed a substantial base both for the political struggles of the decade of the 1780's and for their climax, the contest over ratification. These struggles took several forms, partly along the lines suggested by the first hypothesis, partly along those of the second hypothesis.

For five states, Delaware, Virginia, North Carolina, South Carolina, and Georgia, none of the three hypotheses stated seems to have any considerable applicability. Indeed, the influence of economic forces of any kind seems to have been small.

One is struck by the fact that four of these states were geographically contiguous and that all five lay below the Mason and Dixon line. At the other end of the scale, the four states in which economic systems of interpretation seem to be most applicable were northern states (three of them geographically contiguous) which were relatively advanced economically—the criteria being complexity of the economy, the state or degree to which the division of labor had progressed, the variety of economic functions performed, and, in so far as it can be considered a product of these, density of population.

Three general propositions suggest themselves as a possible

explanation of this distribution of states with respect to the applicability of economic interpretation.

1) Perhaps it is attributable to mere coincidence. The scholar is reluctant to accept coincidence as the explanation for any fact of history, but this possibility must be considered seriously. To establish coincidence as the explanation it must be proved that the conduct of each state was based on conditions peculiar to it and not fundamentally analogous to those in other states. It is obvious that the five states comprising the southern group and the four comprising the northern had certain fundamental similarities to one another and at the same time certain unique features. It seems clear that the unique elements in each of the five southern states were the determining factors in shaping attitudes toward the Constitution, and that the elements they had in common were not. But in the four northern states, while unique elements in each likewise determined the *outcome* of the contests, the elements that were analogous in them (primarily economic "advancement" as defined) channeled the *course* of the contests along parallel economic lines.

Since those elements that were analogous in the four northern states were absent in the five southern states, it follows that an additional characteristic shared by the five southern states was a negative one, the absence of the elements which the four northern states shared. Furthermore, it seems reasonable to infer that this may have been a vital element, the one which determined that the course and outcome of the contests should turn on unique noneconomic local factors in the five southern states and on unique economic local factors in the four northern states. Coincidence, therefore, hardly seems the explanation of the interesting distribution of states on this question of the applicability of economic interpretation. This element, the degree of economic "advancement" as defined, seems to be definitely, though not necessarily measurably, related to the applicability of economic interpretation.

2) Perhaps the making of the Constitution had a more direct effect on the economies, or on something in the economies, or on the economic interests prevailing in the North in general and

in the four "advanced" states in particular. In myriad ways such was obviously the case.[2]

3) With due allowance for the fact that to generalize from inadequate particulars is inherently dangerous, one may tentatively postulate a much broader proposition. Perhaps the likelihood that some form of economic interpretation will render a given historical phenomenon intelligible, other things being equal, increases with the increasing complexity or "advancement" of an economy. Or perhaps this may be true within given limits, that is, in economies above some primitive level and/or below some highly advanced level. Verification of this proposition would depend upon studies of many other historical phenomena.

FOURTH HYPOTHESIS

A FOURTH possible economic interpretation of the making of the Constitution is that it was the expression of the prevailing popular ideology of the socially desirable or normal relationship between government and economy. This ideology did not necessarily coincide with the philosophical systems of theorists and other thinkers, but was rather a broad mosaic of folk values, assumptions, myths, and ideals, a vaguely defined mold which ordinary individuals unconsciously used as a frame of reference in judging whether any proposed political or economic action was acceptable.

Few will be disposed to deny the existence of such a general mold of popular opinion, but it may seem difficult or impossible to reduce it to concrete terms. For the period under study it is particularly difficult. In many historical situations there is a substantial clue to such patterns of opinion in the public utterances of persons seeking to justify or rationalize given political measures. The United States of the 1780's, however, fails to offer such clues, for the reason that, as a long-range view of the period reveals, a fundamental transition was taking place both

---

[2] This, of course, was suggested by Beard. As has been demonstrated, however, Beard's analysis of the ways in which the Constitution affected economic interests and the ways various interest groups behaved bears little relation to the facts.

in the nature of the American economy and in these basic popular attitudes and assumptions. Nonetheless it is possible to devise methods of gaining an adequate *working* knowledge of
prevailing opinion on the principles of political economy that
were current.

The most obvious and probably the safest means of gaining
such insight is to study the systems of polity devised by the
various states. These systems may be viewed in two perspec-
tives: as systems in operation in 1787 or 1788, and as systems
growing and changing throughout the eighteenth century under
the stimulus of changing conditions. A reasonably adequate criterion of the character of such systems is the legislative programs—including, wherever pertinent and ascertainable, legislation by local governmental units inside states—worked out by
the several states from the time of the Declaration of Independence to the inauguration of the government under the Constitution.[3]

In either perspective—the short-range or the long-range view
—one striking fact is to be observed: that there is a unifying
thread running through the legislative programs of the several
states, namely the theme of mercantilism. This is not to imply
identity of policy. Mercantilism was geared to the economic
needs of the community comprising the sovereign jurisdiction,
and those needs were not the same in different communities at a
given time, nor were the needs of a given community the same
at different times. The mercantilist system devised for Virginia
in the 1780's, for example, differed from the one developed
there forty years earlier, and from the French and British systems at that or any other time. In short, mercantilism had always
engendered a wide range of regulatory and promotional measures. Furthermore, the American states had in practice departed
a long way from two of the principal assumptions of classical
mercantilism. The concept that gold constituted wealth was

---

[3] The following observations are derived from systematic analysis of all the
public and private acts of each of the thirteen states, 1776–1789. The statutes
of most of the states during the period have also been systematically analyzed
by seminar students of Professor Fulmer Mood at the University of Texas, and
I have examined these analyses.

often challenged on a philosophical level, and in practice, as was indicated earlier (pages 385–393), the American states had developed a relatively sophisticated monetary system. That the success of a system was to be judged by the balance of trade, measured by accumulation of specie, was no longer universally subscribed to, at least in the carrying states. Even these two assumptions of mercantilism were not actually abandoned, however, but were merely modified to fit local conditions; and most of its other underlying assumptions were unreservedly, if often unconsciously, accepted. The forms that mercantilism took (for example, bounties, protective tariffs, inspection of products for quality, regulation of the flow of specie) were precisely the forms in which the American states cast their systems of polity. Most important, the fundamental concept underlying these state systems was that of mercantilism: the concept of governmental regulation of the economy with a view to the welfare of the sovereign community as a whole rather than that of its individual members.

If the Constitution, to the extent that it was an economic document, had to fit into this general mold to be acceptable, it would seem that it contemplated a governmental system with broad powers to regulate economic life. Yet study of the arguments and propaganda for and against the Constitution reveals that opponents attacked it most persistently on the ground that it did create just such a government, and defenders expended enormous efforts to prove that it did not. The frequency and vehemence of these exhortations would seem to attest to the widespread realization that the voting population at large distrusted and feared strong government. This fact is indeed self-evident and is accepted by virtually all students of American history.

What seems to be a paradox is, however, only an apparent, not a real one. Americans were accustomed to fairly extensive governmental interference in their economic lives, but only on the part of local governments. It was not governmental power as such that Americans feared, but the centralization of power, especially in a government far removed from local supervision and control. A division of power along both horizontal and vertical lines—a federal system with the principle of the separation of powers incorporated into each level of government—was broadly and deeply rooted in the complex of political, economic, and social traditions in Anglo-Saxon America. Such a division had existed prior to the Revolution and during the period between the Declaration of Independence and the ratification of the Articles of Confederation in 1781; it had been continued under the Articles; and it was perpetuated in the political system established by the Constitution. It was not the sum total of governmental power being exercised that varied with these changes in organization, but the distribution of power, the equilibrium of the federal system.

Hence, while the general mold of opinion on matters of political economy was a mercantilistic one, it did not in America imply national mercantilism, but a group of local mercantilisms. The mold varied as to details in the several states, sometimes subtly, sometimes glaringly. Each state required and had in operation a system of its own to meet its own economic needs. In the face of these facts two inferences are inescapable, inferences which resolve the paradox: 1) That the Constitution was not "essentially an economic document," if by this is meant that it created a new system of political economy. 2) That the states—that is, the people thereof, acting in their capacity as citizens of the states—assumed that they would retain control over these and all other matters not manifestly the concern of all the states.

METHODOLOGY

THE methodological implications of the foregoing explorations into economic analysis of the making of the Constitution are clear, and from them it is possible to pose some general propositions regarding the role of economic interpretation in historical analysis.

The events of American history are intrinsically pluralistic in that they take place simultaneously on personal, local, and state levels as well as the general level. The contest over ratification was on one level a single contest, on another thirteen separate contests, and on still another, that of the local units which elected delegates to the various conventions, a series of almost two thousand separate contests. In view of the three-part federal system of political organization in the United States (general, state, and local jurisdictions), and of the not dissimilar structure of the economic and social order, it seems likely, if not certain, that any historical phenomenon above the local level has this pluralistic character.

Research may take place on any of these levels. The findings and conclusions derived from an investigation made on one level can be valid only for that level, and it is always possible that even these findings and conclusions will be upset by new knowledge derived from research on another level. Since there is one level—the personal—on which investigation is inevitably limited to superficialities, and since on all levels it is limited to the study of inevitably fragmentary relics of the past, absolute certainty in historical study is unattainable. The closer the investigator comes to the primary constituents of a phenomenon, the higher the probability of accuracy, but it must be recognized that a historical phenomenon is more than the sum total of its manifestations on local levels, just as it is more than the phenomenon as it manifests itself on the general level. Ideally, all levels will be perceived, studied, and kept in mind simultaneously. The extent to which the historian accomplishes this is, by and large, the extent to which the results of his research can be reliable.

Inside the framework of this pluralistic concept any number of systems of interpretation—economic or otherwise—may prove useful. But it must be recognized that:

1) Whatever the interpretive system, a carefully drawn operational procedure must be consciously formulated at the time the system is formulated. If any approximation of the ideal of objectivity is to be achieved, the procedures of investigation, particularly the basis for selecting and arranging data, must be

strictly defined, in terms of the requirements for verification of the hypothesis. The earlier in the process of gathering data that hypothesizing and selection begin, the greater the dangers of both subjectivity and error; the further along they begin—the more data are in hand before selection and interpretation begin—the greater the probability of accuracy. The more carefully the specifications are drawn, and the more rigorously they are adhered to, the closer the investigator comes to objectivity. This ideal of objectivity would be achieved if one observer could be replaced by another in the course of an investigation without altering the outcome of the observation. The extent to which this replaceability of the investigator is achieved is the measure of the degree of objectivity obtained.

2) No single system of interpretation can explain all historical phenomena; it is even unlikely that a single system can adequately explain all aspects of a single historical event. Obviously romantic as the quest for such single systems may seem, few readers will need to be reminded that it is just such quest that has occupied a very large part of the efforts of American historians. As one critic has phrased it, we have emulated the medieval alchemist, who sought to transmute base elements into gold before learning how to handle simpler things. In working with the simpler things it is useful to be aware that one system of interpretation may work—that is, render intelligible and compatible all the discoverable and verifiable facts—in one aspect of a multi-faceted phenomenon and not in another. That is to say, it should be recognized that a full explanation of one complex event may require several systems of interpretation, or even that several systems which are apparently contradictory may be required for a full explanation.

3) In interpreting a given facet of a given event, any system may prove useful, but the conditions and circumstances of a given situation will ordinarily make it better adapted to interpretation by one system than by another. To cite a simple and obvious analogy, the mathematician has several methods for describing various physical phenomena. For example, when he

wants to describe physical vibrations in a rectangular space, he uses one method, the mode of description, or coordinates, best suited to that kind of space. When he wishes to describe vibrations in a cylindrical space he uses a different method or set of coordinates, and for a spherical space he uses still another set. Theoretically he can use any set for any kind of space if he does not mind making an unnecessarily large number of calculations and arriving at an obscure result; but there is an easy way, a natural system, for each kind of space.

The historian has at his disposal several interpretive systems comparable to these systems of coordinates, and he is limited in devising additional systems only by his own imagination. For any set of historical conditions, circumstances, situations, and phenomena there may be an interpretive system naturally adapted to it. If there is and one begins with an "unnatural" system—which would not necessarily preclude arriving at a satisfactory answer—one will have chosen the hard way. Before the system of interpretation can be made to work (assuming that the historian is proof against the distortion of facts and editing of data to make them conform to his thesis), much labor will be required and the interpretive system itself will require modification.

For this reason the whole idea (expounded by Beard and many others) of beginning research with a system of interpretation and basis of selection, or with a hypothesis, or even with a question, breaks down. However it might be evaluated in terms of philosophy and pure logic, the fact is that it was developed largely for practical reasons, and it is precisely from the practical standpoint that it is weakest. If one guesses wrong, if one investigates a phenomenon in terms of a system of interpretation and selection which proves to be unworkable, all one's efforts may be wasted. An equal amount of effort, applied inductively, might have covered less ground, but it would at least have brought the investigator to a stage at which a more tenable system of interpretation could be induced from the body of particulars, and would at least have taught him to ask meaningful questions.

Outlines for Pluralistic Study of the Constitution

ECONOMIC interpretation renders intelligible many of the forces at work in the making of the Constitution. It is far from adequate to explain it in its entirety, however; this would require that countless noneconomic factors be taken into consideration. The present study, focused as it is on economic factors, does not present sufficient data for a pluralistic interpretation adequate to explain the event, but it does permit of conclusions which suggest synthesizing and organizing principles that might be fruitful of meaningful results in further study of the making of the Constitution.

The Philadelphia Convention which framed the Constitution was made up of fifty-five men. These delegates were officially and primarily the representatives of the several states. They were also unofficial representatives of the geographical areas, political factions, and economic interest groups in those states.

Represented in the convention were twelve of the thirteen American states and virtually every geographic subdivision except the new areas west of the mountains, which had not yet produced significant leadership in any state. Almost all the important political factions in ten states were represented; the delegates from the other two states were drawn primarily from the factions that were momentarily dominant. The representation of economic groups was less complete. Most of the important economic groups were represented by at least one delegate, but a great majority of the delegates were drawn from the three groups that furnished most of the leadership in each state: lawyers, planters, and merchants.

Each individual delegate was also a unique human being with his own *Weltanschauung* as well as his own material interests. Inside the convention each delegate could vote and make proposals as he saw fit. Some delegates, a dozen at the outside, clearly acted according to the dictates of their personal economic interests, and about as many more according to their philosophical convictions, even when these conflicted with their economic interests. But the conduct of most of the delegates, while partly a reflection of one or both of these personal considerations, was to a much greater extent a reflection of the interests and outlooks of the states and local areas they represented.

The document framed by the Philadelphia Convention was thus the product of a number of conflicting elements. Except for a few minor innovations designed to adjust colonial custom and experience to the immediate political and economic milieu, the Constitution contained no provisions that were new to Americans. The one radical feature of the Constitution was that it created a general government to replace the Congress of the Confederation.

If the American people were to have a general government at all, they must accept it on the terms laid down in the Constitution. The states were called upon, through the medium of conventions elected expressly for the purpose, to accept or reject the Constitution in its entirety. Involved as the issue was, countless as were its ramifications, each state could answer in only one of two ways: yes or no.

Its answer to the question—to reject or to accept—depended upon what measure of satisfaction its citizens derived from the federal system of the existing Articles of Confederation, under which the separate states were, in practice, responsible for their separate fates. The extent of that satisfaction, in turn, depended largely upon two primary considerations: the endowments with which a state could expect to cope with its particular problems of sovereign existence, and the skill with which its people had met the problems that had faced them during the brief period of the experiments in independence. In short, those states that had done well on their own were inclined to desire to continue on their own, and those that found it difficult to survive independently were inclined to desire to cast their several lots with a general government.

As independent entities, five states (Delaware, New Jersey, Georgia, Connecticut, and Maryland) had faced problems that had proved insurmountable to them. These states ratified quickly, the first three unanimously and the other two by majorities of 75 and 85 per cent, respectively.

Four states (Pennsylvania, Massachusetts, South Carolina, and New Hampshire) were considerably better equipped for sovereign existence than the first five and were, by and large, faring well on their own. Each of them, however, was dissipating its energies in internal factional or areal disputes, ranging from legislation designed by one group for the destruction of another to organized physical violence. Over considerable opposition, after considerable debate, and/or through various political stratagems, each of these states ratified the Constitution. The majorities in their ratifying conventions ranged from barely over 50 per cent to 67 per cent.

Four states (Virginia, New York, North Carolina, and Rhode Island) were successful enough as sovereign entities to satisfy the greater part of their populations. Three of them were large, populous, and economically powerful states, and the fourth compensated for its deficiencies by the exercise of considerable ingenuity. The delegates elected to the ratifying convention in Virginia favored the Constitution by a slim majority, and the delegates from each of the three other states were opposed to ratification by majorities of about 70 per cent. Virginia ratified only after a vigorous campaign and much debate, maneuvering, and exercise of personal influence. New York ratified only after the City of New York threatened to secede from the state. North Carolina rejected the Constitution in one convention and ratified it in a second convention only after the government of the United States had been in operation for several months, and after twelve amendments had been proposed by Congress. Rhode Island refused seven times even to call a convention, refused to ratify when the convention did meet, and finally ratified only after the principal town in the state seceded and other towns threatened to follow suit.

The general outlines of the struggles for ratification are thus clear and relatively simple. The details which form and fill in the outlines constitute a large, intricate mosaic. The interplay of these details will become understandable only through extensive and intensive study on the state and local levels, areas hitherto largely neglected.

Index

Index